THE EUROPEANIZATION OF CENTRAL AND EASTERN EUROPE

A volume in the series

Cornell Studies in Political Economy

Edited by Peter J. Katzenstein

A full list of titles in the series appears at the end of the book.

THE EUROPEANIZATION OF CENTRAL AND EASTERN EUROPE

EDITED BY

Frank Schimmelfennig and
Ulrich Sedelmeier

Cornell University Press

Ithaca and London

First published 2005 by Cornell University Press
First printing, Cornell Paperbacks, 2005

Printed in the United States of America

Library of Congress Cataloging-in-Publication Data

The Europeanization of Central and Eastern Europe / edited by Frank Schimmelfennig and Ulrich Sedelmeier.
    p. cm.—(Cornell studies in political economy)
  Includes bibliographical references and index.
  ISBN 0-8014-4334-2 (cloth : alk. paper)—ISBN 0-8014-8961-X (pbk. : alk. paper)
  1. European Union—Europe, Eastern. 2. European Union—Europe, Central. 3. Europe, Eastern—Economic conditions—1989– 4. Europe, Central—Economic conditions. 5. Europe, Eastern—Politics and government—1989– 6. Europe, Central—Politics and government—1989– 7. Europe, Eastern—Economic integration. 8. Europe, Central—Economic integration. I. Schimmelfennig, Frank, 1963– II. Sedelmeier, Ulrich, 1967– III. Series.
  HC240.25.E852E975 2005
  337.1′42′0943—dc22
                                                      2004023898

Cornell University Press strives to use environmentally responsible suppliers and materials to the fullest extent possible in the publishing of its books. Such materials include vegetable-based, low-VOC inks and acid-free papers that are recycled, totally chlorine-free, or partly composed of nonwood fibers. For further information, visit our website at www.cornellpress.cornell.edu.

Cloth printing   10 9 8 7 6 5 4 3 2 1
Paperback printing   10 9 8 7 6 5 4 3 2 1

CONTENTS

v

CONTRIBUTORS

LILIANA B. ANDONOVA is an Assistant Professor of Government and Environmental Studies at Colby College, Waterville, Maine.

ANTOANETA L. DIMITROVA is a Lecturer at the Department of Public Administration, Leiden University, the Netherlands.

STEFAN ENGERT is a Ph.D. candidate at Darmstadt University of Technology, Germany, and a researcher at the Mannheim Center for European Social Research.

RACHEL EPSTEIN is an Assistant Professor at the Graduate School of International Studies, University of Denver, Colorado.

HEATHER GRABBE is Deputy Director of the Centre for European Reform, London, and a non-stipendiary fellow of Wolfson College, Oxford University.

ADRIENNE HÉRITIER holds the Chair of Public Policy at the European University Institute, Florence, Italy.

WADE JACOBY is an Associate Professor of Political Science at Brigham Young University in Provo, Utah.

HEIKO KNOBEL is a Ph.D. candidate at Darmstadt University of Technology, Germany, and a researcher at the Mannheim Center for European Social Research.

FRANK SCHIMMELFENNIG is a Fellow of the Mannheim Center for European Social Research, Germany.

viii   Contributors

GUIDO SCHWELLNUS is a Ph.D. candidate at the School of Politics and International Studies, Queen's University of Belfast, Northern Ireland, and a researcher at the Mannheim Center for European Social Research.

ULRICH SEDELMEIER is an Associate Professor of International Relations and European Studies at the Central European University, Budapest, Hungary.

BEATE SISSENICH is an Assistant Professor of Political Science at Indiana University, Bloomington.

ACKNOWLEDGMENTS

This book is the result of three years of intensive collaboration that developed around a series of workshops. The idea to investigate the impact of the EU on the candidate countries was born at a workshop on "Governance by Enlargement" at the Darmstadt University of Technology in the summer of 2000. It received a further boost in the 2001–2002 European Forum "Europe in the World: the External Dimensions of Europeanization" at the Robert Schuman Center for Advanced Studies of the European University Institute in Florence, in which the editors participated. We discussed a first set of papers in the context of the Joint Sessions of Workshops of the European Consortium for Political Research (ECPR) in Turin in March 2002; the final book-making workshop was hosted by the Schuman Center in July 2003. We gratefully acknowledge generous financial support from the Volkswagen Foundation for the Darmstadt, Turin, and Florence workshops and the Schuman Center for our Jean Monnet fellowships and the Florence workshop. We owe special thanks to Alfred Schmidt of the Volkswagen Foundation and Helen Wallace, director of the Schuman Center. In addition, we are grateful to the Mannheim Center for European Social Research for a visiting fellowship for Ulrich Sedelmeier, which greatly helped with the writing of the introductory and concluding chapters and facilitated the editorial process at a crucial stage. Ulrich Sedelmeier thanks Central European University for a sabbatical and the Max Planck Institute for the Study of Societies, Cologne, for hosting him.

We thank those colleagues who presented work at the workshops without contributing a chapter to the final volume: Dorothee Bohle, Martin Brusis, Dorota Dakowska, Adam Fagin, Asuman Göskel, Abby Innes, Petr Jehlicka, Jan-Hinrik Meyer-Sahling, Dimitris Papadimitriou, Nieves Perez-Solorzano Borragan, Gwendolyn Sasse, and Milada Vachudova. We have benefited greatly from their ideas and insights. We presented preliminary versions of the introduction and the conclusions for this book at conferences in Bordeaux (ECPR Standing Group on the EU), Budapest (ISA Convention), and Marburg (ECPR Conference) and in research seminars at the Universities of Bremen, Hanover, and Queen's University, Belfast as well as at the Max Planck Institute for Social Research in Cologne and the Mannheim Center for European Social Research. We thank audiences and discussants for their helpful comments.

Roger Haydon at Cornell University Press steered the project through the review and revision process with the right mixture of criticism and advice. We also thank the two anonymous reviewers for Cornell University Press for their useful criticism and suggestions for improvement, and Stefan Engert for preparing the index. Most of all, however, we are grateful to our authors, who have not only met our increasingly short deadlines and agreed to address a common set of questions, concepts, and hypotheses but, above all, made the preparation of this volume a highly stimulating intellectual exercise and a great learning experience.

THE EUROPEANIZATION OF CENTRAL AND EASTERN EUROPE

Introduction: Conceptualizing the Europeanization of Central and Eastern Europe

Frank Schimmelfennig and Ulrich Sedelmeier

$\mathbf{M}$uch of the literature on European integration refers to the domestic impact of the European Union (EU)[1] as "Europeanization."[2] In this sense, a far-reaching process of Europeanization is currently under way in Central and Eastern Europe.[3] In the aftermath of the fall of communism, international organizations have become strongly involved in the political and economic transformations in the Central and Eastern European countries (CEECs). The impact of international organizations has been most obvious in the case of the EU.

The desire of most CEECs to join the EU, combined with the high volume and intrusiveness of the rules attached to membership, allow the EU an unprecedented influence in restructuring domestic institutions and the entire range of public policies in the CEECs. For member states, the EU sets over 80 percent of economic

For extensive and helpful comments on previous versions of this chapter, we thank Dorothee Bohle, Markus Jachtenfuchs, Gwendolyn Sasse, Guido Schwellnus, Milada Vachudova, and Jaap de Wilde, as well as the two anonymous reviewers for the Cornell University Press.

1. For the sake of simplicity, this volume refers throughout to the EU, even if in particular instances the terms "European Community," or EC, would be more accurate (such as events before the entry into force of the Treaty on European Union in November 1993, or policy activities under the EC pillar of the Union).

2. An exception are Cowles, Caparaso, and Risse, who use the term as a synonym for "European integration"; yet as with the bulk of studies of "Europeanization," their volume also analyzes the impact of EU rules on domestic change (2001).

3. We underline that we do not subscribe to the overly EU-centric notion of "Europe" that the term implies. Indeed, as Helen Wallace has noted, the term "EU-ization" would be more accurate to denote the impact of the EU on the CEECs (2000). However, we go along with the widely used term "Europeanization," while noting its obvious inaccuracy; we supply a pragmatic definition for the purpose of our analysis below.

regulations,[4] and the EU's membership requirements include proof of the ability to implement the entire range of the *acquis communautaire*, regularly cited as including over 80,000 pages of legislation. The impact of alignment on the legislative process in the CEECs is unmistakable. In Hungary's June 1999 parliamentary session, for example, 152 of the 180 laws passed were not subject to any debate because they were part of the *acquis*.[5] The EU has issued increasingly detailed and binding statements of its requirements since the European Commission published its 1995 White Paper on regulatory alignment (see, e.g., Grabbe 1999). The Commission actively monitors the progress of candidate countries in annual reports, starting in 1997 with its Opinion on the CEECs' membership applications.[6] The EU has also become directly involved in the process of alignment. It provides funding for the implementation of particular accession-related legislation as well as technical expertise through its Technical Assistance Information Exchange Office (TAIEX). The most direct form of assistance is the "twinning program," which organizes, upon the request of the CEECs, the placement of member state civil servants in the CEECs' administrations, where they directly advise their counterparts in their areas of expertise. Similar policies of alignment, assistance, and conditionality are part of the EU's relations with the western Balkans and of its "new neighborhood" policy toward the western successor states of the Soviet Union.

In view of the various activities that the EU directs toward the CEECs aspiring membership, most commentators argue that the influence of the EU is pervasive. However, to what extent and in which ways the EU exercises its influence on the accession countries is much less clear. Despite its indisputable relevance, the process of Europeanization in the CEECs and its outcomes have rarely been subjected to a systematic, theory-oriented and comparative analysis.[7]

EU policy in the CEECs is generally described as predominantly a policy of conditionality (see, e.g., Checkel 2000; Grabbe 2001a; Schimmelfennig, Engert, and Knobel 2003a). However, the impact of conditionality is often merely asserted and not made the subject of careful analysis. Thus, on the one hand, we need to distinguish analytically between the use of "conditionality" as a political strategy and its causal impact on domestic politics. EU conditionality might be encompassing, but it might not be effective in particular issue areas or countries, and policy or institutional changes in particular issue areas might not be causally related to it. On the other hand, the term "conditionality" is often used rather loosely in

---

4. See, e.g., Peterson and Bomberg for a discussion of this point and the limited usefulness of such measurements (2000, 4).

5. See Kopstein and Reilly, who cite *Magyar Nemzet*, 19 June 1999 (2000, 27).

6. For the development of EU policy toward the CEECs, see, e.g., Sedelmeier and Wallace (2000).

7. Exceptions are Keohane, Nye, and Hoffmann (1993), which only covers the immediate post–Cold War period, and the looser collections of case studies in Katzenstein (1997) and Linden (2002). However, the situation is starting to change with the recently published and forthcoming books by Andonova (2003), Jacoby (2004), Kelley (2004) and Vachudova (2004).

accounts of the EU's influence on the CEECs, without clear analytical specification what it entails and under what conditions it has an impact.

The absence of conceptual analysis is particularly striking if we consider the heated normative debate about the desirability of the EU's influence on the CEECs. Some analysts see the EU as akin to a colonial power that exploits its superior bargaining power to the disadvantage of socioeconomic and democratic developments in the CEECs (see, e.g., Bohle 2002; Hughes 2001; Innes 2002a). Others see the influence of the EU as much more benign. These commentators consider the EU's push for political and market economic reforms as an overall positive influence and a distinct advantage for the CEECs in comparison to other transition countries (see, e.g., Hyde-Price 1994; Huntington 1991; Kopstein and Reilly 2000, 28; Pravda 2001, 14; Vachudova 2001; 2003) or even argue that the EU has a moral obligation to use its leverage in order to foster the development of democracy and human rights (see, e.g., Rollo et al. 1990). Despite their markedly different assessments of the appropriateness of the EU's influence, both sides in the debate take it very much as a given that the EU has, or at least could have, a pervasive influence on the domestic politics of the CEECs. Similar assumptions are manifest in the accounts of politicians and journalists. Only a few analysts have made an effort to ascertain whether the actual influence of the EU is indeed as ubiquitous as assumed in these debates. Haggard et al. (1993, 188–89), for example, consider the power of the EU to be much more limited and argue that factors other than the obvious power asymmetry between the EU and the CEECs shape the influence of the former.

This volume outlines a theoretical research agenda to study the impact of the EU on the accession countries and presents the findings of comparative analyses. First, the volume provides a framework of analysis for the Europeanization of the CEECs by suggesting three alternative models for the domestic impact of the EU in these countries. Second, the authors seek to bring more analytical rigor to the study of conditionality. We spell out an "external incentive model" that captures the dynamics of the EU's conditionality. We clearly specify the factors that affect its effectiveness and evaluate the explanatory value of this model against two main alternative models: "social learning" and "lesson-drawing." Finally, our agenda is not only theory-driven but also aims to provide a broader picture of the impact of the EU on the CEECs. We selected our case studies not simply in order to ensure variation in explanatory factors but also to present studies of a broad range of issue areas and countries, some of which have received little attention, even in more descriptive studies.

Literature: Lacunae and Synergies

The study of "Europeanization East" contributes to and links several bodies of literature and addresses systematic lacunae in all of them: the literature on enlargement, transition, EU governance and Europeanization, and international institutions (see also Schimmelfennig 2002, 2–5; Sedelmeier 2001).

Enlargement

The theoretically informed literature on the eastern enlargement of the EU generally focuses on the member states' enlargement preferences and the EU's enlargement decisions and policies (for an overview, see Schimmelfennig and Sedelmeier 2002). By contrast, even though it is generally agreed that the adoption of EU rules is a central condition of membership and the most relevant subject matter of the accession negotiations, the process of adoption in the candidate countries is seriously understudied in this literature. Part of the explanation for this lacuna is that it takes some time before the impact of EU rules in the candidate countries can be assessed. It may also have to do with the fact that, to study the transfer of EU rules, it is necessary to look into the CEECs' domestic political systems—something that the International Relations and EU scholars who make up the majority of enlargement researchers are rarely prepared or equipped to do.

Transition

The literature on the transformation of the former communist systems of the CEECs and their more or less successful transition to democracy looks at the adoption and institutionalization of liberal norms and the consolidation of democratic systems from the other angle—that of national political systems and domestic politics. Yet the international environment and the impact of international organizations have traditionally been regarded as secondary in the literature on transitions (see especially O'Donnell, Schmitter, and Whitehead 1986). Although the obvious international influences on Eastern European transitions have spurred comparativists to begin looking at the "international dimensions of democratization" (see, e.g., Pridham, Sanford, and Herring 1994; Whitehead 1996), the transition literature has generally focused on domestic factors in explaining the divergent paths of development in the CEECs and their different degrees of success in liberal democratic consolidation. Summary evaluations stress, for instance, the continuity of elites and mass political culture (Beyme 1994, 355), the initial balance of power between democrats and dictators (McFaul 2002), the newly created political institutions and systems of government (Elster, Offe, and Preuss 1998; Merkel 1999, 443), or the institutional structure of the communist systems and the strategic constellations that shaped the starting points and pathways of transition (Bunce 1999; Elster, Offe, and Preuss 1998; Stark and Bruszt 1998). Although it is an open question whether international factors really matter for transition outcomes, what is missing in these accounts is a systematic integration of international factors into the research design and explanations.[8] Moreover, while certain effects are sometimes ascribed to external influences, these arguments are often mere assertions rather than the result of careful analysis and often do not distinguish between impact of the EU and other external factors.

8. For a recent exception, both with regard to the systematic integration and the causal relevance of international influences, see Kurtz and Barnes (2002).

EU Governance

"Governance" has become a major focus of European integration studies—representing a shift in interest and focus away from the explanation of "grand bargains" and general integration dynamics and toward the study of the EU as a multilevel political system with specific features of policymaking (for a recent overview, see Jachtenfuchs 2001). The governance school should therefore be particularly well suited to refocus the study of enlargement from the explanation of intergovernmental enlargement decisions to the study of the "consequences of enlargement for EU governance, EU institutional development and governance in applicant countries" (Jachtenfuchs and Kohler-Koch 2004, 112). Through association and the preparatory stages of the accession process—and the concomitant regulatory alignment and EU technical and financial assistance—the candidate countries have become part of this governance system long before their formal membership. According to Lykke Friis and Anna Murphy, the governance approach provides "the analytical tools necessary to understand the interplay between EU policies toward the CEEC and its internal development as a system of governance" but "has not been directly applied to studies of the external role of the Union" (1999, 212). This is deplorable, because the external dimension is likely to add interesting variation to the study of EU governance. For instance, Antoaneta Dimitrova suggests that the asymmetrical, hierarchical "governance by enlargement" deviates significantly from the modes of "new" or "network governance" assumed to characterize governance within the EU (2002, 176).

Europeanization

The field of "Europeanization" is closely linked to the governance school of European integration studies. It is concerned with the impact of policy outcomes and institutions at the European level on domestic polities, politics, and policies (for overviews, see Börzel and Risse 2003; Hix and Goetz 2000; Radaelli 2000). Again, this literature has focused on the Europeanization of member states. Rare exceptions focus on some West European nonmember states (see, e.g., Kux and Sverdrup 2000). Including the CEECs would not only make the empirical picture more complete but, above all, permit us to test the established findings in a new context and check some new variables. For instance, does nonmember status facilitate the transformation of domestic institutions and policies, since states aspiring to membership are particularly eager to comply with EU rules and are in a weaker position vis-à-vis EU institutions than member states? Or does it inhibit the domestic impact of EU rules, given that states that have had a say in EU decision-making will also be more ready to comply? Put more generally, do we see a co-variation between the degree and duration of integration into the EU and the degree of the EU's impact in the domestic sphere? Moreover, do the specific features of the CEEC nonmember states that collectively distinguish them from western member states have an influence on their Europeanization? For instance, are the legacies of

central planning an inhibiting factor? Or does institutional inertia, the most important factor reducing the impact of EU rules in the member states, play a lesser role
in the CEECs because political institutions and organized interest have not yet taken
root in the same way as in the West European countries? Will candidate responses
to EU influence be less "differential" (Héritier et al. 2001) and more homogeneous
than member state responses?[9]

International Institutions

For a long time, research on international institutions has focused on the questions
of how and under what conditions international regimes are established and
become durable in an anarchical international environment. In the course of the
1990s, research interest has shifted toward questions of regime effectiveness and
rule compliance (Chayes and Chayes 1995; Young 1999). Moreover, the study of
international institutions has become firmly embedded in the "great debate"
between rationalist and constructivist institutionalism (Katzenstein, Keohane, and
Krasner 1999; Carlsnaes, Risse, and Simmons 2002). Whereas rationalist institu-
tionalists explain compliance by the use of positive and negative incentives, which
constrain or empower states and domestic actors by allocating differential costs to
alternative courses of action, constructivists emphasize processes of international
socialization, in which domestic actors change their identities and preferences as a
result of imitation or argumentative persuasion. Meanwhile, the debate has
reached a high level of theoretical sophistication. Based on different institutionalist theories, authors have specified alternative mechanisms of institutional effects
and the conditions under which they are supposed to work (for overviews, see, e.g.,
Börzel and Risse 2002; Schimmelfennig 2003b). These conceptual insights and
ideas have been already introduced to the Europeanization literature (see, e.g.,
Börzel and Risse 2003) and would also give useful theoretical guidance to the study
of Europeanization in the CEECs, which has so far lacked theoretical coherence
(see, e.g., the contributions to Linden 2002 or Goetz 2001a). At the same time,
having been the site of probably the most massive international rule transfer in
recent history, post–Cold War Central and Eastern Europe offers rich empirical
material for testing theories of institutional effects.

   Of course, the most concrete contribution of this volume is to the literature on
international conditionality, which focuses mostly on the lending conditionality of
international financial institutions (IFIs). This literature also works with rationalist bargaining and constructivist social learning models but generally arrives at a
skeptical assessment of the effectiveness of conditionality (see, e.g., Checkel 2000;
Kahler 1992). The study of conditionality in the EU enlargement process extends
this research to a different context and allows us to test the factors it identifies as
undermining conditionality.

---

9. Adrienne Héritier revisits these questions in chapter 10. For related questions of convergence,
see also Mair and Zielonka (2002) and in particular Bruszt (2002).

In sum, the study of the Europeanization of Central and Eastern Europe has the potential to cover empirical blind spots in the study of enlargement, EU governance, and Europeanization. It allows us to probe into the findings of transition, EU governance, and Europeanization research by introducing new variables and/or increasing variation in existing ones. Finally, it provides new and rich data to test the mechanisms and conditions of international institutional effects. To make the most of it, however, it should be guided by institutionalist theory, take up important explanatory factors from neighboring fields, and share these fields' substantive interest in democratic consolidation and the adoption of international norms and rules.

Rule Adoption: The Dependent Variable

We define "Europeanization" as a process in which states adopt EU rules.[10] Two items in this definition of the dependent variable require further clarification: "EU rules" and "adoption." The "rules" in question cover a broad range of issues and structures and are both formal and informal. To name just a few, they comprise rules for regulation and distribution in specific policy areas, rules of political, administrative, and judicial process, and rules for the setup and competences of state and sub-state organizations.

"Rule adoption" is generally compatible with the explanandum of Europeanization and international socialization literature. Nominally, there is a great variety of dependent variables in the Europeanization literature, but the core is domestic change or transformation (see, e.g., Héritier 2001a, 1; Hix and Goetz 2000, 2; Risse, Cowles, and Caporaso 2001, 4; Risse and Sikkink 1999, 4). By analyzing rule adoption, we focus on the *institutionalization* of EU rules at the domestic level—for instance, the transposition of EU law into domestic law, the restructuring of domestic institutions according to EU rules, or the change of domestic political practices according to EU standards.

We propose to measure and classify "rule adoption" on two main dimensions: (1) The most basic dimension is the *likelihood* of adoption.[11] The conditions under which a nonmember state will adopt EU rules constitute the core dimension for the hypotheses we will subsequently develop. (2) However, as the Europeanization literature emphasizes, implementation and enforcement of rules, rather than simply the legal transposition of rules, is a key aspect of assessing the impact of the EU on domestic politics. We thus distinguish different *forms* of adoption, based on the different conceptions of norms discussed in the literature on international

10. The term "state" in this definition does not imply that we conceive of states as unitary actors. In the following, we usually refer to "governments" to denote the actors who adopt EU rules and "states" as the political-institutional structures into which EU rules are integrated.

11. In this dimension, we could further distinguish between different *degrees* of rule adoption. The case study chapters thus evaluate either the likelihood of full rule adoption or the likelihood that any, including only partial, rule adoption might take place.

institutions: the formal, the behavioral, and the communicative or discursive conception (Hasenclever, Mayer, and Rittberger 1997, 14–21; Raymond 2000, 70–71).

According to the *formal* conception, adoption consists in the transposition of EU rules into national law or in the establishment of formal institutions and procedures in line with EU rules. According to the *behavioral* conception, adoption is measured by the extent to which behavior is rule-conforming. By contrast, according to the *discursive* conception of norms, adoption is indicated by the incorporation of a rule as a positive reference into discourse among domestic actors. Such a reference may indicate that domestic actors are truly persuaded of a norm. Alternatively, it may merely imply that domestic actors "talk the talk," pay lip service to the norm, or use it strategically in "rhetorical action" (Schimmelfennig 1997; 2000, 129–32; 2001; see also Jacoby 2002; Risse and Sikkink 1999, 2–28).

All of these forms of rule adoption can lead to institutionalization, that is, exhibit rule-conforming patterns of domestic rules and procedures, behavior, and discourse. Even though one form of adoption does not exclude another, these categories give rise to several theoretically interesting questions. Is there a *dominant form* of adoption? Are there *actor-specific* forms of adoption? Can we specify conditions under which we would expect to see one form of adoption rather than another? Or can we detect a typical *sequence* in the adoption of rules? Answers to these questions should greatly improve our understanding of the Europeanization processes in the CEECs, although the recent nature of the adoption of EU rules in most cases should caution us to the limitations of current assessments.

Explanatory Models and Mechanisms of Rule Adoption

We develop three main explanatory models that specify different mechanisms of Europeanization and the conditions under which nonmember states adopt EU rules. These models differ on two key dimensions (see table 1.1).

First, the process of Europeanization can be either EU-driven or domestically driven. In the former case, the EU induces the process of rule adoption, while in the latter, the nonmember state takes the initiative. Superficially, it might appear that the former process characterizes all issue areas in which the EU exercises adaptation pressures, and hence all areas in which the EU has competences, since

Table 1.1   Alternative mechanisms of Europeanization

Principal actor in rule adoption process	Logic of rule adoption	
	Logic of consequences	Logic of appropriateness
EU-driven	External incentives model	Social learning model
CEEC-driven	Lesson-drawing model	Lesson-drawing model

the EU demands that new members comply in full with the *acquis*.[12] However, the EU has not been very vigorous in enforcing its conditionality in some policy areas, such as the Social Dialogue, as Beate Sissenich shows in chapter 8. Moreover, while the EU might demand adjustment and actively promote the adoption of its rules in a particular issue area, its actions might merely coincide—and possibly reinforce—a process of rule adoption that a state has embarked on independently. This was the case, for example, with air pollution policies in the Czech Republic, as Liliana Andonova demonstrates in chapter 7, or with regional policies in Hungary, as Wade Jacoby suggests in chapter 5. We therefore emphasize the extent to which the import of EU rules is EU-induced or domestically driven as the more useful distinction. In simple terms, we consider rule adoption as EU-driven in those cases in which a state would not have adopted these rules if it had not been for a particular action by the EU.

The second distinction that our typology emphasizes concerns different logics of action that rule adoption follows. In line with the debates between rationalism and constructivism in IR theory and between rational choice institutionalism and sociological institutionalism in Comparative Politics, we distinguish between a "logic of consequences" and a "logic of appropriateness" (March and Olsen 1989, 160–62). The former assumes strategic, instrumentally rational actors who seek to maximize their own power and welfare. According to the latter logic, actors are motivated by internalized identities, values, and norms. Among alternative courses of action, they choose the most appropriate or legitimate one. Correspondingly, arguing about the legitimacy of rules and the appropriateness of behavior (rather than bargaining about conditions and rewards), persuasion (rather than coercion) and "complex" learning (rather than behavioral adaptation) characterize the process of rule transfer and rule adoption.

If we pair these two distinctions, we can broadly distinguish between the mechanisms of Europeanization depicted in table 1.1. In this book, we focus on three models. The "external incentives model" captures the dynamics underpinning EU conditionality and forms the point of departure of this volume. It follows a logic of consequences and is driven by the *external* rewards and sanctions that the EU adds to the cost-benefit calculations of the rule-adopting state. We contrast this model with two main alternative models that differ from it according to one of the two key dimensions.

The "social learning" model follows a logic of appropriateness. In contrast to the external incentive model, it emphasizes identification of the CEECs with the EU and persuasion of the CEECs by the EU of the legitimacy of its rules as key

---

12. Hence, even before the EU actively promotes its rules in a certain issue area, nonmember states might engage in "anticipatory adaptation," i.e., adopt EU rules in anticipation of the membership requirements (Haggard et al., 1993, 182). For the distinction between such a "passive leverage" of the EU and its "active leverage" (i.e., explicit conditionality) over accession states, see Vachudova (2001). Note, however, that in our typology, both types of EU leverage would fall under "EU-driven" rule adoption.

conditions for rule adoption, rather than the provision of material incentives by the EU. The "lesson-drawing" model differs from the two other models through its focus on the adoption of EU rules as induced by the CEECs themselves, rather than through any activities of the EU. The key difference to the external incentives model is that in this case, states adopt EU rules because they judge them as effective remedies to inherently *domestic* needs and policy challenges, rather than out of considerations about the incentives that the EU might offer for rule adoption. For this model, we do not distinguish between different logics of action. The desire of public policymakers to import rules from abroad might be either the result of pressure from societal groups and the "simple" learning of policymakers, or learning from abroad might be the result of changes in policy paradigms and "complex" learning processes. In the latter case, the key difference to the social learning model is that the learning processes are not induced by the EU.

The External Incentives Model

The external incentives model is a rationalist bargaining model.[13] It is actor-centered and based on a logic of consequences. In a bargaining process, actors exchange information, threats, and promises to their preferences. The outcome of the bargaining process depends on the relative bargaining power of the actors. Bargaining power is a result of the asymmetrical distribution of (1) information and (2) the benefits of a specific agreement compared with those of alternative outcomes or "outside options." Generally, those actors that have more and better information are able to manipulate the outcome to their advantage, and those actors that are least in need of a specific agreement are best able to threaten the others with noncooperation and thereby force them to make concessions.[14]

According to the external incentives model, the EU sets the adoption of its rules as conditions that the CEECs have to fulfill in order to receive rewards from the EU. The EU offers two kinds of rewards to nonmember countries: assistance and institutional ties. The EU's most important assistance program for the CEECs is PHARE. From 1989, it initially offered technical and financial assistance for the transition to market economies and was later redesigned to support more specifically their preparation for EU accession. Institutional ties range from trade and cooperation agreements via association agreements to full membership. These institutional ties provide progressively more market access to the EU with the prospect of gains from trade and investment and increasing participation in EU decision-making.

---

13. For the assumptions and main propositions of rational-choice approaches to Europeanization, see Héritier (2001a, 4–5); Hix and Goetz (2000, 10–13).

14. The external incentives model is the standard model in the study of international financing (World Bank or IMF) conditionality (see, e.g., Haggard and Webb 1994, 25–27; Kahler 1992, 92–123).

EU conditionality mainly follows a strategy of reactive reinforcement or reinforcement by reward (Schimmelfennig 2000, 125–27; Schimmelfennig, Engert, and Knobel 2003a, 496–97). Under this strategy, the EU pays the reward if the target government complies with the conditions and withholds the reward if it fails to comply. It does not, however, intervene either coercively by inflicting extra costs ("reinforcement by punishment") or supportively by offering extra benefits ("reinforcement by support") to change the behavior of the target government. Countries that fail to meet the criteria are simply denied assistance, association, or membership, and are left behind in the competition for EU funds and the "regatta" for accession. The EU regularly exhorts the CEEC governments that it is their own responsibility to create the conditions to be rewarded. A strategy of reinforcement by reward thus avoids the "moral hazard" problems of reinforcement by support: governments cannot count on receiving EU assistance by just remaining "needy" and not adapting to EU rules. On the other hand, and in contrast to reinforcement by punishment, this strategy alone will do little (ceteris paribus) to change the minds and behavior of governments that have come to the conclusion that the domestic costs of rule adoption outweigh the benefits of EU rewards and that EU sanctions will not go beyond withholding those rewards. The following theoretical considerations start from the assumption, and hold under the condition, that the EU pursues a strategy of reinforcement by reward.

The analytical starting point of the bargaining process is a domestic status quo, which differs to some extent from an EU rule. This difference is often measured as the "goodness of fit" in the Europeanization literature (see, e.g., Risse, Cowles, and Caporaso 2001, 6–7). The status quo is conceived as a "domestic equilibrium" reflecting the current distribution of preferences and bargaining power in domestic society and, possibly, the constellation of bargaining power between international and domestic actors and different international actors promoting divergent rules. EU conditionality upsets this domestic equilibrium by introducing additional incentives for compliance with EU rules into the game. Conditionality can work in different ways (Schimmelfennig, Engert, and Knobel 2003a, 497–98; Vachudova 2001, 10).

(1) *Intergovernmental bargaining.* First, it may work directly on the target government, which then calculates whether the benefits of the promised EU rewards outweigh the domestic adjustment costs of adopting the EU rule and the opportunity costs of discarding the rules promoted by other international actors.

(2) *Differential empowerment of domestic actors.* Second, conditionality may work indirectly through the differential empowerment of domestic actors. In this case, certain domestic actors have independent incentives to adopt EU rules, which might stem from the utility of EU rules in solving certain policy problems to the advantage of these domestic actors or, more generally, in increasing their influence in the political system. However, in the previous domestic equilibrium, these actors did not have sufficient power to impose their preferred rules on the other domestic actors. Conditionality then changes the domestic opportunity structure in favor

of these domestic actors and strengthens their bargaining power vis-à-vis their opponents in society and government—to the extent that these opponents share the goal of EU membership and expect to benefit from the EU's rewards (cf. Börzel and Risse 2003, 63–64; Knill and Lehmkuhl 2002, 268–71).

Whereas intergovernmental bargaining produces a "top-down" process of rule adoption, the differential empowerment of domestic actors is more "bottom-up." At the end of the day, however, rule adoption requires the authoritative decision of the target government, which seeks to balance EU, domestic, and other international pressures in order to maximize its own political benefits. At the same time, differential empowerment might also strengthen the bargaining power of the government vis-à-vis societal actors or party rivals. The most general proposition of the external incentives model under a strategy of reinforcement by reward, therefore, is: *A government adopts EU rules if the benefits of EU rewards exceed the domestic adoption costs.*

To make this proposition more concrete and formulate testable hypotheses for explaining variation, we suggest that the cost-benefit balance depends on four sets of factors: the determinacy of conditions, the size and speed of rewards, the credibility of threats and promises, and the size of adoption costs.

Determinacy of Conditions

Generally, the external incentives model suggests that—given a domestic equilibrium in the nonmember country—the adoption of EU rules will be absent if the EU does not set them up as conditions for rewards. In addition, the determinacy of the conditions set by the EU and the determinacy of the rules from which they are derived enhances the likelihood of rule adoption by the candidate countries. Determinacy refers both to the clarity and formality of a rule. The clearer the behavioral implications of a rule and the more "legalized" and binding its status, the higher its determinacy.[15] Jacoby and Cernoch distinguish between high and low "density of norms" as an important factor shaping the impact of the EU in the CEECs (2002, 320). Dimitrova (2002) and Grabbe (2001, 1025) see the lack of rule clarity as one main inhibiting factor in the enlargement governance.

Determinacy matters in two respects. First, it has an informational value. It helps the target governments know exactly what they have to do to get the rewards. For example, as Heather Grabbe shows in chapter 6, the evolving nature of the Schengen *acquis* was detrimental to rule adoption. It initially created uncertainty in the CEECs as to whether these rules were part of the accession requirements, and then about which particular rules they had to adopt. Second, determinacy enhances the credibility of conditionality. It is a signal to the target countries that they cannot manipulate the rule to their advantage or avoid adopting it at all. At the same time, however, it binds the EU. If a condition is determinate, it becomes

---

15. For discussions of "determinacy" or "specificity" of rules and norms, see Franck (1990, 52–83) or Legro (1997, 34). For an explication of the concept of "legalization," see Abbott et al. (2000).

more difficult for the EU to claim unjustly that it has not been fulfilled and to with-hold the reward. The link between determinacy and credibility is reflected in an episode in the run-up to the Copenhagen European Council in June 1993. Despite their diametrically opposed preferences concerning the speed of enlargement, both the French and the Czech government were pressing for the EU to use quantita-tive membership criteria—for example, relating to GDP/capita—the former in order to avoid politically motivated decisions in favor of an early enlargement and the latter to avoid that political bias would lead to a postponement of enlargement. On the basis of these considerations, we formulate a *determinacy hypothesis*:[16]

> *The likelihood of rule adoption increases, if rules are set as conditions for rewards and the more determinate they are.*

Size and Speed of Rewards

Another source of variation under a strategy of reinforcement by reward is the size and speed of the conditional rewards. Accordingly, the promise of enlargement should be more powerful than the promise of association or assistance, and the impact of the EU on candidates for membership should be stronger than on outside states not considered potential EU members (cf., e.g. Smith 2001, 37–38).

Moreover, the longer the temporal distance to the payment of rewards, the lower the incentive to comply—at least swiftly. Conversely, rule adoption becomes more likely the closer the day of EU enlargement decision-making gets. A gradual process with several levels of progress at which compliance is checked and inter-mediate rewards are paid reduces this problem even if the ultimate reward—EU membership—is distant.[17] A sequencing of trade and cooperation agreements, association agreements, pre-accession support, and inclusion in accession negoti-ations serves this purpose of intermediary rewards. The Commission's Opinions and its Regular Reports on the progress of the candidate countries toward meeting the accession conditions provide regular occasions for the EU to reward the can-didates or to withdraw benefits. The corresponding *rewards hypothesis* is:

> *The likelihood of rule adoption increases with the size and speed of rewards.*

Credibility of Conditionality

A third set of factors has to do with the credibility of the EU's threat of with-holding rewards in the case of noncompliance and, conversely, the credibility of the EU's promise to deliver the reward in the case of rule adoption. In other words, given a strategy of reinforcement by reward, rule adoption requires both the supe-rior bargaining power of the rule-setting agency (otherwise threats would not be credible) and certainty on the part of the target states about the conditional pay-

---

16. Here, and for the following hypotheses, the ceteris paribus clause applies.
17. See Kelley (2004) and, on a more skeptical note, Grabbe (1999, 8–9).

ments (otherwise promises would not be credible). A discussion of credibility therefore has to address the conditions under which bargaining power and certainty are enhanced or impaired.

The first issue is the *capabilities and costs* of the agency employing conditionality. On the one hand, the EU must be able to withhold the rewards at no or little cost to itself, and it has to be less interested in giving the reward than the target government is in getting it. If a target government knew that the EU would prefer unconditional assistance to no assistance or unconditional enlargement to no enlargement, conditionality would not work. In general, this condition is present in EU-CEEC relations. Interdependence is highly asymmetrical in favor of the EU. Whereas the CEECs are only of marginal importance to the EU economy, the CEECs are heavily dependent on the EU market and will benefit much more strongly from accession than the EU member states (Baldwin, Francois, and Portes 1997; Moravcsik and Vachudova 2003, 46–52). On the other hand, however, the EU must be capable of paying the rewards—at a low cost to itself. Promises are not credible if they go beyond capabilities. The higher the costs of the rewards to the EU are, the more doubtful their eventual payment to the target countries will be. On the basis of this reasoning, assistance and association have been more credible rewards than accession. Eastern enlargement involves substantial costs to the organization, which—although far from being prohibitive—are likely to exceed the marginal benefits of most member states (Schimmelfennig 2003a, 52–62). The credibility of threats and promises thus varies also across countries, according to the net costs of a country's membership to the EU.

However, one also has to take into account the "sunk costs" of rewarding. In contrast to assistance, which requires comparatively small investments on the part of the EU and can be stopped rather easily, enlargement involves costly, long-term negotiations and preparations and a restructuring of EU institutions and policies. The more the pre-accession process advances, the higher the costs are of withholding the reward, that is, the investments that would be lost if the process was broken off or postponed to sanction a candidate state. The credibility of conditional rewards therefore increases considerably with the opening of accession negotiations, since, in the words of Commission officials, they "require a large input of political and human resources [and] because opening them implies a willingness to conclude them" (Avery and Cameron 1998, 27). Even for countries not yet involved in accession negotiations, the opening of accession negotiations with, and the subsequent accession of, a first group of candidate countries increases the credibility of rewards for the remaining candidates, as it demonstrates that the EU is serious about enlargement. On the other hand, however, just as the credibility of rewards in enlargement conditionality increases over time, the credibility of threats decreases. Antoaneta Dimitrova observes in chapter 4 that the EU's requirements for administrative reforms had little effect on the Czech government that considered itself a front-runner for accession and thus did not consider as very credible the threat of exclusion in case of failing to adopt EU rules in this area.

Second, credibility depends on the *consistency* of an organization's allocation of rewards. If the EU were perceived to subordinate conditionality to other political, strategic, or economic considerations, the target state might either hope to receive the benefits without fulfilling the conditions or conclude that it will not receive the rewards in any case. In both cases, the target state will fail to adopt EU rules. In this sense, the decision of the Helsinki European Council in December 1999 to include Slovakia, Latvia, and Lithuania into accession negotiations as a reward for their progress with meeting the accession criteria increased the credibility of the EU's conditionality. By contrast, the politically motivated inclusion of Romania and Bulgaria rewarding them for their support of NATO action in Kosovo damaged its credibility.

Another source of inconsistency would be internal EU conflict about conditionality. If target states learn about such internal conflict and receive inconsistent signals, they will be tempted to manipulate it to their advantage or simply be confused.[18] Beate Sissenich shows in chapter 8 that differences in the degree of importance attached to the EU's social policy between the Council and the Commission, as well as between the Commission's DGs for Social Policy and Enlargement, had a negative impact on the adoption of EU rules in this area.

Third, *cross-conditionality* must be absent or minor. EU conditionality would not be effective if the target government had other sources offering comparable benefits at lower adjustment costs (Kahler 1992, 104, 111; Killick 1996, 221, 224). In the terminology of bargaining theory, cross-conditionality enhances the outside options of target countries. Yet, given their strong dependency on the EU market and the strong incentives of potential transfers from the EU budget, for most of the CEECs there is no credible alternative to EU integration. Conversely, conditionality will be more effective if other international actors—like NATO or the IFIs—offer the government additional benefits in return for fulfilling the same conditions (parallel conditionality) or if other international actors make their rewards conditional upon prior fulfillment of EU conditions (additive conditionality).

Fourth, *asymmetries in information* reduce the effectiveness of conditionality (see Kahler 1992, 114). If the EU does not possess the capacity to monitor the target state, if information by other monitoring agencies is inconsistent, or if the target state is able to conceal its compliance record from the monitors, the credibility of conditionality is weakened. Monitoring presented the EU with an entirely new challenge in the case of eastern enlargement. The Commission does not usually proactively monitor the compliance of members with the *acquis*. Given the magnitude of the changes required in the CEECs and the fear of the disruptive effect on the internal market of an avalanche of court cases against new members after enlargement, the Commission invented new instruments of monitoring, including questionnaires, "harmonigrams," extensive "screening," and progress reports.

---

18. The effect of this kind of inconsistency is similar to that of indeterminacy (see Grabbe 2001a, 1026–27).

However, it often still had to rely on the applicants themselves as important sources of information.[19]

In sum, we formulate a general *credibility hypothesis* together with some more specific conjectures:

> *The likelihood of rule adoption increases with the credibility of conditional threats and promises.* (1) The credibility of threats increases and the credibility of promises decreases as the benefits of rewarding or the costs of withholding the reward decrease; (2) credibility increases with the consistency of, and internal consensus about, conditionality policy; (3) credibility decreases with cross-conditionality and increases with parallel or additive conditionality; and (4) credibility decreases with information asymmetries in favor of the target government.

Veto Players and Adoption Costs

If nonmember states are confronted with determinate rules and conditions and credible conditionality and if they are offered equally beneficial rewards, the external incentives model postulates that the size of domestic adoption costs and their distribution among domestic actors determines whether they will accept or reject the conditions. The external incentives model assumes that rule adoption is always costly—otherwise it would have taken place in the absence of conditionality. Adoption costs can have various sources: First, they may take the form of opportunity costs of foregoing alternative rewards offered by adopting rules other than EU rules. Second, they may produce welfare or power costs for private and public actors. On the other hand, adoption costs are balanced by the benefits of EU rewards. As a result, adoption costs may become negative. They turn into net benefits for some, or all, domestic actors. Given that EU rules have to be adopted and implemented by the government, the effectiveness of conditionality then depends on the preferences of the government and of other "veto players," defined as "actors whose agreement is necessary for a change in the status quo." According to veto players theory, "the difficulty for a significant change of the status quo . . . increases in general with the number of veto players and with their distances" (Tsebelis 2002, 37).[20] For the purposes of this study, we reformulate this condition as the number of veto players with significant net costs of rule adoption.

---

19. The credibility problems stemming from both the lack of a clear consensus in favor of enlargement inside the EU and information asymmetries favoring the CEECs are captured in the standing joke among CEEC officials that the enlargement process was sustained through a double hypocrisy: "You pretend that you want us and we pretend that we are ready."

20. As Tsebelis points out, however, the number of veto players alone is not an accurate predictor of policy stability. A new veto player does not affect policy stability if it is located within the unanimity core of the existing set of veto players; or if a political system with a higher number of veto players is ideologically less heterogeneous than one with fewer veto players (2002, 28–31). For the use of the veto player hypothesis in Europeanization studies, see Börzel and Risse (2003) or Héritier (2001a, 5).

Generally, the number of veto players is considered to be small in the CEECs (see, e.g., Dimitrova 2002, 176; Schimmelfennig, Engert, and Knobel 2003a, 498–99). However, veto players may still vary in causally relevant ways across issue-areas (see, e.g., Jacoby and Cernoch 2002, 320). The scarcity of veto players increases the influence of the government as the main target of EU conditionality as well as the causal relevance of its cost-benefit assessment.[21]

However, if the government incurs net adoption costs, this is not the end of the story. Adoption may still occur later as a result of elections and a change in government. In this case, conditionality can be influential by providing the electorate and interest groups with information about the chances of incumbent governments to attain EU rewards and with incentives to vote for reform-friendly parties, for which the balance of EU rewards and adoption costs will be positive (see Vachudova 2001, 27–30; 2003).[22] In sum, we formulate the following *adoption cost hypothesis*:

> *The likelihood of rule adoption decreases with the number of veto players incurring net adoption costs (opportunity costs, welfare, and power losses) from compliance.*

In sum, then, according to the external incentives model, given a strategy of reinforcement by reward, conditionality will be most effective if rules and conditions are determinate; conditional rewards are certain, high, and quickly disbursed; threats to withhold the reward are credible; adoption costs are small; and veto players are few. Even if these conditions are conducive to rule adoption, target states will still choose the form of adoption that minimizes their costs. Usually, we would expect discursive adoption—understood as rhetorical "talking the EU talk"—to be the least costly option. Formal adoption is a more costly form of adoption but may still result in "Potemkin harmonization" (Jacoby 1999), the creation of "EU conform" laws and institutional structures for external consumption with little or no impact on actual domestic state politics and outcomes. Only in the case of behavioral adoption do the target states come to bear the full costs of compliance. The differential costs of adoption are also a function of the distribution of information between the EU and the target states of conditionality. If information is symmetrically distributed, it will be difficult for the target state to get away with merely discursive or formal adoption. If, however, it is distributed asymmetrically in favor of the target state, the EU may not be able to detect the "Potemkin villages" the candidates have erected. In sum, the deepening of rule adoption requires continuous and effective monitoring and sanctioning.

---

21. Cortell and Davis also propose that in centralized states with distant state-society relations, "state officials serve as the primary means by which international norms and rules affect national policy choices" (1996, 455).

22. For a more critical assessment of the significance of electorates, see Schimmelfennig, Engert, and Knobel (2003a, 499).

Alternative Explanation I: The Social Learning Model

The social learning model is based on core tenets of social constructivism. It has informed studies of international socialization in general (Checkel 2001) and constitutes the most prominent alternative to rationalist explanations of conditionality (Checkel 2000; Kahler 1992) and Europeanization (Börzel and Risse 2003). In contrast with the rationalist model of conditionality, the social learning model assumes a logic of appropriateness. In this perspective, the EU is the formal organization of a European international community defined by a specific collective identity and a specific set of common values and norms. Whether a nonmember state adopts EU rules depends on the degree to which it regards EU rules and its demands for rule adoption as appropriate in terms of the collective identity, values, and norms (Schimmelfennig 2003a, 83–90). The most general proposition of the *social learning* model, therefore, is:

> *A government adopts EU rules if it is persuaded of the appropriateness of EU rules.*

Several groups of factors impinge upon the persuasive power of the EU: legitimacy, identity, and resonance. Moreover, social learning can take the two routes outlined in the external incentives model. The EU may either persuade the government of the appropriateness of its rules—or societal groups and organizations, which then lobby the government for rule adoption. The EU further empowers these societal actors domestically through external legitimacy and authority.

Legitimacy of Rules and Process

The first group of factors refers to the quality of the rules themselves and the process through which they were established and are transferred to the target states. According to Thomas Franck, rule adoption depends on "the clarity with which the rules communicate, the integrity of the process by which they were made and are applied, their venerable pedigree and conceptual coherence. In short, it is the legitimacy of the rules which conduces to their being respected" (1990, 38; cf. 1990, 49). Just as in the conditionality model, determinacy is an important factor but works somewhat differently. Obviously, the minimal condition of determinacy is that the EU must have rules for a given issue area. Even if an EU rule exists, its compliance pull will be reduced if it is defined ambiguously or used inconsistently. Moreover, the rule's capacity to obligate nonmember states suffers if the member states do not generally accept it or apply it incoherently. In addition, the extent to which a rule is tied to the constitutive values and norms of the community and the result of a legitimate rule-making process strengthens its legitimacy.

Nonmember states usually do not participate in the EU's rule-making processes. Any EU rule is thus likely to have the stigma of foreign imposition. By the same token, the way in which EU rules are communicated and transferred to the nonmember states is therefore all the more important. If the EU simply demands the adoption of established rules, the legitimacy problem is likely to increase. If, however, the EU engages the target states in a deliberative process, takes into account their concerns and special needs in the interpretation and application of EU rules, and relates its demands to higher principles and general international standards, the perception of imposition will be mitigated (Checkel 2001, 563). In the terminology of the international assistance business, the more the EU is able to increase the perception of "ownership" of EU rules in the target states, the higher the legitimacy of EU rules and the more likely these rules will be adopted (see, e.g., Killick 1996, 218–19). The EU accession process should then be beset by considerable legitimacy problems: it is a one-way process in which the new member states have to accept the entirety of the *acquis*. Negotiations only concern the terms under which the applicants will adopt and enforce these rules. They might lead to the granting of transitional arrangements that allow new members to phase in their compliance with certain rules by a date agreed during the negotiations, but they "can in no way involve amendments to Community rules" (Avery 1995, 5).

Finally, the absence of alternative and conflicting rules in the international environment is a helpful condition. As in the case of cross-conditionality and credibility, the legitimacy of EU rules will be undermined if other international actors, such as the United States or organizations of the UN or Bretton Woods system, challenge these rules, provided that they also enjoy the confidence of the target states. Conversely, rule adoption will receive a boost if EU rules are in line with the rules of these other external actors. Finally, even in the case of international rule contestation, EU rules may be more persuasive if the density of interaction between the EU and the target state is significantly higher than that between the target state and other international actors (Checkel 1999a, 549). Thus, one basic hypothesis of the social learning model is the *legitimacy hypothesis*:

> *The likelihood of rule adoption increases as the legitimacy of the rules increases.* (1) Legitimacy increases with the clarity of rules, their adherence to a rule hierarchy based on the constitutive values and norms of the community, their degree of acceptance and the legitimacy of the rule-making procedures; (2) decreases if there are special rules for nonmember states or they are not accepted and applied in all member states; (3) increases with the deliberative quality of the process of rule transfer; and (4) increases with international rule consensus.

Identity

Nonmember states are more likely to be persuaded by the EU to adopt its rules if they regard the community of states represented by the EU as a valid "aspiration group" whose collective identity, values, and norms they share, whose recognition they seek, and to which they want to belong (Checkel 2001, 563; Johnston 2001, 499). The *identity hypothesis* is:

> *The likelihood of rule adoption increases with the identification of the target government and society with the community that has established the rules.*

Resonance

In addition, the social learning perspective emphasizes domestic factors that facilitate or inhibit persuasion and can be subsumed under the term "resonance."[23] First, the openness to accept and adopt new and external rules increases if domestic rules are absent—for instance, if an issue is new—or have become delegitimated as a result of a crisis or a clear and serious policy failure (Checkel 2001, 562–63). It also increases if the principles on which EU rules are based correspond to beliefs of "good policy" and due process in domestic political and legal culture and if EU rules tie in with existing or traditional domestic rules. Conversely, conflicting domestic rules that enjoy high and consensual domestic legitimacy, perhaps as symbols of the national political culture, complicate rule adoption. The final social learning hypothesis, then, is the *resonance hypothesis*:

> *The likelihood of rule adoption increases with domestic resonance.*

In sum, according to the social learning model, the likelihood of rule adoption increases with the legitimacy of rules and procedures, identification, and domestic rule resonance. With regard to the form of rule adoption, the social learning model suggests that actors do not instrumentally exploit the cost difference between alternative forms. Nevertheless, since social learning starts with a process of arguing and persuasion, adoption is likely to remain initially discursive. According to the logic of appropriateness, we would, however, expect discursive adoption to be sincere, and formal and behavioral adoption to follow suit quickly. The congruence of forms of adoption, however, only applies to persuaded actors. If only part of the relevant actors in a target state are persuaded, these actors will seek to adopt and implement EU rules but may founder on the opposition of the unpersuaded actors.

Alternative Explanation II: The Lesson-Drawing Model

Nonmember states might also adopt EU rules without inducement from the EU. This is the case with a particular type of "policy transfer" in which knowledge of EU rules is used in the development of rules in the political systems of the CEECs.[24] The literature on policy transfer draws a key analytical distinction between voluntary and coercive forms of transfer. While "conditionality" lies at the more "coercive" end of this continuum, the "ideal type" of voluntary transfer is "lesson-drawing" (Dolowitz and Marsh 2000, 13). The concept of "lesson-drawing" has been developed in the work of Richard Rose (1991, 1993). The "lesson-drawing model" that we present here departs from Rose's concept to

---

23. See the importance of "cultural match," "salience," or "resonance" emphasized in studies of international norm transfer (Checkel 1997 and 1999b; Cortell and Davis 1996 and 2000).

24. This adapts the definition of policy transfer by Dolowitz and Marsh (2000, 1).

create an "ideal type" of Europeanization on the basis of which we elaborate hypotheses.[25]

Lesson-drawing is a response to domestic dissatisfaction with the status quo (Rose 1991, 10–12). Policymakers review policies and rules in operation elsewhere and make a prospective evaluation of their transferability, that is, whether they could also operate effectively in the domestic context (Rose 1991, 23–24). Our lesson-drawing model includes both a rationalist and a more sociological variant. The common point is that domestic dissatisfaction with current policies leads policymakers to engage in a process of learning from abroad. In the rationalist version, this learning process is characterized by "simple learning," that is, new information leads to a change in means but not in ends; in the sociological variant, "complex learning" includes a modification of underlying goals (Deutsch 1963, 92; Levy 1994, 286). These differences notwithstanding, the key analytical distinction from the other two models is that the activities of the EU—either the rewards that it attaches to the adoption of particular rules or its efforts at persuasion—are not the decisive factor in the decision to adopt EU rules.

Lesson-drawing does not imply that rules or programs are transferred without any adaptation to the domestic context. As with other types of policy transfer, there are four basic degrees of lesson-drawing (Dolowitz and Marsh 2000, 13; see also Rose 1991, 21–22): copying (direct and complete transfer), emulation (adoption, with adjustment to different circumstances, of a program already in effect elsewhere, or the transfer of the ideas behind the program), combination (mixtures of policies from different places), and inspiration (another program inspiring policy change with the final outcome not drawing on the original).

Particular cases of rule adoption in the CEECs lie at the borderline between domestic choice and EU-induced rule adoption. For example, a government might be dissatisfied with certain policies at home. However, if the rules in question are subject to EU conditionality, policymakers might only look as far as the EU's model rather than searching among a broader range of different models abroad for potentially superior programs. In this case, EU conditionality limits the boundaries of the search, but the mechanism is still one of lesson-drawing, albeit in a "bounded" form: rules are imported voluntarily as the result of perceived domestic utility rather than of a thorough weighting of EU rewards versus adjustment costs.

In other cases, EU conditionality might lead CEEC policymakers to adopt EU rules rather than maintaining incompatible domestic rules, but EU requirements might be rather loose and allow a choice among a range of "EU conform" rules. In such cases, policymakers might scan a number of different models across the member states in order to identify the rules that they expect would operate most effectively in their domestic context. In this case, the external incentives model

---

25. Rose is less concerned with developing a systematic explanatory model that specifies the conditions under which lesson-drawing occurs, notwithstanding the discussion in Rose (1993, 118–42). For a critical review, see James and Lodge (2003).

might best explain rule adoption, but the choice of *specific* rules within a larger universe of conforming rules is best explained by the lesson-drawing model. The most general proposition of the *lesson-drawing model* is:

> *A government adopts EU rules if it expects these rules to solve domestic policy problems effectively.*

Whether a state draws lessons from EU rules depends on the following conditions: a government has to (1) start searching for rules abroad, (2) direct its search at the political system of the EU (and/or its member states), and (3) evaluate EU rules as suitable for domestic circumstances.

These conditions in turn depend on four sets of factors: policy dissatisfaction, EU-centered epistemic communities, rule transferability, and veto players.

Policy Dissatisfaction

The most fundamental condition for a government to search for policy models elsewhere is a (perceived) policy failure and domestic dissatisfaction with the status quo. Policy failure and dissatisfaction with domestic rules can result from changes in the policy environment or in political values, both of which concern most public policies in the CEECs after 1989. The rationalist variant primarily emphasizes the threat of domestic sanctions, such as the loss of support or public office, expected by policymakers to be the main stimulus for the search (Rose 1991, 12). The more sociological variant also considers that policy failure might discredit the ideas underlying a policy domain (Hall 1993, 291). The ensuing search for new rules might result in a process of "complex learning" that changes the belief systems of policymakers and thus leads to changes in policy paradigms that concern not only the setting of instruments and questions of efficiency but also underlying policy objectives and questions of legitimacy, for example of the hierarchy of goals.

We can thus formulate the following *policy dissatisfaction* hypothesis and two more specific conjectures that draw respectively on a rationalist and a sociological variant of lesson-drawing:

> *The likelihood of rule adoption increases as the perception that domestic rules are working satisfactorily decreases.* (1) Policymakers' dissatisfaction with domestic rules increases as the threat of domestic sanctions for maintaining the status quo increases, and (2) dissatisfaction increases as policy failure discredits the ideas underpinning policy.

EU-Centered Epistemic Communities

For a government to draw lessons from EU rules, it does not only have to engage in a search for lessons, it also has to direct its search at the EU or its member states. Since policymakers do not have the time and capacity to search everywhere, familiarity with other political systems is a key factor influencing where they direct their search (Rose 1991, 13).

Geographical proximity can foster familiarity, but a key factor that increases familiarity are professional contacts across institutional and geographical boundaries.[26] Especially in policy areas that depend on technical expertise and specialist knowledge, "epistemic communities" (Haas 1990 and 1992) are an important source of ideas involved in lesson-drawing (see also Rose 1991, 15–16). The influence of epistemic communities on policymakers, then, depends on factors relating to the specific issue as well as the characteristics of the domestic institutional structures that mediate the policy impact of new ideas (see, e.g., Adler and Haas 1992).

We can thus formulate a general *epistemic community hypothesis*, as well as more specific conjectures:

The likelihood of rule adoption increases the more that public policymakers have institutionalized relationships with epistemic communities that promote EU rules and the more that domestic structures are conducive to the influence of new ideas. (1) The influence of epistemic communities increases as uncertainty about cause and effect relationships in a certain policy area among policymakers and with the consensus among the experts involved increases, and (2) influence increases as the institutionalization of expert advice in the policy process and the receptiveness of domestic structures to new ideas increase.[27]

Transferability of Rules

A key condition for a state to draw a "positive" lesson from scanning rules in operation elsewhere is the perception that these rules are successful in solving policy challenges similar to those at home. However, the effectiveness of rules abroad is only one necessary condition. Actors also have to assess whether these rules will still work successfully if they are transferred into a different political system. The likelihood of a positive assessment is higher if the conditions that affect how these rules will work in a given political system are more similar. These conditions include the suitability of institutions needed to implement the rules or the equivalence of resources between governments (Rose 1993, 122–31). In general, we

---

26. For arguments emphasizing the importance of geographical proximity in the case of the CEECs, see Kopstein and Reilly (2000); Orenstein and Haas (2002).

27. The literature specifies further characteristics of the domestic structures that affect the policy impact of ideas from abroad. Most authors focus on the structure of state-society relations. Checkel argues that a statist, and in particular a "state above society" structure is most conducive to elite learning (1999b, 88–91). Risse-Kappen distinguishes between the impact of structures on the access of new ideas to the political system and the ability of an idea that has gained access to find a sufficiently strong following; a liberal structure facilitates the former, a statist structure the latter (1994, 208–12; 1995, 20–28). Cortell and Davis further distinguish different domestic structures not only according to the pattern of state-society relations but also according to the extent to which decision-making authority in an issue area is centralized (1996, 454–57). Hall focuses on the structure of communications between policymakers and professional bodies of experts and emphasizes factors that structure interactions both within expert bodies and the state administration, such as the influence of younger experts within the profession or the extent to which permanent civil servants enjoy a monopoly of access to expertise (1989, 378–79).

would expect transferability to be problematic in the case of the CEECs due to legacies of socialism that led to divergent socioeconomic and institutional developments. The institutional infrastructure to implement and enforce EU rules has to be developed from scratch, and financial and administrative resources are scarce. A CEEC government's evaluations of rule transferability might, however, also draw on historical similarities, for example pre–World War II administrative traditions.

Furthermore, transferability does not only depend on the fungibility of rules. In addition to their technical viability, EU rules also have to be politically acceptable (Hall 1989, 373–75; Rose 1993, 44–46). Even rule changes that are designed to correct dissatisfaction with domestic policy might still adversely affect certain societal groups. As in the external incentives model, the number of domestic veto players and the heterogeneity of their preferences thus also affect the ability of public policymakers to implement lessons learned from EU rules. A key difference to the external incentives model is that while the latter assumes a domestic equilibrium that is upset by the incentives that the EU provides, the lesson-drawing model takes as its starting point a domestic disequilibrium in which the balance of domestic pressures favors a departure from the status quo. On balance, domestic actors opposed to rule changes *as such* are therefore less politically significant. Nonetheless, significant domestic veto players might oppose the choice of *particular* rules among a larger universe of alternative policy changes. Governments thus calculate not only the opportunity costs of adopting EU rules over maintaining the status quo but also between different rule changes.

Finally, transferability does not only depend on material resources, and veto players are not only provoked by the material costs of adopting EU rules. Similar to the concept of "resonance" in the social learning model, more sociological accounts emphasize that EU rules and the ideas that underpin them have to be compatible with the terms of the domestic political discourse. National political discourses are structured by the "network of associations that relate common political ideals, familiar concepts, key issues, and collective historical experiences to each other" and that give most political terms their collective meaning (Hall 1989, 383; see also Hall 1993, 289–90).

These considerations lead us to formulate the following *transferability hypothesis* and more specific conjectures:

> *The likelihood of rule adoption increases with the rule's success in solving similar policy challenges in the EU and the transferability of this success.* (1) Transferability increases with the similarity or substitutability of the institutional, administrative, and financial resources required for their implementation; (2) transferability increases with the compatibility of rules vis-à-vis the national political discourse; and (3) transferability decreases with the number of veto players incurring net adoption costs.

In sum, according to the lesson-drawing model, nonmember states are most likely to adopt EU rules when there is domestic dissatisfaction with the policy status quo, interactions with epistemic communities promoting EU rules are dense, the transferability of rules is high, and veto players are few. If rule adoption follows the lesson-drawing mechanism, the *form of rule adoption* that governments prefer is behavioral adoption rather than merely formal or discursive adoption. As the motivation behind rule adoption is to redress domestic policy failures and not EU rewards, governments have a keen interest in the effective operation of these rules. Still, rule adoption might start with discursive or formal adoption, which can be viable in the short term, to the extent that the main interest of governments is to be *seen* doing something to dispel domestic dissatisfaction with the status quo in a certain area.

Organization of the Volume

The contributions to this volume evaluate the external incentives model of Europeanization against the social learning and lesson-drawing models in comparative case studies covering a wide variety of CEECs and issue areas. We emphasize that these models are not necessarily competing; they might also be complementary.[28] On the one hand, in the ideal case for EU influence, the EU would offer credible and sizeable external incentives for the adoption of rules that enjoy high legitimacy and high lesson-drawing appeal. One the other, some conditions, such as the number of veto players, are relevant in more than one model. Generally, however, conditions differ. According to the external incentives model, we would expect a high likelihood of rule adoption even in the absence of legitimacy, identity, and resonance—which the social learning model emphasizes as necessary conditions— if the conditions specified by the external incentives model were favorable. Likewise, high and credible external incentives should be effective in the absence of policy dissatisfaction and EU-centered epistemic communities, which are emphasized by the lesson-drawing model. On the other hand, the other models would expect rule adoption in the absence of conditionality and of credible and sizeable net benefits—if the conditions of social learning and lesson-drawing were present. Finally, we look for "scope conditions" that specify when one model rather than another works best.

Table 1.2 gives an overview of the countries and issue areas covered in the individual case study chapters. While the authors focus predominantly on the Czech Republic, Hungary, and Poland, many contributions either include these countries in a comparison involving all eight CEE candidate countries that joined in May 2004 or add particular CEECs that are less well researched. The issue areas covered range from basic issues of democracy and human rights via administrative reform and regionalization to a broad selection of economic, social, and environmental policies. In doing so, we seek to avoid biased country-specific or issue-specific findings and to achieve some degree of generalization. All contributions engage in

---

28. For a discussion of designs of theory competition and synthesis, see Jupille, Caporaso, and Checkel (2003).

Table 1.2 Overview of chapters

Chapter	Countries	Issues
Schimmelfennig, Engert, and Knobel	Latvia, Slovakia, Turkey	Liberal democracy
Schwellnus	Hungary, Poland, Romania	Minority rights
Dimitrova	All candidates	Administrative reform
Jacoby	Czech Republic, Hungary	Regional policy, health policy
Grabbe	All candidates	Movement of persons
Andonova	Czech Republic, Poland	Environmental policy
Sissenich	Hungary, Poland	Social policy
Epstein	Poland	Central banking, agricultural policy

testing the external incentives model. However, individual studies might test the explanatory power of the external incentives model explicitly against only one of the alternative models or focus on particular explanatory factors that emerge as especially salient in the cases under investigation.

Frank Schimmelfennig, Stefan Engert, and Heiko Knobel (chapter 2) study the EU's impact on basic democratic and human rights reforms in Slovakia, Turkey, and Latvia. They find that the likelihood of rule adoption varies mainly with the size of domestic adoption costs—provided that the credibility of EU conditionality is high. By contrast, they argue that neither the determinacy of rules nor the factors emphasized by the social learning model—legitimacy, identity, and resonance—significantly affect the likelihood of rule adoption.

Guido Schwellnus (chapter 3) compares the implementation of nondiscrimination and minority rights legislation in Romania, Hungary, and Poland. These cases vary both with regard to the legitimacy of the rules and the strength of EU conditionality. In a two-cuts analysis, he argues that the external incentives model gives a good *prima facie* account of rule adoption in applicant states. However, for a comprehensive explanation, the resonance of EU rules with domestic institutions and legacies and their role in the discursive norm construction within the domestic arena have to be considered. These factors are particularly important in cases where conditionality is weak or EU rules are unclear and contested.

Antoaneta Dimitrova (chapter 4) examines the EU's administrative conditionality in the accession countries. She argues that rule adoption mainly varies with the credibility of both threats of exclusion and promises of inclusion. Her analysis of variation in administrative reform finds that administrative conditionality worked best with states that were neither too far from joining the EU (weakening the promise of membership) nor too close to membership (weakening the threat of exclusion).

Wade Jacoby (chapter 5) derives scope conditions for the applicability of the external incentives and lesson-drawing models from an analysis of two policy areas, namely, regional and health policy, in the Czech Republic and Hungary. He finds that the lesson-drawing model explains rule adoption best in the time period in which EU conditionality was less determinate (prior to the publication of the Commission's 1995 White Paper on alignment with internal market rules) and in policy areas in which the low density of EU rules resulted in a rather light application of conditionality (such as health policy). The external incentives model explains rule adoption best after the EU explicitly formulated its conditionality and particularly in those policy areas in which the EU applied significant pressure on CEECs (regional policy). His study shows that both the availability of alternative models and the number and structure of veto players surviving from the communist period play important roles in determining the likelihood that the CEECs will adopt EU rules.

Heather Grabbe (chapter 6) examines how the EU has influenced the regulation of the movement of people in the CEE candidate states during the accession process. She tests the hypotheses of the external incentives model with regard to two different frameworks: the regulation of the free movement of workers under the single market framework and passport-free travel under the rules of the Schengen agreement. The external incentives model explains the single market case well, less so with the adoption of the Schengen rules. In a second cut, then, Grabbe explores some factors that might explain this special case.

Liliana Andonova (chapter 7) conducts a longitudinal analysis of Europeanization in the area of environmental policy. She argues that while social learning accounts for the EU's influence on environmental policy in the early 1990s, external incentives became dominant with the onset of accession preparations and later on in the process of accession negotiations. She finds that air pollution reforms in the Czech Republic largely completed in the early 1990s were strongly influenced through the "Environment for Europe" process, which provided a forum of policy learning and leveraging of financial assistance. By contrast, Poland adjusted its air pollution policies to the EU only in the late 1990s through the institutional mechanisms prevalent in the pre-accession environmental cooperation between the EU and candidate countries.

Beate Sissenich (chapter 8) tests the explanatory power of the external incentives and social learning models in the case of the transfer of EU social policy to Poland and Hungary. Her finding that rule adoption in this field has been primarily formal, with behavioral adoption lagging behind, is largely consistent with the cost-benefit calculations emphasized in the external incentives model. However, neither external incentives nor social learning can explain why nonstate actors have no input in either country's rule adoption, despite the existence of direct ties to EU and government institutions. She concludes that two domestic factors—weak state capacity and civil society—need to be considered in understanding cross-national rule spread.

Rachel Epstein (chapter 9) compares two cases of successful formal rule transfer in Poland's postcommunist economic policy: central bank independence and agricultural policy. However, she asks why Poland ultimately institutionalized central bank independence despite domestic opposition, while the restructuring of Polish agriculture in compliance with EU demands remained a contentious domestic political issue. She argues that the mechanism of rule transfer matters for the form of rule adoption: whereas processes of social learning tend to foster rule and norm adoption at multiple levels, external incentives tend to elicit formal acceptance accompanied by multilevel resistance.

Adrienne Héritier (chapter 10) comments on the differences and similarities between the research on the Europeanization of accession states in this volume and the Europeanization literature that focuses on EU member states.

In the concluding chapter, we draw together the findings of the case study chapters and formulate conclusions about the conditions under which nonmember states adopt EU rules. We find that the external incentives model generally explains the broader patterns of rule adoption well. However, a key insight that we derive from the contributions is that the influence of the EU depends crucially on the context in which the EU uses its incentives. We thus suggest distinguishing between the context of *democratic conditionality* and the context of *acquis* conditionality. Depending on the context, a more limited set of factors explains variation in rule adoption. In the context of democratic conditionality, credible conditionality and adoption costs are key variables. In the context of *acquis* conditionality, the scope conditions are a credible membership perspective and the setting of EU rules as requirements for membership.

After drawing together the analytical implications of the empirical findings, we assess the contribution of our conceptual insights to related bodies of literatures, namely those dealing with EU enlargement, transition, EU governance and Europeanization, and international institutions. We conclude with an outlook on the prospects of Europeanization in the CEECs and some implications for further research.

CHAPTER TWO

The Impact of EU Political Conditionality

Frank Schimmelfennig, Stefan Engert, and Heiko Knobel

Human rights, liberal democracy, and the rule of law are the fundamental rules of legitimate statehood in the European Union (EU). They are the core conditions that states have to fulfill before they are allowed to enter into accession negotiations and are expected to adopt the specific rules of the *acquis communautaire*. "Political conditionality" is the core strategy of the EU to promote these fundamental rules. In this chapter, we examine the conditions of effective political conditionality and evaluate the explanatory power of the external incentives model in a comparative longitudinal and cross-sectional study of three nonmember states: Slovakia, Turkey, and Latvia. We compare Slovak reactions to political conditionality under the Mečiar (1994–98) and Dzurinda governments (1998–), Turkish rule adoption before and after Turkey was accorded "candidate status" at the Helsinki summit of 1999, and Latvian policy toward the Russian-speaking minority in the early and late 1990s. In each of these cases, rule adoption improved over time.

We argue that the likelihood of rule adoption has varied mainly with the size of adoption costs. Provided that the credibility of EU political conditionality is high both with regard to the promise of membership and the threat of exclusion, it is the size of domestic political costs for the target government that determines its propensity to meet EU demands. Generally, these costs increase the more that EU conditions negatively affect the security and integrity of the state, the government's domestic power base, and its core political practices of power preservation. On the other hand, we argue that the determinacy, legitimacy, and resonance of EU conditions do not affect the likelihood of rule adoption in any systematic way. The analysis corroborates the external incentives model of Europeanization, in particular its credibility and adoption cost hypotheses.

EU Political Conditionality

Since the end of the Cold War in 1989, the EU (then EC) has made assistance and institutional ties—first informally and later formally—conditional on the fulfillment of democratic and human rights standards (see Smith 2001, 37–40). Generally, these conditions become more stringent as external countries seek to upgrade their institutional ties with and assistance by the Union.

Already in January 1989, the European Parliament demanded that "reference to human rights should figure" in the Trade and Cooperation Agreements the EC was beginning to negotiate with the Central and Eastern European countries (CEECs) and should be mentioned specifically in the negotiating mandates given to the Commission (*Agence Europe*, 20 January 1989). In April, the Council made resumption of the negotiations with Romania conditional upon the country's compliance with its human rights commitments in the CSCE framework (*Agence Europe*, 24–25 April 1989). In November, the Paris summit established that "initiatives aimed at the countries of Eastern Europe as a whole are applicable only to those which re-establish freedom and democracy" (*Agence Europe*, 22 November 1989). During his visit to Belgrade in May and June 1991, Jacques Santer, president of the Council, stated that Yugoslavia's passage from the Cooperation Agreement to association "hinges on political conditions such as . . . progress in establishing democracy and respect for human rights and the rights of minorities" (*Agence Europe*, 1 June 1991).

After the dissolution of the Soviet Union, the Commission confirmed that "negotiating . . . new types of agreements has to be subject to political conditions (respect of human rights and democratic freedoms, guarantees for minorities, etc.)" (*Agence Europe*, 27 February 1992). In May 1992, the Council underscored that respect for democratic principles and human rights . . . , as well as the principles of a market economy, constitute essential elements of cooperation and association agreements between the Community and its CSCE partners" (*Agence Europe*, 14 May 1992). Henceforth, the EU added a clause to the agreements that stipulated a suspension of the agreements if partner countries failed to comply with these principles. In November of the same year, the Council approved guidelines for PHARE, the EC's main program of assistance to the CEECs, which made aid conditional upon the "state of advance of the reforms in each of the beneficiary countries" (*Agence Europe*, 16–17 November 1992). On this basis, Croatia and Serbia-Montenegro have long been denied PHARE aid. In July 1993, the new regulations of the aid program for the former Soviet republics (TACIS) strengthened conditionality too: "The level and intensity of the assistance will take into account the extent and progress of reform efforts in the beneficiary country" (*Agence Europe*, 24 July 1993).

Finally, at its Copenhagen summit in June 1993, the European Council established the "stability of institutions guaranteeing democracy, the rule of law, human rights and respect for and protection of minorities" as the *sine qua non* for accession to the EU. In its 1997 Opinions on the applications and in its subsequent

annual progress reports, the Commission has regularly evaluated the political conditions in all candidate countries. In 1997, its negative assessment temporarily
deleted Slovakia from the list of first-wave candidates; until 2004, Turkey's failure
to fulfill the political criteria has been the most serious obstacle to the opening of
accession negotiations with this country.

In sum, the fact that the EU has made basic liberal democratic norms essential,
nonnegotiable conditions for the most important tangible benefits it has to offer—
from aid to membership—fulfills the basic condition of the external incentives
model: that rule adoption is set as a condition for rewards.

Political Conditionality and Adoption Costs:
The Theoretical Argument

In this chapter, we argue that the likelihood for a candidate government to adopt
the basic norms of liberal democracy mainly varies with the size of its domestic
adoption costs. The analysis thus corroborates the adoption cost hypothesis of the
external incentives model.

In the Europeanization literature, adoption costs are often associated with the
strength of the domestic opposition against an EU rule and operationalized as the
number of veto players (cf. Börzel and Risse 2003; Héritier 2001a, 5; see also
chapter 1). For two reasons, however, we focus on the costs for the government
more narrowly. First, in the CEECs we examine here, the number of societal veto
players is generally considered to be small (Dimitrova 2002; Schimmelfennig,
Engert, and Knobel 2003a). Political parties have been organized top-down, are
weakly rooted in society and social organizations, and depend on the state for their
resources. Industrial relations are generally characterized by a state-dominated corporatism (in many cases even patrimonial networks), and an active civil society has
failed to emerge despite promising beginnings in the revolutions of 1989. Rather,
levels of political participation have declined.[1] This characteristic of societal weakness also holds for Turkey (Turan 2002, 6–8; Yavuz 2000, 33–35).

Second, it is in the nature of the liberal democratic rules of political conditionality that they mainly limit the autonomy and power of executives while
expanding that of societal actors. We may therefore assume that veto players are
most likely to be found at the level of governments and that rule adoption will
depend on the effect of EU rules on the power of the executive. Generally, power
costs increase the more that EU conditions negatively affect the security and
integrity of the state, the government's domestic power base, and its core political
practices for power preservation. In the area of human rights and democracy, these
costs will be perceived as high, for instance, if the government relies on authoritarian practices to preserve its power or if it expects minority rights to encourage

---

1. For general assessments along this line, see, e.g., Ágh (1998, 52, 106); Birch (2000, 15–16); Kaldor
and Vejvoda (1999, 11, 19–22); Merkel (1999, 494–532); Sitter (2001, 75–76, 87).

separatism or to make minority parties major players in domestic politics. Thus, it is our central hypothesis that *the likelihood of rule adoption increases as the target governments' domestic political costs decrease.*

On the other hand, we hold that alternative factors will have no relevant or systematic effect on the variation in rule adoption. In discussing alternative factors, we focus on the external incentives and social learning models.

Determinacy and Legitimacy

We argue that variation in the determinacy or legitimacy of rules has had no systematic effect on rule adoption. Many observers point to the lack of determinacy and legitimacy in EU political conditionality. First, the EU has set political conditions that are not part of the *acquis* and are not even shared and met by some of its members (Grabbe 1999, 8). This is particularly true for minority rights (De Witte 2000, 3; Schwellnus, chapter 3). Second, the concrete EU demands for minority rights and protection varied significantly between candidate countries (see also Schwellnus, chapter 3). As the case studies in this chapter will show, the EU accepted the situation in Latvia, where a large part of the resident population will be deprived of Latvian citizenship for a long time to come, while it heavily criticized the Slovak government under Vladimír Mečiar for its treatment of the Hungarian minority, which enjoyed the full rights of Slovak citizens.[2] Finally, as Mineshima showed for the rule of law principle, the political conditions are so vaguely and broadly defined that target governments might not know precisely which changes are required of them and which measures will satisfy EU conditions (2002). Under these circumstances, the effectiveness of political conditionality should suffer according to both the external incentives and the social learning models.

These shortcomings are correctly observed, in principle. We argue, however, that they did not matter for two reasons. First, the general lack of determinacy was offset by concrete demands for changes in state rules and behavior in all kinds of EU communications including, above all, the Commission's Opinions and annual progress reports. The continuous stream of EU evaluations of the political situation in the candidate countries provided them with sufficiently clear feedback to know whether they were meeting the necessary conditions and which further steps were required of them. Thus, determinacy—although not a quality of the rules as such—was indeed high.

Yet the clarifying communications did not imbue EU conditions with higher legitimacy. In line with the external incentives model, we argue, however, that the incentive of membership was so strong that it overrode any concerns and criticisms the candidate countries might have had with the appropriateness of EU conditions. The only reasons for not complying with EU conditions were tangible domestic political costs, not an intangible lack of legitimacy.

---

2. We thank one of the anonymous reviewers for alerting us to this point.

Size and Speed of Rewards

The EU offered membership to all countries analyzed in this chapter. Thus, the size of rewards was constant across cases and cannot explain variation in rule adoption. Moreover, even the huge benefits of EU membership do not produce rule adoption if domestic power costs for governments are high. Moreover, in the case of political conditionality, rewards are generally distant. The liberal democratic political conditions are a prerequisite for opening accession *negotiations*. Hence, even if they fulfill these conditions, the candidate countries need to go through the entire accession process and adopt the EU's more specific *acquis communautaire* before they can reap the benefits of membership.

Credibility

We suggest that while the credibility of threats and promises is a core prerequisite of any effective bargaining process, it cannot in and of itself explain the success of political conditionality. In other words, credibility is a necessary but not a sufficient condition of rule adoption. Political conditionality will not work without credibility, but even if credibility is high, rule adoption will depend on the size of governmental adoption costs.

Generally, high credibility has been a constant feature of EU political conditionality. First, despite the fact that some of the political conditions were understood and applied inconsistently among the member states, they were not contested as conditions of membership and thus could not be manipulated by the candidate countries. Most conspicuously, France, probably the most skeptical EU member state with regard to minority protection on its own territory, has been at the same time most active in demanding the settlement of minority conflicts in the East as a precondition of membership (see, e.g., the Balladur plan of 1993). Second, parallel and additive conditionality have generally been high. EU political conditions have been in line with recommendations and demands of the Organization for Security and Cooperation in Europe (OSCE) and the Council of Europe (CE), that is, those European organizations most directly concerned with the human and minority rights situation in the CEECs. Moreover, they were reinforced by the fact that NATO had made accession subject to the same conditions as the EU. Third, we assume a high degree of transparency across Europe because international organizations as well as NGOs extensively monitor democratic and human rights practices. Thus, the (constant) level of EU-internal and international unity cannot account for variation in rule adoption across the target states. Rather, we would expect effective conditionality across the board.

It is sometimes suggested that the EU cannot credibly threaten some countries with withholding assistance and membership even if they violate its political conditions. For instance, because of its strategic relevance, Russia was rewarded with aid and institutional ties despite severe human rights violations in Chechnya (see Smith 2001, 39). When it comes to membership, however, the political criteria are applied rigidly. On the other hand, the EU might not give some countries—such as Ukraine or Belarus—a credible membership promise even if they fulfilled the political conditions (see Pravda 2001, 22–23; Smith 2001, 37–39, 54). In our sample of cases, however, all countries were associated with the EU and given a membership perspective. Thus, credibility was generally high in this respect, too.

The only variation in credibility in our sample concerns Turkey: here, the credibility of the EU's membership promise to Turkey increased significantly when the European Council officially accorded Turkey candidate status in 1999.

Identification and Resonance

Finally, we claim that identification and resonance cannot explain the variation in rule adoption. Generally, identification with the European and the wider western international community is high in the candidate countries and among their political elites. The "return to Europe" has been their most important postcommunist foreign policy orientation. We claim, however, that strong identification is not sufficient for rule adoption but must be complemented by low domestic adoption costs. Moreover, despite high general identification, the resonance of specific rules may be low. This is especially true for minority rights. We will show, however, that it is the adoption costs of specific rules, not their resonance, that matters for the degree of rule adoption.[3]

We substantiate our theoretical claims in a comparative analysis, both longitudinal and cross-sectional, of three countries, each at two different points in time. The design is comparative statics—that is, we compare the conditions at these time points without explaining why they changed. The selection of cases is guided by two criteria. First, we selected "problematic cases" for the methodological reason that the impact of political conditionality will be most discernible where there is substantial conflict, in comparison to cases in which rule adoption only requires technical adaptation on the basis of normative consensus. Problematic cases are more easily observed and traced because they involve sustained public exchanges, get greater attention by the political institutions, and receive better media coverage. Moreover, in these cases, it is easier to distinguish the impact of the EU from endogenous change, that is, change that would have occurred in the absence of EU conditionality.

This case selection comes at a cost, however.[4] By excluding the "easy cases" from the analysis, we risk biasing the analysis against the model of lesson-drawing, which may well capture the adoption of democracy and human rights rules in countries in which the EU did not have to apply political conditionality to bring about change. For this reason, we limit of our findings to cases of initial conflict

---

3. In Schimmelfennig, Engert, and Knobel (2003b) we argue that whereas resonance does not matter for behavioral rule adoption, it shapes the argumentative verbal reactions to EU conditions by candidate governments.

4. We thank Uli Sedelmeier for discussion of this point.

in which the EU used political conditionality. We study the impact of political conditionality rather than the adoption of fundamental political EU rules in general.

The second criterion of case selection is variation of the independent variables. We selected three countries in which the test variable, the size of domestic political costs, has changed over time from high to low (or lower) costs. This selection allows us to trace and analyze the effects of change in the test variable on the dependent variable (rule adoption) while holding other country-specific conditions constant. As far as possible, we tried to avoid cases in which the test variable co-varied with one or more of the control variables. Finally, where possible, we also differentiate between issues and their legitimacy and adoption costs within the case studies, thereby adding to the number of cases and the variation.

For an overview, see table 2.1, in which the negative sign indicates a hypothesized negative effect of the variable on rule adoption, and a positive sign indicates a positive effect. At first glance, the signs for "rule adoption" perfectly match the signs for the "size of adoption costs," indicating that the size of adoption costs is both a necessary and a sufficient condition of rule adoption. Moreover, in most of our cases, credibility was high and therefore qualifies as a necessary but not sufficient condition of rule adoption. The relevance of this variable is emphasized by the Turkish case, in which rule adoption was preceded by an increase in credibility.

By contrast, the variables emphasized by the social learning model—legitimacy, identification, and resonance—are not systematically related to rule adoption. In the following case studies, we substantiate the results summarized in table 2.1 with empirical evidence. The case studies mainly consist of descriptions of the negative and positive signs for the independent variables and rule adoption.

Slovakia

Initial Conflict

In September 1994, the Movement for a Democratic Slovakia (HZDS), the party of Mečiar, won the parliamentary elections and formed a coalition with the Slovak National Party (SNS) and the Association of the Workers of Slovakia (ZRS). Immediately after the elections, the coalition embarked upon an authoritarian course. Above all, it sought to concentrate political power in the hands of the prime minister. It curbed the rights of the opposition in parliament and harassed its members; it defamed, ignored, and tried to force out of office President Michal Kováč; it ignored decisions by independent courts; and it brought public administration at all levels under the control of its followers. Moreover, it expanded governmental control of the audiovisual media, applied financial pressure on the private media, and restricted the freedom of the press. Finally, it was hostile toward any autonomous rights of the Hungarian minority that makes up around 12 percent of the population. In sum, the political style of the Mečiar government between

Table 2.1 Overview of case study conditions and results

Countries	Size of adoption costs	Determinacy and legitimacy	Credibility	Size of rewards	Speed	Identification	Resonance	Rule adoption
Slovakia (Meciar)	–	Mixed	+	+	–	Mixed	+	–
Slovakia (Dzurinda)	+	Mixed	+	+	–	+	+	+
Turkey (1990s)	–	Mixed	–	+	–	+	–	–
Turkey (from 2000)	Mixed	Mixed	+	+	–	+	–	Mixed
Latvia (early 1990s)	–	–	+	+	–	Mixed	–	–
Latvia (late 1990s)	+	–	+	+	–	Mixed	–	+

1994 and 1998 is safely characterized as a "tyranny of the majority" (see, e.g., Bútora and Bútorová 1999, 84; Schneider 1997).

Conditionality

Almost immediately after the 1994 elections, the Commission began to express its "doubts and fears" with regard to the domestic behavior of the new majority (*Agence Europe*, 7 December 1994). A year later, in October 1995, an EU *démarche* initiated a continuous stream of criticism on all aspects of "Mečiarism" and appeals to Slovakia to comply with its obligations as an EU associate. The *démarche* already reminded the Mečiar government that "Slovakia is an associated country in a pre-accession period and . . . the criteria of approval at the Copenhagen Summit are applicable to it" (*Agence Europe*, 27 October 1995). In 1996, then, the Slovak government received increasingly concrete signals that its chances of joining the EU had diminished sharply. Even after the Commission and the European Council decided not to invite Slovakia to accession negotiations in 1997, the EU continued to assure Slovakia that it was eligible and in principle welcome to become a member. At the same time, however, the EU was increasingly explicit about the need for a change in government as a precondition (*Agence Europe*, 31 May 1997, 15 October 1997).

Conditions

The Slovak case combines variation in the test variable (size of adoption costs) with constant values for most of the control variables. It is thus a suitable case for testing the impact of the size of adoption costs on rule adoption. There is, however, a potentially confounding influence because identification improved together with the size of adoption costs. Finally, determinacy and legitimacy vary among the EU conditions.

(1) *Determinacy and legitimacy.* The EU took issue both with the authoritarian tendencies in the Mečiar government's general domestic politics and with its policy toward the Hungarian minority. According to the social learning model, democratic conditionality should have been more successful than minority rights conditionality.

(2) *Credibility.* Together with the other CEECs—the Czech Republic, Hungary, and Poland—Slovakia had always been named a "most likely" candidate for the first round of EU enlargement. Thus, the credibility of the EU promise of membership was comparatively high. Some observers even argue that the Mečiar government perceived it as so strong that it underestimated the EU's threats to exclude Slovakia if it failed to fulfill the political conditions (Kelley 2004; Samson 2001). Although the 1997 EU decision to exclude Slovakia from accession negotiations certainly enhanced the credibility of EU political conditionality, the EU had made it clear since 1995 that Slovakia would not qualify without a thorough change in its domestic politics. The threat signals were so clear and consistent, and the

strategic or economic importance of Slovakia for the EU so small, that we consider the credibility of promises *and* threats throughout to have been high.

(3) *Identification.* The identification of the Mečiar government with the western international community was mixed at best. Whereas the SNS and the ZRS were both staunchly antiwestern parties and represented the far right and the far left of the Slovak party spectrum, the HZDS is best understood as a populist party representing "the older, less educated, and less reform-minded part of the population" (Bútora and Bútorova 1999, 81). It had neither been antiwestern nor profoundly nationalist at first but embraced Slovak nationalism to mobilize its supporters, to create its own power base in a separate Slovak state, and to forge a coalition with the SNS (Schneider 1997, 20). By contrast, the ten parties of the opposition alliance that won the 1998 elections "all support[ed] Slovakia's integration into the European Union and NATO" (Bútora and Bútorova 1999, 82; cf. Kirschbaum 1999, 600). Finally, the ratings for the image of the EU and the support for membership in Slovak public opinion were, by Central and Eastern European standards, comparatively high.[5]

(4) *Resonance.* The resonance of the EU's basic political rules in Slovak society was high by Eastern European standards. Support for democracy in Slovakia was as strong as it was in the more consolidated democracies of the Czech Republic, Hungary, and Poland.[6] Moreover, Slovak society was highly concerned about the deterioration of the human rights situation in their country. Of all the EU candidate countries, Slovaks saw the political development of their country most negatively between 1993 and 1997 (Stankovsky, Plasser, and Ulram 1998, 78).

(5) *Size of Adoption Costs.* For the Mečiar government, the adoption costs were high. The main motivation for Mečiar's authoritarian policies was the preservation of power in a potentially volatile political environment. In particular, by establishing a firm control over the parliament and isolating the president, he sought to prevent a repetition of the events that had brought down his government in early 1994 (Schneider 1997, 11). Moreover, giving in to EU democratic conditionality, especially with regard to the autonomy of the Hungarian minority, would have endangered the coalition with the SNS, which in the absence of other partners was crucial for the HZDS.

By contrast, in 1998, the opposition parties had been elected on a platform to advance democratic reform and western integration, and—in addition to preventing Mečiar from returning to power—these issues were the glue of an otherwise programmatically diverse coalition of reformed communists, Christian Democrats, and parties of the Hungarian minority. Thus, EU integration—and, by extension, compliance with EU demands—was in the immediate domestic political interest of the coalition parties. For these reasons, and despite severe coalitional conflict,

---

5. *Central and Eastern Eurobarometer*, No. 8, 1998, http://europa.eu.int/comm/public_opinion/archives/ceeb/ceeb8/ceeb08.pdf. Accessed July 2004.

6. Some figures were even better than in the neighboring CEECs (Stankovsky, Plasser, and Ulram 1998, 80, 81, 83).

repeated threats of coalition parties to leave the government, and a breakup and restructuring of some of them, the government of Prime Minister Mikuláš Dzurinda managed to survive its entire four-year term.

Rule adoption

In spite of the unambiguous warnings from the West and the high stakes of EU membership involved, EU political conditionality had no major or lasting impact on the behavior of the Mečiar government. Even the single most important success of western conditionality policy, the signing of the Basic Treaty between Slovakia and Hungary, which committed Slovakia to the CE guidelines for the treatment of national minorities and to the granting of autonomy rights to its Hungarian population, was compromised and rendered ineffective by domestic measures. Signed at the Stability Pact conference in March 1995, the treaty met with the fierce resistance of the SNS, Mečiar's main coalition partner at home. Slovakia finally ratified the treaty in March 1996, but only after the government had planned several laws to dilute the treaty provisions (see, e.g., Leff 1997, 250; Schneider 1997, 20–24).

By contrast, the Dzurinda coalition government immediately declared its commitment to the constitutive rules of the EU and its willingness to meet EU political conditions. A few days after having been elected prime minister, Dzurinda went to Brussels and afterwards vowed to move quickly to meet two concerns expressed during the talks, "that a law on national minority languages be drawn up and that an investigation into the 1995 abduction of former President Kováč's son be launched" (*RFE/RL Newsline*, 9 November 1998). Generally, government representatives declared they would "do everything" for the EU to decide in favor of inviting Slovakia to membership negotiations in 1999 (*RFE/RL Newsline*, 28 December 1998, 22 January 1999).

In parallel, the new coalition set about to resolve the constitutional conflicts and to rectify the authoritarian tendencies of the Mečiar years. For instance, the parliament immediately proceeded with the election—blocked by Mečiar—of a new state president and restored the rights of the parliamentary opposition. Hungary and Slovakia quickly reached agreement on implementing the Basic Treaty (*RFE/RL Newsline*, 16 November 1998). In July 1999, the Slovak parliament approved a minority language law in line with OSCE recommendations; it was welcomed by the EU (Kirschbaum 1999, 600). Finally, in December 1999, the European Council decided to open accession talks with Slovakia.

Results

In Slovakia, rule adoption was a result of a change in government. From 1994 to 1998, Slovakia was ruled by a coalition that relied on authoritarian practices to preserve its power and whose identification with the West was mixed at best. In 1998, it was replaced by a coalition that had been elected on a platform of democratic reform and EU integration and, despite its political heterogeneity, was united in its identification with the western community and was stabilized by the need to work together to achieve EU membership. Thus, the Slovak case study does not fully discriminate between the impact of costs and identification. It seems, however, that for Mečiar, the potential power costs of rule adoption were more relevant than identification with the West. Although Mečiar did not share the anti-western orientations of his coalition partners, he was prepared to give in to them to remain in power.[7]

By contrast, the different legitimacies of general democratic norms and minority norms did not have the expected effects. If anything, the Mečiar government made stronger (tactical) concessions to the EU on minority policy than on domestic liberalization in general, and the Dzurinda government began to comply immediately with both kinds of EU demands.

The credibility of EU promises was high during the entire period of examination and thus cannot by itself explain the change in rule adoption. It also seems that societal resonance, another constant, cannot account for rule adoption. The change in Slovakia suggests, however, that both factors together had an impact on rule adoption that is obscured by our research design of comparative statics.

Although neither credibility nor resonance had any major effect on the Mečiar government while it lasted, public opinion polls indicate that they were relevant factors in the election of a reform- and integration-oriented government in 1998 and its confirmation in 2002. A majority of Slovak citizens were aware of and preoccupied with the deterioration of their country's standing in Europe and its exclusion from EU enlargement. This concern was only second to the concern about the growth of violence (Bútorová 1998, 35; Bútorová and Gyárfásová 1998, 54, 59, 62). In addition, the opposition overcame their fragmentation and cooperated to make the most of the votes they received and to isolate the HZDS, which remained the strongest party in the country.

Thus, the transition from a "high cost/weak identification" government to a "low cost/strong identification" coalition, one that brought about a significant improvement of rule adoption, can itself be partially attributed to a credible policy of conditionality, which caused a prowestern and prodemocratic electorate to reassess the costs of having a government, which proved to be an obstacle to the western integration of their country.

Turkey

Initial Conflict

Turkey's state doctrine of "Kemalism" is partially based on values alien to western liberal democracy and, on a wide range of issues, has led to authoritarian domes-

---

7. Interview with member of the Slovak mission to NATO, NATO headquarters, Brussels, 18 May 1999. See also Goldman (1999, 169) and Michael Frank, "Die Slowakei droht abzudriften," *Süddeutsche Zeitung (SZ)*, 15 November 1994.

tic political practices that conflict with core European norms.[8] First, through the National Security Council (NSC), composed of the highest military and civilian leaders of the country, the military has had an enormous, albeit informal, influence on day-to-day politics (Rouleau 2000; Tank 2001). It generally assumed the self-defined task of guarding Kemalist principles in Turkish politics. It intervened four times in domestic politics to restore "democratic rule": 1960, 1971, 1980, and indirectly in 1997. Second, general human rights and the rule of law have been systematically violated for decades. Turkey upheld the death penalty, which runs against the European norm. Torture has been widespread. The freedoms of expression and association were restricted, and the judicial system includes a strong role for military courts, which did not meet European standards of independent and fair justice. Finally, the Kurdish minority has suffered from violent repression and lacked minority rights and protection.

Conditionality

Turkey is subject to the same conditionality regime as the CEECs. Whereas a general membership perspective was already included in the association agreement of 1964 (Ankara Agreement, Article 28), it only became more concrete when the EU granted Turkey candidate status at the Helsinki summit of December 1999. Just as in the case of the CEECs, Turkey was included in the Commission's annual progress reports, and the EU promised that membership negotiations would begin as soon as the country fulfilled the Copenhagen criteria. At its Copenhagen Council of December 2002, the European Council agreed to review the state of political reforms and decide about the opening of accession negotiations in December 2004.

Conditions

In contrast with the other cases, credibility increased but adoption costs decreased only partially in Turkey. As a result, we expect to see differentiated instead of wholesale rule adoption over time. This would also be the expectation given the different degree of legitimacy and determinacy of EU political conditions. (High) identification and (low) resonance remained constant.

(1) *Legitimacy*. As in the case of Slovakia, EU conditionality has targeted rules with different degrees of determinacy and legitimacy. They range from the abolition of the death penalty, one of the most determinate and legitimate European human rights norms, to the less institutionalized and more contested minority rights norms. The norm of civilian control of the military is located somewhere in between: although it is widely shared, it is neither clearly specified in the Accession Partnership Document nor formally institutionalized in the *acquis*.

(2) *Credibility*. Although the EU had given Turkey a general membership perspective in the association agreement of 1964 and had never explicitly withdrawn

8. The Kemalist model is based on the following six principles: republicanism, nationalism, secularism, reformism, statism, and populism. For an excellent short discussion, see Kramer (2000, 3–10).

its commitment, the credibility of the EU promise was doubtful. First, the sheer length of the probation period raised doubts as to whether Turkey would ever meet the accession criteria. Second, some European leaders not only questioned the ability of Turkey to meet the political membership conditions but also contested Turkey's general status as a "European country" for cultural, historical, geographical, and religious reasons.[9] The credibility problem became especially acute when, at the Luxembourg summit of 1997, the first CEECs were invited to accession talks—but Turkey was not. In reaction, Turkey suspended its participation in the Association Council. Credibility was strongly enhanced when the EU granted Turkey candidate status at the Helsinki summit in 1999 and subsequently began to develop a pre-accession strategy and accession partnership with Turkey.

(3) *Identification.* The Kemalist elites have always emphasized their European identity and have consistently striven to be part of all European organizations.[10] In fact, the EU is the only major European organization in which Turkey is not yet a full member. The Turkish state elites conceive of themselves as western and regard the West as their primary "in group" in international relations (Kubicek 1999a, 159). As indicated by their strong reaction to the rejection of their candidacy for EU membership at Luxembourg in 1997, the elite policymakers find it painful not to be recognized as worthy of membership.[11] In addition, there is strong support for EU membership and a generally positive image of the EU in Turkish society.[12]

(4) *Resonance.* Yet this strong identification is in remarkable contrast to the lack of rule resonance. First, the role of the military as the guardian of the heritage of Kemal Atatürk has remained unquestioned. The military has traditionally received high rates of approval within society and continues to be the most trusted institution (see, e.g., Kramer 2000, 32). Second, ethnic minority protection is alien to Turkey's notion of nationalism which emphasizes the homogeneity, unity, and indivisibility of the state, its people, and its territory. Finally, a majority of the people supported keeping the death penalty (Rouleau 2000, 113; Schönbohm 2002).

(5) *Size of Adoption Costs.* The political demands of the EU have been widely perceived in the Kemalist state elites as a danger to the internal security of the Turkish state and to the foundations of its power. However, the size and change of adoption costs has varied for the different issues of EU political conditionality.

9. A recent example are remarks by Valery Giscard d'Estaing, head of the Convention on the Future of Europe, who declared that the inclusion of Turkey would spell "the end of the European Union." He claimed that Turkey had "a different culture, a different approach, a different way of life" (*Turkish Daily News*, 11 November 2002). Similar sentiments were voiced by the parliamentary group of the European People's Party in 1997.

10. See, e.g., the National Programme for Adoption of the Acquis (NPAA) of March 2001.

11. *Agence Europe*, 13, 15/16, 19 and 20 December 1997; *SZ*, 15 December 1997.

12. See *Applicant Countries Eurobarometer*, 2001. The figures are comparable to those of Slovakia. Support for membership is at 59% (Slovakia 58%) and 51% of respondents have a positive image of the EU (Slovakia 48%).

First, the Kemalist elites have generally feared the prospect of the disintegration of the Turkish state (as happened to its predecessor, the Ottoman Empire) were all minorities to be granted specific status or regional autonomy (Kuniholm 1996, 358). In addition, the terrorist guerrilla war of the PKK against the Turkish state has raised the stakes and made it even harder for the Kemalist elite to consider minority rights. Conversely, adoption costs decreased significantly when the armed struggle subsided in the late 1990s: after the Turkish military had captured the head of the PKK, Abdullah Öcalan, he called upon his followers to refrain from violence, advocated a political solution to the Kurdish problem, and offered to withdraw his fellow insurgents from Turkish soil (Gunter 2000, 852–59). The PKK and the death penalty issues were closely linked. Although the Turkish government had already established a moratorium on the death penalty in 1984, it reserved the right to execute the state's foremost enemy, namely Öcalan.

However, EU demands still challenged the powerful position of the military. On this issue, adoption costs have remained high. On the one hand, hardly any politician could risk openly challenging the role and position of the military without facing the threat of personal persecution. On the other hand, however, the Kemalist political elites regarded the military as the ultimate protection against the challenge of radical Islamism—such as in 1997, when the military forced an Islamist government to step down and returned the Kemalist parties to power (Dembinski 2001, 19).

Rule adoption

During the 1990s, Turkey did not make any substantial progress on the EU's political conditions. Since 2000, however, Turkey has embarked on a series of reform activities. The current (2003) overall picture of rule adoption is mixed.

When the EU accorded Turkey candidate status in 1999, accompanied by a long list of political conditions to fulfill prior to accession negotiations, it triggered numerous legislative activities. However, the first set of reforms in October 2001 mainly consisted of limited formal changes that left fundamental issues and the Kemalist power base intact. Formal concessions, such as further limitations of the death penalty to terrorist and war crimes, a substantial increase in the number of civilians in the NSC, and the use of Kurdish in radio and television broadcasts, still fell far short of EU demands. On the other hand, the legislative package of August 2002 included the abolition of the death penalty in peacetime and cultural rights for the Kurdish minority (the addition of Kurdish in schools and broadcasting). In January 2003, Turkey also signed Protocol 6 to the European Convention on Human Rights (ECHR), which outlaws the death penalty. For the first time, the EU, in its annual progress report of 2002, as well as international NGOs like Human Rights Watch, acknowledged significant change in these areas (Commission 2002a, 46; *Turkish Daily News*, 9 August 2002). Nevertheless, the Commission pointed out that the practical implementation of the new laws still remained and that the issue of civilian control of the military needed to be addressed adequately (2002a, 47). In sum, we need to explain both the improvement in Turkish compliance with EU demands and its variation across issues.

Results

Some of the explanatory factors obviously explain neither compliance nor non-compliance: identification and resonance have remained constant over time and across issues. Whereas high identification with the EU community did not by itself promote rule adoption in the 1990s, the lack of resonance of the EU conditions did not prevent partial progress in recent years.

Legitimacy varies across issues, but the match with compliance is imperfect. Whereas the most progress has indeed been achieved with regard to the most legitimate rule, the prohibition of the death penalty, there has been more progress on the least legitimate rule (minority protection) than on the more legitimate issue of civilian control of the military. Moreover, legitimacy cannot explain the change in compliance because it remained constant throughout the period of study.

"Costs" and "credibility" are the most promising candidates for an explanation of rule adoption in Turkey. There is no doubt that the increased credibility of the EU's promise of membership after the Helsinki summit was a necessary catalyst for change. But if it had been a sufficient condition of rule adoption, it should have had a uniform effect across issues. A full account of change in Turkey, therefore, needs to be based on the differential size of adoption costs: the higher the costs, the less effective conditionality has been.

Although the latest changes on the death penalty and minority protection mark a significant break with the past, the domestic power costs they imply are comparatively small. First, Turkey already had a moratorium on the death penalty in place since 1984. Second, the PKK had renounced armed combat. Given the fact that the vast majority of the Kurds in the southeast oppose the establishment of a separate state (Kuniholm 1996, 357–58), recognition of cultural and linguistic rights as well as the prospect of cashing in the peace dividend comes at a historically low price to solve the long-lasting, bitter Kurdish problem by peaceful means. Moreover, the (Kurdish) People's Democracy Party (HADEP), Turkey's only "minority party," has virtually no chance to cross the 10 percent threshold in national elections.

By contrast, the power of the military has not been curbed. The symbolic measure to increase the number of civilians in the NSC does not diminish the military's de facto influence. As General Hüseyin Kivrikoglu, chief of the General Staff, commented: "If they want 100 civilians as members of the National Security Council, so be it. They asked us, and I told my friends, 'There will be no objections.' . . . In any case MGK [NSC] decisions aren't taken through voting" (*Turkish Daily News*, 26 July 2000). In sum, the Turkish case strongly supports the conditionality model of Europeanization.

Latvia

Initial Conflict

In contrast with Slovakia and Turkey, Latvia has not been criticized for violating democratic principles in general. Yet its policy toward the non-Latvian population did not meet the standards of European organizations on minority rights. Latvia is the Baltic state with the highest proportion of "Russian speakers," who migrated to Latvia as part of the policy of "Russification" during the Soviet era (Haab 1998, 4). When Latvia became independent from the Soviet Union in 1991, parliament granted automatic citizenship only to the citizens of the interwar Latvian Republic and their descendants. Moreover, the government set high conditions for naturalization. Since the Russian-speaking immigrants lost their Soviet citizenship with the end of the Soviet Union, this policy deprived 30 percent of the population of their political rights—and a state (Hanne 1996, 72). In the two following years, the government enacted additional laws on the use of the Latvian language, education, and economic rights, the bulk of which indirectly discriminated against the non-Latvian population (Pabriks 1999, 151). Here we concentrate on two central issues of conflict, the citizenship law and the language law.

Conditionality

The EU did not develop its own minority rights policy on Latvia but followed the lead of the OSCE and its High Commissioner on National Minorities (HCNM), Max van der Stoel. While the HCNM did not take issue with the requirement of a naturalization process for "Soviet immigrants" itself (including a test of Latvian language), he demanded that the naturalization process and the language requirements be regulated as liberally as possible. Yet the HCNM did not have any tangible political or material rewards to offer in return for compliance and thus could not credibly pursue a strategy of conditionality.

By contrast, the CE and the EU linked rule adoption with membership. In December 1993, the CE stated that Latvia would not be admitted as a member if it did not change the citizenship law. In its Copenhagen criteria of the same year, the EU established respect for minority rights as a political accession criterion. In July 1997, in its Opinions on the applicant countries, the Commission mirrored the concerns of the HCNM by noting that "Latvia needs to take measures to accelerate naturalization procedures to enable the Russian speaking non-citizens to become better integrated into Latvian society" (Commission 1997a).[13]

---

13. In March 1997, the Commission asked the HCNM to contribute in drawing up the Opinions (*Agence Europe*, 19 March 1997).

Conditions

The Latvian case combines change in the test variable with constant values for the control variables. It therefore provides a model quasi-experimental setting for examining the impact of adoption costs on rule adoption.

(1) *Legitimacy.* In Latvia, political conditionality focused exclusively on the less legitimate minority rights. In comparison to other basic democratic norms of the western community, the international consensus on minority protection was weak and less formalized. However, with regard to the language issue, international actors could also rely on various more legitimate international antidiscrimination norms.

(2) *Credibility.* Soon after achieving independence in 1991, Latvia embarked on a path of progressive integration into the EU. The EU and Latvia signed a Trade and Cooperation Agreement in 1992, a Free Trade Agreement in 1994, and a Europe Agreement of association in 1995. The Commission evaluated Latvia's application for membership in its 1997 Opinions together with that of the other CEE candidates. Thus, in contrast to Turkey, the Latvian government had no reason to doubt the general membership promise of the EU and the member governments. At the same time, the EU had emphasized the importance of respect for minority rights in general—and that of the recommendations of the HCNM on Latvia in particular—early on.[14] The fact that, in 1997, the Commission recommended Estonia but not Latvia for accession negotiations proved both the credibility of the membership promise for the Baltic states, which were generally otherwise treated as a group, and the credibility of the threat to exclude individual countries for political reasons. Thus, we consider credibility to have been high throughout.

(3) *Identification.* The ruling Latvian political elite identified itself strongly with the western international community throughout the decade. All centrist and conservative parties were strongly pro-European. They regarded Latvia as a part of western civilization, and they were committed to the westernization of their political and economic systems as well as to Latvia's integration in western organizations (Plakans 1997, 285; Jubulis 1996, 69; Smith et al. 1998, 108). Extremist groups that did not share the western orientation remained overall weak in parliament and society.[15] However, opinion polls show that support for EU membership and a positive image of the EU have consistently been weak in Latvian society compared with other candidate countries.[16] Therefore, we rate identification as mixed.

14. For instance, at a meeting of the EC Troika with the Baltic states in April 1993 (*Agence Europe*, 21 April 1993) and in an EU Communiqué on the Draft Latvian Citizenship Law in June 1994 (*Agence Europe*, 23 June 1994).

15. A coalition between extreme nationalists and communists failed shortly after the 1995 elections.

16. *RFE/RL Newsline*, 31 July 1998, 18 March 1999; *Central and Eastern Eurobarometer*, No. 8, 1998. This applied even after the start of accession negotiations. The figures for both items are 33 percent, according to the *Applicant Countries Eurobarometer* 2001.

(4) *Resonance.* As in the Turkish case, the specific resonance of western rules of minority rights and protection has been low. Among the political forces that have dominated Latvian politics, nationalism has had a strong influence. They shared the belief that the new Latvian state must ensure the survival and revival of the Latvian nation, identity, and language after decades of "Russification." In essence, the national trauma of "Russification" and the nationalist ideology of the elites in power reduced the resonance of western standards applicable to the minority policy (Pabriks 1999; Wälzholz 1998, 92–93). Moreover, anti-Russian orientations were strong in the Latvian population—at any rate, there was no societal pressure on the government to improve the situation of the non-Latvian population.

(5) *Size of Adoption Costs.* The costs of adoption to minority rights conditionality were high at the beginning and decreased from the mid-1990s on. At the beginning of the decade, all governments emphasized the risk that a policy aiming at a change in the composition of citizens would cause a dramatic shift in Latvian politics, because it would strengthen the political power of people considered loyal to Russia (Birckenbach 1997, 21–23; Holoboff 1995, 121), threaten the independence of Latvia—especially since Russian troops were still present on Latvian territory (Holoboff 1995, 112–15; Jubulis 1996, 61)—and undermine the survival and revival of the Latvian culture and language (Pabriks 1999, 150; Wälzholz 1998, 88; Melvin 2000, 145). Since the Latvians were unwilling to support substantial concessions to the non-Latvian population, electoral defeat was a substantial risk for all governments. Building stable coalitions in parliament was impossible without parties from the conservative spectrum; therefore, proposing a liberal minority policy carried the risk of coalition breakdown and thus of a loss of power.[17]

From the mid-1990s onwards, however, the Latvian political elite realized two things. First, a liberalized policy would not lead to mass naturalization, since the majority of non-Latvians were actually hesitant to apply for citizenship. Furthermore, "Russian speakers" did not form a unitary political front. Hence there were no signs of a political upheaval on the horizon.[18] Second, the Latvian elite saw the progressive integration of Latvia into European structures as a guarantee of Latvian independence.[19] Thus, once the Russian troops had left and Latvian association with the EU and NATO deepened, the perceived threat diminished. In addition, the people of Latvia increasingly made welfare their political priority, which also reduced the risk of electoral defeat to some extent (Bungs 2000, 244). Altogether, domestic adoption costs decreased considerably.

17. As late as October 1997, the governing coalition under Prime Minister Guntars Krasts was on the brink of collapse because of the minority rights issue (see *Frankfurter Allgemeine Zeitung*, 17 October 1997).

18. See Rose (1997, 12); and State President Guntis Ulmanis's address to the Parliament of Latvia, 22 June 1998, http://www.am.gov.lv/en/news/speeches/1998/jun/3745. Accessed July 2004.

19. See, e.g., the 1995 "Foreign Policy Concept of the Latvian Republic" cited in Jubulis (1996, 61).

Rule adoption

The Latvian parliament, called the Saiema, repeatedly ignored the HCNM's suggestions in practice and accepted them in the second half of the 1990s only when they were directly linked to EU membership. In response to the arbitrary quota system of naturalization envisioned in the 1993 draft law, van der Stoel suggested that it be replaced by a law with a guaranteed annual naturalization quota. But in June 1994 the Saeima hardly modified the draft law, revising it only to ensure Latvian membership in the CE, which was perceived among the CEECs as an antechamber to the EU and NATO (Jubulis 1996). Still, the new conditions for naturalization did not meet the expectations of the western organizations. In its letters of October 1996 and May 1997 to Foreign Minister Valdis Birkavs, van der Stoel therefore made several recommendations to overcome the "stagnation of the naturalization process": the reduction of naturalization fees, the simplification of the tests required of new citizens, and, above all, the granting of citizenship to stateless children and the abolishment of the naturalization windows, which allowed only a fixed small number of noncitizens to acquire citizenship each year. In his immediate answer, Birkavs was evasive and defensive on the main recommendations.[20]

Later in the same year, however, the Commission published its Opinion on Latvia, which mirrored the HCNM's demands. In response, the Latvian government introduced a package of laws to the Saiema that partly followed the HCNM recommendations. On 1 June 1998, Foreign Minister Birkavs urged the parliament to comply with the OSCE recommendations because Latvia would otherwise risk losing allies in Europe and the United States (*RFE/RL Newsline*, 2 June 1998). Later the same month, the amendments as proposed by the government were approved and hailed by both the Clinton administration and the EU as furthering Latvia's integration into European and transatlantic structures (*RFE/RL Newsline*, 23 and 24 June 1998).

The second case is the Latvian state language bill. In 1998, the Saeima drafted a law that was criticized by the OSCE and the CE because it not only required the use of the state language in the public sector but also asked private bodies and enterprises to conduct their activities in Latvian.[21] In April 1999, van der Stoel warned that passages of the bill in its current form might impair Riga's chances of integration into the EU (*RFE/RL Newsline*, 19 April 1999). The Finnish EU presidency reiterated the warning but a large majority of the Saeima voted in favor of the law nevertheless. However, new president Vaira Vike-Freiberga refused to sign the law and asked the parliament to revise it to conform to EU legislation (*RFE/RL Newsline*, 7, 9, 15 July 1999, 1 September 1999). On 9 December 1999, a few days before the Helsinki summit of the European Council was to decide about

20. See http://www.arts.uwaterloo.ca/MINELRES/osce/counrec.htm.
21. See Parliamentary Assembly of the Council of Europe, "Honouring of obligations and commitments by Latvia," Doc. 8426, 24 May 1999.

the opening of accession negotiations with the next group of CEECs, the Saeima finally passed a revised law. As a result, Latvia was invited to begin accession talks in 2000.

Results

The analysis shows that, given a credible conditionality strategy of the EU—and despite low legitimacy and resonance of EU rules of minority protection as well as a comparatively low degree of societal identification with the EU—the decrease in the size of domestic adoption costs furthered progressive rule adoption. However, each major step in the process of rule adoption required the use of concrete linkages with membership in the EU and other regional organizations.

In this chapter, we analyzed a very basic process of Europeanization—the conditions under which the EU has been able to transfer its constitutive political rules to the CEECs: democracy, the rule of law, and human rights. Together with the end of communism in this region, the EU developed a strategy of political conditionality, offering the CEECs aid and institutional ties on the condition that they respect human and minority rights and continue on the path of democratization and democratic consolidation. Since the EU assumed a proactive role early on— and since we focused on cases of initial noncompliance and rule contestation—an account of rule adoption via lesson-drawing could be excluded from the start. Therefore, the main question we address is whether the impact of EU political conditionality is adequately explained by the external incentives model or, alternatively, the social learning model of rule adoption.

The analysis corroborates the conditionality model of Europeanization. First, credibility proved to be a necessary condition of rule adoption. This is best seen in the case of Turkey, where the granting of EU candidate status—a more credible promise of membership—triggered a wave of unprecedented reform activities. But even in the cases of Slovakia and Latvia, where credibility had been higher from the beginning, the actual exclusion of both countries from the shortlist of candidate countries in 1997 enhanced the credibility of the EU political conditionality, which helped mobilize the electorate (Slovakia) or lead legislators to accept EU conditions grudgingly (Latvia). Credibility, however, was not sufficient.

Second, the size of adoption costs needs to be taken into account to explain why even highly credible promises of membership and threats of exclusion sometimes failed to bring about rule adoption. In our selection of cases, low adoption costs qualified as a necessary and sufficient condition of rule adoption. Improvement in compliance was regularly preceded by a significant decrease in the domestic political costs of compliance: in Slovakia, the demise of a coalition that relied on authoritarian practices to preserve its power; in Turkey, the subsiding armed struggle with the PKK; and in Latvia, the changing perception of naturalization as a threat to Latvian independence and identity.

Finally, the lack of clarity and determinacy of the constitutive EU rules was compensated by the resolve with which the EU defended them as the *sine qua non* of inclusion and by its regular communications to the candidate states, in which the Commission specified what it expected them to do to meet the conditions and indicated when it was satisfied with their progress.

By contrast, the conditions of the social learning model proved less successful in explaining the variation in rule adoption. The legitimacy of rules did not matter for compliance at all. Nor was high resonance in any way consistently correlated with rule adoption. It seems plausible, however, from our selection of cases, that resonance has an influence on the path of conditionality: where resonance was low (as in Latvia and Turkey), conditionality had to work through intergovernmental bargaining; where it was high, it could have an impact via the empowerment of domestic actors (as shown by the reaction of the Slovak electorate to the exclusion of Slovakia from the EU accession negotiations).

Finally, overall identification has not had any systematic impact on rule adoption either. It may only be interpreted as a necessary condition of rule adoption if we restrict it to political *elites*: there were no cases of rule adoption without strong identification of the governing elites with Europe and the West. In addition, the case of Slovakia under Mečiar adds plausibility to the conjecture that low governmental identification results in noncompliance. A closer analysis of the Slovak case reveals, however, that it was the interest in preserving political power rather than any antiwestern orientation that motivated the prime minister and his party to ignore EU conditions. Moreover, identification does not qualify as a sufficient condition of change. None of the conditions of the social learning model accounts for the improvement of rule adoption in any of the three countries.

In sum, high EU credibility plus low governmental adoption costs appears to be the key to successful political conditionality.

CHAPTER THREE

The Adoption of Nondiscrimination and Minority Protection Rules in Romania, Hungary, and Poland

Guido Schwellnus

W hen the Copenhagen criteria for the EU membership of Central and Eastern European countries (CEECs) were set out, the list of political conditions included respect for and protection of minorities. However, the meaning of minority protection remains highly contested on the international level, not only between supporters and reluctant states, but also regarding the concepts to be applied in order to guarantee minority protection. Furthermore, since the EU has not itself developed any minority standard to be applied to existing member states so far, there exists a discrepancy between the internal and external application of the minority norm by the EU (De Witte 2000, 4).

The contested and non-EU minority norm can be contrasted with a related but distinct and well-established EU standard: nondiscrimination is required generally as part of the *acquis communautaire*, but it is also specifically demanded to address minority problems in certain applicant countries, in particular with regard to the large Roma population in some CEECs. Moreover, the EU applied differentiated pressure across applicants with regard to both norms, depending on whether minority protection or nondiscrimination issues were regarded as problematic and relevant to security (Brusis 2003b; Hughes and Sasse 2003; Kymlicka 2001).[1]

I thank the editors, the two anonymous reviewers at Cornell, and especially Rachel Epstein, Marika Lerch, David Phinnemore, Milada Anna Vachudova, and Antje Wiener for their helpful comments. The responsibility for this version is mine. Financial support by UACES in the form of a research scholarship is gratefully acknowledged.
1. The question why the EU took a "security-based" rather than a principled "justice-based" approach to promoting minority protection (Kymlicka 2001, 372) and differentiated conditionality according to perceived security risks and not according to one of the other possible patterns, e.g., closeness to accession, is in itself an interesting question. I thank one of Cornell's anonymous reviewers for alerting me to this point. Its discussion lies, however, beyond the scope of this chapter, which investigates rule adoption by applicant states, not strategy choice on the part of the EU.

Therefore, rule adoption can be fruitfully compared across the two norms as well as across countries.

The Impact of EU Rules and Conditionality in Applicant Countries

As outlined in the introductory chapter, rule adoption can be driven by external or internal forces, i.e., it rests either on active rule promotion and conditionality by the EU (external incentives and social learning models) or on a voluntary adoption of EU rules on the part of the applicants (lesson-drawing model). Of course, since the EU's policy of conditionality is one of "reinforcement by reward" (Schimmelfennig, Engert, and Knobel 2003a, 496) and does not include direct imposition or coercion, rule adoption is never entirely EU-driven. The external incentives model therefore also includes domestic factors at the receiving end of EU conditions. There are, however, good reasons to assume that, in the case of EU enlargement, domestic obstacles should be overcome by conditionality. Indeed, the Union seems to be in a particularly strong position vis-à-vis the applicant states. The material asymmetry in favor of Western Europe and the lack of alternatives for the CEECs gives the EU a strong bargaining position. The ideational factors stressed by the social learning model also point strongly toward a high degree of EU leverage: in most of the applicant states, EU membership enjoys both high rates of public support and strong elite commitment. The end of the Cold War gave western norms of liberal democracy and market economy a high degree of legitimacy (Schimmelfennig 2000, 124).

Accordingly, the first cut put forward in this chapter tests assumptions of the external incentives and social learning models, starting with the "supply side" of EU conditionality and rule promotion, namely the existence and quality of EU conditions. The main assumption is: the stronger and clearer EU conditionality, the higher the probability of rule adoption. To distinguish this hypothesis based on the determinacy of EU conditions (as put forward by the external incentives model) from the legitimacy hypothesis of the social learning model, an additional distinction can be made between strong and weak EU rules. Congruence between well-established EU rules and conditionality can be seen as a measure of the legitimacy of EU conditions. On the basis of these distinctions, four configurations are possible:

Strong EU rule and conditionality/promotion: In this case, both the external incentives and social learning models would predict at least good "supply side" conditions for rule adoption, since applicants face strong incentives and clear demands, and conditions are based on legitimate rules shared and applied by all EU members. Internally driven lesson-drawing is rather unlikely, because if domestic actors were actively looking for EU models to copy, explicit and prolonged conditionality on the EU's part would hardly be necessary to trigger rule adoption.

Weak EU rule, but strong conditionality/promotion: There are several possible cases of the EU promoting rules that are not part of the *acquis* and no shared standard among member states. One is the development of conditions specifically designed for the transition countries in Central and Eastern Europe applying for membership, a second the "import" of rules established in other European institutions like the Council of Europe. The predicted likelihood of rule adoption in the face of "double standards" differs between the external incentives and the social learning models. From the perspective of the external incentives model, no significant difference in the probability of rule adoption compared to conditionality based on EU rules is to be expected as long as conditions are clear and determinate, because it is the benefit connected with compliance that counts. In principle, the CEECs can try to exploit the situation rhetorically, but since EU conditions are predetermined and nonnegotiable, and since the EU remains in a position to provide authoritative interpretations of these conditions, there is no real potential for "rhetorical entrapment" (Risse 2000; Schimmelfennig 2000). From the social learning perspective, by contrast, the legitimacy of EU conditionality and the conditions for genuine persuasion are impaired if the EU as the promoter of a norm does not apply it in a coherent way, either internally or externally (Franck 1990). As in the case of strong EU rules and conditionality, the lesson-drawing model would not expect rule adoption under these conditions.

Strong EU rule, but weak conditionality/promotion: Narrowly understood, if an EU rule is not required or promoted, adoption cannot be explained as driven by external incentives or social learning but must rely on internal driving forces. In a basic sense, of course, any existing EU rule is part of EU conditionality, via the demand of complete adoption of the entire *acquis communautaire*. However, the general condition to adopt the *acquis* is a rather weak form of conditionality compared to explicit, specific, and persistent demands, probably with the exception of the final phase of accession negotiations, when the remaining gaps in implementing the *acquis* are clear and sanctions after EU membership (e.g., infringement procedures) are impending. Considering the amount of EU legislation to be implemented, it is likely that EU rules that are not explicitly spelled out or prioritized by the EU face the risk of dropping down the agenda of applicant state elites. It follows that from the external incentives perspective, rule adoption is possible, but its likelihood is diminished. The social learning perspective would also predict lower chances for rule adoption, but not because of a lack of legitimacy (which is high), but because no real attempt to persuade is made. The lesson-drawing model, for its part, would see at least the necessary conditions for rule adoption fulfilled, although it has to be noted that this model would not expect rule adoption unless domestic factors direct the search for policy solutions toward the EU.

Weak EU rule and conditionality/promotion: In this case, EU influence of any sort cannot explain the development of rules in the applicant states. Externally driven rule adoption is either unlikely or unnecessary under both the external incentives and the social learning model because there is no adaptational pressure or active attempt to persuade on the part of the EU. There is also no basis for

Table 3.1 "Supply side" conditions for the likelihood of rule adoption

	EU conditionality or rule promotion	
EU rules	Weak	Strong
Weak	External incentives: (−) Social learning: (−) Lesson-drawing: (−)	External incentives: (+/−) Social learning: (−/+) Lesson-drawing: (−)
Strong	External incentives: (−/+) Social learning: (−/+) Lesson-drawing: (+)	External incentives: (+) Social learning: (+) Lesson-drawing: (−)

domestically driven lesson-drawing, since there is no EU rule that could serve as a model. If change takes place, it must be explained by alternative factors, e.g., domestic politics or lesson-drawing from states or international institutions outside the EU.

Nondiscrimination and Minority Rights: International, European, and EU Rules

For the use of this chapter, nondiscrimination and special minority rights shall be treated as two distinct norms. While the norms do not necessarily contradict each other and can be combined in a comprehensive approach to minority protection (Open Society Institute 2001, 16), they can still be distinguished and follow different rationales: First, nondiscrimination is a general human rights principle (so that "belonging to a national minority" is only one among many reasons for discrimination to be eliminated), whereas special minority rights are group-specific, i.e., targeted at particular persons or groups.

Second, while nondiscrimination aims at the removal of all obstacles to the enjoyment of equal rights and full integration of persons belonging to minorities into society, special minority protection requires permanent positive state action in support of the specific minority group in order to preserve its identity and prevent assimilation. Nondiscrimination is therefore predominantly a negative, minority protection a positive right.[2] Third, nondiscrimination is mostly viewed as an individual right. By contrast, the question whether special minority rights should be conceptualized as individual or collective rights, i.e. as rights granted to

2. Although the interpretation of the nondiscrimination principle has changed from a formal to a substantive reading, which allows "affirmative action" to counter de facto inequalities (Thornberry 1991, 126), the aims of nondiscrimination and minority protection remain different: positive measures under nondiscrimination are by definition only to be employed temporarily and are put into place to remove the underlying distinction, while special minority rights are essentially permanent and aim at the preservation of the distinctive character of the minority group.

persons belonging to minorities (e.g., to mother-tongue education or official language use) or as rights granted to the groups as such in the form of self-government, autonomy, or self-determination remains highly contested. Hence, the special minority rights norm can conceptually be further subdivided into individual and collective minority protection concepts.[3]

EU Rules and Conditionality in the Field of Nondiscrimination

Nondiscrimination has been a fundamental principle within the European Community from the outset, in the form of gender equality and the abolition of discrimination on the basis of nationality between member states. Furthermore, although the original treaties did not contain human rights provisions, the European Court of Justice (ECJ) established a competence for human rights issues within its case law, which was later codified in the Maastricht Treaty with the introduction of Article F (now renumbered as Art. 6) into the "Treaty on European Union" (TEU) (Betten and Grief 1998, 56–59).

Since the Amsterdam Treaty, the nondiscrimination framework has been expanded to include ethnic and racial discrimination: Article 13 of the "Treaty Establishing the European Community" (TEC) enables the Community to "take appropriate action to combat discrimination based on sex, racial or ethnic origin, religion or belief, disability, age or sexual orientation." On this basis, a Directive on equal treatment between persons, irrespective of racial or ethnic origin, known as the "Race Equality Directive" (Council Directive 2000/43/EC; OJ L180, 19 July 2000, 22–26), was adopted. Furthermore, "membership of a national minority" was included in the nondiscrimination article (Art. 21) of the Charter of Fundamental Rights.

It follows that nondiscrimination can be regarded a clear and well-established norm at the EU level. Moreover, it is largely congruent with international nondiscrimination norms as laid down in the Universal Declaration of Human Rights and the UN Charter; Article 26 of the UN International Covenant on Civil and Political Rights (CCPR), which prohibits discrimination on the ground of race and national origin; the UN Convention on the Elimination of All Forms of Racial Discrimination (CERD); as well as Article 14 of the Council of Europe's European Convention on Human Rights (ECHR), which includes national minorities in a general nondiscrimination clause.

Nondiscrimination is also part of EU conditionality, but there is variation with regard to its strength across different CEECs. On the one hand, since all applicant countries are subjected to the general requirement of complete adoption of the *acquis*, they all face the general obligation to develop nondiscrimination legislation and specifically to implement the Race Equality Directive. On the other hand, the Commission reports make explicit and constant reference to the discrimination of

---

3. For an overview on collective minority protection concepts, see Brunner (1999) and Niewerth (1996).

Roma in particular candidate countries, where their situation is considered to be especially problematic. Hence, we can make a distinction between general but rather weak and implicit conditionality (at least until the final accession phase) for all applicants and consistently strong and explicit conditionality in "problematic" cases.

EU Rules and Conditionality in the Field of Minority Protection

In sharp contrast to the principle of nondiscrimination, the EU has neither developed a minority standard within the internal *acquis communautaire*, nor do the member states subscribe to a single European standard (Pentassuglia 2001; De Witte 2000; Toggenburg 2000). In the accession *acquis*, the minority criterion also remained ill-defined, failing to develop a clear and common standard for all the applicant states. This is in part because, despite considerable attempts of the UN, the OSCE, and the Council of Europe to develop a minority standard after the end of the Cold War, it remains a contested norm that is not consensually shared internationally and is susceptible to a wide range of interpretations.

In the absence of internal minority protection rules, the EU has mainly referred to standards developed by other European organizations. While early references were made to the politically binding norms developed in the CSCE/OSCE context and specific demands followed the recommendations of the OSCE High Commissioner on National Minorities, which often invoke international standards but follow a case-to-case approach aimed at crisis prevention (Brusis 2003b; Hughes and Sasse 2003; Kymlicka 2001), the standard generally expected from the applicants can be deduced from the Agenda 2000, which stresses that a "number of texts governing the protection of national minorities have been adopted by the Council of Europe, in particular the Framework Convention for the Protection of National Minorities and recommendation 1201 adopted by the Parliamentary Assembly of the Council of Europe in 1993. The latter, though not binding, recommends that collective rights be recognized, while the Framework Convention safeguards the individual rights of persons belonging to minority groups" (Commission 1997b, 44).

While Recommendation 1201 was rejected as an additional protocol to the ECHR precisely because it includes collective provisions in the form of territorial autonomy, the individualist approach taken by the Framework Convention seems to codify the highest achievable standard beyond nondiscrimination shared by at least the majority of European countries (Blumenwitz and Pallek 2000, 45). Accordingly, the EU's external promotion of collective minority rights declined during the accession process, and the focus also shifted, along with the security concerns underlying the promotion of minority protection in the CEECs, from the protection of national minorities as a remedy to the threat of ethnic conflict to issues of nondiscrimination in order to prevent mass migration, specifically with regard to the Roma population (Hughes and Sasse 2003; Kymlicka 2001).

In summary, minority protection is not an EU rule and in the accession *acquis* it remains a weak rule not following a common standard, while conditionality varies greatly across applicant states. Some countries with problematic minority situations are under continuous scrutiny and face explicit and determinate, though not necessarily legitimate, EU demands; others—notably those with small and hence "unproblematic" minorities—have to comply with the minority criterion in general, but are not confronted with any particular concept offered for adoption.

Rule Adoption in Romania, Hungary, and Poland

The following section sets out to give an overview of the implementation of nondiscrimination and special minority rights legislation in three applicant countries in order to determine whether and to what extent the EU's policy of conditionality has led to formal legislation in the candidate countries in line with the *acquis* or rules demanded by EU accession criteria.[4] The case selection follows variation in the independent variable, i.e. in both EU rules and conditionality. The first dimension is addressed by the fact that, as developed in the previous part, nondiscrimination is considered a strong and clear EU rule, while minority rights are contested and not established at the EU level.

The country cases are then selected according to variation in the strength and determinacy of EU conditionality: Romania has been under explicit and persistent pressure to implement both special minority rights and measures to counter Roma discrimination; Hungary is a mixed case, in which only the Roma issue was addressed, while the minority protection standard was considered sufficient and even exemplary; Poland was confronted with low conditionality in both areas. In line with the focus on the "supply side" of the conditionality model, the cases cover all four combinations of EU rules and conditionality. They do not control for domestic variables, which vary considerably across the three countries.[5] Domestic factors are, however, considered as alternatives to explain variation unaccounted for by the "supply side" hypotheses.

Romania

As a state with a considerable amount (over 10 percent) of internal and small external minorities,[6] Romania traditionally belonged to the opponents of minority pro-

---

4. By focusing exclusively on legislative measures, it follows a purely formal conception of rule adoption, being fully aware that this is not to be equated with de facto implementation or social acceptance, for which social in addition to legal internalization would be needed (Koh 1997). It also does not mean that the situation of minorities is fundamentally better in states with adopted minority legislation than in those without.

5. They especially do not control for the size of the minorities, which varies greatly across the three cases. I thank one of Cornell's anonymous reviewers for alerting me to this point. Minority size alone is, however, largely indeterminate as to the choice of the minority protection concept. It features, however, both on the "supply side," since large minorities are deemed much more "problematic" by the EU and therefore trigger stronger conditionality following the security-based differentiation, and as a domestic factor, in the form of adoption costs.

6. The only significant group of ethnic and linguistic Romanians abroad are the Moldovans in the Republic of Moldova, where they do not constitute a minority but are in fact the majority population.

Table 3.2 EU rules and conditionality in Romania, Hungary, and Poland

EU rules	EU conditionality or rule promotion	
	Weak	Strong
Weak	Minority rights: Hungary, Poland	Minority rights: Romania
Strong	Nondiscrimination: Poland	Nondiscrimination: Romania, Hungary

tection (Bartsch 1995; Hofmann 1992). Furthermore, the relation between the state and its minorities can also be characterized as a conceptual clash between a "unitary and indivisible nation state" and radical claims to collective protection and autonomy by the Hungarian minority (Shafir 2000).[7] Given these conflicting domestic conditions, the positive developments achieved since the mid-1990s are best explained with the strong and persistent promotion of minority protection by international organizations, linked with explicit EU conditionality (Kelley 2001; Ram 2001). However, the most profound improvement only occurred after the 1996 elections, when the former government, which depended heavily on nationalist forces, was replaced with a democratic and emphatically prowestern coalition that included the Hungarian party (cf. the similar development in Slovakia; see Schimmelfennig, Engert, and Knobel, chapter 2).

There were, moreover, limitations to the effectiveness of EU conditionality, which are related to the contested character of the minority rights norm and its resonance within the domestic context. This is most obvious in the failure of international pressure and conditionality to induce a collective minority standard against strong domestic resistance. Although Romania accepted Recommendation 1201, first in relation to its accession to the Council of Europe and then in a bilateral treaty with Hungary (signed under international pressure and EU conditionality), it rejected the notion of collective rights and autonomy included in the document by insisting on an additional footnote to be added to the treaty (Ram 2001, 72). This reinterpretation was criticized by the western organizations and by Hungary and the Hungarian minorities themselves. It could, however, be justified on the basis of the existing European standard as represented by the Framework Convention, so in the end it was accepted. Conversely, in the name of maintaining good-neighborly relations between the two countries, the EU strongly discouraged Hungary from continuing its advocacy of collective minority rights and autonomy for the Hungarian minority in Romania (Williams 2002, 239); and later

7. Quotation drawn from Articles 1/1 and 4/1 of the Romanian Constitution of 21 November 1991; cited in Andreescu 2001, 273. Accordingly, the constitution does not include collective minority provisions despite initial promises of the new post-1989 government to "guarantee individual and collective rights and freedoms for ethnic minorities" (Shafir 2000, 102; Tontsch 1999, 235). It does entail a positive individual minority protection clause (Art. 6), which is, however, circumscribed by a restrictive formula that "protective measures . . . shall conform to the principles of equality and nondiscrimination in relation to the other Romanian citizens" (Art. 6/2).

it dropped Recommendation 1201 from the agenda to support the individualist approach of the Framework Convention.

In the following years, EU attention shifted from special minority rights to the issue of discrimination, especially with regard to the Roma population. The Commission report in 2000 concluded that "the treatment of minorities in Romania is mixed. The lack of progress with regard to tackling discrimination against the Roma is a subject which has been raised in previous regular reports but which has still not been adequately addressed. On the other hand, a series of progressive initiatives have greatly improved the treatment of other minorities" (Commission 2000e, 24–25). Thus, the EU explicitly spelled out nondiscrimination as a missing element in the Romanian minority protection system. The Romanian government responded to this assessment with the adoption of an Ordinance on the Prevention and Punishment of All Forms of Discrimination in November 2000, which "gives Romania the most comprehensive anti-discrimination framework among EU candidate countries" (Open Society Institute 2001, 393) and includes many aspects of the Race Equality Directive. Consequently, it has been praised as a major development in the 2001 Commission report (Commission 2001f, 22).

In sum, both minority protection and nondiscrimination legislation in Romania seem to have been in large part triggered by external conditionality and rule promotion, especially by the EU. However, externally driven rule adoption was limited to minority protection concepts that resonated with Romanian institutions, ensuring that "the treatment of individuals rather than groups as the subject of minority rights legislation has been fairly consistent over the past decade" (Horváth and Scacco 2001, 253). This individualist preoccupation could not even be altered by a combination of minority mobilization, kin-state support, and EU conditionality.

Hungary

With regard to minority protection, Hungary can hardly be viewed as an instance of western norm transfer in any meaningful sense. The minority protection system, guaranteed by the constitution and specified in the Minority Act of 1993, was well developed before the minority criterion in the EU accession *acquis* was formulated. Furthermore, Hungary has long been a promoter of minority rights and was in fact among the main driving forces to put minority protection on the international agenda after 1989. On the other hand, Hungary largely failed in its attempts to "internationalize" the internally developed collective minority protection standard, given the predominantly liberal-individualist character of the current European and global human rights norms and the strong opposition against collective minority rights in some West European countries.

Two main reasons account for the unique Hungarian approach to minorities. First is Hungary's specific minority situation. Not only the existence of large external minorities, i.e. fellow Hungarians living as minorities in neighboring countries and a relatively low percentage of internal minorities (Preece 1998; Bartsch 1995),[8] but also the fact that the external minorities are territorially concentrated, while the internal minorities are dispersed, well integrated and to a large extent assimilated (Krizsán 2000, 247)—this amounts to a strong incentive to promote collective rights. Second, the cornerstones of the system go back to an intellectual tradition based on the concept of "personal autonomy," which was first proposed as a model for the Austro-Hungarian empire and subsequently developed by Hungarian scholars (Krizsán 2000).[9] Thus, it is domestic conditions and legacies and not European norms that were the driving force behind the development of the Hungarian minority system. However, as the level of minority protection in Hungary is perceived to go beyond European standards, this conceptual difference was not criticized in the EU assessments.

The purely domestic factors accounting for the Hungarian minority protection system gain importance for a study of EU influence only when combined with an assessment of the Hungarian record on nondiscrimination. The Hungarian constitution includes a general nondiscrimination clause, and several laws feature antidiscrimination clauses, but a general antidiscrimination law did not exist and NGOs have criticized that apart from being scattered, "Hungary's anti-discrimination legal framework is largely inoperative" (Open Society Institute 2001, 224). The issue of Roma discrimination has been repeatedly addressed by the Commission, beginning with the initial accession opinion and throughout the annual reports. Furthermore, countering Roma discrimination has been included in the accession partnership. Therefore, the nondiscrimination issue has been backed not only by rather clear European standards but also by persistent EU conditionality.

These demands have not, however, been transposed quickly into antidiscrimination legislation. Although a draft has been proposed by the Ombudsman for Minorities, the Minister of Justice in 2000 explicitly rejected the introduction of legislation in this field after the Constitutional Court ruled that such legislation was unnecessary. Rather, the external pressure to implement antidiscrimination measures seems initially to have been reinterpreted and "diverted" into measures within the positively assessed collective minority protection system. This was reinforced by the Commission's judgment that, despite the legal shortcomings, Hungary had fulfilled its short-term priorities on the issue (Open Society Institute 2001, 218). In the end, rule adoption followed, but with a considerable time lag compared to Romania. Only on 22 December 2003, just before accession, a comprehensive Act on Equal Treatment and the Promotion of Equal Opportunities was passed.

8. The number of internal minorities in Hungary is small relative to the size of the Hungarians living abroad, although it reaches with around 10 percent (including Roma) almost the percentage of the minorities in Romania.

9. Personal autonomy as a collective form of minority protection is the counterpart to territorial autonomy. In the case of territorial autonomy, self-government rights are granted to a territorially based (local or regional) authority in which the minority is numerically dominant. Personal autonomy, by contrast, grants these rights to a person-based authority, i.e. to an organization in which all persons belonging to the minority are members (Brunner 1999).

Poland

Specific EU conditionality on Poland with regard to minority rights and nondiscrimination has been low, since throughout the accession process the Commission considered the political criteria fulfilled. Nonetheless, NGOs have described Polish nondiscrimination legislation as falling "far below the requirements of the EU Race Equality Directive" (Open Society Institute 2001, 346). The constitution includes a general nondiscrimination clause, but simple legislation focusing on racial discrimination is virtually absent. This has not, however, raised much EU concern. Significantly, despite the legal shortcomings, the issue of nondiscrimination was not connected to the situation of the very small and therefore "unproblematic" Roma community, which "has not been a focal point in Poland's EU accession negotiations" (Open Society Institute 2001, 345). Ultimately, it has to be concluded that the low adaptational pressure on Poland in the nondiscrimination area has contributed to the neglect of the issue in Polish domestic legislation, the "robustness" and clarity of the norm in the EU context notwithstanding. Partial rule adoption in the form of a new Labor Code (adopted on 14 November 2003) covering the grounds and types of discrimination addressed by EU directives only followed shortly before accession and explicitly in order to implement the EU *acquis*.[10]

In the area of minority rights, no rule adoption (absent purely domestically driven rule development) might be expected, given that in this case low EU pressure was combined with ill-defined rules. Indeed, after external concerns—especially from Germany—were settled early on through bilateral treaties (Lodziński 1999; Mohlek 1994) and some legislative measures concerning preferential representation and education for minorities were introduced, the development of comprehensive minority legislation was (and still is) slow and contested (Vermeersch 2003, 19–20). However, even the Polish reluctance to ratify the Framework Convention, which the EU considers to be the central European minority rights instrument, was hardly criticized.[11]

While the Polish case so far fits into the external incentives model, it remains a puzzle when it comes to explaining the emerging minority protection concept as enshrined in the constitution and proposed in the (still pending) Draft Law on

10. Also, the issue of Roma discrimination has recently been addressed in the Sejm Committee on National and Ethnic Minorities, and in 2001 the government adopted the "Małopolska" program to support the small Roma minority in this region (Vermeersch 2003).

11. Although Poland signed the Framework Convention on the first day it was opened for signature in 1995, it was not before 1999 that the ratification document entered parliament for the first reading. The Convention was ratified in December 2000 and came into force in April 2001, which made Poland one of the last applicant countries to do so (only Latvia has still not ratified it, for which it was severely criticized by the EU). As an example of the almost nonexistent EU criticism, the 2000 progress report simply stated that "Poland has ratified the major Human Rights conventions with the exception of the Council of Europe's Framework Convention on the protection of National Minorities . . . and has an established track record of providing appropriate international and constitutional legal safeguards for human rights and protection of minorities" (Commission 2000b, 57).

Minorities. The concept is described as following the principle of "positive support and protection of individual rights of persons belonging to minorities (positive individual approach) . . . based on OSCE and Council of Europe standards" (Lodziński 1999, 1). This outcome, while obviously not a result of external pressure, can also not be accounted for by a domestic macro-explanation, for no clear national preference for a specific minority protection model can be deduced either from the minority situation or from national institutions or legacies.[12] Furthermore, far from having an established view on the issue, Polish political elites faced a high degree of uncertainty as to the form of protection to be implemented when the minority problem was "re-discovered" in 1989, since they were rather taken by surprise by the mobilization of minorities believed to be marginal or even nonexistent (Lodziński 1999, 3). For their part, the minorities themselves also had no clear idea as to the minority protection concept they preferred (Gawrich 2001, 255–56).

Discussion of the Results: The Importance of Domestic Factors and Norm Resonance

The findings of the first-cut case studies can be summed up as follows: First, explicit and determinate conditionality mattered. In all three cases, where it was applied (minority rights and nondiscrimination in Romania, nondiscrimination in Hungary), rule adoption of some sort followed in the end. Second, legitimacy and EU rules alone were not sufficient. The mere existence of the rather clear and well established EU nondiscrimination standard did not trigger domestically driven rule adoption in the Polish case. Only in the final phase before accession, when the general condition of *acquis* implementation became paramount, did partial rule adoption follow. Third, lack of legitimacy did not prevent rule adoption. The contested nature of minority rights and the problem of double standards on the part of the EU did not lead to noncompliance in the Romanian minority rights case.

Although these findings largely corroborate the external incentives model, the case studies also cast some doubts on the explanatory power of purely "supply side" arguments and point toward the importance of domestic factors. In the cases of rule adoption in reaction to explicit conditionality, successful Romanian resis-

---

12. Since Poland has a low level of internal minorities (3–5 percent) and its external minorities do not necessarily benefit from international minority protection, as they are not recognized as minorities (e.g. in Germany), no clear preference for or against collective minority rights can be deduced (Bartsch 1995). Polish history includes a wide variety of experiences with minorities ranging from being a tolerant multinational federation in the early modern age, through a hugely troubled interwar period, to the communist era, where Poland was transformed into an almost homogeneous nation state that denied the existence of minorities. While all three experiences are used (positively or negatively) as arguments in the Polish debate, they also do not lead to a clear preference with regard to individual or collective minority rights.

tance to collective minority provisions and the delay of rule adoption in the case of nondiscrimination in Hungary remain to be explained. In these cases, domestic factors can figure as intervening variables, because "international norms must always work their influence through the filter of domestic structure and domestic norms, which can produce important variations in compliance and interpretation of these norms" (Finnemore and Sikkink 1998, 893).

Two sets of domestic factors are highlighted by the models focusing on EU-driven rule adoption: adoption costs and veto players in the external incentives model and resonance in the social learning model. The evidence presented in the case studies suggests a complementary rather than competing role of these factors. In the case of minority rights in Romania, high adoption costs and resistance by veto players against collective minority rights can be explained rationally by the large size and territorial concentration of the Hungarian minority. Acquiescence to individual minority rights can be seen as a bargaining compromise between a "maximalist" Hungarian demand for collective minority rights and a "minimalist" unitarian position of the Romanian government. Resonance adds to this rationalist explanation an account for why individual minority rights were the acceptable compromise solution from the Romanian perspective.

With regard to the nondiscrimination cases, a comparison of the different timing of legislation in Romania as compared to Hungary and Poland is instructive: while the delay in Hungary can be described as a result of veto players (e.g., the Constitutional Court) resisting rule adoption, resonance seems to give a better account of why decisive actors deemed legislative steps toward a general nondiscrimination framework unnecessary, alternatively opting for addressing the Roma problem within the collective minority rights system until consistent EU pressure and domestic lobbying could overturn this decision. The almost simultaneous rule adoption in Hungary (where specific demands to counter Roma discrimination were made throughout the accession process) and Poland (where this was not the case) shortly before the accession date also suggests that in the final phase the general requirement of adopting the EU *acquis* (which has been coded as low conditionality) has received a decisive boost. In Romania, on the other hand, introducing nondiscrimination legislation was not only responsive to EU demands but also much more in line with domestic norms, as laid down in the constitution, for example. It is far less convincing to assume that objective adoption costs were higher in Hungary than in Romania.

Domestic factors serve as alternative explanations in cases where no rule adoption was to be expected by any of the proposed models, simply because both EU rules and active rule promotion or conditionality were absent. This is most obvious in the Hungarian minority rights case. Here, domestic institutions and legacies go all the way to explain rule development independent of any EU influence. This does not contradict the external incentives or social learning models, because conditionality and rule promotion may be absent precisely because rule adoption had already occurred beforehand for domestic reasons. Also, the absence of external incentives or active attempts to persuade in no way discourages or prevents

Table 3.3 Explanatory factors and outcomes of rule adoption

		Conditionality (determinacy)	EU rule (legitimacy)	Domestic factors (resonance)	Rule adoption
Romania:	ND[1]	+	+	+	+
	MR[2]	+	−	−	(+)[3]
Hungary:	ND	+	+	−	(+)[4]
	MR	−	−	+	+
Poland:	ND	−/+[4]	+	−	−/+[5]
	MR	−	−	unclear	+

[1] Nondiscrimination.
[2] Minority rights.
[3] Rule adoption, but not following EU demands (individual instead of collective MR).
[4] No specific conditionality, but general requirement to adopt the acquis.
[5] Partial rule adoption (Labor Code), but only in the end phase before accession.

domestically driven rule development. Explaining this kind of rule development, however, is clearly beyond the scope of these models.

Again, more rationalist (adoption costs, veto players) and more constructivist (resonance, ideational legacies) factors seem to complement each other among domestic explanations. While favoring collective minority rights in Hungary with its large external and small internal minorities is consistent with rationality assumptions, and political consensus on this issue suggests the absence of veto players, purely rationalist analyses remain indeterminate as to the specific minority concept developed to serve the interests (Garrett and Weingast 1993).[13] This is best explained with reference to resonance with ideational legacies such as the minority concepts dating back to the Austro-Hungarian empire. In the Polish minority rights case, however, even considering this kind of domestic macro-explanation leaves the main puzzle unsolved, for unlike in Hungary no clear-cut domestic preference seems at hand.

Epistemic Communities and the Discursive Construction of Resonance

In order to address this gap, it is helpful to focus on the process of domestic norm construction. Following the assumption that the norms in question are not necessarily stable, unproblematic, and with a fixed and commonly known meaning

13. This rational basis can be contested by pointing out that because the states with large Hungarian minorities have all the costs and risks to bear, Hungary could not rationally expect them to reciprocate. Indeed, they have always rejected the Hungarian claims, especially regarding collective rights—see the Romanian position with regard to Recommendation 1201. I thank one of Cornell's anonymous reviewers for pointing this out to me. However, support for collective minority rights is consistent with (subjective) rationality assumptions on the Hungarian part in the form of "rhetorical action" (Schimmelfennig 2000): internally institutionalizing a comprehensive collective minority protection system at relatively low costs and risks gives them an argumentative tool to pressurize the neighboring countries. Whether this "reversed reciprocity" strategy succeeds is, of course, a different matter.

(Wiener 2003, 266), contested interpretations of norms and the discursive construction of intersubjective meaning come to the fore. In this view, resonance is not only a structural precondition for rule adoption, it also includes an agency-oriented, dynamic, and interactive element, insofar as "the meanings of any particular norm and the linkages between existing norms and emergent norms are often not obvious and must be actively constructed by proponents of new norms" (Finnemore and Sikkink 1998, 908). It therefore also means the ability to create compelling and coherent arguments within a social context with regard to the norm and relate it positively to institutions, traditions, and ideas that are prevalent in this context. In other words, the question is how European norms are introduced and presented in the process of domestic norm construction.

One factor highlighted by the lesson-drawing model is the involvement of domestic or transnational experts acting as "epistemic communities" (Haas 1992), which promote EU rules internally as a model for domestic legislation. While work on epistemic communities has so far focused mainly on scientific expertise in highly technical policy areas, the concept has recently also been extended to lawyer communities (Van Waarden and Drahos 2002). The influence of epistemic communities relies on favorable domestic conditions: experts depend on the demand for expertise by political elites as a precondition for being included in the process. Specialists are included voluntarily by political elites in the domestic process of norm construction if they can provide expertise and consensual interpretations to overcome uncertainty in the absence of clear obligations and models. Expert advice is rather unlikely to be sought or to have a deep impact in situations of open political contestation between established and well-known alternatives, or where clear domestic legacies and norms clash with European rules, but it can have a crucial effect in cases when political elites face high uncertainty regarding the "right" legislative decision, and when the experts are able to present a consensual definition of what "the law" is. Also, transnational communities of legal specialists can exert an important function as catalysts or mediators of meaning (Wiener 2001; Ratner 2000), given their knowledge both of international and domestic norms. Therefore, not only can epistemic communities direct policymakers toward EU rules in order to solve domestic problems, their arguments can also help to enhance the resonance or transferability of EU rules.

The Polish Case Revisited: Contested Minority Concepts in Domestic Norm Construction

To explain the congruence between the emerging Polish minority standard and European norms, this part takes a closer look at the process of domestic norm construction. The central focus is the debate over minority protection concepts, namely general nondiscrimination and individual and collective minority rights. Most notably, the resulting "positive individualist" approach was initially not the favored model of any of the political actors. Rather, it emerged in the process of domestic norm construction as a consensus position among the supporters of minority protection, who were in the early phases split between advocates of collective rights and champions of general nondiscrimination.

Methodologically, the following case study conducts a more detailed process-tracing of the development of minority norms in Poland, based on a qualitative content analysis of draft and final documents as well as an argument analysis of parliamentary debates and committee sessions concerning two issues central to the evolution of Polish minority protection after 1989: the drafting period of the new constitution and the work on the Draft Law on National and Ethnic Minorities.

The first drafts of a new constitution proposed in 1991 by constitutional committees of both chambers of the Polish parliament, the Sejm and the Senate, contained special minority clauses on the basis of collective formulations (Chruściak 1997, 1:141–42; Kallas 1995, 179; Hofmann 1992, 50–51). The minority provisions contained in the constitutional proposals brought forward by the major political parties in 1994 reflected a clear dichotomy between individualist approaches promoted by liberal parties, which focused mainly on nondiscrimination, and positive minority provisions included in the drafts handed in by the postcommunists and different groups of the Solidarity right based on the collective formula of the Senate draft (Chruściak 1997; Kallas 1995; Mohlek 1994).[14]

A third option resembling the "positive individualist" approach taken by the Framework Convention was developed within the Sejm Committee on National and Ethnic Minorities. The committee initially also based its work on the Senate draft. However, after consultation with legal advisors, the collective formulation was replaced by an individualized formula (Kallas 1995, 180). This version was adopted by a group of legal specialists set up to develop a unified document building on the different constitutional drafts (Chruściak 1997, 2:11–12; Tkaczynski and Vogel 1997, 170–71), and was subsequently confirmed by the Constitutional Committee of the National Assembly in March 1995. However, the discussion of the article was initially conducted along the old front line, with representatives of the Solidarity trade union (NSZZ-Solidarność) favoring a collective formulation[15] against strong opposition by the liberal Freedom Union (UW).[16] Again, the

14. The proposals focusing on nondiscrimination were handed in by the liberal Democratic Union (UD) and on behalf of President Wałęsa; the latter featured as the fundamental rights section a Charter of Rights and Freedoms elaborated by the Helsinki Committee, a Warsaw-based human rights NGO. Cf. Chruściak (1997, 1:75, 267); Kallas (1995, 182); Mohlek (1994, 63).

15. Piotr Andrzejewski (NSZZ-S) reiterated the draft article proposed by his party, which "stands on the basis of the protection of minority rights also as group rights." Komisja Konstytucyjna Zgromadzenia Narodowego, II kadencja, no. 14, 7 March 1995, 62 (author's translation). Hereafter cited as Constitutional Committee. In addition, another member of the NSZZ-Solidarność proposed the original version elaborated by the Senate. Alicia Grześkowiak, in: Constitutional Committee II/14, 7 March 1995, 68.

16. "We cannot include into the Constitution rights in collective form, because we would entangle ourselves in problems that are extremely difficult to resolve. We know from our history that the granting of group rights and their inclusion in state laws led to nationality conflicts instead of resolving problems. . . . I am against all formulations . . . that propose the protection of group rights in the Constitution of the Republic of Poland." Hanna Suchocka (UW) in Constitutional Committee II/14, 7 March 1995, 69–70 (author's translation).

"positive individualist" consensus was reached only after the intervention of legal advisors[17] and the invocation of international and European standards as examples for individual formulations of minority rights.[18]

The individually formulated minority clause was included with some minor changes in the final version of the constitution adopted on 2 April 1997 (Lodziński 1999, 8; Chruściak 1997, 2:389). It has been widely recognized that the "protection of minority rights prescribed by this article goes beyond general principles of equality and non-discrimination of citizens as embodied in the old (communist) Constitution of 1952" (Lodziński 1999, 8), while upholding "an individualized approach to the protection of minorities by using a phrase 'Polish citizens belonging to national or ethnic minorities,' which is consistent with the currently existing international standards" (Lodziński 1999, 8; cf. Bajda, Syposz, and Wojakowski 2001, 211).

A parallel development can be observed in the drafting period of a law on national minorities. An initial text worked out by a group of specialists from the Helsinki Committee, a Warsaw-based human rights NGO with strong transnational links, was based entirely on an individualist approach to minority rights (Kallas 1995, 184). In the following discussions within the Sejm Committee on National and Ethnic Minorities, the question of group rights emerged several times but was dismissed by the legal advisor from the Helsinki Committee. Finally, they came to a consensus that "the legislative project regulates the individual rights of minorities, i.e. the rights of persons belonging to a minority" as opposed to "group rights, which are practically impossible to codify."[19] In the final version of the draft, the explanatory note stressed that "by using the construction of individual rights, the bill contains, in accordance with European standards, a catalogue of fundamental rights. . . . Thereby group rights are excluded."[20]

This consensus on the minority protection concept united the pro-minority parties, formerly split along the individual/collective rights line as well as between special rights and general nondiscrimination, in support of the "positive individualist" formula. When the law was discussed in the first parliamentary reading, support was based predominantly on two arguments: the individualist character of the draft and its "fit" both with the Polish constitution and European standards. Opponents of the bill had two major arguments to back their rejection: First, in reply to the "positive individualist" presentation of the draft, special minority rights as such were equated with group rights and attacked as privileges violating

17. Cf. the contributions of Andrzej Rzepliński and Leszek Wiśniewski in Constitutional Committee II/14, 7 March 1995, 72.

18. The examples cited included the CCPR, the CSCE documents and the Framework Convention. Czesław Śleziak (SLD) in Constitutional Committee II/14, 7 March 1995, 66.

19. Henryk Kroll in Komisja Mniejszości Narodowych i Etnicznych, III kadencja, poszedzienie no. 12, 17 March 1998 (author's translation). Hereafter cited as: Sejm Committee on National and Ethnic Minorities.

20. Komisyjny projekt ustawy o mniejszościach narodowych i etnicznych w Rzeczpospolitej Polskiej (druk nr 616 wpłynął 22-09-1998), uzasadnienie, 2 (author's translation).

the principle of (formal) nondiscrimination.[21] Second, mainly to counter the "European standard" argument of the camp in favor, reciprocity was invoked by comparing Poland, which supposedly already "ensures a very high standard of minority rights protection,"[22] with the status of Polish nationals in other countries, complaining that "everything that happened after 1989 from the Polish side with regard to national minorities living in Poland is sadly not reciprocated by our neighbors."[23]

It can be concluded that the consensus position among the pro–minority parties focusing on a "positive individual" version of special minority rights, which started from a contestation between individual nondiscrimination and collective minority rights positions, was forged by the desire to comply with the European standard under the strong influence of legal advisors acting as catalysts for the formulation of a shared minority norm conforming to the emerging European standard. The Helsinki Committee was a particularly key player, forming an epistemic community promoting the "positive individual" model as the only solution in line with European norms and applicable to the Polish situation.

Finally, although the question of EU conditionality was raised on some occasions during the debates, it did not play a major role in the domestic norm construction and functioned rather as background knowledge about the general importance of minority protection in the accession procedure.[24] But given the lack of a coherent EU model for minority protection and the absence of high adapta-

---

21. For example: "The law has to be equal for everybody, not differentiated, so that one group of citizens has other rights than another group, because such a situation would be discriminatory. I concur with the opinion that the bill would differentiate and privilege minorities on the basis of granting them group rights, thereby violating the equality of all citizens of this country. . . . I think that we do not need group or minority rights." Ewa Sikorska-Trela (AWS) in: Sejm III kadencja, 46 posedzienie (18.03.1999) (author's translation). Further cited as: Sejm. In the same vein, Andrzej Zapałowski, speaking for the extreme rightist KPN and ROP groupings, insisted that "every Polish citizen, independent of his declared nationality, independent of his opinions or world views, has rights guaranteed in the Constitution. . . . The rights proposed in the law on national and ethnic minorities privilege the minority against the rest of the Polish citizens." (author's translation).

22. Marian Piłka (AWS) in: Sejm III/46, 18 March 1999 (author's translation).

23. Janusz Dobrosz (PSL) in: Sejm III/46, 18 March 1999 (author's translation). Comparable arguments were brought forward by members of the center-right AWS and the right-wing KPN opposing the bill. On the other hand, only one supportive AWS member brought forward the reverse argument, that Poland could serve as a model for other countries by adopting far-reaching minority legislation. Mirosław Kukliński in: Sejm III/46, 18 March 1999.

24. After the debate of the minority provision in the Constitutional Committee in 1995, the outcome was presented in the Sejm Committee on National and Ethnic Minorities with the remark that "this article has been adopted unanimously. All the indications are that it will be kept, and this will be the key to the European Union." Jerzy Szteliga (SLD) in: Sejm Committee on National and Ethnic Minorities II/32, 5 October 1995, 3 (author's translation). In the parliamentary debate over the Framework Convention, the question was raised whether there was "a certain link with regard to the ratification in the process of negotiation with the European Union." Tadeusz Iwiński (SLD), in: Sejm III/65, 3 December 1999 (author's translation). Although the government representative did not see a direct connection between ratification and accession, she replied, "This is undoubtedly one of the most important points, which is monitored all the time in the negotiations." Undersecretary of State in the Foreign Ministry Barbara Tuge-Erecińska in: Sejm III/65, 3 December 1999 (author's translation).

tional pressure to adopt specific model, the EU option could not play a decisive role in deciding the argumentation about which approach to minority protection should be chosen. Therefore, the standards formulated above all by the Council of Europe had a much bigger impact on the development of an intersubjective meaning among Polish politicians in order to establish a minority norm consistent with European standards.

I have compared the development of nondiscrimination and minority protection legislation in three applicant countries: Romania, Hungary, and Poland. My analysis proceeded in three steps: Initially, the "supply side" conditions for rule adoption were established. Distinguishing between EU rules on the one hand and EU conditionality and rule promotion on the other, the test hypotheses regarded the determinacy of EU conditions as assumed by the external incentives model (explicit and clear conditionality) and the legitimacy of EU rules and conditions as set out by the social learning model (existence of commonly shared EU rules and absence of double standards, i.e. congruence between internal and externally promoted rules).

Applied to the three case studies, this first-cut account led to the following results: First, whenever explicit and determinate conditionality was applied (minority rights in Romania, nondiscrimination in Romania and Hungary), it led to rule adoption of some sort in the end, although not necessarily quickly and not entirely in line with EU demands. Second, legitimacy and EU rules alone were not sufficient to trigger domestically driven rule adoption. Poland neglected the nondiscrimination issue for most of the time when it was not specifically demanded by the EU and adopted legislation in this field only very late, when the general requirement of implementing the *acquis* became more pressing than during the accession process. Third, lack of legitimacy and double standards did not prevent rule adoption in the case of minority rights in Romania, although rule adoption deviated from initial EU demands. Although these findings largely corroborate the external incentives model, the case studies also cast some doubt on the explanatory power of "supply side" arguments and point toward the importance of domestic factors to explain timing of and variation in rule adoption.

These findings so far largely correspond to the conclusions drawn by Schimmelfennig, Engert, and Knobel (chapter 2) on the EU impact on basic democratic and human rights reforms in Slovakia, Turkey, and Latvia. In contrast to their study, the domestic factors discussed in the second step of this chapter place a stronger emphasis on the concept of resonance as put forward by the social learning model, which is not, however, explicitly tested against the domestic variables derived from the external incentives model (adoption costs, veto players) but is seen as a complementary rather than competing explanation. Still, it was argued that the inclusion of resonance gives a more convincing account of both the successful resistance of Romania against the EU's promotion of collective minority protection and rule adoption along the lines of individual minority rights, and the delay of Hungarian nondiscrimination legislation in comparison to the swift rule adoption in the same area in Romania, despite roughly equal EU conditionality and domestic adoption costs in both cases.

Furthermore, I not only included "hard cases" for the effectiveness of explicit conditionality but also instances where conditionality and rule promotion was weak or absent. The development of minority rights in Hungary and Poland highlight alternative, domestically driven explanations that do not necessarily contradict but lie beyond the scope of the external incentives and social learning models. In this regard, my findings correspond to those of Jacoby's account of rule adoption (chapter 5). Jacoby also finds different processes at work under different "supply side" conditions: the external incentives model applies to cases with strong and explicit EU conditionality, while domestically driven lesson-drawing explains cases where it is absent. The Polish and Hungarian minority rights cases examined in this chapter, however, see not so much the adoption of EU rules (which are weak in this issue area), but point toward purely domestic explanations (Hungary) and lesson-drawing from other institutions like the Council of Europe (Poland).

In a third and final step, the detailed process-tracing of the Polish minority rights case reveals an indirect and mediated but nevertheless decisive role of European norms in the process of domestic norm construction. Consistent with the lesson-drawing model, the development of the Polish minority protection system is explained as the domestically driven adoption of Council of Europe standards under the influence of legal advisors acting as an epistemic community and forging a consensus on a "European" minority protection model.

CHAPTER FOUR

Europeanization and Civil Service Reform in Central and Eastern Europe

Antoaneta L. Dimitrova

As a number of Central and Eastern European countries (CEECs) took their place as full members of the European Union (EU) in May 2004, they brought to its final stages one of the longest and most intensive periods of accession preparation in the history of the EU. The candidates have undergone a process of complex and demanding adjustment to the rules of the club they have been eager to join since 1989. With its requirement that the candidates transpose most of the *acquis communautaire* before accession, the EU seemed to strive to make "ideal members" (Mayhew 2000; 2002). The forging of "ideal members" through the extensive process of adjustment resembles widely discussed processes of Europeanization, defined by some as "the emergence and the development at the European level of distinct structures of governance" (Risse, Cowles, and Caporaso 2001, 1) or, in another important study, as "the process of influence deriving from European decisions and impacting member states' policies and political and administrative structures" (Héritier 2001a, 3). A fundamental difference, however, is that since candidate states have not been part of EU decision-making, their "Europeanization" has not, in the accession period, included the important first step, the creation of EU rules, but only the second stage, the implementation of these EU rules influencing domestic structures and policies. Given the absence of the candidates from the process of rule-making and essential asymmetry of the enlargement process, we can identify distinct patterns of enlargement governance, one of which is conditionality, an element not present in the relations between the EU and its member states (Dimitrova 2002).

I thank Martin Brusis, Frank Schimmelfennig, Ulrich Sedelmeier, and the participants of the "The 'Europeanization' of Eastern Europe: Evaluating the Conditionality Model" workshop held at the EUI, Florence, 4–5 July 2003, for their helpful comments.

This chapter tests the explanatory power of the external incentives model defined in chapter 1 regarding rule adoption in the area of administrative reform and, more specifically, civil service reform. In particular, I focus on the impact of administrative conditionality on the associated countries that prepared to join the EU after the invitation issued by the Copenhagen European Council in 1993[1] and negotiated for membership since 1998 or 2000, namely Bulgaria, the Czech Republic, Estonia, Hungary, Latvia, Lithuania, Poland, Romania, Slovakia and Slovenia.[2]

The External Incentives Model

In accordance with the external incentives model defined in chapter 1, I assume that governments in the CEECs make strategic calculations regarding the adoption of rules for which the benefits of complying with EU demands are set against the costs of losing EU funding and institutional ties (see chapter 1). Since civil service reform requires the initiative of governments and the passing of legislative acts, I focus on governing parties or coalitions in the 1989–2003 period as the relevant actors.

Conditions for administrative adaptation were set out by the EU fairly late in the accession process, added to the already existing Copenhagen criteria. The credibility of administrative conditionality is an important variable to consider when applying the external incentives model to civil service reform. Based on the game theoretical assumption that actors ignore incredible threats (cf. Hargreaves-Heap and Varoufakis 1995, 116), we can expect EU conditionality to work only when the EU's *threat* of withholding benefits appears credible to the candidate states. And on the other end too: as Steunenberg has noted (2002, 6), the credibility of the EU's *promise* to complete the enlargement process is a crucial element in the sequence of moves involving reforms in the candidate states, which presuppose that enlargement would be the reward for these reforms.

As suggested in chapter 1, credibility varies across countries. One way to evaluate credibility is to take into account the signals candidate states have been receiving throughout the enlargement process. It is to be expected that states that have been singled out as forerunners would find the credibility of a threat of exclusion from the process low. Such signals can come via official EU policies or as an informal ordering of candidates at various stages of the process of enlargement or even from individual member states, such as Germany. Since the EU as a whole has to reach unanimity at the various decision points of enlargement, both EU institu-

---

1. The Copenhagen European Council invited the states with which the EC had or considered plans to conclude Association (Europe) agreements—at the time, the group included Poland, Hungary, Czech and Slovak republics, the Baltic states, Bulgaria, Romania, and Slovenia. See Baun (2000, 45).

2. I exclude Cyprus and Malta, since they have very different institutional starting positions from the postcommunist states, and Turkey, since it has only has been subject to enlargement conditionality in the last few years.

tional signals and member state signals would affect the credibility of EU's promises and threats. One would, however, expect institutional signals to be more important, as they would reflect some level of internal consensus.

Since the decision of the Copenhagen European Council in 1993 to invite the CEECs to join, there have been several different orders of preference affecting the credibility of conditionality. In 1995, when the discussion on whether to invite a smaller or larger group of states was most intense, the Commission and member states were divided between the "big bang" and the small group approach to the start of negotiations. As Baun reports, Germany ignited this debate when Chancellor Helmut Kohl promised in Poland in 1995 that Poland, Hungary, and the Czech Republic would be EU members by 2000 (2000, 67–70; see also Friis 1998). This provoked a reaction from the other member states, which insisted on equal treatment for all candidates (Friis 1998). Nevertheless, this promise must have sent a signal to the states favored by Germany, namely Poland, Hungary, and the Czech Republic.

Another ordering of the candidates with regard to future membership emerged with the Commission's recommendations in the "Agenda 2000" document in 1997. A division between the "ins" and "not yet ins" was introduced by the Commission's initial assessments of the readiness of the candidates to start negotiations in the Agenda 2000. These divided the candidates between those deemed ready to start negotiations—Estonia, Hungary, Poland, the Czech Republic, and Slovenia—and those evaluated as not yet ready for negotiations—Bulgaria, Latvia, Lithuania, Slovakia, and Romania. Following the credibility hypothesis, we should expect conditionality to have the most impact on the states from the second group, as their accession appeared less secure. Yet credibility cannot be measured solely on the basis of the Commission's ordering at various points in time. Widespread assumptions that this enlargement would be impossible without Poland, the Czech Republic, and Hungary should also be taken into account. If the EU were to exclude these states, the EU stood to lose enough in terms of trade and reputation for the threat of applying conditionality to these states to be less than credible.

The first five states started membership negotiations with the EU in 1998, the "Luxembourg group"; the next five, the "Helsinki group," started in 2000. The Union adopted a "regatta" approach as the guiding principle of the negotiations, meaning that states were to be judged on their own merits and would become members at different times, when they were ready. This approach appears to have been adopted with credibility in mind, since it ran counter to a historically established principle of enlargement, that the EU preferred to negotiate with and accept groups of states at the same time (Preston 1997).

On the whole, the credibility hypothesis of the external incentives model would lead us to expect that EU conditionality works best with states which are neither too far from nor too close to joining the EU at the moment when conditionality is applied. An important final caveat is that the condition examined, in this case the EU criterion linked to administrative reform, had to be considered sufficiently important in the overall set of EU conditions in order to be credible.

Having established the parameters of the external incentives model and the credibility variable, both of which are particularly relevant for this analysis, a few words need to be said about the way in which rule adoption can be traced and about the starting point of Europeanization in the context of administrative reform.

Europeanization in the Context of the Postcommunist Candidate States

In order to test the effects of the independent variable, EU conditionality, on the dependent variable, rule adoption, I will consider the state of these rules at t_0, before they were affected by EU conditions. To observe the crucial difference between "before" and "after," a starting point needs to be determined and the status quo in domestic transformations defined. Thus, a clear definition of the temporal limitations of conditionality is crucial for delimiting the period in which we can seek EU influence. Such a definition involves a choice between a minimalist and a maximalist approach to what we call Europeanization in the CEECs.

A maximalist approach would define all changes after 1989 as Europeanization. More specifically, some authors have argued that the changes from 1989 until about 1993 can be seen as anticipatory adaptation or Europeanization (Haggard et al. 1993). There are several reasons why this is not a useful approach for the purposes of testing the effects of conditionality. Even if Europeanization is defined here as the adoption of "EU rules," it would be misguidedly West European–centric to assume that all change in the postcommunist states in Central and Eastern Europe occurs as a result of adopting EU rules. It is important to distinguish between the reforms of the immediate aftermath of the fall of communism during which the most basic institutions of democracy were established and those occurring in the later period that were more responsive to EU concerns.[3] The 1989–90 period was a period of intense institution-building during which the EU was doing little more than reacting to the rapid changes in Central and Eastern Europe. In this initial period, the EU did not exert much of an influence, except possibly as a model on a par with the United States, Canada, New Zealand, and other successful democracies. We cannot search for the impact of the external incentives model with regard to these processes, as the EU did not systematically target any of the states in question with specific and elaborate conditions in that period. Indirect influences of Western Europe were of course present, but the process of rule adoption was much more domestically driven, and rule adoption is more likely to have been the result of lesson-drawing than external incentives. Even so I hesitate to label

---

3. The earlier reform period has been described and analyzed in the literature on democratic transitions and on postcommunist transformations. See Linz and Stepan (1996), Elster, Offe, and Preuss (1998), Offe (1998), Anderson et al. (2001).

these early processes Europeanization—given the importance of the United States as a model for the young democracies, they could just as well be called "Americanization."

A minimalist approach, involving a more precise delineation of the transformation period and the enlargement period, would be more helpful. It would follow for example Ágh, who suggests that the distinction between democratization and Europeanization corresponds to the two-stage model of systemic change, namely transition and consolidation. Democratization, defined as a period of constitutional choices, is the first period, followed, in some but not all cases, by consolidation. It is in the period of consolidation that Europeanization started playing a significant role. These periods, as Ágh also stresses, differ greatly and need separate treatment to avoid overdetermining the effects of the EU (2002, 5).

Overall, it is important to make the distinction clear between the effects of conditionality, Europeanization, and postcommunist reform. Not every process of transformation taking place in every postcommunist CEE can be called Europeanization. Rule adoption resulting from EU pressure through conditionality should be defined in a much narrower sense and linked to the EU's concrete criteria and requirements in order to be able to arrive at any meaningful results indicating whether or not EU's incentives have led to rule adoption.

Late Emergence of Administrative Conditionality

If we look at how the EU has developed its policy of conditionality over time, we can distinguish several periods. In the first period, 1989–93, the EU was finding its way with regard to conditionality, and its development was based on the experience in development policies or input from other international organizations. The main elements of conditionality were to be found in the Association agreements concluded with the postcommunist states and in the assistance program PHARE. Conditionality in this period focused on human rights and democratic principles and democratic stability as a whole. The most significant moment in the development of EU enlargement conditionality was undoubtedly the Copenhagen European Council in 1993, establishing the well-known Copenhagen criteria and stating that the candidates are invited to join when they and the Union were ready. The Copenhagen criteria remain central in the EU's policy of conditionality, and most subsequent developments were influenced by these criteria.

In the second period, 1993–97, conditionality focused not only on democracy and human rights but started dealing with the internal market *acquis* and its potential implementation by the candidates. The pre-accession strategy approved by the member states at the Essen European Council in 1994 started this process and shaped economic conditionality. The main focus of the pre-accession strategy was preparing the candidates for taking part in the internal market (Baun 2000, 59). This was done via the Commission's White Paper on the internal market, adopted by the Cannes European Council in 1995.

From 1997 until the Copenhagen European Council in December 2002, conditionality became stronger and more complex as the Commission evaluated the progress of the candidates every year in the regular reports and as the EU set goals for them in the Accession Partnerships. There were multiple focal points to which the Commission drew the attention of the candidates, with administrative reform, reform of the judiciary, and regionalization coming more to the fore.

Administrative conditionality first emerged as part of the EU's enlargement governance in 1995, defined by the Madrid European Council (Dimitrova 2002); however, it was not enforced in any meaningful way until 1997. This is the starting point from which we should seek traces of its impact. Before proceeding with the empirical examination of administrative reform before and after EU conditionality, a discussion of the potential mechanisms via which conditionality impacts domestic structures is necessary.

Variables Mediating Domestic Responses

What determines the response of candidate states faced with *credible* conditionality? When considering the variables discussed in chapter 1, such as the fit with existing rules and the number and distribution of veto players, we must bear in mind that rationalist Europeanization approaches that utilize these variables need to be reassessed to take into account the asymmetry underlying enlargement, specifically the weaker position of the candidate states. During the enlargement period and in contrast to incumbent member states, the candidates have little choice concerning the rules they adopt and a great deal of pressure and monitoring from the Commission. Furthermore, as mentioned above, the postcommunist candidate states had already initiated wide-ranging transformations in a number of areas. The fit between already existing reforms and EU conditionality determines the level of adaptation pressure from the Union.

Adaptation Pressure and Fit with Domestic Institutions

The Europeanization framework developed by Héritier et al. explains diversity in Europeanization by using an actor-oriented institutional approach, one that also takes into account the "reform state" of a sector as well as actors' preferences and policy beliefs (2001). In the same vein, one should consider the "goodness of fit" between the state of reform of an area in the candidate states and the requirements for rule adoption via EU conditionality. Obviously, several scenarios are possible:

(1) The candidate has already reformed a particular area, and reform has been implemented along lines similar to EU conditions and criteria. In such cases we would expect little change, as adaptation pressure should be low.
(2) The candidate has reformed an area, but follows a model very different from EU requirements. Adaptation pressure would be high.

(3) The candidate state has not started or implemented reforms in a particular area. Adaptation pressure would be high, and changes can be expected within the parameters specified in the external incentives model.

When discussing goodness of fit, some of the Europeanization literature takes a distinctive historical institutionalist turn, arguing that existing institutions are robust and would resist change when adaptational pressure exists (Caporaso, Cowles, and Risse 2001, 6–8). Morlino identifies an important reason why we should not automatically follow this assumption in the case of the CEECs (2002, 9–10). While core domestic institutions may be well entrenched in EU member states, this is not the case in democracies undergoing long crises or transitions, so actors' strategies influenced by domestic institutions may not be fixed. Given the fundamental and multiple transformations that have been under way in Central and Eastern Europe, there are few established institutions that enjoy high levels of legitimacy and efficiency. On the contrary, as suggested by Dimitrova (2002) and Morlino (2002), in the case of the CEECs, institutions are new and recently established. As Morlino notes, we do not yet know what might happen when high adaptational pressure is applied to institutions that have very poor legitimacy (2002, 10).

As we know from the Europeanization literature, lack of a good fit and adaptational pressure is not a sufficient condition for domestic change to occur. If we can establish that adaptational pressure exists, we have to consider another important variable mentioned in chapter 1, namely, veto players.

While earlier discussion in the policy literature focused on veto *points*, which a proposal has to overcome in order to become law (Immergut 1992), more recently scholars have stressed the importance of veto *players* in particular in the theoretical framework developed by Tsebelis (1995; 2002). Tsebelis defines veto players as "individual or collective actors whose agreement is necessary for a change in the status quo" (2002, 19). The number and configuration of veto players defined by the constitution and other parameters of the political system determines the possibility of departing from the status quo and, therefore, the potential for change (Tsebelis 2002, 2).

The structure of the enlargement process, heavily dominated by the executive (Grabbe 2001a), leads us to reexamine the importance of veto players when conditionality is in play. Typically, when a condition arises in the enlargement context, the Commission transmits it to a candidate's government, which would be the agenda-setter and would have some freedom as to the way in which the required policy change is brought about. EU-related legislation has been discussed in parliamentary committees before adoption, as in Bulgaria and the Czech Republic (Malova and Haughton 2002, 111), but generally this has been done at great speed, which makes debate more difficult.[4] This does not change the fact that parliaments

---

4. This has been the situation during the early stages of the enlargement process and negotiations, but as the moment for concluding accession treaties drew near, the possibility for certain issues to become highly politicized and provoke wider societal debate and the opposition of certain actors became more real. In the case of Poland, such an issue was the assistance for farmers; in Bulgaria, the agreement for closing certain reactors of the nuclear power station Kozloduy; and so on.

remain veto players and that party majorities and coalitions play a role in determining the configuration of veto players and, therefore, policy stability (Tsebelis 2002, 5). When considering parliaments and political parties, it is important to take into account the distance between the various veto players (irrespective of what the status quo is). Some veto players, depending on their preferences, can be absorbed and therefore will not increase policy stability (Tsebelis 2002, 26–27).

In order to establish what the external incentives model would lead us to expect, we have to consider actor preferences in the candidate states more specifically. It would appear at first that the difference in preferences that needs to be taken into account is that between enthusiastic reformers and slow reformers or those opposed to reform. However, to show that actors' attitudes to reform matter for their response to EU conditionality, we have to assume that actors who are antireform also oppose joining the EU. This has most emphatically not been the case—in fact, many slow reformers or even former communists such as Iliescu in Romania have taken up the EU membership cause. Actors from any ideological background can hold preferences in favor of the EU, having understood that embracing European integration brings them greater material and other benefits than isolationist positions do (Hanson 2001, 145). Thus I assume that the preferences that matter are whether actors are in favor or against accession to the EU.

In this respect, the preferences of political actors in the candidate states are grouped very closely together, since acceding to the EU has been known to have the support of all major political parties, give or take some bargaining rhetoric. Since the Union has used the reward of membership as the incentive for governments to carry on reforms, I expect that only governments or other actors that do not value membership would be prepared to veto reforms required by the EU (again assuming credible conditionality). In other words, we can expect veto players to make EU-driven reform more difficult or veto it altogether only if they are located far from other players with regard to EU accession—that is, if they are Euro-skeptical. All other veto players would be "absorbed," to use Tsebelis's terminology, in the set of actors with similar preferences for EU accession.

Given the small number of Euro-skeptical veto players, we may expect a high degree of uniformity in the adoption of EU rules in the enlargement period, provided, of course, that we can assume that EU pressure on the candidates can be taken as uniform.[5] In terms of administrative conditionality, this high degree of rule adoption would be restricted by credibility in the way described in the previous sections.

The hypotheses with regard to administrative conditionality can be summarized as follows:

---

5. Other chapters in this book rightly draw attention to the supply side of EU conditionality. It is actually not clear whether the pressure exerted from the EU via conditionality has really been uniform, or, in other words, whether the EU has cared equally about Romania and about Slovakia and put the same amount of pressure on them. But for the purposes of this chapter and given the existence of common criteria applied in a roughly similar ways in the Commission's Regular Reports, I will assume candidates have been treated in uniform fashion.

(1) Conditionality would be credible when it presents a credible threat of exclusion from the enlargement process *and* the promise for accession remains credible as well.

(2) Given credibility of conditionality, we can expect to see rule adoption in a specific area when this area has not yet been reformed along the lines required by the EU. If it has been reformed, adaptation pressure would be lower and little change would be seen. Other factors or models such as social learning or lesson-drawing may have played a role.

(3) If (1) and (2) obtain, conditionality would result in rule adoption in almost all cases regardless of actors' preferences on an issue, as long as the relevant veto players are in favor of accession to the EU.

Last but not least, the question arises whether, if all actors declare that they are prepared to adopt EU rules, this would signify changing patterns of behavior? The distinctions among discursive, formal, and behavioral adoption made in chapter 1 are important in this context. I will only test the external incentives model and explain *formal* rule adoption in the case of administrative reform in the candidate states. As for *behavioral* adoption, this is an issue for which we cannot test at this stage of enlargement, although it is useful to start speculating about potential scenarios based again on the status quo in the candidate states—a topic that will be discussed in the concluding part of this chapter.

Civil Service Reform before and after EU Administrative Conditionality

EU Administrative Conditionality

As mentioned above, EU conditionality covers a range of issues, which come to the fore at different points in time and have various weights and importances ascribed to them. Some are sufficiently important that, if breached, they can stop or delay considerably the process of accession; these include instability and violation of democratic institutions, war, human rights violations, torture.[6] Others are defined as important but their potential to stop a country from acceding is left deliberately unclear; these include such items as administrative and judicial reform and treatment of the Roma minorities. One can treat the separate sets of conditions linked to the EU's Copenhagen criteria as partial conditionalities or subconditions. Some of these partial conditionalities have clearly become more important over time.[7] It is also likely, although evidence is scarce, that if a candidate does not

6. The EU introduced conditionality linked to human rights and democratic principles in 1992–93 in the Trade and Cooperation agreements with the Baltic states and the Association agreements with Bulgaria and Romania. Conditionality took the form of suspension clauses that were later introduced in all agreements with third countries, including the renegotiated Association agreements with the Czech Republic and Slovakia.

7. To illustrate this, we need to look at the Commission's progress reports, which are divided into sections, following the Copenhagen criteria: democratic, economic, and *acquis*–related conditions.

progress very well with one set of conditions but is evaluated as progressing well in general, then this set of partial conditionalities may not have central importance in the state's cost-benefit calculations.

Conditionality with regard to administrative reform, capacity and ability to implement the *acquis* is a partial conditionality that grew in importance in the late 1990s and has been linked to both the democracy criterion (rule of law) and the implementation of the *acquis*. The following paragraphs discuss the development of the administrative capacity criterion in this enlargement as a way to evaluate the determinacy and clarity of conditions that, as specified in chapter 1, would be important for rule adoption under the external incentives model.

The administrative conditionality criterion was first formulated by the Madrid European Council in 1995, but there was little follow-up in terms of defining what it meant until the Commission included it in its Opinions in 1997 and gave it increasing weight and importance in the Regular Progress Reports of 1998, 1999, and 2001 (Dimitrova 2002).[8] In its Opinions, the Commission invited the candidates to make major efforts in reforming their administrations to improve administrative capacity to implement the *acquis*. Later, administrative capacity was defined as including sectoral capacity to implement the *acquis*, horizontal capacity, development of structures for the coordination of negotiations with the EU, and, last but not least, increased capacity of regional governments and local administration. Reform of the judiciary became a closely related criterion singled out in the Commission's Regular Reports in the last years before accession.

While sectoral capacity was linked to particular parts of the *acquis*, horizontal capacity, emerged as synonymous with administrative reform. However, having decided at the Madrid European Council that candidates should have the administrative capacity to implement the (Single Market) *acquis*, the EU and especially the Commission could not easily define horizontal administrative capacity requirements. The reason for this was first and foremost that the Union had no *acquis*, no common rules regarding the capacity of administrations or the administrative organization of member states. As for the development of informal rules and potential convergence of administrative practices in the European Union in order to form a kind of European administrative space, the debate whether there is any degree of convergence due to Europeanization is still very much open (cf. Olsen 2002b).

The absence of EU rules and a common model made the Commission's work in specifying administrative conditionality, and especially conditions for improving horizontal capacity, more difficult. Nevertheless, administrative conditionality

---

Despite a somewhat blurred hierarchy among the criteria, it is clear that the democracy criterion was evaluated first, followed by the economic and *acquis* criteria. In recent years, in evaluating Turkey, the Commission has specified that a country has to fulfil the first criterion, the stability of institutions guaranteeing democracy and human rights before starting negotiations, a position consistent with the exclusion of Slovakia in 1997.

8. The following several paragraphs draw heavily on Dimitrova (2002).

emerged as a separate criterion in the 1997 Opinions and the regular reports that followed them. The Commission requested the Support for Improvement in Governance and Management in Central and Eastern European Countries (SIGMA) group of the OECD to develop criteria for administrative reform. The questionnaires for evaluation and baseline criteria developed by SIGMA in the late 1990s constituted the basis for the EU's horizontal capacity requirements. This was an interesting case of absence of rules at the EU level but an existence of these rules as a condition for benefits or accession.

Following the assumption specified in chapter 1, one could argue that the lack of common EU rules created a lack of clarity and determinacy of conditions, which prevented any meaningful rule adoption. Johan Olsen, for example, predicted a lack of convergence in administrative structures and practices: "Probably, the most significant factor impeding convergence on a model transferred from the EU has been the absence of an agreed-upon exemplary organizational model and a coherent reform policy in the Union. The EU has wanted reforms and improved capabilities, but exactly what kind of administration and capabilities are needed has not been clear" (2002b). However, the Commission's strong insistence on the passing of civil service legislation as a start of administrative reform made the conditions determinate enough over time, even though candidates remained aware that the EU has no administrative *acquis*.

The content of administrative conditionality, in other words the substance of the rules the EU required the candidates to adopt, was influenced by the ambiguity created by the lack of a common EU model and the perceived need for the candidates to (re-)create their administrations almost from scratch. Remarkably, the administrative criterion of the EU did not endorse the New Public Management model (NPM), which has been the most influential model for civil service reform in Western Europe in recent decades (cf. Toonen 2001, 184). Instead, the Commission and SIGMA promoted requirements for passing legislation establishing civil services in the CEE candidates as independent professional bodies and protecting civil servants from dismissals and extensive political interference. The model endorsed by the administrative conditionality requirements is thus closest to the classical Weberian bureaucracy model, although some subsequent advice related to the adoption of performance-oriented criteria in personnel policy brings it closer to NPM and therefore, according to some, it is a mixed model.[9]

Even though the focus of EU's administrative criterion has always remained the somewhat elusive "ability to implement the *acquis*," the horizontal capacity requirements can be evaluated as a kind of an institutional healing approach (the more common Commission term is "institution building") in which the EU tries to fix the ills and problems of postcommunist administrations. To see how successful the EU has been, one must look at the reform state of the postcommunist

---

9. For a discussion of the model promoted by the EU in the candidate states, see Fournier (1998), who evaluates it as a classical Weberian model and Bossaert and Demke (2003, 1–9), who disagree, calling it a mixed model.

administrations before administrative conditionality came into play, that is before 1997.

Postcommunist Administrations before Conditionality

Postcommunist administrations could not, in most cases, develop as independent Weberian bureaucracies, instead suffering from numerous problems linked to the overarching, all-encompassing role of the state in communist regimes.[10] As Verheijen aptly puts it, "systems of public administrations as they functioned in the previous system of governance were at best an 'implementation machine' for decisions taken by the Communist party apparatus and at worst a means of suppression of citizens by the state." One implication of this is that "the notion of a professional civil service . . . had been eliminated in most states" (Verheijen 2003, 490).

As a result, the postcommunist administrations shared a number of common problems linked to their communist legacy (see Goetz 2001; Goetz and Wollmann 2001; Verheijen 2001). The communist party domination and penetration of bureaucracies of the CEE states in the past and the resulting dual hierarchies left postcommunist administrations after 1989 openly partisan and unable to get away from political interference (see Sootla 2001, 117). The use of the state apparatus for the purposes of repression by the communist regimes created serious challenges to the legitimacy of public institutions (Coombes 2001). One has to agree with Vidláková's bold assessment that, "administrative reform in Central and Eastern European countries involves nothing less than the definition of a new concept of statehood" (2001, 106).

Goetz and Wollmann point to another feature of the communist legacy, namely that administrations were underpoliticized in terms of policymaking capacity—weak executives—but overpoliticized in terms of personnel policy—politicization of the civil services (2001, 865). Adding the perception of corruption and an almost universal lack of accountability provides a short but significant list of some of the common problems of postcommunist administrations at the outset of the CEE transitions. These also became the ills that the EU tried to address after 1997 through the administrative conditionality criterion in its various incarnations.

The main components of the EU's approach regarding at least horizontal capacity were the insistence on the adoption of legislation defining the roles of the civil service and the civil servants, the requirement of creating a strategy for public administration reform and a training program for civil servants. In addition were the sectoral capacity requirements linked to the application of various sectors of the *acquis*. Before looking at how these rules were adopted by the candidates, their initial reform state, that is, the state of administrative reform before the EU applied conditionality, will be established.

10. With the possible exception of Hungary, where the civil service had a Weberian tradition and remained relatively separate from the Communist party (Vass, 1999).

The existence of the challenges the CEECs had in common tends to obscure the differences, which were important as they represent the different states of reform on which EU pressure came to bear from 1997 onwards. In the early period of general institutional formation (1989–93) when the EU did not play a role, the status of postcommunist administration reforms in the CEECs analyzed in this chapter differed to a considerable degree. We need to take this difference into account when considering adaptation pressures from the EU.

Candidate states can be categorized according to the various stages of their civil service reform development. Even though there is no disputing the argument that institutional reform, in this case administrative reform, is an undertaking far larger and more complex and multifaceted than merely passing certain legislation, the adoption of legislation provides a useful first cut on reform. More specifically, I consider the passing of laws on the civil service, on administrations, as well as secondary legislation creating a professional civil service and defining the role of civil servants in relation to society and politics as a clear case of reform.

None of the states examined here, with the exception of Poland, had legislation defining the role of the civil service or civil servants in the communist period. We can thus consider legislation adopted in the early period (1989–93) as early reform, part of the multiple institutional transformations defined above. This does not in any way exclude the possibility of such reforms being influenced by the EU or West European states, which may have served as models for new legislation. However, since I look at conditionality formulated after 1995 and enforced after 1997, for the purpose of testing the external incentives model, we can treat reforms passed up to 1995 as the initial "reform state."

I differentiate among several types of reform or rule adoption: full, partial, or no reforms. Given that the main elements of this round of reform have been the separation of civil servants from politics and the issues of personnel policy on the one hand and the conceptualization of the place and role of the civil service on the other, full reform can be defined here as being underpinned by both civil service and public administration laws and possibly reform strategies, secondary implementing legislation, training, or other measures, such as access to information laws. Consequently, cases where both basic laws and strategy and training were in place can be deemed full reforms. Cases in which one piece of legislation regarding civil service had been passed but not implemented and no other acts followed for several years can be classified as partial reforms. If no basic legislation regarding the civil service has been passed, we can state that no reform had started. Thus the picture of reform in CEE candidates emerges as follows: few early reforms and only one clear case of full reform, some backtracking, and an almost complete lack of implementation of the laws adopted, except in Hungary, Poland, and Estonia.

Early Reformers, 1989–1993. Hungary was a clear forerunner in reform (Meyer-Sahling 2001). The Hungarian government started with a civil service law in 1992 and was reasonably successful in implementing it. Experts describe the 1992 law as "stable, working legislation," although it did not prevent the Hungarian civil service from suffering from excessive politicization and manipulation by politi-

Table 4.1   Civil service reforms in the CEECs until 1997

| | Legislation passed 1990–93 on | | Legislation passed 1993–97 on | |
| | | Civil service/public | | Civil service/public |
Country	Civil servants	admin.	Civil servants	admin.
Bulgaria				
Czech Republic				
Estonia			1995	
Hungary	1992	1992		
Latvia			1995	
Lithuania			1995	
Poland			1996	
Romania				
Slovenia	1990			
Slovakia				

cians.[11] Slovenia had a law defining the position of civil servants starting in 1990, but the law was not followed by any other legislation in that period and was regarded as incomplete. Therefore, we can describe Slovenia's reform status quo as early but incomplete reform.

Partial Reformers, 1993–1997. Poland adopted a civil service law in 1996 but, as Goetz reports, "its implementation was aborted" and new legislation replaced it in 1998 (2001, 1036). Estonia adopted a public service act in 1995. It introduced the difference between career civil servants and state civil servants, but since the law did not have a clear public administration concept, it has been considered incomplete (Sootla 2001, 122). In Latvia, civil servants legislation was adopted but not implemented. Subsequent governments abandoned the push for reform and did not pass other essential legislation for civil service reform, such as the civil service or public administration legislation (Reinholde, forthcoming). In Lithuania, similarly, the law on officials was passed in 1994, but again it was reportedly never fully implemented, and administration reform did not progress much further until 1997 (Verheijen 2003, 492).

Rhetorical Reformers: No Major Changes in Administrative Legislation until 1997. Despite the rhetoric of reform in these states, no civil service legislation was passed in Bulgaria, Romania, the Czech Republic, and Slovakia in the initial period examined here. These states had either no reform legislation or limited postcommunist regulation. The Czech Republic and Slovakia incorporated civil service provisions into their Labor Codes, and reform was seen as necessitating Labor Code amendments. Furthermore, the Czechs were locked into a longstanding political battle over lustration, which also involved the civil service. In all of these states there had been plenty of rhetorical statements by politicians regarding the need of public administration reforms, but little had happened in Bulgaria, Romania, the Czech Republic and Slovakia to follow up such rhetoric. Table 4.1 summarizes what we

11. E-mail interview with Laszlo Vass, 4 March 2003.

Table 4.2   Civil service legislation and EU conditionality

Candidate state	Start of membership negotiations	Laws on the civil service Laws on civil servants
Bulgaria	2000	State Administration Law 1998, amended 2001, 2003 Civil Service Law adopted 1999, in force 2000
Czech Republic	1998	Civil service legislation adopted May 2002 (most provisions to come in force 2004), job security legislation aborted
Estonia	1998	Public Service Act adopted 1995, in force 1996; Law on the Public Administration 2001 (in force 2003)
Hungary	1998	Civil Service Law/Legal Status of Public Officials 1992, amended June 2001
Latvia	2000	Law on civil service 1994; Law on the state civil service adopted 2000 (in force 2001); draft law on public administration; draft law on administrative procedures
Lithuania	2000	Law on officials 1995 Civil service law 1999 (several amendments, latest 2002) Law on the organization of the state administration 1998
Poland	1998	Law adopted 1996, revised; new law on civil service adopted 1998
Romania	2000	Law on the Statute of Civil Servants 1999
Slovakia	2000	2001 Civil Service Law adopted after protracted debates and amendments, Labor Code oriented
Slovenia	1998	Package of civil service laws passed in 2002, in particular Public Administration Law and Law on the Civil Servants.

Source: Reproduced, with some changes, from Dimitrova (2002).

can call the status quo of reform before the EU started applying administrative conditionality in 1997.

Given this reform "status quo," did conditionality make a difference? In other words, did conditionality after the Madrid European Council formulated the administrative criterion, and especially after the Commission elaborated it in 1997, lead to rule adoption? The summary of adopted legislation in table 4.2 suggests that, indeed, conditionality and especially the pressure for reform linked to the start of negotiations for membership did make a difference.

Comparing table 4.1 and table 4.2, it is easy to see that states that had not adopted civil service legislation or completed reforms did do so in a relatively short period of time after 1997 (1998–2002). This was the case with Bulgaria, Romania, Slovakia, Slovenia, Lithuania, and Latvia, while even states that already had legislation, such as Poland or Estonia, adopted new laws in this period. Latvia's law of 2000, for example, was fundamentally revised in comparison with the one of 1995 (Verheijen 2003, 492).

Furthermore, most candidates adopted or amended civil service legislation in the period near the start of their negotiations with the EU. Even though the number of cases examined here is too small to draw a general conclusion, it appears that there is evidence of widespread rule adoption among candidate states, similar to other studies finding convergence among the candidates for EU membership (Malova and Haughton 2002, 101; Ágh 2002). This seems, on the whole, to indicate compliance with conditionality rather than lesson-drawing to suit specific situations in domestic administrations, which may have been expected to occur at any time and not specifically in the run-up to the start of negotiations.

The variation in the adoption of reform legislation is mostly observed in the exact timing and less in the content of laws adopted. Nevertheless, while some details differ, in most cases the new legislation has defined the civil service and the position of civil servant, established some form of career civil service system, provided for the protection of civil servants from political interference by favoring competition and limiting political appointments. Elements of performance-oriented personnel policy were limited, especially in the first versions of legislation, which may have been amended later, as in Hungary, Poland, Latvia, and Bulgaria. The state that appears to have responded in the most minimal fashion to conditionality in terms of both timing and content—and in which political actors have openly doubted the rules suggested by the Commission—is the Czech Republic. Slovenia and Estonia have also been slow to introduce or change legislation, while Hungary made few changes but its early 1992 reform to a great extent corresponded to the rules and conditions suggested by the Commission.

How can existing variation be accounted for? As indicated in previous sections of this chapter, credibility of administrative conditionality may have been lowest for the Czech Republic, Hungary, and Poland. The expectation that when credibility is low external threats and incentives would play less of a role is confirmed. Rule adoption in 1997–2000 has been rather limited in Hungary and the Czech Republic, while in Poland the amendments to the mid-1990s legislation create a more blurred picture.

As shown above, Poland had already started administrative reform and made some progress when administrative conditionality became a central issue. The 1995 law, which came into force in 1996, established a system of qualifications that promoted a neutral, carrier civil service. The 1998 law, however, completely revised the earlier law and made changes that established political positions and introduced some elements of a spoils system. This system provided more opportunity for political appointments by the Buzek government, a change that was not preferred by the EU. This can be explained by the fact that with regard to Poland the credibility of a potential threat of exclusion was quite low.

The Europeanization mechanisms at play appear different in the other two cases. In the case of Hungary, reforms had been well under way when administrative conditionality came into play. Thus, adaptation pressure was low. Hungary was the only CEEC that started reform early, in 1992, along lines not too far from the model later suggested by the EU. Hungarian public administration reform had taken off well before the EU started focusing on administrative conditionality (Verheijen 2003, 491–92) and has been characterized by a relative stability of the civil service, which is much needed across the region. Even though the EU informally criticized amendments in the Hungarian legislation in 2001 that created a special "political" category of 350 civil servants to be appointed by the prime minister, Hungarian reform is still seen as the most advanced in the region.[12] While my focus is the importance of the external incentives model for rule adoption, the early development of administrative reform in Hungary suggests that other explanatory models can make a significant contribution in explaining rule adoption. Experts assess the Hungarian reform process as domestically driven but with strong influences from other systems, notably the French cabinet system (Vass 2001, 156). Thus, lesson-drawing may have been the dominant mechanism for rule adoption in Hungary.

The case of the Czech Republic can be classified as resistance and delay of rule adoption. One of the major political parties, Václav Klaus's ODS, repeatedly rejected the civil service package of legislation, although it was finally adopted in 2002. The ODS's position has been that no laws are needed to reform the civil service and that reform can be achieved through other means. This position was clearly informed by political and ideological preferences for a system in which the job security of civil servants would not be guaranteed. Experts have indicated that it has been one of the most contentious issues in the Czech Republic's preparation for EU membership. Vidláková describes the situation as follows: "Since 1993 public administration reform was repeatedly postponed because of the lack of 'political will.' Civil servants were powerless at that time, all documents and drafts of laws were prepared, but the politicians did not act, but quibbled over details. It is only at present that we see that it was not 'a lack of capacity' or 'lack of political will' but rather the fear of political elites that too much power had been 'handed out' to municipalities and the central state power began to dislike it" (2001, 103). When the law on the civil service was finally passed in 2002, provisions regarding civil servants job security were dropped by the parliament and other provisions were delayed and devised to come into force in 2004. It must be noted, however, that the Czech Republic did proceed with administrative reform by other channels and means, with a strong focus on local and regional government reform. The issue in evaluating the Czech efforts, however, is not the ultimate suitability or effectiveness of reform, but simply the response to EU conditionality. This response was the most negative of all member states, and rule adoption was minimal.

Both low credibility and the presence of an important veto player can account for the developments in the Czech Republic. It has been one of the states considered in the forefront of accession. Elites have had a clear and strong sense of the Czech Republic's importance in the whole enlargement process. Even more importantly, there has been a player on the Czech political scene, the ODS under Klaus, which, even if not against accession, has been sufficiently Euro-skeptical to count as a veto player that cannot be absorbed. The criticism of the EU by Klaus and other ODS members has been sufficiently explicit as to provoke doubts in some EU circles as to the commitment of the Czech Republic to the EU institutions. Klaus was thus a viable veto player whose perception of the credibility of the EU's threat and cost-benefit calculations was affected by his position on European integration.

12. Ibid.

The other state where a delay can be noted, Slovenia, has been among the first five selected to start negotiations in 1998, so credibility of conditionality appeared to be low. Still, Slovenia did respond to EU conditionality, albeit in an unhurried way, by adopting a civil service legislation package in 2002. This represents an interesting contrast with Bulgaria, Romania, and Latvia, where the adoption of such legislation was one of several remaining conditions linked by the Commission directly to the start of negotiations, to be undertaken in a very short period of time. All of these states adopted rules for which there had been little political consensus beyond rhetoric before the EU stepped in. In the words of one Latvian official, "Nothing would have happened here without the EU pressure on politicians" (Interview, December 2002).

Evidence from some experts that Latvia has been influenced by the New Zealand model (Jansone and Reinholde 2001, 209) makes the country a very interesting mixed case. Interviews have indicated that there had been stagnation in reform after the 1994 law was adopted and that the push for the adoption of new legislation and other measures came from the EU. At the same time, measures introduced in 2000, such as the management contracts for civil servants, indicate the mechanism of lesson-drawing has been important with regard to the contents of reform at its later stages. This suggests the need to elaborate further potential complementarity between the external incentives and the lesson-drawing models.

The picture of the CEE governments' attitude to the definition of the civil service as a separate and independent body immune from political interference grows more complex when one looks at subsequent changes in the adopted rules. Several candidate states have passed amendments that run contrary to EU conditionality and re-introduce a larger degree of political influence via political cabinets or special staff. This seems to be the spirit of the amendment of the Hungarian law in 2001 and, according to at least some experts, the changes in Poland. This is an early indication that rule adoption driven by external incentives may not result in lasting changes. Given that EU conditions required substantive and important domestic reform to install a certain type of administration, often against the preferences of governments favoring a NPM approach, conditionality has to be evaluated as having been remarkably successful in bringing about formal rule adoption. But what about behavioral rule adoption?

Some Propositions about Behavioral Adoption

To evaluate the potential for behavioral adoption following the formal adoption of EU rules or, in the language of the European Commission, the chances for implementation of the *acquis*, one can speculate that, under certain circumstances, implementing formally adopted EU rules will bring losses or less benefit than other strategies to significant actors who could be seen as informal veto players. Evaluating such a possibility requires a closer look at the political landscapes and political dynamics of postcommunist states and at theories that attempt to explain the dynamics of postcommunist democratic consolidation. The role of the state in democratic transitions and consolidation has become an important issue in recent debates. Linz and Stepan stress that a functioning state and usable bureaucracy are a prerequisite for consolidation (1996, 7). Stephen Hanson goes further, claiming that even if not all societal groups accept the rules of the democratic game, "it is still meaningful to speak of democracy as 'consolidated' whenever the enforcers of democratic institutions themselves can be counted on with very high probability to behave in ways compatible with, and oriented toward, the perpetuation of formal institutional rules." (2001, 141) He goes on to make the rather convincing claim that consolidation in Central and Eastern Europe can be explained by the "increasingly reliable enforcement of formal legal norms governing state boundaries, political contestation and citizenship rights by party and state officials" (2001, 145).

There are, however, formally consolidated democracies whose progress with reforms seems to proceed at a painfully slow pace or even to backslide. This can be explained by a framework that suggests the coexistence both of "staffs" that enforce the legal norms embraced by prowestern elites and of officials or whole networks that function according to other, informal rules. The existence of such networks, not instead of but parallel to the official state structures, suggests that state weakness is a danger for the functioning of new, formally established rules, which may not be adopted behaviorally by important actors. If we link conditionality to possible state penetration by organized interests, we can envisage a cleavage after accession between organized interests that might lose from a set of reforms and EU membership and those who stand to gain from it, such as modernizers, free market reformers, minority leaders, pro-European groups, or legitimate business groups. Thus we might expect that if organized interests exist that do not see sufficient payoffs in the EU enlargement process, we will not see widespread behavioral adoption of already adopted formal rules. Organized interests might stall the implementation of EU formal rules and reforms if members of shadow networks and connected political elites anticipate the payoff to be smaller than the costs, for example the costs of bringing shadow economies into the open.

In all of the ten cases studied in this chapter, considerable changes in formal rules regarding the functioning of civil services occurred in a relatively short period of time. In some cases these changes occurred without any evidence of prior existence of actor coalitions in favor of reform. Given empirical evidence not only of rule adoption but also in some cases of a direct link between administrative reform legislation and the start of the respective candidate state's negotiations for membership, we can conclude with reasonable certainty that conditionality matters. The relative uniformity of the type of measures adopted also suggests that the changes are not a result of imitation (since not all the bureaucracies of EU member states are shaped by such legislative measures) or lesson-drawing, both of which imply that candidates would be most likely to pick the legislation that they find most relevant to their situations. If the driving mechanism behind the changes were lesson-drawing, we would expect the adoption of a greater variety of rules for administrations in the candidates, as legislators would have selectively chosen from existing (and very different) EU models and traditions. I would also argue that the external incentives model has more explanatory power than social learning, since the latter would require shared norms and identities by the politicians dealing with administrative reform. As evident from the debate on the existence of a European administrative space mentioned in this chapter, shared norms and coherent identities may not yet be present with regard to administrations.

Given the limitations imposed by credibility, the external incentives model can also explain cases in which political actors have not complied with EU administrative conditionality or have complied in the most perfunctory fashion (such as the Czech Republic). Low credibility of the threat of exclusion from the enlargement process made rule adoption more difficult in countries perceived as forerunners and enabled changes in adopted rules at a later stage.

Last but not least, not only does conditionality matter, it matters more than Europeanization mechanisms in the existing EU member states. The EU's influence on core domestic structures is much more significant in the candidate states than in the EU member states where, as Cowles and Risse conclude, "[t]he core structures of member states are often resistant to Europeanization" (2001, 236). The influence of the EU on rule adoption with regard to basic "rules about the rules" in the candidate states is impressive. However, the endurance of the formally adopted rules after the candidates become members is a different issue, one that can be explored in future research.

CHAPTER FIVE

External Incentives and Lesson-Drawing in Regional Policy and Health Care

Wade Jacoby

How does rule adoption differ in cases in which the EU drives it and cases in which a CEEC drives it? This chapter pursues this question by focusing on two policy areas that, according to the propositions in the introduction, ought to have extremely different dynamics. I look at regional policy, where several external incentive propositions predict rapid rule adoption, and show that while outcomes generally fit the broad predictions of this model, there are some anomalies that do not fit. I then introduce the lesson-drawing model as a possible complement to the external incentives model and show that it accounts well for the pattern of rule adoption in other policy areas. I look at health care to demonstrate these mechanisms in detail.

This "two-cut" research design does not focus equal attention on all four propositions in each explanatory model. Instead, this chapter emphasizes the consequences of two variables that appear in both the external incentives model and the lesson-drawing model, albeit in different guises. The first variable is the availability of alternative models of organization. For the external incentives model, this is operationalized through the determinacy of conditions; where determinacy is high, states have clear cues about which rules to adopt. For the lesson-drawing model, alternatives come through EU-centered epistemic communities. The second common variable is the structure of interest representation. In both models, this variable is operationalized through the size of adoption costs incurred by veto players, although the models differ on the extent to which these costs must be exclusively material ones.

I thank Frank Schimmelfennig, Ulrich Sedelmeier, Antoaneta Dimitrova, and the other participants in the Turin workshop for helpful comments on a previous draft and Matthew Jennejohn and Steve Page for their research assistance.

Each case study covers two periods divided by the Commission White Paper on the preparation of the CEECs for the internal market: from the late 1980s to mid-1995 and mid-1995 to the present. The White Paper was the first document that provided concrete guidelines to aspirant members on the transposition of the one thousand or so directives that stood at the heart of the internal market. Before 1996, for my purposes, Europeanization was generally CEEC-driven. After that date, external incentives began to enter the calculus.[1] Because even this simplified model requires detailed qualitative research, my study is focused on two countries, Hungary and the Czech Republic. These two countries share several important features: both have had long experience with broader European institutional developments and have relatively high levels of economic development. Both are unitary states with long-term integration into the traditions of the Germanic subfamily of civil law. Both have had alternations of government between center-right and center-left within parliamentary regimes with similar electoral thresholds. Both have had a domestic elite consensus that joining the EU was a central foreign policy goal, although that consensus was clearly stronger in Hungary. The countries are about the same size, with populations around ten million, and inside CEE both have been among the front-runners for EU membership. In short, if there is any place in CEE where conditions for rule adoption are propitious, it is here. Most important, both the external incentives and the lesson-drawing logics should have been possible.

The chapter starts with a case that should be among the "best case" scenarios for finding EU-driven rule adoption (e.g., the external incentives model) because the *acquis* is significant and determinate and because potential veto players are few.[2] This case study fits well—but not perfectly—with the external incentives explanation, but it has certain anomalies that are better explained with the lesson-drawing logic. The chapter then moves to health policy, a likely "worst case" for the external incentives model because the EU has little leverage and the obstacles—in the form of ministerial bureaucrats, providers, and patients—are many.[3] That said, the case does have some propitious conditions for lesson-drawing and thus can help us explore the relevance of the role of epistemic communities and the structure of interest groups for that model.

In order to focus on rule adoption, I say less about parallel reforms that do not reflect Europeanization. In phase one of each policy area, I look at rule adoption under conditions where rule adoption, if it occurred, would have to be CEEC-

1. Note that any such chronological dividing line (e.g., Europe Agreements, Essen Summit, White Paper, Accession Partnerships, etc.) would be somewhat arbitrary. But the alternative would oblige the researcher to get inside the heads of policymakers to determine whether they were engaged in some form of anticipatory rule adoption (e.g., pre–White Paper but still somehow conditioned by the EU).

2. The other two external incentives propositions also point to significant external influence, since rewards were very substantial and the EU's PHARE program could, at least in principle, disburse them quickly and the structural fund rules do credibly threaten the exclusion of actors who do not follow the rules. I will return to these issues briefly later in the paper.

3. By "worst case," I simply mean that the tenets of the external incentives model would lead us to expect little rule adoption.

driven. Since such rule adoption was not an obligation at that point, the states often used the EU or member state rules as rough guides or templates without trying to copy them exactly. In phase two, I look at the EU-driven rule adoption that occurs after the publication of the White Paper and especially after the onset of screening. In keeping with the notion of the determinacy of rules, I make a simple division between "thresholds" set by the EU—where rules are looser—and "patches"—where the EU requires very specific reforms.[4] Both empirical cases emphasize formal and behavioral rule adoption more than discursive rule adoption.

Rule Adoption in Regional Policy

The structural and cohesion policies are the second most expensive component of the EU's budget, trailing only agriculture.[5] And because of restrictions on their receipts from the Common Agricultural Policy (CAP; see also Epstein, chapter 9), CEECs will actually receive *more* money from the structural funds than from CAP in the first several years of membership. The EU's structural and cohesion funds contribute financially to the regional policies (RP) of the member states as they seek to create appropriate conditions for investment and job creation. The CEECs are far poorer than the EU average, and this enlargement is the most ambitious ever in terms of integrating poorer economies. For example, in each of the three previous EU enlargements, three new states joined and lowered the total EU GDP per capita from 3 to 6 percent. This enlargement, by contrast, lowered GDP per capita across the EU by about 9 percent.

Rule determinacy is substantial, but within limits that generally respect the rights of member states to develop their own basic RP structures. The cofinancing role of the EU requires that individual projects funded by the EU respond to priorities set by the Commission, especially regional competitiveness, social cohesion and employment, and the development of urban and rural areas (Commission 1999c).[6] Moreover, access to these funds is predicated on planning competence and administrative mastery of complex procedures. These controls are sufficiently strict that many subnational governments in longtime member states are unable to gain access to monies to which their region is nominally entitled. That is, certain administrative competences and the ability to follow an extensive set of rules are a prerequisite for receiving structural funds. Thus, while the EU is reluctant to specify how nation states configure subnational units, both its functional demands and its administrative procedures generate a web of requirements and quasi-

4. For an extended discussion of the concepts of thresholds and patches, see Jacoby (2004).

5. On EU structural funds, see Hooghe (1996) and Allen (2000). For an overview of the link between macroeconomic stabilization, privatization, and regional policy, see Bachtler et al. (2000).

6. Of course, member states can have *other* programs that do not respond directly to these priorities, so long as they do not run afoul of single market provisions on, for example, subsidies to industry.

requirements that make this case very much one in which external incentives are apparent and determinacy is relatively high.

Initially, it appeared that few veto players populated this policy domain, which was relatively underdeveloped in the early postcommunist period. During the communist era, many of the policy functions that would fall under the RP domain were instead addressed by sectoral promotion policies at the aggregate level and income standardization policies at the individual level. Such policies were highly centralized. In the immediate postcommunist period, reformers focused their attention on macroeconomic policy and gave little, if any, attention to microeconomic issues besides privatization.

There is no single EU RP model, and, indeed, a few states (Ireland and Portugal) distribute regional funds from a single central fund. But most EU member states, whether unitary or federal, have some form of administrative devolution to constituent units, and it was this notion that has occupied the Commission from the time of its initial Opinions in 1997. One of the main tasks in this policy sector has been to build up actors at regional levels who are competent enough to engage in the demanding tasks of planning and implementing RP. While the number of formal laws that must be transposed is actually small—RP is a policy area where "direct effects" dominate—the rules and norms around the EU structural and cohesion funds are many and strict (Brusis 2003; Sasse and Hughes 2002). The EU has pushed the creation of new regional and local actors. The Czechs had more to build and less to start with because, unlike Hungary, there had been no efforts to regionalize politics in the waning years of communism. And while the Hungarian government did take an interest in broader European RP developments even prior to the 1994 Essen Summit, the Czech government did not. This difference complicates any easy attribution of rule adoption to external influences because some of the rule adoption occurred prior to the presence of such incentives.

Hungarian Regional and Cohesion Policy: A Brief Overview

Like much of the CEE region, Hungary suffers from two glaring patterns of economic disparity—an urban-rural divide and a West-East divide. For much of the 1990s, foreign direct investment in Budapest constituted up to 75 percent of that for the whole country, while unemployment in the eastern counties bordering Slovakia and Romania was 2–4 times the rates in the western counties that bordered Austria, Slovenia, and Croatia.[7] Hungarian regional policy began changing even before the end of communism. From the early 1970s, Hungary had explicit programs to promote the economic development of rural villages, while a 1985 parliamentary decree and subsequent ministerial resolution marked the first effort for systematic regional (as opposed to economic sector-specific) development in Hungary. This program, starved for resources and focused on only two eastern

7. For detailed data on both issues, see Hungarian Ministry of Agriculture and Regional Development (hereafter, HMARD) (1998).

counties, had little lasting effect, but it did indicate some indigenous impulses to attack economic disparities in something other than sectoral terms. An important consequence of the mainly sectoral orientation of all communist-era development policies was that the large heavy industrial factories that were one hallmark of such policies were among the first to close after the onset of market liberalization. Thus the main instruments of communist-era development were often most vulnerable to new market forces and gave only temporary relief to affected regions. As a result, Hungarian policymakers had both an indigenous platform and some incentives to investigate other European RP models.

A burst of activity in the mid- and late 1990s led to a situation in which Hungarian RP came much closer to the formally decentralized structures the Commission had been requesting since the mid-1990s. Hungary's first major step to address EU concerns over centralization and underfunding came in 1996 with the passage of the Law on Regional Development and Physical Planning (Act XXI). This law, to the development of which PHARE programs had already contributed significantly, served as the primary referent for screening Hungarian policy with EU directives. Act XXI's main principles were decentralization, subsidiarity, partnership, programming, additionality, transparency, and concentration, which already implied that these EU RP norms had passed beyond the level of discourse to at least the formal level. On the other hand, we shall see that behavioral changes still lagged behind the formal adoption of EU rules (Horváth 1998, 16; Sasse and Hughes 2002).

The year 1996 also brought the formation of Regional Development Councils (RDCs) and, as subsets of the councils, Regional Development Agencies (RDAs). These bodies responded to EU demands by devolving decision-making and management control to the regional level and were meant to be key actors in implementing regional development programs in Hungary. By 1999, there were seven RDCs set up at the so-called NUTS II level. In a few cases, these RDCs had different boundaries and different competences than when first set up on a voluntary basis. Yet although they remain a weak link in the overall administrative structure (dominated by the central state and local government), these intermediate-level bodies have been far more effective than in the Czech case (see below).[8] EU involvement continued with the National Regional Development Concept (1998), the National Programme for the Adoption of the Acquis (updated in 2001) and the National Development Plan (2001). Negotiations were finalized in December 2002 and set preliminary spending corridors for the period 2003–06.

Czech Regional and Cohesion Policy: A Brief Overview

Although Czechoslovakia was "the strictest follower of equalization policy among the former communist states," a mere five years after the end of communism the traditional economic gradient separating more prosperous Bohemia in the West

8. For an extensive discussion, see Downes (2000, 334–35).

from less prosperous Moravia in the East had reappeared (Blažek 1996, 63). The vast majority of foreign investment flowed into Bohemian regions, while average income was nearly 50 percent higher and unemployment almost 2 percentage points lower than in Moravia (Blažek 1996, 66–67). And, as in Hungary, the capital city was by far the strongest economic core. Per capita GDP in Prague is actually above the EU average, while *every* other region's GDP is below the Czech *national* average. And although income for Prague residents was only 6.4 percent above the national average in 1989, by 1997 it was 31.5 percent higher (Cervený and Andrle 2000, 89–95).

Czech RP got a later start than in Hungary.[9] In the early 1990s, some officials in the hardest hit Czech regions, such as North Bohemia, began to call for policies to address R&D, retraining, and restructuring. Rising unemployment figures revealed a growing cleavage between regions. Through the early 1990s, overall Czech unemployment was remarkably low, but aggregate unemployment and regional disparities grew sharply throughout the second half of the 1990s. In July 2000, the unemployment rate had reached 9.0 percent, but in the worst affected areas of North Bohemia, unemployment had reached 20.7 percent (Most District); in North Moravia, it reached 18.4 percent (Karviná District) (Czech Republic, Ministry of Regional Development 2000, 8). Early on, the government of Václav Klaus chose not to use regional policy to buck the unemployment trend. The Klaus government did focus on some industrial crisis points but neglected both interministerial coordination at the central level and coordination with actors at the regional and municipal levels. As such, early Czech regional policy tended more toward "bailouts" than development.

The reform government of Petr Pithart abolished the regional communist party committees in 1990, although the seven regions lived on as territorial and statistical units. But the regions had no powers of self-government and were simply the (weakened) administrative arms of the central state (Innes 2002b). The resulting lack of regional authority was apparent in comparison with that of many EU member states, even strongly unitary states. But this form of Czech exceptionalism hardly bothered Klaus, whose ODS Party emphasized the defense of the nation state as the main source of political identity and vigorously fought efforts to create strong Czech regions. The Social Democrats (ČSSD) saw growing unemployment in structurally weak regions as a potential source of votes, however, and they responded with a stronger RP emphasis. In contrast to the ODS, pro-EU arguments began to appear in the ČSSD election campaigns and later found a prominent spot in the party program (Czech Social Democratic Party 1997).

There were almost no established RP actors in the Czech case, and Czech privatization cut off and allowed to atrophy those networks that had existed (McDermott 2002). Only when the ODS left the government did circumstances shift. In January 1996, the Czech Republic applied for EU membership, and, as

---

9. For detailed case studies of the EU influence on Czech regional policy, see Jacoby and Černoch (2002) and Blazek (1997).

noted above, the Commission prepared the required opinion on the readiness of the Czech Republic to join. As a consequence of the lack of interest in regional policy by the ODS-led government, the Commission's initial assessment in this area was blunt: "Currently, the Czech Republic has no regional policy. Indeed, regional development initiatives are implemented through sectoral policies at national level" (Commission 1997c, 83). The Commission pointed at the functional *necessity* of authorities able to formulate regional development priorities. It also specified the need for some kind of partner on the Czech side able to develop and articulate such plans. On these points, the Commission noted that

> Czech authorities still have to introduce important reforms to comply with EC's structural policies. . . . Financial resources at the disposal of regional policy should be increased and efficient instruments need to be created. . . . Czech authorities have to determine the future legal basis of a Czech regional policy in order to provide the appropriate legal structure for the actions envisaged to counteract regional disparities and for financing structural policy expenditure. (Commission 1997c, 84)

Phase 1: CEEC-Driven Rule Adoption

If the Klaus government allowed little space for any adoption of West European rules in this policy domain during the period through the Essen Summit, in Hungary there is more of a story to tell. As noted, CEEC-driven rule adoption of western RP models began in Hungary even before 1989. The 1985 Act on "Long Term Tasks of Regional and Settlement Development" is, in fact, indebted to western models. The Act approximated the following key western elements: first, "cooperation between settlements instead of hierarchical relations"; second, "wider use of local resources, together with the strengthening of local independence"; and third, "a new, decentralized financing system of settlements" (Lackó 1994, 151, 153–54).

After the collapse of state socialism, the Hungarian government introduced the Regional Development Fund in 1991. The Fund used EU financing guidelines, but with the crucial difference that it retained management with the central government in Budapest rather than dispersing management authority. Here we see an echo of the Czech case: the EU RP practices were *appealing* if they promised techniques or resources for dealing with growing unemployment. But those same practices were *threatening* if they seemed to erode central state authority. Far more than the Czechs, the Hungarians made real use of the PHARE instruments for regional policy, signing their first agreement in 1993 and following up with a second set of pilot projects in 1994 (Hungarian Ministry of Agriculture and Regional Development 1998, 61–68). In the Czech case, we cannot point to any substantial and sustained use of EU rules during the period. The first Czech pilot programs got off the ground only in 1998 (Czech Republic, Ministry of Industry and Trade 1999, 184). Though some officials took a discursive interest in western ways, formal rule adoption was limited to a very few cases and even there, behavioral adherence to norms of decentralization was virtually nil.

Phase 2: EU-Driven Rule Adoption

The EU began to set RP reform thresholds—less determinate warnings that improvement was needed—in 1997, and each of its subsequent Regular Reports contains a multitude of such reminders. For instance, in the 2001 Regular Report on Hungary, the Commission calls for improvements in interministerial cooperation, technical preparation for fund management, partnership structures and local participation in policymaking, project evaluation, financial management, and regional statistics (Commission 2001b, 74–75). Other thresholds are that budgeting must be multi-annual, expenditures concentrated on "priority objectives," and that EU spending not reduce member state spending ("additionality"). Finally, the Structural Funds contain a novel form of "area designation" that emphasizes as "objectives" areas of social and economic underdevelopment, industrial restructuring, and high unemployment (Downes 2000, 340). The EU insists that states follow these guidelines, though it typically recognizes that such thresholds can be met in a number of different ways.

Hungary was more responsive to such suggestions than was the Czech Republic. Already by the time of its major 1996 RP reform, Hungary had enshrined, in word if not yet in deed, the EU's favored principles of decentralization, subsidiarity, partnership, programming, additionality, transparency, and concentration. The Commission's 1999 Regular Report noted that Hungary needed to reform its mechanism for RD financing (1999a, 71). In response, in 2000 the parliament's Budget Law introduced two new regional financing tools (2000c, 63). The Commission set a threshold by warning implicitly that if the regional financing system was not fixed, the Commission would decide not to fund its pilot programs. The Hungarians, in meeting this threshold, then chose a funding mechanism that followed the EU insistence that *regional* approaches take priority over *sectoral* ones.

EU pressures also led to the heavy use of what we can call patches—the faithful adoption of existing EU or member state rules and practices. Here, determinacy was clearly higher than it was with the thresholds. For example, Bachtler et al. report the use of new bookkeeping and payment procedures, control checklists, internal control systems, data systems, and evaluation methodologies (2002, 12, 22). Because large-scale RP programs are unprecedented in these countries, the complex monitoring systems required have to be set up essentially de novo. To encourage CEECs to make these patches, the Commission earmarked a certain *range* of funds for ISPA, SAPARD, and PHARE programs, so that better performance would be rewarded with spending at the high end of the range and lower performance with lower spending. In many cases, Hungary dealt with EU thresholds not by innovating on existing institutions or policies but by quickly adopting EU-conform practices learned about through screening or the vetting of draft Regular Reports.[10]

10. The Commission often allowed the candidate countries to have drafts of the reports some months in advance and in many cases would soften the final language if it was convinced that the candidate was ready to make more progress in a specific area.

As Hungary was implementing Act XXI, the EU was looking in vain for Czech partners to implement PHARE projects aimed at preparing the ground for RP reform. Not until the Klaus government fell did the Josef Tošovský government unblock the RP issue and pave the way for future reforms. Most important, in late 1997 the Constitutional Act on the Formation of the Higher Territorial Administrative Units was passed by both chambers of parliament. This represented the first major step toward fulfilling the provisions of Article 99 of the constitution. When a Social Democrat minority government emerged from the April 1998 elections, it eventually adopted *The Principles of the Government on Regional Policy*, a document that discursively reflected the principles of regional policy of the EU.[11] It used EU parlance to identify two types of problem regions according to the classification of structural funds: economically weak regions (what the EU calls objective 5b regions) and structurally weak regions (objective 2). The new government hewed closely to EU norms on its definitions of these regions (Blažek and Boekhout 2000, 302–3). In the Commission's eyes, these moves constituted real progress, even if only on paper.

In response, the EU started a PHARE-financed pilot project for North Bohemia. This project was run by the MRD, which now began to develop a regional policy according to the EU framework. The Ministry's First Regional Operational Program involved not just the central government but also actors from the regional and municipal levels. Before the creation of the higher territorial units in January 2000, these regional actors were mainly mayors and representatives of Regional Development Agencies, some of whom were also set up with PHARE financial support. In 1999 the regional actors formed special Regional Coordination Committees (RCCs), which also included representatives of the state administration. These committees assumed the de facto role of informal, unelected governments on the subnational level. With regional elections in fall 2000 leading to the establishment of the higher territorial units on 1 January 2001, the regions then incorporated the RCCs into their administrative structures. Thus did Commission thresholds, PHARE seed money, a latent constitutional provision, and a change of government produce new momentum for Czech RP (Marek and Baun 2002).

As in the Hungarian case, we can identify the key RP thresholds the Czechs faced. First, the EU presumed that states had formal regional actors in place with the authority to formulate regional policy objectives. Second, the EU promoted the coordination of regional policy between the central government and the regions concerned. Third, the EU pushed the expectation that the allocation of structural funds would be based on competitiveness among regions. Fourth, the EU insisted that states separate management and monitoring of regional policy. And fifth, the EU understood regional policy as an instrument of job-creation and investment incentives, instead of a mere redistribution mechanism (Commission 2000a, 60–62).

---

11. Innes (2002) shows that the ČSSD initially continued the ODS policies.

How precisely did the EU exploit the chance to affect Czech practices? Once the Commission launched the negotiation process with the first group of candidate countries in March 1998, the *acquis* was divided into thirty-one chapters, and each became subject to a screening process. During this period, the Commission explained to the candidate countries what the *acquis* contained in the individual policy areas. The candidate countries in turn responded by describing the extent to which they already complied with EU law and further specified time periods over which they could likely achieve full compliance. After completion of screening in 1999, substantial negotiations began on each chapter. The RP chapter was provisionally closed in 2002, and at the Copenhagen Summit of December 2002, the EU committed €21.7 billion for the Structural and Cohesion Funds for the ten new member states in 2004–06. By 2006, average per capita RP spending across this region is projected to reach €117.

Both exercises—screening and the negotiations—were instrumental in establishing a reform agenda and timetable in the candidate countries.[12] In its regular reports, the Commission assessed the progress of each country in meeting the norms and the institutional requirements it had laid out. And in addition to mere explication of the *acquis* in this highly structured process, the EU made substantial funds available to support the development of necessary administrative structures for a successful implementation of EU policies and also to start concrete work by financing pilot projects. Thus, while the Hungarian case contained a small degree of more voluntaristic lesson-drawing, the key routes to rule adoption are best explained by the external incentives model. This chapter has further specified that this model is compatible with two very different modalities, namely by responding to less determinate thresholds or by implementing very determinate patches.

Summary of the External Incentives Hypotheses

Table 5.1 summarizes the external incentives model as applied to the RP case. Variations in external incentives are arrayed on the top, and variations in rule determinacy are arrayed just below these. Since most (but not all) of the Hungarian case accords well with the external incentives model, the table highlights six phases of the cases that point out some limitations of the model. In particular, the table notes in italics the two anomalies described above: first, in the lower left cell, there was in the Hungarian case (but not the Czech) a certain amount of lesson-drawing that occurred well before any external incentives were applied. Thus, while the external incentives model (EI) correctly predicted Czech pre-1997 rule adoption as very unlikely (coded as −−), it missed the Hungarian case, where a moderate amount of rule adoption did occur (coded as a +). Second, in the upper right cell, despite significant external incentives and some determinate rules, the Klaus government—a clear veto player—refused to make significant movement on RP reforms despite what might be coded a "medium likelihood" (coded as +) that it would do

12. For a discussion of screening, see Baun 2000, 105–10.

Table 5.1   The external incentives model applied to regional policy

Relevant incentives	Few external incentives (pre-1997)	Significant external incentives (post-1997)	
Relevant rules	No relevant rules	Less determinate rules	More determinate rules
Strong veto players	Czech RP before 1997 EI: rule adoption (RA) very unlikely (−−) Outcome: −−	CZ RP thresholds during Klaus government EI: RA unlikely (−) Outcome: −	*CZ RP patches during Klaus government* *EI: medium likelihood (+)* *Outcome: −*
Weak veto players	*HU RP before 1997* *EI: −−* *Outcome: +*	RP thresholds after 1997/Klaus EI: + Outcome: +	RP patches after 1997/Klaus EI: RA high likelihood (++) Outcome: +

Note: Normal type indicates that the outcomes match predictions of external incentives model. *Italic type* indicates outcomes do not match the model.

so. The logic is that one variable—determinacy—points toward rule adoption while the other—veto players—does not.

While this chapter has focused on the twin aspects of rule determinacy and the structure of veto players, the other two propositions linked to the external incentive model are unlikely to explain these anomalies. The size of the RP rewards is obviously quite substantial. Though the EU often did move too slowly in rewarding progress in rule adoption, the lags and delays are irrelevant to the first anomaly (since Hungary adopted rules without promise of external reward) and seem far too short to fully explain the Czech unwillingness to adopt rules in spite of incentives to do so. The other proposition—that rule adoption follows when external threats and promises are most credible—seems to run afoul of the same two objections. It is irrelevant to the first case and does not explain the second because, in this case, it is in fact quite plausible that a state might be able to join the EU and yet receive little access to the structural funds. Thus, the Klaus government should not have expected to be able to flout EU rules and still reap the rewards of the structural funds. On the other hand, the external incentives model correctly predicts the other four Czech outcomes, as well as the rest of the Hungarian trajectory. In terms of the counterfactual, then, it seems best to conclude that a more competent regional political layer of government is emerging in the Czech Republic—a development difficult to imagine without the external incentives from the EU. And even in Hungary, where EU pressure met fewer veto points, the EU practices, norms, and administrative rules played a decisive role.

Rule Adoption in Health Care

In health care reforms CEE elites have looked to western models, yet the EU has played a minor role. Here, rule adoption has been mostly CEEC-driven. The lesson-drawing model best explains rule adoption in the absence of external incentives (though a few relatively weak incentives do appear late in the enlargement process). Since the basic premises of the external incentives model are not present, this section will evaluate the lesson-drawing model as an explanation. It again focuses attention on the availability of alternative models (here, through epistemic communities that draw in experts from CEECs) and veto players. The covering hypothesis for the lesson-drawing model is that governments adopt new EU rules—which, by this volume's definition, include the rules of individual member states—when they expect to thereby avoid domestic sanction.

There is little doubt that lesson-drawing has occurred among the CEECs in this policy area. Indeed, some have asserted that the reform of the Hungarian, Czech, and other CEE health care systems equaled a move "back to Bismarck." That is, these states had Bismarckian insurance-based health care systems until the Soviets imposed their model through the national communist parties. Today, these states seek to implement models based on contemporary Bismarckian models (Marrée and Groenewegen 1997). This image serves as a useful starting point. In addition to insurance systems, CEECs also emulated western systems of provider payment. Since 1990, a variety of systems have been introduced, though with mixed success.

Health care reforms in the Czech and Hungarian cases share two important features: there are many interest associations present, and the EU's very sparse health policy *acquis* provides the EU little leverage.[13] It is clear that well-established actors have complicated health reforms. The World Bank remarks on the "highly fragmented nature of health policy in the Czech Republic. . . . There is no clear leadership in the sector, and the myriad of amendments to the original Act is testament to the lack of clear vision" (World Bank 1999, 227). In Hungary, health reforms have been hindered by "endemic conflict" among the Ministry of Health (MoH), the National Health Insurance Fund (HIF), and the Ministry of Finance (MoF), who have had "overlapping responsibilities in the financing, policy preparation and administration of healthcare" (Orosz and Burns 2000, 43). Since the communist system relied on high numbers of specialists, interest representation of health care workers is also highly fragmented (e.g., primary care versus specialized care, doctors versus other health care workers, private practice versus public-sector employment) (Nelson 2001, 257).

The Hungarian Case: A Brief Overview

Though coverage of Hungarian industrial workers in insurance funds was mandatory by 1891, access to insurance and services lagged far behind for the large rural population. Traditionally, Hungarian health insurance funds employed their own medical personnel and actually delivered services to their subscribers. These funds and most private health care provision were ended by the Communist Party in the

---

13. For a comprehensive overview of EU health programs, see Commission (2000d).

late 1940s. The Soviet Semashko model provided for state allocation of all health care services and coverage through a centralized MoH. Thus, the same organization both *funded* health care and *provided* it. The weaknesses of the Semashko systems were evident throughout the 1970s and 1980s. Long before the collapse of communism, Hungarian officials had to confront the declining health of the population, the poor quality of health care, and the shortages of financial means (Marrée and Groenewegen 1997, 84; Nelson 2001, 254–55).

The late 1980s and early 1990s saw a series of modest reforms, though experts continue to lament a host of remaining inefficiencies and shortcomings of central planning (Orosz, Ellena, and Jakab 1998, 225; Orosz and Burns 2000). The most important reform replaced the old central state health budget with an insurance-based system funded primarily by a levy on wages.[14] The compulsory HIF has its roots in the reform communist era (1988–89) and was built on the foundation of two remaining vestiges of the precommunist insurance system.[15] The government's 1990 *Programme for National Renewal* noted that "we will establish a Hungarian health care system that functions on the insurance principle" and went on to speak of its desire to change other health institutions "in the way accepted throughout Europe" (Government of Hungary 1990, 15). The HIF pays for recurrent expenses while capital costs are still paid for by taxes from the general fund. The HIF covers virtually all Hungarians, and in 2002 accounted for 80 percent of all medical payments, with the rest being out of pocket expenses.

Hungarian health care is supervised by the central state but provided by local government entities. The state transferred ownership of most health care facilities to local governments in 1990. Public providers in county- and city-owned facilities now provide the vast majority of medical services, and they are reimbursed by the HIF. The state regulates the HIF, covers most capital investment, and regulates public health. During the 1990s, Hungary spent around 7 percent of its GDP on health care, which is just under the EU average of 8.5 percent (European Observatory on Health Care Systems 1999, 9–12, 26, 33–34). A 2000 OECD study concluded that the Hungarian health care system is "broadly in line with that of other OECD countries" but that it "remains in serious need of reform."[16] Hungarians have the OECD's lowest life expectancy, and "the effectiveness of the nearly universal national health insurance system is greatly reduced by systemic inefficiency, perverse incentive structures, and perennial overspending in pharmaceutical expenditures." Hungary also has an "excess supply of specialists" that results in an "excessively hospital-centric and specialist-based pattern of treatment." The study also noted that difficulties plague the payment systems for inpatient (diagnostic resource groups) and outpatient hospital (points) care. As we shall see, both systems owe something to the inspiration of specific western models.

14. Employers pay 11 percent, and employees pay 3 percent.
15. The health and pension section of this "Social Insurance Fund" were separated in 1992.
16. All quotations in this paragraph are from Orosz and Burns (2000).

The Czech Case: A Brief Overview

The Czech system is less troubled. Like the Hungarians, the Czechs had a Bismarckian insurance-based system in the interwar period and ultimately shifted to a socialist centralized system by the 1950s. Unlike Hungary, however, there was no real period of experimentation with the health care system in the 1980s, and Czechs entered the post–Cold War period with little in the way of usable reform antecedents. Yet beginning in 1991, the Czech reforms have been substantial and have opened up a variety of insurance funds as opposed to the single fund in Hungary. The Klaus government allowed some facilities to become legally and financially independent and also permitted patients a free choice of providers. As in Hungary, most provider facilities are owned by local government entities, but, unlike in Hungary, private-practice physicians (rather than salaried physicians) renting space in the facilities provide the bulk of primary care (over 90 percent of family physicians, dentists, and pharmacists are in private practice).

Scheffler and Duitch note that the reforms were designed to achieve, among other things, the "creation and promotion of competition among non-profit, employment-based health insurance plans in the private sector" (2000, 5). In January 1992, a General Health Insurance Fund (GHIF) was formed. In 1993, the GHIF became autonomous in a way very analogous to the German funds. Subsequently, several other autonomous insurance funds were formed (e.g., Škoda-Volkswagen). But for reasons explored below, by 1995, most of these privatized insurance funds faced severe financial difficulties, and GHIF took over many of them. Starting with as many as twenty-seven funds, there were only nine by 2000 (European Observatory on Health Care Systems 2000, 11). The GHIF covers about 80 percent of Czech health care expenses, with taxes covering 11 percent and out-of-pocket expenses the rest. Czech spending as a percentage of GDP is just slightly above the Hungarian level, but the larger GDP means that per capita expenditures on a PPP (purchasing power parity) basis reached $943 in 1997 (versus $642 for Hungary and $1771 for the EU) (European Observatory on Health Care Systems 2000, 24–28).

Phase 1: CEEC-Driven Adoption of Insurance and Provider Payment Mechanisms

The Insurance Model Early in the 1990s, the German and Austrian models were clearly a significant point of reference for CEE reformers, and Cox describes the epistemic communities in which postcommunist health care debates took place (1993). These debates included many Czech and Hungarian policy experts who had had contact with these expert communities during the late communist period as well. In fact, some of these experts had participated in significant reforms in the waning days of communism. For example, in Hungary, the last socialist government separated the health system from the general fund. The insurance model was politically attractive to those who thought it might insulate the health sector from the decline of state revenues by tapping wage and nonwage employer contributions as new sources of finance. Crucially, it was also attractive to health care providers, who earned low salaries compared to other professionals in the CEECs and, compared to providers in Western Europe, were strong advocates of the move to insurance-based systems (European Observatory on Health Care Systems 2000, 19).

Many CEECs have made a similar choice, though Hungary went farther toward the German model by also placing major social groups, including unions and employers, into top management positions in the HIF. Kornai and Eggleston pinpoint the timing of a more general shift in the direction of the German model to 1991 in Hungary and 1992 in the Czech Republic (2001, 145–46). Both Hungary and the Czech Republic voluntarily implemented certain functional characteristics of the German model. The mechanism the two states chose drew on the German model in two ways. First, the social insurance fund for health care has its own source of revenue that lies outside the general fund; second, the fund purchases services from health providers, from whom it is institutionally distinct (Kornai and Eggleston 2001, 145, 148). Yet rule adoption was approximate, not exact, and the omissions were revealing. In Hungary, the HIF, unlike most western systems, lacks the ability to negotiate, as a purchaser of health services, with providers. Instead, it is obligated to buy services from all existing providers.

Like their Hungarian counterparts, Czech reformers took a keen interest in western health care models. According to Dr. Martin Bojar, who served in the Czechoslovak government from 1990–92, Czech health care reformers were "definitely inspired by the experience of German speaking countries, the Benelux and a number of EU member states." During 1990–91, he explains, "the general attitude was to follow trends and recommendation by the WHO and the EC [EU] in order to understand underlying trends in Western European heath care." According to Bojar, EU accession was "immaterial at the time—the prime focus was reform along the lines of general health care reforms in Europe." Germany was not the only influence. Rather, Belgian government experts were also helpful in "providing details for the development of health insurance companies and the shift away from financing health care from the state budget to the launch of private sector health care operators."[17]

In short, CEE experience with insurance-based health systems emphasized approximation and negotiation. Certain features of western models appealed to important reform constituencies—many politicians apparently saw the models as ways to stabilize health care spending while providers saw the models as a way to increase their income and prestige. Those features of the model that appealed to powerful constituencies and potential veto players were taken over while other aspects of the model were downplayed or not emulated at all. But even such politically contingent and approximate rule adoption could not guarantee stable outcomes, for both Hungarian oversight mechanisms and Czech insurance providers

17. Author interview with Martin Bojar, Czech Ministry of Health, Prague, November 2002.

have been quite unstable. In the Hungarian case, ministerial oversight has actually changed twice since 1998. In the Czech case, though one initial rationale for multiple funds was to promote competition, a thin financial footing left many funds unable to cover even basic services. In 1997, competition on the basis of supplemental benefits was abolished (European Observatory on Health Care Systems 2000, 21).

Payment Systems Other reforms also have foreign roots.[18] Among the most convoluted is the reform of the systems of payment in Hungary and the Czech Republic. Here too, attenuated rule adoption and institutional turbulence went hand in hand. The shift to insurance-based systems to raise health care revenues raised the related question of how to allocate these revenues to providers of health care. Here too western models were used selectively. The aim was to move away from allocating budgets on the basis of political negotiations and move toward some system of allocating spending based upon services performed by providers.

Because postsocialist states have much higher investments in hospitals (as a percentage of their overall health spending) than do West European states, the most important financial reforms were in inpatient care. Under the first postsocialist government, Hungary adopted and adapted the practice of "diagnostic resource groups" (DRGs) for hospitals. These DRGs, which set insurance payments to hospitals for groups of related medical conditions, are widely used in the United States, Germany, Norway, Sweden, Portugal, and Austria. In Hungary, German health consultants played a key role in articulating the virtues of DRGs. DRGs were to promote competition among hospitals, as some hospitals would respond to the new financial incentive to raise their efficiency and quality while others would fail, thus reducing sectoral overcapacity. As with the insurance system, rule adoption had the support of many providers. Hungarian doctors anticipated that DRGs would boost their official salaries, but they also expected that the system's incentives to treat higher numbers of patients as quickly as possible would increase the number of unofficial "gratuities" they received from patients (Orosz and Holló 2001, 22). DRGs were first introduced on a pilot basis in 1987; after the HIF gained independent status in 1993, they were extended to all Hungarian hospitals.

As with the insurance system, this rule adoption was not faithful but approximate. The American DRG system was adapted to reflect major historical differences. First, reformers noted the much higher use of technology and longer stays in U.S. hospitals than in Hungary. Second, Hungarian hospitals built into the DRGs the employment costs of doctors, typically billed separately in U.S. hospitals, where doctors often have privileges without being employees. Third, DRGs were adapted to take into account different epidemiological patterns in Hungary. Given the incentives to discharge patients as early as possible, the DRG system did indeed cut the average hospital stay. On the other hand, hospital admittances rose (Orosz and Holló 2001, 23). And overuse reached remarkable proportions as some obstetrics departments performed cesarean sections on over half of their deliver-

---

18. On Czech use of western models of health care management, see Prymula et al. (1997).

ies, while other units invited males 20–25 years of age for annual screenings for Prostate Specific Antigen despite widespread doubts about the effectiveness of such screening even in much older men (Kahan and Gulácsi 2000, 2).

The Czechs also made significant modifications when they adopted fee-for-service methods of payment in which points are distributed for each procedure. The Czech point system drew very closely on German models (Marrée and Groenewegen 1997, 63; Scheffler and Duitch 2000, 6). But unlike in most existing fee-for-service systems, the Czechs made no initial provisions for copayments, so insurance companies lost an important cost control lever, and health care costs increased dramatically. Providers rushed to maximize their number of points, which, given the caps in place and the lack of brakes that copayments would have represented, devalued the worth of an individual point. This development fed back to undercut the insurance-based principle in the following way: where the initial expectation of liberal Czech reformers was that funds would compete in part by negotiating reduced rates with providers, the inflation in the point system removed all room for maneuver for providers. The result was the failure of several individual funds and the consolidation noted earlier (Scheffler and Duitch 2000, 6). Here, rule adoption in one area undercut rule adoption in another.

While official Hungarian health sector incomes have changed little, those in the Czech Republic have clearly grown. Scheffler and Duitch (2000, 7) show that rapid privatization has made a big difference in Czech medical incomes, tripling those of physicians and doubling those of nurses. Again unlike Hungary, the cumulative effect has been for much more health care spending. And private doctors are billing at a much higher rate than similarly specialized doctors who remain in the public sector; indeed, it has become common for Czech doctors to bill over 100 hours a week. In response, since about 1997 the Czech government has been trying to introduce a capitation-based component to the payment system to reduce the incentives for physicians to overuse procedures. As in Hungary, then, the Czechs have not really been able to get a handle on the incentives for physicians to overprovide services, nor have they been able to shift patient care away from hospital specialists and to general practitioners.

Phase 2: The EU Enters the Picture

The previous section sketched those moments in which Czech and Hungarian officials relied on CEEC-driven emulation of western models for specific health reforms. The reforms usually merely approximated existing western models. While West European experts gave a great deal of advice on health care reforms, CEECs were perfectly free to take that advice or leave it. But later in the 1990s, the EU began to take a more active role in promoting institutional modifications. At first, relatively little was done in the field of health, but the Commission has gradually developed a presence in this policy area, and the two main tools for doing so have been first, a small *acquis* in the area of public health, and second, what might be called the "health spillover" from other policy areas where the Commission had an active agenda. The most important areas to generate spillover effects in health care are the CAP, food safety regulations, environmental protection, and employment and social policy.[19] Keenly aware that existing member states guard their prerogatives in health and social policy, the Commission must take a cautious approach. Still, it tries to squeeze maximum leverage from a minimal health *acquis*. While the Commission talks of "health issues which are relevant to accession," it has yet to institute a program that explicitly defines the steps that states must take to reform their health care systems, both in terms of policy and structure, prior to EU accession (Commission 2001e, 3). The Commission's Regular Reports were not very specific with respect to health. The 2001 Czech Report mentioned MoH disarray and problems with fiscal surveillance (Commission 2001d, 69), while the report on Hungary complained of "major shortcomings" and fretted about the fiscal demands of health care and the overreliance on hospital stays (Commission 2001b, 32). But absent detailed leverage, the EU was left to emphasize that without reforms, the CEECs' fiscal situation might deteriorate.

Summary of the Lesson-Drawing Hypotheses

In this case, the lesson-drawing model's covering hypothesis—a government adopts EU rules if it expects the rules to be effective and dispel the threat of domestic sanctions—is roughly confirmed. Three further conclusions stand out, however. First, the light *acquis* (which meant low determinacy) and the high number of established actors (many potential veto players) meant rule adoption took the form of a process of what might be called continuously negotiated inspiration in the Hungarian and Czech health care systems. The lack of EU leverage meant that CEEC politicians were free to take foreign advice only where they chose to. Openness to this advice was highest early in the 1990s, and the CEECs have made few significant reforms in health care since then. To be sure, when the Czech MoH did put forward a major reform proposal in 1997, health care experts from the United States and a number of European countries—including the United Kingdom, Germany, the Netherlands, Belgium, Austria, and Switzerland—had consulted on the reforms.[20] But if the engagement of an epistemic community of policy professionals seems clear, there is less evidence of direct rule adoption at this later stage. Thus, contact is clearly not a sufficient condition for rule adoption, although it may make it more likely. Health care reforms in the middle of the decade were much less radical than the first round of reforms, even though contacts had increased. This conclusion implies that some aspect of "openness" to foreign models may be more important than mere contact with foreign experts.

---

19. Author interview with David Rath, Czech Medical Chamber, Prague, November 2002. See also Szilágyi (2001, 81).

20. Author interview with Martin Bojar, Czech Ministry of Health, Prague, November 2002.

Second, early in the decade, the political weight behind health care reforms was often significant. The initial impetus clearly came from health care workers themselves, who associated institutional reforms with the opportunity for better material and technological conditions in their daily work (Figueras, McKee, and Lessof 2002). This aspect is crucial, for foreign models must provide some "docking point" for well-established interests (Jacoby 2000). They must also avoid the threat posed by veto players. Since many potential beneficiaries are also potential veto players, the organization of civil society and the state cannot be reduced to a structural variable. Rather than simply counting the number of actors involved, it is crucial to understand the preferences of these actors before making predictions about whether lesson-drawing is likely to lead to a functional form of rule adoption or to an empty ritual in which formal institutional changes have little behavioral effect.

Third, while health care initially showed more behavioral rule adoption than did regional policy, there remain large gaps between the CEE practices and those in Western Europe. At one level, this finding is expected, since it would be surprising to see health care systems change fundamentally in just over a decade. But a related issue has been getting the support of state elites, most of whom understand that health reforms cost money now and take time to pay dividends. Thus they have ranked health care reform as a low priority (see Szilágyi 2001). State power is also a consideration. The tendency to run at full speed away from the paternalist state has often so diminished state capacities that in many countries it cannot oversee reforms. In some cases, this was a result of personnel losses to the private sector; in other cases, it was a result of administrative decentralizations that left the MoH without authority or resources. In short, governments often have been too weak or too temporary to carry out good reform designs.

This chapter has not directly tested the external incentives and lesson-drawing models against one another because it used cases in which one model had a clear advantage over the other from the very outset. The regional policy case clearly had strong external incentives; just as clearly, the health care case did not. The chapter's purpose has been to expand our understanding of the two models by using them in cases where they were likely to perform relatively well. A fuller test could go on to further develop the lesson-drawing model on the regional policy case and the external incentives model, at least after 1998 or so, on the health care case. Certainly, there are some issues still to explain—for example, in Hungary there did seem to be more early interest in EU-style regional policies even before there were any explicit EU conditions or even informal pressures to do so. Is this better explained by the lesson-drawing model? In health care, the "open method of coordination" is growing increasingly important (see McKee, Mossialos, and Baeten 2002). Should we view this as a kind of soft conditionality or does it belong entirely outside the external incentives model? Some of this test has, however, already been done in this chapter, and little additional insight of a fundamental nature would be gained by a lengthier investigation. Instead, this chapter complements other chapters in the book, some of which investigate policy areas that provide tougher tests for one model or the other. At the same time, it provides several insights of its own.

We see that the kind of rule adoption pursued and the results achieved are likely to vary by policy domain. Specifically, the determinacy of the rules and the structure of pre-existing actors at the level of both state and society both matter for understanding outcomes. The extensive and detailed *acquis* and the absence of any policy legacy in the field of regional policy gave the EU both the leverage to ask penetrating questions and the space to suggest very specific answers. By contrast, the light and loose *acquis* and the significant number of established actors in both state and society caused rule adoption to take the form of a process of what I called continuously negotiated inspiration in the Hungarian and Czech health care systems. The lack of EU leverage meant that CEE politicians were free to take advice where they chose to. In short, while each model has four major propositions (and several sub-propositions), a great deal of insight can be gained from just two variables common to both models: the availability of other rules (whether through a menu of determinate practices or contact with epistemic communities) and the structure of veto players. By no means are these two variables always enough—we have seen, for example, that the preferences of veto players also matter—these twin "leverage and legacy" variables can often take us a long way.

Both cases also shed new light on the specific explanatory models. The health care case does seem to add a new dimension to our discussions of external incentives, which obviously cannot explain the pattern we have seen. The case shows both that significant amounts of rule adoption can occur without the EU's significant involvement and that non-European (e.g., U.S.) practices play at least some role in the broader story. The external influences model also cannot explain rule adoption in Hungarian regional policy to the extent that it occurred well before any conditionality was articulated by the EU. We also saw that once external incentives were put in place, their determinacy did not matter as much as the activities of veto players.[21] This was most clear in the upper right cell of table 5.1, where variation in the determinacy of rules had no effect on outcomes while the Klaus Government was in place.

Unlike the regional policy case, the health care case had no major variation on the dependent variable of rule adoption. To be sure, there were some differences in the way both the insurance systems and the payment mechanisms developed in each state, but these differences seem relatively minor in comparison to the striking similarities across the two country cases. This finding is all the more surprising in light of the almost complete absence of any "homogenizing" EU pressure until very late in the postcommunist era and despite the wide diversity of West European health care models. We saw that while a sense of policy failure did exist in both states, government officials could more likely expect domestic sanctions for

21. This finding is consistent with that of Schimmelfennig, Engert, and Knobel (chapter 2).

failing to reform in the future than for having established a failed system in the past. For example, there is little evidence of a wholesale public rejection of the inherited communist-era health systems, but much evidence that specific interest groups hoped that more stable provision systems would be resistant to major budget cutbacks in the face of a fiscal crisis of the state. Thus, a fascinating open question for future research is the extent to which interest groups not only motivate politicians to draw certain lessons but also capture those designs as they do so. We saw also that this capture—or "attenuation"—is easy to miss if one looks only at the formal structure of health care institutions. Detailed knowledge of the systems is required to show how apparently subtle changes lead to major advantages for certain interests.

In sum, the picture presented in this chapter is complex, and it defies easy characterizations of either EU imperialism or of CEEC governments as slavish imitators of western practices. The EU's leverage varies widely across policy areas and, even where it is strongest, must still take into account the domestic politics of each state.

CHAPTER SIX

Regulating the Flow of People across Europe

Heather Grabbe

This chapter is about how the European Union (EU) has sought to influence regulation of the movement of people in the candidate states of central and east Europe (CEE) during the accession process. It explores processes of Europeanization in public policymaking in CEE. The aim is to show both the scope of EU influence and the limitations on the use of that influence. In particular, I focus on Europeanization in cases where the EU's rules are inconsistent—either in how they are framed or in how they are applied to the candidate countries—and how that inconsistency affects rule adoption and the outcome of negotiations.

This chapter tests the hypotheses of the external incentives model with regard to how movement is regulated under the single market framework and under the rules governing the Schengen area, the EU's zone of passport-free travel. These are two cases where the conditionality operates under different conditions. They thus allow testing of the external incentives model under different circumstances in what is substantially the same policy area.

I argue that the principal hypotheses of the external incentives model are confirmed by two cases concerned with the regulation of the movement of people by the EU. However, I conclude that external incentives models need some refinement with regard to how it treats EU accession negotiations because they are not cases of pure bargaining. Both social learning and lesson-drawing models provide necessary additional parts of the explanation of how the EU influenced the regulation of movement of persons in the candidate countries—so the analysis in this chapter takes two cuts, mainly testing the external incentives model but also bringing in elements of the other models considered in this volume.

Applying the External Incentives Model to the Regulation of Movement of Persons

I seek to use the external incentives model under investigation in this book to explain why the candidates accepted apparently suboptimal outcomes in negotiations in these two areas. In 2001, the EU closed a key chapter in accession negotiations with several CEE applicants for membership. In doing so, it secured their agreement on a transitional period of up to seven years before citizens of new member states could work freely anywhere in the fifteen existing member states. The EU also put forward a negotiating position on justice and home affairs (JHA) that required the applicants to implement its border policies prior to accession but did not make any reciprocal commitment that the existing member states would remove frontier controls with the new members immediately after enlargement. In both cases, the candidates agreed to an EU position that explicitly denied them the benefits accorded to existing members for some years after accession.

I analyze these outcomes of the negotiations as cases of rule adoption in the areas of:

- Free movement of workers (FMW) in the single market; and
- Control of movement of persons across the external borders of the Union under the Schengen provisions.

In both of these cases, the external incentives model is appropriate. It is rationalist, actor-centered, and based on a logic of consequences—all suitable characteristics for the study of these two policy areas. In their presentation of the external incentives model in the introduction to this volume, Schimmelfennig and Sedelmeier discuss three groups of factors that condition the degree of rule adoption: the determinacy of conditions, the credibility of conditionality, and the relative size of domestic adoption costs.

The Dimensions of Rule Adoption

Table 6.1 summarizes the dimensions of rule adoption for these two policy areas. In both cases, the degree of rule adoption was high. In the first case, the single market *acquis* is fundamental to EU membership. The primary actor on the EU side is the Commission, because it is a credible enforcement agency in policing application of single market rules across the member states. In the second case,

Table 6.1   Rule adoption for the movement of persons

	Degree of adoption	Form of adoption
FMW in the single market	Medium/high	Formal
Schengen	High	Formal and behavioral

application of Schengen rules was of great political interest not just to the Commission but also to the member states. Bulgaria and Romania had an additional incentive to comply with the Schengen *acquis* in that they wanted to have the visa requirements on their citizens lifted—which indeed happened in 2001 for Bulgaria and 2002 for Romania.

In both cases, the dominant form of rule adoption was formal, in that it involved the transfer of EU rules and the establishment of formal institutions and procedures. However, it is not yet clear empirically whether the formal adoption of the rules has led to fully rule-conforming behavior on the part of CEE actors in the case of the single market *acquis*. As far as the accession conditionality is concerned, formal adoption of the relevant EU legislation and its implementation by national authorities constitute Europeanization in this policy field. My fieldwork revealed that individuals working in the public administration of the candidate countries displayed internalization of rules and habitualization of rule-governed behavior as well. However, enforcement of single market rules by individual bureaucrats or Schengen rules by frontier guards is not necessarily uniform. Just as in the current member states, the internalization of rules may be incomplete even after the central process of legislative transfer has been completed. The extent to which this has happened is hard to measure until the candidates become member states, at which point the Commission and the European Court of Justice will gain a role in reviewing the adequacy of enforcement.

The Degrees of Rule Adoption

The previous section has shown that the degree and form of adoption are similar for the regulation of movement of people under the single market and under Schengen. However, the degrees of adoption are likely to be different because the factors that condition the degree of rule adoption are very different in the two case studies.

The Determinacy of Conditions. The candidates were quite certain about the single market rules that had to be adopted, so the determinacy of conditions was high. As explained in the next section, the EU has clear common rules in this area. They were clearly set as conditions for membership in the Commission's Single Market White Paper in 1995. The rules are fairly tight, owing to their firm basis in EU law and the long practice of using them among the current member states. Candidate country policymakers thus had little room for maneuver in determining which domestic rules would be compatible. Finally, target governments understood what they had to do to adopt them, and the rules were clearly specified. In this case, all three hypotheses presented in the introduction on the determinacy of conditions were borne out.

The only uncertainty was whether the EU would apply its own rules reciprocally to the new member states. This uncertainty did not affect the determinacy of conditions as regards getting into the EU, but it strongly affected the cost-benefit calculation that policymakers had to make in deciding how fast and how thoroughly to adopt the EU rules. These rules were part of the *acquis* for membership, but the EU's insistence that they must be adopted prior to accession was undermined by the likelihood that the current member states would not offer reciprocal benefits to CEE citizens. Candidate country governments could have made a strong case that they need not implement and enforce the free movement of labor until the EU member states lifted their own restrictions on the movement of CEE workers. For example, they could have argued for a "canal-lock" system whereby they would progressively remove barriers to entry to their labor markets for each member state bilaterally, according to when the member states removed the obstacles to CEE workers.

With regard to Schengen, by contrast, the determinacy of conditions was low. The EU was developing a set of common rules over the course of the candidates' preparations for accession, thus creating parallel processes of policy development in the EU and the applicant countries. Second, it was not clear which of the Schengen rules would be conditions for accession and which only had to be implemented when the new members fully joined the Schengen area, which would be at least several years after accession. Third, the rules were fairly loose to begin with in the early to mid-1990s because the *acquis* was still evolving and because Schengen was not brought into the EU's treaty structure until the Amsterdam Treaty in 1997. Finally, many of the rules were unclear even after the incorporation of the Schengen Convention into the treaties. It was not until 1999 that the EU finally published the Schengen *acquis* so that the candidates could see a definitive statement of what the rules were.[1] Even then, most of the rules referred to other legal documents and texts, some of which were overlapping and potentially contradictory. The set of rules had not been rationalized into a single consistent framework for adoption by the candidate countries prior to the end of negotiations.

This low determinacy of conditions would suggest that rule adoption would also be low, according to the hypotheses advanced in the introduction to this volume. However, that is not what happened. In fact, as the next section will discuss, the candidate countries in some cases adopted EU rules with greater enthusiasm and a greater degree of compliance than these hypotheses would suggest.

The Credibility of Conditionality. There is a similar disjuncture between the two cases with regard to the credibility of conditionality and the legitimacy of the EU's rules. For the single market, the EU could have withheld the rewards at low cost to itself because the candidate countries' economies were small relative to the those of the EU (accounting for about 7 percent of EU GDP at purchasing power parity), so the benefits of economic integration accrue mostly to the candidate countries (see Grabbe 2001b). The EU generally did not subordinate conditionality to other considerations, there was no significant cross-conditionality, and there were few asymmetries in the information garnered through monitoring.

---

1. The Schengen *acquis* was published as Council of the European Union (1999), "Council Decision of 20 May 1999 concerning the Definition of the Schengen Acquis," *Official Journal of the European Communities* (L 176/1, 1999/435/EC, 10 July 1999).

However, there was one source of internal conflict that affected the credibility of the EU's rules: the fact that free movement of labor was presented as an economic benefit even though it would not apply on accession. The EU had presented a clear policy paradigm to the candidate countries: that the four freedoms of the single market were essential to membership and that they were indivisible. A "policy paradigm" is the idea underlying a policy, which gives it a cognitive logic and shapes its interpretation (see Sedelmeier 2002 on the use of policy paradigms). In the case of the EU's single market policy, one of the most fundamental paradigms is that there is free movement of goods, services, capital, and labor across borders in Europe.

The idea underlying this policy is long-established in the EU's treaties, and the principle of the four freedoms underpinned the Single Market Program pursued by the EU in the late 1980s and 1990s. But now the EU was going against its own paradigm. That inconsistency did not fundamentally undermine the credibility of the EU's conditionality. Applicant governments knew that it was likely that if the single market *acquis* were not implemented, the candidate country would not be allowed to join. But the inconsistency of the application of the rules did undermine the EU's intellectual case for the policy paradigm of the four freedoms. The EU's policy looked very hypocritical to policymakers in the candidate countries because the EU was applying its rules inconsistently. As a result, many of the policymakers I interviewed expressed disillusionment about the principles underlying the single market. They were prepared to comply with the single market rules for free movement owing to a logic of consequences—in order to get into the EU.

For Schengen, the situation was different. The credibility of the conditionality was low until 1998 because of two factors: it was not certain whether all the Schengen rules had to be adopted before accession, and the EU's commitment to pay the ultimate reward of full Schengen membership was uncertain, because there was little indication of when each candidate might be admitted to the zone of passport-free travel. The political dynamics of border control among the member states were highly sensitive. Many politicians and policymakers were extremely wary of making any commitment to a date when the new members could join Schengen, for fear that the prospect of passport-free travel would increase the threat of illegal migration and illicit goods coming unchecked over the EU's new eastern borders. The temporal distance between the fulfillment of the conditions and the payment of the reward was uncertain, but during the negotiations it looked likely to be at least several years after accession. By the end of negotiations, it was clear that new members could not become full members of Schengen until at least 2006, because the necessary technical modifications to the Schengen Information System will not be complete before that year at the earliest. Policymakers in France, Germany, and the United Kingdom, speaking off the record, made estimates of between five and fifteen years before citizens of all the new member states would be allowed to enjoy passport-free travel around Schengen.

Despite the low credibility of the EU's arguments, however, the candidate countries went to enormous efforts to comply with the EU's demands regarding Schengen. This seems to contradict the hypotheses advanced in this volume about the effects of the inconsistency of EU conditionality policy (which should decrease rule adoption) and the size, speed, and certainty of rewards (which should increase rule adoption). This outcome can partly be explained by a logic of consequences. The candidates knew how sensitive the issue of movement of persons was in the domestic politics of the member states. The JHA chapter was one of the few credible veto points in the accession process—member states really might prevent a country from joining if it could not control movement of persons and goods across its borders with non-EU countries. Not only were the fifteen existing member states likely to deny new members full membership in the Schengen zone, but the candidates could be denied membership completely if they could not guard their external borders effectively.

Moreover, individual member states might impose visa requirements on CEE citizens if they considered them to pose a significant threat of illegal migration and likely to produce many asylum claims. The EU maintained visa requirements on Bulgaria and Romania for more than a decade, and several member states demanded visa provisions for particular candidate countries, especially Slovakia and the Czech Republic, owing to asylum claims and concerns about border control. Such requirements were lifted only when these countries had demonstrated to the EU's satisfaction that they could control their own frontiers and that their citizens would not claim asylum in the EU. This process demonstrated both to these countries and the other candidates that the EU would not grant interim rewards for compliance with its demands on border control unless they met the conditions it had set. The factors that limited the credibility of conditionality—particularly inconsistency and uncertainty—did not stop the candidates from complying because other factors were more important—particularly the interim costs of noncompliance (visa requirements) and the long-term risk of being denied entry to the Union.

Relative Domestic Adoption Costs. The adoption costs in the two cases are different. For the candidates, adoption costs for free movement of workers are low because implementation of the rules on mutual recognition of qualifications does not involve complex bureaucratic procedures, it is not expensive to implement, and it is not politically controversial in CEE. The EU's negotiating position was also affected by the low adoption costs in its member states. In the final negotiations at the Copenhagen European Council in December 2002, the EU agreed to Poland's demand that the qualifications of its nurses be regarded as equivalent to those of nurses trained in EU member-states. This agreement will allow Polish nurses to work in the EU with mutual recognition of qualifications. This last-minute concession emerged because Poland was able to slip in some small demands at the last minute when the EU was trying to secure the overall package deal. In the context of all the other costly issues that were on the table—such as agricultural subsidies

Table 6.2 Factors affecting the likelihood of rule adoption

	Determinacy of conditions	Credibility of conditionality	Size of adoption costs
FMW in the single market	*High*: common rules that are conditions, with strict and clear rules	*High*: low cost to EU, consistent, no sources of comparable benefits, reward credible, information consistent and dependent on monitoring	*Low*: not bureaucratically complex, financially expensive, or politically controversial
Schengen	*Low until 1998, then high*: evolving set of rules, not clear when all of them will apply, changing strictness of application	*Low*: commitment to pay the reward uncertain because of the politics of border control in the EU	*High*: financially and politically costly

and regional aid—this concession seemed fairly inexpensive to the EU member states.

By contrast, the Schengen rules are very expensive for the candidates to implement because they involve building new border infrastructure and retraining a swathe of public officials; in addition they are politically controversial in those member states that have long borders with the EU's new eastern and southern neighbors. The main means by which Hungary and Poland—where political controversy was greatest—tried to resist the conditionality was through delaying the introduction of visas for people in neighboring countries. Table 6.2 summarizes the factors affecting the degree of rule adoption in these two cases.

Rule Adoption in the Case of Movement of Persons

This section discusses how the candidates adopted EU rules in more detail, and how rule adoption was affected by the accession negotiations that ran in parallel with implementation of much of the *acquis*. The methodology adopted follows that of other chapters in this volume. The case of movement of persons is considered in the framework of the external incentives model. In a second cut, the analysis draws briefly on the social learning model and then turns to the lesson-drawing model to provide missing parts of the explanation of the outcome in this case. The research design is forward-looking and cross-sectional.

The Rules of the Game in the Free Movement of Workers in the Single Market

From the EU's point of view, the accession conditions for this policy area were a fairly simple matter of demanding compliance with a clear EU *acquis*. The free movement of workers is a founding principle of the European Union and it has a well-developed legal basis. It has a long-standing treaty base and legal instruments have accumulated which confirm its scope and application. By contrast, much of the *acquis* on social policy and on justice and home affairs—which are the other areas related to movement of persons—has evolved recently and has an uncertain legal status. It involves traditional mechanisms of integration based on legal instruments and institutional requirements. The EU therefore has a very clear and detailed agenda to present to candidates. Because the free movement of workers forms part of the single market, it was also presented early in the accession process, starting with the Europe Agreements. It was of relatively low political salience on both sides until negotiations on this phase began, when it rapidly moved up the political agenda.

The essential components of the *acquis* are freedom to move around the Union, freedom of establishment and freedom to provide services (the right to practice a trade or profession in either an employed or self-employed capacity), which in turn are facilitated by the mutual recognition of professional qualifications and the coordination of social security systems. The health, architecture, and legal professions have specific legislation. The approach to social security is not harmonization of national systems but rather coordination to ensure that people moving across frontiers retain their rights to social security benefits. Related to the free movement of workers provisions in the single market *acquis* are those in the social and employment policies of the Union. There is a "nexus between the market and social policy," which was at least partially acknowledged at the outset of European integration, when social policy in the Community was addressed largely in relation to reducing restrictions on labor mobility (Leibfried and Pierson 2000, 277). The key tasks presented to the candidates are summarized in table 6.3.

Given the spread of a complex patchwork of regulations and court decisions over forty years, there is little room for member states to insert their own methods and preferences into this policy area, because the *acquis* is well established. Implementation happens by "downloading" policy with little possibility of "uploading" domestic policy preferences, to adopt a distinction made by Jordan (2000). For the applicants, there was still less room for maneuver in implementation, because the EU presented full application of the single market *acquis* as essential right from the start of the eastern enlargement process. Both official statements (e.g., European Council 1993) and academic analyses (e.g., Baldwin 1994; Faini and Portes 1995; Smith et al. 1996) have stressed that strict implementation is essential for the single market to function in an enlarged EU.

Nevertheless, in the development of the single market, mobility of labor has remained more limited than mobility of capital and goods. Indeed, the Schengen area was established with the aim of facilitating the free movement of people in order to ensure the free circulation of labor in the Union. The limitations on labor mobility are partly the result of continuing barriers to workers seeking recognition of their qualifications, which is imperfectly assured across the current EU-15. The *acquis* provides some room for maneuver in implementation, where member states

Table 6.3 Summary of tasks to ensure free movement of workers in the single market

Task to be undertaken	Aim of task	Instruments of transfer	First introduced	Timescale
Equal treatment of CEE and EU workers (and spouses and children) regardless of nationality	Removal of barriers to free movement of workers—extending existing single market *acquis* to applicants	Legally binding agreement (accompanied by technical assistance)	Europe Agreement 1993	Implementation of the EAs from 1993
Coordination of social security systems	Removal of barriers to free movement of workers—extending existing single market *acquis* to applicants	Legally binding agreement (accompanied by technical assistance)	Europe Agreement 1993	Implementation of the EAs from 1993
Legislation for mutual recognition of professional qualifications	Removal of barriers to freedom of establishment and freedom to provide services	Provision of legislative and institutional templates	Single Market White Paper 1995	Implementation prior to accession
Efforts to ensure the necessary legislative and enforcement measures for mutual recognition of professional qualifications	Implementation of established *acquis*	Benchmarking and monitoring	Accession Partnership 1998 (annex)	Short-term (1999) and medium-term (5 years)
Further efforts to ensure the necessary legislative and enforcement measures for coordination of social security schemes	Implementation of established *acquis*	Benchmarking and monitoring	Accession Partnership 1998 (annex)	Short-term (1999) and medium-term (5 years)
Complete alignment of mutual recognition of diplomas (and also professional qualifications for Hungary)	Implementation of established *acquis*	Benchmarking and monitoring	Accession Partnership 1999 (and update 2000)	Medium-term (5 years)
Assessment of administrative capacity to implement mutual recognition of professional qualifications	Clarification of institutional requirements by unofficial communication	Advice	"Main administrative structures" document from the European Commission	From 1999

Source: Author's summary compiled from EU documents.

may protect national labor markets, either for political reasons or simply to prevent bureaucratic inefficiency. In addition, the *acquis* specifies only the broad parameters for the institutional arrangement for mutual recognition, leaving room for national professional bodies to discriminate against foreigners. For the applicants, this means that the EU's institutional preferences are well-defined in comparison with other accession requirements, such as the vague condition of having a "functioning market economy." But even in this core element of the single market, there is some margin for national differences to persist and there remain considerable obstacles to free circulation in practice in many member states.

Similar obstacles may well emerge in the new member states now that they have joined and implementation and enforcement of the *acquis* can be tested by workers from the old EU-15 countries who try to get jobs in the candidate countries. However, it is difficult to assess the degree of enforcement until complaints arise.

From the candidate countries' point of view, the rules to be adopted in the area of free movement of workers under the single market are relatively clear in comparison with other parts of the *acquis*, which were more uncertain because they were open to interpretation or evolving rapidly. Implementation of the rules also involved little cost—either financial or political—in comparison with many other parts of the *acquis*. The administrative framework required the candidate countries to set up mutual recognition of qualifications—the prerequisite for implementing free movement of workers—which was neither highly complicated nor costly in comparison with some of the free movement of goods and capital, such as standards and certification bodies or financial services regulators. Politically, the institutional changes required and the principle of allowing workers from the EU-15 member states access to their labor markets did not run against domestic interests. The "goodness of fit" might be described as neutral, in that it required changes, but it did not significantly disrupt the domestic equilibrium.

Political attention to this area only grew during the negotiations, when it became clear that the EU would ask for a transitional period of its own in this area—a very rare exception—owing to the domestic politics of enlargement in several of its member states. At that point, the structure of incentives for the candidates changed—with implications for the compliance of the CEE candidates with EU demands. The candidates were faced with a nonreciprocal adjustment whereby the main incentive to comply with the *acquis*—which was full access to the single market—was substantially reduced by the transitional period imposed by the EU. However, the candidate countries had already taken most of the required measures by that point, making the cost of further compliance relatively low—unlike in the case of compliance with the Schengen *acquis*.

The Rules of the Game in Regulating Movement of Persons under Schengen

The regulation of movement of persons under Schengen involves a much larger and more complex *acquis* than that for the single market presented above. The precise institutional and policy requirements for the candidates were unclear until late in negotiations because they had not been defined and most of what had been defined had been kept secret. The EU's impact in this area was lessened by the contradictions in its cognitive logic for regulating movement of people. Its policy paradigm for movement of workers within the single market is the opposite of that for movement across external frontiers.

The EU employed a range of instruments to transfer its policies connected with controlling and regulating the movement of persons across external frontiers (see table 6.4). A large variety of different instruments were involved because JHA is a "composite policy"—one encompassing a wide range of different policies that are not necessarily related in logical or practical terms (see Sedelmeier 1998). Moreover, although prescriptive policy transfer is an important mechanism by which JHA cooperation works in the EU, its use in the candidate countries was probably well below the potential policy transfer because the EU did not establish what would count as compatible models and standards until late in the accession process.

The origins of EU border policies lay in the aspiration to get rid of obstacles to the free circulation of goods, services, and people, rather than the tighter regulation of frontiers (Bigo 1998). In the 1980s, immigration and asylum policies were matters for national authorities, with European-level policies confined to partially liberalizing movement of workers in the single market. The first moves toward common frontier policies were motivated by frustration with the slow removal of obstacles between countries that were geographically close and had tightly integrated economies. This led to an agreement outside the European Community framework signed at Schengen in 1985, which was elaborated and implemented as the Schengen Convention by five countries (Belgium, France, Germany, Luxembourg, and the Netherlands) in 1990. The original aim of Schengen was "the gradual abolition of controls at common frontiers," and indeed such controls were finally abolished in 1995.[2] By that time, most of the other EU members had entered Schengen, leaving only Ireland, the United Kingdom, and Denmark partially outside it.[3]

The EU's institutional framework for "justice and home affairs"—a portmanteau term for issues ranging from refugee protection to organized crime to citizens' rights—has changed enormously over the past decade, moving from intergovernmental negotiations in the 1980s to the "third pillar" plus the extra-EU Schengen area after the 1992 Maastricht Treaty. By the mid-1990s, justice and home affairs was governed by a complex policy network among national enforcement agencies. The Schengen agreements on the abolition of internal border

2. Border controls were abolished in 1995 among seven Schengen countries; Austria and Italy became full members of the Schengen zone in 1998, while Greece was admitted in 2000.

3. The UK and Ireland have opt-outs from Schengen that include a "selective opt-in," whereby they do not normally participate in migration policy measures. Denmark is a member of Schengen, but until March 2001 it had a special arrangement whereby it had opted out of the third pillar (Monar 1999), after which it exercised its opt-in right.

controls were incorporated into a new *acquis*, and a new Title IV on migration and asylum was created in the Amsterdam Treaty of 1999 (see Monar 2000; den Boer and Wallace 2000). The Amsterdam Treaty's aim was to create "An Area of Freedom, Security and Justice," with all matters relating to movement of persons placed in the first pillar, following the 1996–97 Intergovernmental Conference.[4] Since 1997, border controls, asylum, visas, immigration, and cooperation on civil justice have been put within the competence of Community institutions (such as the European Commission and Court of Justice), leaving the third pillar containing police cooperation and criminal justice. When the Schengen agreements were incorporated into the Treaty on European Union, the *acquis* was "riddled with soft law, delicate compromises, and reservations by member governments" (den Boer and Wallace 2000).

The Schengen *acquis* is the laws emerging from the incorporation of the Schengen Convention into the EU's treaty structure after the 1997 Amsterdam Treaty came into force: it is now part of the EU *acquis*, but for clarity it is referred to as the "Schengen *acquis*" in this chapter. The *acquis* contains special arrangements for three EU member states (Denmark, Ireland and the United Kingdom), while Norway and Iceland are associated with it despite not being members of the Union. However, candidate states were not offered the opportunity to negotiate similarly flexible arrangements; the European Council made it clear on several occasions that new members will not be allowed opt-outs or other forms of flexible integration. The EU's new area of "Freedom, Security and Justice" under the Amsterdam Treaty thus differentiates between existing and prospective members in its applicability. Defining this emerging "*acquis frontalier*" for CEE has raised new questions about the legal status of EU policies and how they should be applied to nonmembers—both candidates and countries like Norway.

The process of "Europeanizing" border policies in the candidate countries involves the transfer of EU legislation, institutional models, and working practices. It is a complex process, not least because the various measures related to borders and internal security are scattered across different parts of the EU's agenda for the candidate countries.

The candidates have to take on the whole of the Schengen *acquis*—which means harmonizing with EU law and undertaking a range of measures to build the institutions and policies to implement it. They include the EU's common visa regime, common regulations for procedures at land and coastal borders and airports. There is also extensive police cooperation and the "Schengen Information System" (SIS) database, in which details of persons entering the Schengen area are logged; candidates have to establish databases for policy registers and for persons refused entry. The tasks that the Commission sets in its policy documents consist of specific measures with a clear timetable—for example, setting up new reception centers for asylum seekers—and also general exhortations to "improve border management."

4. For details of the Amsterdam negotiations, see Petite (1998).

Table 6.4 Overview of principal measures for justice and home affairs presented in the accession partnerships

Task to be undertaken	Aim of task	Instruments of transfer	Applicable countries	Timescale: short-term defined as 1 year, medium-term as 5 years
Strengthen border controls and coordinate services to prevent illegal immigration and to enable full participation in Schengen Information System, including data and telecommunication infrastructure	border controls	institutional capacity and international cooperation	All	Short
Upgrade border posts and "green border control"	border controls	institutional capacity	Hungary, Latvia	Short
National integrated interagency border management strategy with particular attention to the budgetary requirements of the eastern border	border controls	framing integration	Poland	Short and medium
Adopt new law on National Border Control and complete border demarcation with Belarus; start border demarcation with Kaliningrad	border controls	framing integration, including for foreign relations	Lithuania	Short
Implement law on the state frontiers, including merger of the border guard and border police	border controls	legal and institutional reform	Romania	Short
Adopt, implement, and enforce new legislative frameworks on migration, alien, and asylum procedures	migration and asylum	framing integration: policy development	All	Short
Align legislation and improve administrative capacity for implementation of the asylum and migration *acquis* and international norms	migration and asylum	prescriptive integration and institutional capacity	Latvia, Lithuania, Poland	Medium
Upgrade facilities for asylum seekers and refugees, including reception centers	asylum	infrastructure building	Bulgaria, Hungary	Medium
Amend asylum legislation and improve procedures for dealing with asylum applications, including staffing	asylum	institutional capacity	Hungary, Lithuania, Romania, Slovakia, Slovenia	Short
Progressive alignment of visa legislation and practice with that of the EU	visas	prescriptive integration	All	Medium
Strengthen police cooperation mechanisms with EUROPOL	police	institutional capacity and international cooperation	All	Medium

Task	Category	Type	Countries	Timeframe
Reinforce police and customs authorities and ensure better coordination between law enforcement and judicial bodies at central, regional, and local level	law enforcement	institutional capacity	All	Short or medium
Upgrade and better coordinate law enforcement bodies	law enforcement	institution-building	Bulgaria, Czech Republic, Poland	Medium
Speed up reform of penal law	law enforcement	institution-building	Estonia	Short
Speed up the demilitarization of te bodies subordinated to the Ministry of the Interior	law enforcement	institutional reform	Romania	Short
Create an advanced integrated criminal investigation data system and improve forensic research capacity	crime	institution-building	Estonia, Hungary	Short or medium
Sign and ratify international criminal conventions (OECD Convention on Bribery, European Convention on Money Laundering, European Criminal Law Convention on Corruption, Council of Europe 1990 Convention on Laundering Search, Seizure, and Confiscation of the Proceeds of Crime)	crime	harmonization with international norms	All	Short
Implement policies on organized crime, corruption, drug trafficking (legislation, implementing structures, sufficient qualified staff, better cooperation between institutions, training, and equipment), including national strategies to combat economic crime	crime	framing integration	All	Short or medium
Adopt and apply the international instruments related to the fight trafficking (in particular Agreement on Illicit Traffic by Sea, 1988 UN against drug Convention against Illicit Trafficking in Narcotic Drugs and Psychotropic Substances)	crime	harmonization with international norms	Bulgaria, Estonia	Medium
Strengthen capacity to deal with money laundering	crime	institutional capacity	All	Short or medium
Continue fight against trafficking in women and children, drug trafficking, organized crime, and corruption	crime	exhortation	All	Medium
Implement anticorruption strategy	crime	framing integration	All	Medium
Further intensify international coordination and cooperation in the field of combating trans-border crime, especially in the field of transiting, producing, and selling drugs as well as money laundering	crime	international cooperation	Bulgaria	Medium

Note: The wording for the tasks given in the first column reflects the wording in the individual Accession Partnerships, but it is not necessarily a direct quotation because this table presents a shortened summary of the tasks.

Source: Author's summary compiled from individual Accession Partnerships 1998–2001.

Justice and home affairs did not come onto the agenda until relatively late in the accession process, with its first appearance during the autumn of 1998 in the Accession Partnerships. It was only after the Amsterdam Treaty was ratified and came into force that the EU could start to define the JHA *acquis*, and it is still very unclear in terms of the formal demands to be made. Measures that affect border policies and the regulation of movement of people are also scattered across several different documents that the EU has produced for the eastern candidates. The main JHA measures (including those connected to Schengen) are set out in table 6.4.

The general conditions set out by the EU in its accession policy documents include accession of the candidates to the relevant international treaties, observation of the rule of law, stability of administrative and judicial institutions, and data protection. More specific policy requirements are the establishment of equitable asylum procedures and laws as well as the adoption of restrictive measures to limit immigration and to ensure stringent border controls. The latter include tightening visa regimes and admissions systems (rules on residence and work permits), strengthening enforcement and deportation procedures, introducing penalties for illegal immigration, concluding bilateral readmission agreements with other countries, and improving the control and surveillance of borders.

There are additional responsibilities for the countries located on the outer rim of the Schengen zone, such as Poland and Hungary, that are not faced by member states surrounded by other Schengen members, like Luxembourg. The countries whose borders form the external frontier of the Union not only have to control traffic through land frontiers, they also have a greater burden in keeping data on who and what is crossing their borders and on their legal apparatus to deal with asylum claims and refugees. The countries forming the new external border thus take on major responsibilities, both economic and legal, as they become the EU's front line in dealing with transnational population movement.

None of the candidates was well-adapted to the EU model of regulating movement of persons when adjustment to the EU began. Movement of persons and goods across the Warsaw Pact countries had been tightly controlled before 1989, but the methods used were incompatible with EU procedures. Moreover, a number of visa-free agreements were concluded among the Warsaw Pact states (Laczko, Stacher, and Graf 1999). The whole system of regulating movement of persons and goods had to be adapted to EU norms, which included more complex procedures for the admission of persons. Customs procedures—for regulating the movement of goods—were important too, because the pre-1989 methods used to search vehicles crossing borders in the Council for Mutual Economic Assistance (COMECON) region relied on a heavy-handed approach that discouraged trade and was very prone to corruption.

The candidate countries responded similarly to the Schengen *acquis* requirements at first. Stimulated by EU and bilateral aid and technical assistance, they began work on border controls quickly and made rapid progress in the development of infrastructure and procedures. The EU's hyperactivity in JHA policy in the late 1990s helped to stimulate corresponding activity on CEE borders. The candidates were invited to join new EU initiatives and policies on organized crime, drugs and human trafficking, illegal migration, and so on. They were offered training, aid, political contacts, and a role in EU fora on JHA issues.

In the candidate countries, officials responsible for border controls were largely in favor of the EU's agenda and keen to use EU help to enforce stricter controls on movement of persons. In interviews, they frequently quoted EU policy paradigms to justify their national policies on border control, migration, and cross-border crime. Officials working in the administration of border control—whether in the interior ministry, border guard, or police—used similar language to their counterparts in the member states and talked approvingly of the "new approaches" that the EU had brought in.

Their political masters had clear material incentives to implement EU rules, because of the rewards discussed above. But interviews I conducted with officials suggested that social learning and lesson-drawing were taking place: the CEE officials who were implementing the EU's policies by and large became persuaded of the EU's approach and modeled their practices on those of EU counterparts. However, the practices that they followed varied according to the country of origin of the models: EU member states guard their borders and control movement of persons in very different ways, and this diversity is reflected in the different views of the agents from the member states offering advice and technical assistance in the candidate countries on different aspects of regulating movement of persons.

However, although practitioners seeking to control free movement moved toward a logic of appropriateness, other officials, particularly in the foreign ministries and prime ministers' offices, were more concerned about the misfit of EU approaches to border management with other interests—particularly bilateral relations with eastern and southern neighbors. Officials in Hungary and Poland were most concerned about these issues, as Poland has long borders with Belarus and Ukraine, and Warsaw has pursued an active policy of rapprochement with Ukraine since 1989. Hungary's concern is the several million ethnic Hungarians living in neighboring states and bilateral relations with those countries. However, Hungarian and Polish officials pursued a strategy not of preventing implementation of the *acquis* or resisting EU pressures, but of developing other policies in parallel to try to mitigate the impact: in Hungary's case, a "status law" for external minorities; in Poland's, a reinforced eastern policy based on engagement and political dialogue. A country further back in its preparations was Bulgaria, which tried to meet EU demands but was hampered by problems in the public administration, such as an unreformed judiciary, poorly trained border guards, and unmotivated public officials.

The clearest difference among the countries emerged in their visa policies. This was the one part of the *acquis* where the candidates used timing: most of the candidates stalled on setting dates for ending visa-free regimes with neighboring countries and tried to find ways around the visa requirements, such as seeking bilateral readmission treaties with neighboring countries. The other candidates gave in to EU demands earlier than Poland. Bulgaria and Romania used timing the least, primarily because their governments were also trying to persuade the EU to lift the visa requirement on their own citizens that was still in place until 2001 and 2002, respectively. However, on the whole, all the candidates tried to implement the Schengen *acquis* vigorously because they knew it was a potential veto point to accession.

Explanations: The External Incentives Model and Beyond

Why did the candidates adopt EU demands despite the high adoption costs? This outcome seems to contradict the expectations of the external incentives model. An obvious answer is that the applicants are in a weak position vis-à-vis the Union owing to their asymmetrical dependence on it. They want membership far more than the current member states want to accept them. Indeed, the Union's own collective ambivalence about enlargement strengthens its negotiating power. Moreover, EU accession is a package deal. The EU negotiators can put bargains on the table that, while unattractive, are nevertheless accepted by the CEE negotiators because the overall attraction of joining the Union outweighs the disadvantages of parts of the deal. "Ultimately, accession on any terms is better than no accession," as a Hungarian official remarked to the author.

The EU's upper hand in negotiations and the nature of its accession conditionality are important parts of the explanation for this outcome. In the case of Schengen, it was clear that some of the candidate country negotiators accepted the EU's demands because the high salience of Schengen rules for the award of membership was critical after 1998. In interviews with the author in 1998–2002, the negotiators talked of their fears that some member states were likely to slow down their accession if they could not control the flow of traffic across their borders in accordance with the Schengen regime. Member states did not take much interest in the candidates' compliance with many parts of the *acquis*—such as social policy—and left the assessment of compliance to the European Commission. But issues connected with the movement of persons are much more politically sensitive than other parts of the *acquis*, because the flow of people in the Union has a direct and immediate effect on the member states and can mobilize the domestic press and interest groups. As a result, the member states took an active interest in how the candidates were adopting Schengen border controls.

There is clearly a rationalist solution to the apparent puzzle of the CEE negotiators' compliance: the overall reward of membership still outweighs the costs of adopting suboptimal rules on movement of workers and border protection. Indeed, the high salience of people flow in the 'member states' domestic political debates makes EU conditionality even more credible, because the EU-15 countries could threaten to exclude certain candidates owing to domestic pressure on their governments. This threat was credible because candidate country negotiators could read the debates about drug trafficking through CEE in the German press or hear Austrian trade unionists arguing that CEE workers should not be able to work in the EU until average wage levels in CEE rose to meet the Austrian average. Member states could credibly argue that their hands were tied in the negotiations because of the political salience of the issue at home. In other, nonsalient issue areas, it was not credible that candidates would be excluded just because they did not fulfill the administrative criteria (as Antoaneta Dimitrova discusses in this volume). The credibility of the conditionality was further enhanced by the fact that the decisions were clearly in the hands of the member states, not the Commission. The member states created a JHA working group, for example, in the Council of Ministers in May 1998 to establish the accession *acquis* in the area of justice and home affairs, keeping it out of the Commission's hands.[5] Ultimately, it is the Council that decides whether a country can join Schengen—and it is the member states that ultimately decide whether a country can join the EU.

There were further external incentives because of the rewards associated with complying with the Schengen *acquis*. The new members would almost certainly be able to join the Schengen area at some point, even though it will be several years after joining the EU. Their citizens will then be able to travel without passports across much of Europe, benefiting from the removal of internal borders. So there will be a long-term reward for preparing for Schengen. The EU also offered considerable aid and technical assistance to help with these preparations— both through additional money for Schengen-related measures in the EU's pre-accession funds and bilateral aid from concerned member states, especially Germany. In particular, Germany offered substantial help to Poland in upgrading the protection of its eastern border with Belarus and Ukraine. So there were some other rewards that helped to offset the costs of adopting the Schengen *acquis*— although most foreign ministry officials did not regard these as sufficient to outweigh the damage done to Poland's relations with its eastern neighbors.

But why did the candidates overcomply with both Schengen and free movement of workers? Here we have to look beyond the candidates' negotiating position and disaggregate the countries into different groups of officials. The external incentives model does not fully account for the behavior of the candidate countries' ministries of the interior. Why did candidate country officials not all use what negotiating power they had to argue that there was no point in implementing measures if the benefits would not apply immediately on accession? Why did they not stall or delay implementation to mitigate the impact of these measures?

The lesson-drawing and social learning models provide additional insights that explain what happened in the ministries. In addition to the material incentives discussed above, rule adoption in the case of Schengen followed a logic of appropriateness as well as one of consequences among practitioners and interior ministry officials, who became persuaded of the need for stricter controls on the movement of persons. They were willing to adopt the Schengen rules because this *acquis* suited their policing and security agendas. Lesson-drawing—as used in domestic political debates—thus proceeded in parallel with conditionality. Here, the logic of

---

5. *Agence Europe* 7232, 30 May 1998.

rule adoption varied among the ministries. From the foreign ministries' point of view, the Schengen *acquis* was very damaging, for it undermined their policies of rapprochement with neighboring countries—particularly for Poland's relationship with Ukraine. However, for the interior and justice ministries—whose primary concern is internal security and law and order—this was not a central concern. Instead, the job of the ministers and officials in those ministries was to protect the countries' external borders and reduce cross-border criminal activity. For them, the EU's policies were much more suited to their own agendas. Although border controls had been steadily relaxed after 1989, allowing people to move freely after the end of the Cold War, interior ministry officials were worried about criminals taking advantage of the chaotic situation. The EU's demands for border protection fit in with some of the ministries' policy goals to reduce cross-border crime. Moreover, EU attention to justice and home affairs forced interior ministry priorities up their government's overall policy agenda. EU conditionality thus presented different incentives to different groups of CEE actors. In the cases of people flow, the dominant logic underlying rule adoption varied among the ministries involved. The foreign ministries tended to calculate the overall costs of Schengen compliance as much higher—even if they were outweighed by the reward of membership—whereas the interior ministries saw Schengen measures as a way of partly solving some their own problems.

My fieldwork in three CEE countries (Bulgaria, Hungary, and Poland) revealed discursive change as well. Although this is not a key part of the explanation for the outcome in these two policy areas, it is worth noting. In the case of the single market *acquis*, this change was evident at the level of discourse, with civil servants talking approvingly of the "four freedoms" of the single market. However, the degree of discursive change was affected by the EU's negotiating position. Once it became clear that the EU was going to demand a transitional period before the member states would have to allow CEE workers into their labor markets, the legitimacy of the EU's policy paradigm on single market freedoms was damaged. This did not stop the candidates from complying with the *acquis*, because the external incentives presented to them still made rule adoption attractive because it was necessary for them to gain the much bigger reward of EU membership. But it did affect the discourse in the ministries about why rule adoption was necessary: officials accepted the EU's policy paradigm about free markets, even though they disapproved of the EU's hypocrisy in insisting that it should apply in one direction only for the first few years after accession. That acceptance, in turn, caused them not to demand a transitional period on the free movement of EU workers into their own countries. Only Malta asked for—and obtained—a transitional period in the other direction. Officials in the foreign and finance ministries in the CEE countries argued that free movement of labor was good for their economies—which is a domestically driven incentive, but one that closely follows the EU's own policy paradigm on free markets.

In the case of Schengen, discursive change was slower, because the *acquis* evolved over the period while rule adoption was taking place. Moreover, there was much greater resistance in most candidate countries to adopting EU policies that would force them to change their visa policies and methods of guarding external borders. However, interviews I conducted with officials and politicians in the region between 1997 and 2002 revealed a profound change in their discourse. Civil servants and law enforcement officials adopted many of the assumptions prevalent in the EU about the aims and effectiveness of Schengen-inspired policies. The striking feature of discursive change was the contrast between foreign ministry and interior ministry discourse. Foreign ministry officials in the candidate countries continued to talk about Schengen as a problem for bilateral relations with neighboring countries, referring to the need to develop flanking policies to mitigate its impact on the countries left outside the Union. However, differences narrowed between the views of candidate country officials working in the interior ministries and law enforcement bodies and their counterparts in the EU's institutions and the member states over the period 1997–2002. By the end of negotiations, in December 2002, my interview evidence revealed a much greater difference in the discourse used by foreign and interior ministries in the candidate countries than between that used by candidate and EU officials. The form of rule adoption became behavioral as well as formal.

Inconsistency between the EU's rhetoric and practice made a difference to the outcome of negotiations as well. As discussed above, the candidates accepted the EU's transitional period labor mobility after accession, even though it ran against one of the fundamentals of the single market: the free movement of labor. The EU's inconsistency did not undermine the conditionality, because it did not compromise the EU's capacity to deliver the reward to the candidates. The applicant countries' officials thus followed the material incentives, the incentive to join overrode other considerations, and the EU delivered on the incentive structure it had set up. Although the EU's own hypocrisy damaged the legitimacy of its rules in the eyes of the candidates, its conditionality was still credible because of the likelihood that the member states would exclude an applicant if it did not comply. In this respect, the cases presented in this chapter firmly reject the proposition of the social learning model about the importance of legitimacy. Legitimacy can be damaged without undermining conditionality if it is clear that the international organization will withhold a reward without compliance by the candidate, even if compliance is not justified by the international organization's own internal rules.

However, the conflict between the EU's practice and its policy paradigm produced an inconsistency that did affect the details of the negotiated settlement. According to my interviews with Commission and candidate country officials during the negotiations, the EU made additional concessions to the candidates specifically to offset the political damage that their governments incurred as a result of agreeing to the transitional period on free movement of labor. In particular, the Commission offered most of the candidates a transitional period on the freedom of EU citizens to purchase land in the candidate countries and on the application of some environmental standards (see Grabbe 2001b). According to the actors involved at the time, one of the key reasons that Commission negotiators offered transitional periods in these two other areas was embarrassment at the inconsistency of the EU's negotiating position on free movement of labor with the four freedoms of the single market. Although this inconsistency did not undermine the EU's conditionality—in particular the credibility of the conditionality—it did produce additional concessions when the candidate country negotiators complained about it. Negotiations for accession are not pure and simple bargaining. Rather, they are an iterative process that can produce trade-offs between policy areas even in the absence of a logical linkage.

Moreover, the EU's negotiators are well aware that the negotiations are not just about the EU imposing deals on the candidates by using its asymmetrical bargaining power. "Negotiations did not just concern 'us and them,' but the 'future us,'" as one of the Commission officials put it (Avery 1995). One of the concerns of the EU's negotiators was that disillusionment in the candidate countries about how the rules were applied would mean that the logic of appropriateness, based on persuasion, would have less power than it would otherwise have had. The EU's negotiators were aware that they needed to persuade the candidates to be good citizens and follow EU norms once they had joined. Most of the officials in the negotiating teams of the applicant countries would be involved in implementing the EU's *acquis* in their own countries. The quality of implementation and enforcement is affected by how far the public administrators buy into the EU's logic of doing things. Moreover, later many of the CEE officials involved in negotiations would become Commission officials and representatives of their countries in Brussels. It would not be in the EU's interest for them to be entirely cynical about the application of the Union's rules and see the EU as just about power politics. These concerns were certainly in the minds of the EU's negotiators when I interviewed them, and they affected the concessions offered to the candidates, even if the EU ultimately stuck to its bargaining position. This behavior is in line with the argument advanced by Sedelmeier that the EU's policy is influenced by a diffuse norm of accommodating the candidates' interests in negotiations (1998).

The most general proposition of the external incentives model is that "a state adopts EU rules if the expected benefits of EU rewards for the state are higher than the costs." Is this hypothesis confirmed in the case of free movement of workers in the single market and under Schengen? My conclusion is that the external incentives model works well for analyzing how the EU has transferred its mechanisms to Central and Eastern Europe for regulating the movement of persons in the case of single market regulation, but less well in the case of Schengen. Schengen presents a challenge to the external incentives model because the candidates' behavior contradicts some of the model's key propositions.

The EU's negotiating position on free movement of workers under the single market allowed member states to maintain their national restrictions on the movement of CEE workers for at least two and up to seven years after accession. The candidates were thus told to implement the whole single market *acquis* prior to accession, but with a delay in the application of the reciprocal benefit from many current member states. However, the conditions were clear, the conditionality was highly credible, and the size of adoption costs was low, so the candidates continued to implement this part of the *acquis*. The overall strength of the EU's conditionality overcame the disincentive to comply with this particular policy area—so the logic of consequences still held, because the expected benefits were higher than the costs. The key hypotheses of the external incentives model thus hold.

In the case of Schengen, the EU offered a long and uncertain delay in the application of benefits after accession, as the candidates will not fully join the Schengen area for at least several years now that they have joined the Union. However, unlike with the single market, the conditions were not precisely determined until the very last stage of negotiations, and the size of adoption costs for the candidates was very high. The credibility of the conditionality on Schengen was high for getting into the EU, particularly once the EU published detailed tasks for this area in 1998. But the credibility of the conditionality was low as regards the EU's commitment to rewarding progress—because it was not at all certain that it would allow the candidates into the Schengen area. So why did the candidates comply?

I have advanced an explanation that uses the external incentives model and found it adequate to explain the overall outcome of negotiations on the two areas concerned with movement of persons. The structure of incentives for the candidate countries to meet the EU's conditions changed in both cases when the EU decided not to offer the promised benefits of compliance immediately upon accession—which affected the power of the conditionality. However, in both cases, the candidates carried on implementing the *acquis*—and hence adopting EU rules.

In the case of single market regulation, this was because the costs of adoption were so low that it was not worth challenging the conditionality. Moreover, many of the necessary measures were already in place. This outcome confirms the hypotheses of the external incentives model about the degree of rule adoption.

In the case of Schengen, candidate country governments continued implementation partly because of material incentives. In particular, the high political salience of this issue made the EU's conditionality more credible as regards membership because EU negotiators could plausibly argue that some member states would veto a country's accession if it did not comply with Schengen—even though the EU did not offer the benefits of joining Schengen immediately upon accession. Thus the high salience of Schengen rules for accession trumped the otherwise unfavorable conditions for rule adoption. But candidate country officials and ministers also complied because of the lessons that some of them had already drawn from the EU. Persuasion and transfer of models had been occurring in parallel with the process of negotiations, which meant that candidate country governments generally decided to carry on with implementation rather than to challenge the EU's conditionality. Their decisions were based on interests such as sunk costs and the danger of accession being delayed, but they were also the result of acceptance of the policy paradigms underlying the EU's rules on movement of persons and the support that the Schengen regime offered to interior ministries' own policies in tightening border control. Although the Schengen *acquis* was a particularly expensive and complex way of addressing some of the candidates' internal security problems, it was welcome to some interior ministry officials because it forced their concerns up the government's overall agenda.

However, the EU also offered additional concessions in other areas as compensation for the bad deal on free movement of workers. This outcome resulted from additional concerns on the part of the EU's negotiators about how far they would in future—after the accession of the new members—undermine the logic of appropriateness underlying important parts of European integration.

"Europeanization" is defined as a process of rule adoption for the purposes of this volume. Europeanization processes can certainly include calculation of material interest, but they can also involve changes in the logic of behavior driven by the absorption of EU norms, attitudes, and ways of thinking. These changes in behavior follow a logic of appropriateness, which in the cases of movement of persons explored here works in parallel with the logic of consequences.

CHAPTER SEVEN

The Europeanization of Environmental Policy in Central and Eastern Europe

Liliana B. Andonova

The adoption of European Union (EU) environmental rules in Central and East European countries (CEECs) is strongly dominated by external incentives associated with EU membership conditionality. The environment chapter is one of the costliest parts of the EU *acquis*. It contains over 250 regulations developed over the course of decades, which have to be applied within several years in the relatively poor CEECs. Not surprisingly, the alignment with the EU environmental *acquis* is typically presented as a bitter pill that candidates have to swallow to advance their broader strategic objective of EU membership. EU law approximation and implementation in candidate countries has proceeded through multiple steps of intergovernmental and domestic bargaining, influenced by the linkage among EU markets, environmental regulations, and broader foreign policy objectives (Andonova 2003).

In this context of interest-driven strategic bargaining, has there been space for EU environmental norm diffusion through lesson-drawing or social learning? I will show that such norm diffusion has taken place in the context of East-West environmental cooperation. The influence of normative mechanisms was particularly strong in the early 1990s, when environmental protection was seen as a major policy failure of the fallen communist regimes and western regulations were promoted as the standards to aspire for. While normative diffusion gave way to hard bargaining in the course of accession negotiations, mechanisms of socialization and learning were still maintained to support the internalization of EU legislation in domestic policy systems.

My aim is to disentangle empirically the relative significance of the rationalist external incentives model elaborated in this volume on the one hand and of the constructivist variant of the lesson-drawing and social learning models on the other. I thus contribute to the theoretical agenda that seeks to bridge the constructivist-rationalist divide in the study of international institutions and their effects. I will proceed to elaborate the argument that while lesson-drawing and social learning dominated EU influence in the early 1990s, external incentives became dominant with the onset of accession preparations and negotiations. This temporal variation allows us to specify methods for testing the significance of each mechanism over time. I trace the observable implications of each mechanism in controlled case studies of institutional influence and policy adjustment in the early and late 1990s. The cases cover the Environment for Europe process established in 1991, the framework of pre-accession environmental cooperation between the EU and candidate countries, and policy adjustment to EU air emission regulations in the Czech Republic and Poland.

Mechanisms of EU Influence

Two parallel approaches in international relations theory examine the influence of international institutions on state policies. The "rationalist" or neo-liberal perspective emphasizes the role of institutions in facilitating bargains among rational actors with a given set of interests through mechanisms that decrease the transaction cost of agreements, extend the time horizon of parties, and provide monitoring, issue linkage, and commitment mechanisms. Rationalist accounts that factor in domestic politics examine the change in state preferences as a result of shifts of domestic interests and coalitions under international constraints (see, e.g., Martin and Simmons 1998). The sociological or constructivist perspective, in turn, emphasizes the constitutive role of international norms, which can reshape state identities and even perceptions of interests. This perspective, similar to studies of international policy diffusion, also emphasizes the role of transnational learning, norm diffusion, persuasion, and socialization as mechanisms of institutional influence that are quite distinct from strategic bargaining (see, e.g., Ruggie 1998a, 1998b).

These two approaches to international regimes have developed largely in parallel to each other. Only recently have scholars emphasized the interplay of cognitive and instrumental mechanisms of institutional influence and the need to specify the conditions for their relative significance (Checkel 1997; Christiansen et al. 2001; Schimmelfennig 2001; Tallberg 2002). I look at the EU influence on the environmental policies of CEECs as an opportunity to specify alternative propositions about the role of instrumental and ideational factors of institutional influence. Because of the limited number of explanatory variables that can be analyzed in a set of controlled case studies, the analysis does not emphasize disentangling the conditions for the relevance of the lesson-drawing and social learning models. Instead, I focus on the common points of lesson-drawing and social learning as two models that have affinities with constructivism and compare their relative significance with the rationalist external incentives model. Lesson-drawing and social learning are thus viewed here as roughly the demand and supply side of a broadly defined norm diffusion process in the context of environmental cooperation involving CEECs, the EU, and other international institutions.

As already indicated, it appears that a rationalist external incentives model may be the only argument about the EU's influence on environmental regulations in CEECs that can be seriously sustained. This model would posit that EU conditionality, or more broadly issue linkage of environmental regulations with geopolitical and economic objectives, influences domestic environmental politics and drives policy adjustment in CEECs. Even in the context of strong EU conditionality, however, it may be premature to dismiss the role of cognitive factors and learning in the diffusion of EU environmental rules.

We only need to go back to the early 1990s to discover conditions identified by the constructivist literature as highly conducive to norm diffusion and social learning. First, postcommunist countries inherited significant environmental degradation from communism. There was a public consensus that the environment was a policy failure that requires urgent attention, and thus a demand for lesson-drawing and transnational policy diffusion (Checkel 1999a, 2001; Dolowitz and Marsh 2000; Schimmelfennig and Sedelmeier, chapter 1). Second, environmental improvements were perceived as compatible with the broader democratization process and identity formation of CEECs as responsible to their citizenry. The ideational linkage between democratization and environmental reforms was reinforced by former dissident environmentalists, who became active policy entrepreneurs in postcommunist governments and spearheaded transnational epistemic networks. Third, and very important, western models of environmental governances were both seen and promoted as the "appropriate" models for the newly established democracies to follow. The identification of CEECs with the community of West European states and the desire to "re-integrate" in western institutions increased the salience of EU rules as models for social learning. Finally, the early reforms tackled broad principles of environmental governance set in framework legislations, which amplified the constitutive influence of international norms. As John Ruggie points out, the constructivist perspective is particularly powerful in explaining the shaping and diffusion of basic "constitutive rules" that define identities and practices, while the rationalist perspective has focused almost exclusively on what he calls "regulatory rules" intended to regulate specific actions or behavior (1998b, 22–23).

In sum, at the beginning of postcommunist transition, a number of conditions identified by the lesson-drawing and social learning models as conducive to transnational norm diffusion manifested themselves in CEECs: perception of policy failure, broad agreement on the compatibility of western environmental rules with domestic democratization discourse, transnationally proactive bureaucracies, aspiration for membership in the EU and other western institutions, active promotion of improved environmental governance by western institutions, and emphasis on setting the constitutive principles of environmental governance. While conditions for lesson-drawing shaped the "demand" for environmental policy transfer in CEECs, international institutions and cooperation "supplied"

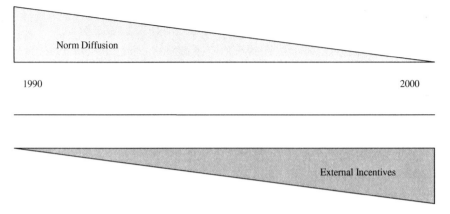

Figure 7.1 Mechanisms of EU influence on environmental policies of the CEECs

mechanisms for social learning by fostering deliberation, information exchange, bureaucratic networks, and technical assistance.

It would be misleading, however, to suggest that East-West environmental co-operation in the early 1990s was devoid of material interests. Efforts of CEE leaders to engage western states and international agencies in a dialogue aimed not solely at consensus-building and learning but also at securing financial assistance. Donors, similarly, tended to disburse aid according to strategic priorities in the region. Nevertheless, the linkage between policy reforms to incorporate western standards and material rewards remained very loosely connected in the early transition period.[1] A considerable portion of the assistance was provided to strengthen capacity for learning rather than for specific environmental reforms or investment, often raising criticism both by policymakers and analysts that expected an outcome-oriented, tit-for-tat cooperation (Connolly, Gutner, and Bedarf 1996). Thus, while both material bargaining and normative diffusion through learning were part of environmental cooperation between East and West in the early 1990s, it is possible to argue that lesson-drawing and socialization were the dominant mechanisms of international influence, as represented in figure 7.1.

As the CEECs signed association agreements with the EU and started to prepare for accession negotiations in the latter part of the 1990s, the focus of environmental reforms shifted quickly to the very specific task of adopting EU environmental legislation as a requirement for membership. Even the general discourse on the adoption of EU law did not focus on the appropriateness of EU environmental regulations for CEE candidates but on the costs and procedures associated with their adoption. The linkages among EU markets, environmental rules, and broader policy objectives shaped domestic responses to EU conditionality and determined

1. An important exception is nuclear safety assistance provided in the early 1990s, which was tied to very specific conditionality.

the speed and level of compliance with EU rules (Andonova 2003). As accession preparation and negotiations progressed, the factors facilitating the influence of external incentives became dominant: conditions became more specific, monitoring intensified, the credibility of EU conditionality increased (both via increased threats to postpone accession and via increased volume of assistance), and parallel conditionality increased as other multilateral institutions such as the World Bank and the European Bank for Reconstruction and Development (EBRD) incorporated the EU accession criteria into their portfolios for the region.

Nevertheless, mechanisms of socialization and learning persisted even in the context of interest-driven negotiations on compliance with the EU environmental *acquis*. EU assistance in the form of capacity-building and expertise-sharing continued throughout the accession period. It served as a social learning tool targeted primarily at CEE bureaucracies as well as an instrumental mechanism to ensure better monitoring (Grabbe 2001a; Sissenich 2002a). Trans-European nongovernmental networks among both industry and advocacy organizations were also strengthened by the enlargement process and became actively engaged in the promotion and diffusion of EU norms. Although such actors, particularly in industry, were often motivated by instrumental reasons, they generally used information-sharing, capacity-building, and suasion (Andonova 2003). In sum, during pre-accession preparations and negotiations, the dominant mechanisms of EU influence were exercised through external incentives, while social learning mechanisms served to ease and legitimize the process of adopting EU environmental legislation (see figure 7.1).

The above discussion of dominant mechanisms of EU environmental influence in CEECs suggests that the external incentives model and the lesson-drawing and social learning models are not necessarily mutually exclusive. These perspectives to institutional influence can be understood as "alternative" in an analytical sense as plausible explanations with observable implications. In reality, however, both external incentives and socialization mechanisms of EU influence coexisted, while the logic of appropriateness dominated in the early 1990s and the logic of consequences became dominant in the late 1990s. The question is then how can we disentangle empirically the relative influence of external incentives and socialization in the Europeanization of CEE environmental policies?

One method to address this question is to focus on the details in the policy-making process, trace specific aspects of the interaction between EU institutions and domestic politics, and examine to what extent these details match the observable implication of the argument specified above. One set of observable implications of the two propositions relates to the tools and mechanisms of cooperation likely to be prevalent in processes of learning and processes of strategic bargaining. In settings where ideation and constitutive influence prevails, we should see greater density of mechanisms such as network-building, capacity-building, framework agreements, and support for transnational expert groups. In a context dominated by the logic of consequences, there should be greater emphasis on institutional mechanisms such as monitoring, strategic information-sharing, dependency of assistance on particular outcomes, and negotiations of follow-up procedures (table 7.1). Examination of the density of suasion and instrumental bargaining mechanisms is one set of evidence suggestive of which logic of influence prevails, but it does not give us sufficient evidence of the impact of these mechanisms and does not rule out the possibility that suasion mechanisms are simply instruments of strategic bargaining objectives.

To provide evidence of the actual impact of alternative mechanisms of international influence, we also need to document the motivations for policy change and policy outcomes as recorded in personal statements, parliamentary records, and government documents (Checkel 1997). We should search for gaps or disconnects among rhetoric, stated motivation, material interests, and policy outcomes to evaluate alternative hypotheses (Johnston 2001). For example, the adoption of EU norms despite recognized failures of financial assistance or rule adoption exceeding formal EU requirements may indicate strong influence of learning and socialization. By contrast, evidence of little policy action in support of principles embraced rhetorically or the reversal of internationally promoted principles as a result of a change in the strategic environment or material interests will indicate a weak impact of transnational learning and norm diffusion. Table 7.1 lists the observable implications of the conditionality and norm diffusion models of EU influence, which can be traced in cases of environmental cooperation and policy change through the 1990s.

Table 7.1   Observable implications of the external incentives and norm-diffusion models of EU influence over the environmental policies of CEECs

	External incentives	Norm diffusion
Tools of cooperation/ influence	Prevalence of instrumentality: —monitoring —assistance against outcomes —enforcement mechanisms —issue linkage	Prevalence of socialization: —networking —expert groups —framework agreements —loose connection between aid and outcomes
Policy motivation	Justified predominantly: —in terms of interests —in terms of strategy	Justified predominantly: —in terms of principles —in terms of group identification
Policy outcomes	—No policy action following agreements in principle or rhetorical action —Reversal of policy learning as a result of change in strategic situation or interests —Policy change reflects closely patterns of interest and power	—Exceeds strategic requirements —Materializes despite disconnect between expected benefits or material interests —Persists after change in material interests/ strategic situation

The argument of the prevalence of lesson-drawing and social learning mechanisms of EU influence in the early transition period and the dominance of external incentives in the process of accession negotiations allows us to construct a longitudinally controlled comparison to trace the observable implications of the rationalist versus the constructivist models. I examine two sets of events at each end of the temporal spectrum identified in figure 7.1. I first look at the "Environment for Europe" process of East-West cooperation, which was initiated in 1991 and continues to this date. I then compare the Environment for Europe process with the pre-accession environmental cooperation between the EU and the CEECs that developed in the second half of the 1990s. The analysis then moves to two specific cases of policy adjustment: air pollution regulations in the Czech Republic and Poland in the early and late 1990s. Both countries started environmental reforms early in the transition period, but the Czech Republic adopted EU rules on air pollution emissions in 1991, while Poland harmonized its air emission regulations with those of the EU in the late 1990s, allowing us to examine the different types of reform incentives across time periods and countries. According to the argument advanced here, in the Environment for Europe process and air pollution regulations of the early 1990s, the influence of EU and other international institutions should exhibit details that support the proposition of predominantly constitutive influence through lesson-drawing and social learning. The EU pre-accession environmental assistance and the harmonization of EU air pollution regulations in Poland during the second half of the 1990s, by contrast, should exhibit evidence of the dominance of external incentives over norm diffusion as a mechanism of institutional influence.

The Environment for Europe Process

The Environment for Europe process was the first pan-European forum of environmental cooperation after the fall of communism. It was initiated in 1991 by the Czechoslovak minister of the environment, Josef Vavrousek, who was a former dissident and active policy entrepreneur domestically and internationally. Vavrousek had originally proposed the creation of a European Environmental Council to steer cooperation. The EU was unwilling to set up a formal institution, instead supporting a more informal high-level process of cooperation and consensus building (Gutner 2002). This gave birth to Environment for Europe—a series of biannual meetings of European environmental ministers, donor agencies, other interested parties, and gradually representatives from the former Soviet Union countries as well. Following the first conference in Dobris Castle near Prague in 1991, ministerial meetings were held in Lucerne (1993), Sofia (1995), Aarhus (1997), and Kiev (2003). A network of policymakers and experts anchored at international institutions such as the Organization of Economic Cooperation and Development (OECD), the World Bank, and the Regional Environmental Center in Hungary, was established to conduct the preparatory and follow-up work for the meetings. Environment for Europe was thus set up as a process driven by transnational policy entrepreneurs.

Since its very inception, the rhetoric and justification of the process focused on advancing a set of constitutive principles, lesson-drawing, and social learning in the region. There was high demand for lesson-drawing motivated by the perception of environmental policy failure in the former communist states, as attested by the Czech initiative to start Environment for Europe and the close epistemic network built around it.[2] Another central motivation expressed at Dobris and subsequent conferences was to generate financial assistance that would facilitate the convergence of environmental standards across Europe (Connolly, Gutner, and Bedarf 1996). Of the two main items on the Environment for Europe agenda—first, policy diffusion and institution-building, and second, coordination of financial assistance—the former became clearly dominant and more successful (Connolly, Gutner, and Bedarf 1996; Green 1991; Gutner 2002; Ferguson 1991; Moldan 2000; World Bank 1994).

Those hoping that Environment for Europe would generate significant financial assistance or even contribute to the better coordination of aid soon became disillusioned. Efforts to increase aid commitments at the Lucerne and Sofia meetings in 1993 and 1995, respectively, produced weak results. Donors ultimately preferred to maintain greater control over the allocation of aid by channeling it on a bilateral basis. Even the International Financial Institutions (IFIs) chose to prioritize environmental assistance according to their own standard procedures and operational rules rather than coordinate it within a broader international forum (Connolly, Gutner, and Bedarf 1996; Gutner 2002; World Bank 1994).

The failure of Environment for Europe to generate significant financial resources did not, however, result in an abandonment of the broader agenda of policy diffusion through social learning. The assistance channeled through the Environment for Europe process most effectively was "soft" money for capacity-building, policy networking, and strengthening of environmental institutions. Assistance was used primarily as a social learning mechanism to export ideas and policy styles, rather than as a means of reducing the transaction costs of specific agreements or of monitoring compliance.

Environment for Europe allowed for the exportation of a variety of policy styles and instruments, mostly from the West but also across transition states. Through its early PHARE program, the EU exported a relatively centralized and legalistic style of environmental policymaking, with emphasis on command and control regulations and the enhanced legal capacity of ministries of the environment. IFIs such as the EBRD, the World Bank, and the OECD promoted a more flexible approach to environmental management, emphasizing economic instruments, cost minimization, and priorities involving measurable health effects and cost-benefit

2. Author interviews with close associates of Josef Varvrousek and with representatives of Green Circle, Prague, November 1997. See also Meadows (1996) and the speeches by Joseph Vavrousek published in Huba and Novacek (2000).

analysis. The United States promoted its own regulatory style emphasizing eco-nomic instruments and tying environmental assistance to democratization and a stronger civil society. The Regional Environmental Center, which has its head-quarters in Hungary, was funded with U.S. assistance to support environmental NGOs and public participation across the region (Francis, Klarer, and Petkova 1999; Moldan 2000; World Bank 1994).

The specific policy outcomes associated with Environment for Europe also attest to the dominance and success of transnational norm diffusion and learning. The forum, along with supporting institutions like the World Bank and the OECD, pro-vided assistance for the development and adoption of National Environmental Plans that set priorities for reforms. Although the National Environmental Plans were only programmatic documents with no legal force, they were important in strengthening capacity for the young environmental administrations, especially in states that did not have the resources or management expertise to produce national programs. The existence of National Environmental Plans and review procedures within the Environment for Europe framework also enabled societal advocates to monitor more closely the work of governments and to hold them accountable for delays in environmental reforms.

The collaboration of experts within Environment for Europe also accelerated the adoption in the CEECs of framework legislations for environmental protec-tion. Both donors and recipients of assistance established a shared understanding and support for shared environmental norms such as the "polluter pays" princi-ple, the precautionary principle, and the right of access to information, all of which were reflected in the newly adopted framework legislations of the transition coun-tries. In most cases, framework laws closely followed the constitutive principles of EU legislation in anticipatory support of the countries' EU membership aspira-tions, but policymakers and legislators did not engage in the type of line-by-line comparisons with EU legislation that would later be required by the EU harmonization process. A study of the Regional Environmental Center in 1996 on the level of approximation of EU environmental legislations revealed that by 1995, all of the CEECs except Estonia, Latvia, and Romania had achieved well over 50 percent proximity between the domestic general environmental regu-lations and those of the EU. Legislation on nature conservation, in which post-communist countries had strong traditions, and framework environmental legislation were the areas in which the countries most eagerly aligned with EU principles.

Another notable institutional outcome associated with Environment for Europe was the establishment of extra-budgetary environmental funds across the region as mechanisms for soft environmental financing. Such funds were intended to fill the gap between high investment needs for environmental improvements and lack of both private and public resources in transition countries. The funds gen-erated income from pollution taxes, penalties, and, in some instances, budget allo-cations and foreign resources and also offered soft financing for environmental investments. This institutional innovation was developed first by a few leading reformers, such as Poland, the Czech Republic, and Hungary, with the support of experts from IFIs. Thanks to the active support of the Environment for Europe process, the fund system spread to virtually all transition states in Europe and Central Asia. Although environmental funds have different capacity across states, reflecting domestic political and economic constraints, they have been important in generating revenue and indicate internationally induced institutional convergence across the region (Francis, Klarer, and Petkova 1999).

The crowning achievement of Environment for Europe was the adoption of a pan-European convention on access to information at the Aarhus Conference of Ministers in 1997. The convention is an intergovernmental agreement of European states that gives a legal status to Article 10 (covering access to information and environmental justice) of the Declaration adopted at the 1992 World Summit on Sustainable Development in Rio de Janeiro. The Aarhus convention was a result of years of work by networks of NGOs, policymakers, and environmental bureaucracies, supported by the Environment for Europe framework and the Regional Environmental Center (Jendroska 1998). It is notable that this convention went beyond the immediate strategic objectives of the CEECs, which by 1997 were already focused on the environmental requirements of EU accession. The convention established a new and binding pan-European agreement, both for the EU and CEECs.

In sum, the Environment for Europe process initiated in the early 1990s exemplifies the power of normative influences of the EU and other international institutions on the environmental policies of CEECs. In this forum of cooperation, international influence responded to a demand for lesson-drawing and was exerted by donors not so much through strategic bargaining and contracting but through a process of social learning that emphasized networking, deliberation, and the exchange of information, policy advocacy, and institution-building. The process influenced the principles of policymaking in transition states, despite its failure to respond to their strategic objective of a substantial increase in financial support. It resulted in instances of striking convergence of policy and institutional forms, despite the persistent differences in economic development across postcommunist states.

EU Pre-Accession Cooperation

As the CEECs started formal pre-accession cooperation with the EU, the dynamics of environmental cooperation shifted from one predominantly focused on lesson-drawing and social learning to one almost entirely centered on interest-based bargaining over specific regulatory outcomes. In the period between 1993 and 1996, all CEECs concluded association agreements with the EU; by 1996, all had formally applied for EU accession. The 1993 Copenhagen summit specified the broad conditions for future membership: a functioning market economy, democratic institutions, and implementation of the EU *acquis*. The adoption of EU legislation, including environmental regulations, was thus an explicit condition for membership.

By the second half of the 1990s, the European Commission established pre-accession technical assistance programs for environmental approximation. While these programs employed mechanisms of capacity-building and socialization, their ultimate objective was to assure high harmonization levels in candidate countries prior to accession. The types of capacity-building projects funded by the Commission provide evidence of the overwhelmingly instrumental nature of EU-funded technical cooperation.

In the mid-1990s, significant resources were devoted, for example, to assessments of the implementation *costs* of the EU environmental *acquis* for candidate countries. Both the EU and the CEECs had a strategic interest in producing a set of cost estimates on which all could agree. For the European Commission, such estimates identified areas of potential difficulties with national implementation, while for candidates, they provided a figure they could use to bargain for transition periods and investment assistance (Botcheva 2001). No economic analysis of the *benefits* of EU law harmonization in postcommunist Europe was done until 2001, when most countries were already completing their negotiations of the environment chapter (Ecotech 2001a). This indicates that even if there was some scope for lesson-drawing in the context of EU law harmonization, candidate countries had no strategic interest to present any part of the harmonization process as policy changes that would have been undertaken anyway for domestic reasons. Some cost studies funded by IFIs concluded that parts of the EU environmental legislation would present an excessive burden to transition economies and specific sectors, so they recommended a more flexible approach to applying EU rules (World Bank 1997, 1998, 2001).[3] Such policy lessons were plainly disregarded in the process of negotiations, as the EU maintained a requirement of full incorporation of the *acquis* with minimal transition periods.

Another mechanism of strategic learning supported by the EU was the funding of legislative gap studies. The Environmental Legal Approximation Facility (DISAE) was established with the support of the PHARE program to disburse assistance for such legislative analyses and twinning programs. These analyses and programs were implemented with the help of EU consultants and did indeed increase the understanding of EU laws among the environmental ministries of the candidate countries. However, they also provided the Commission with a very specific tool for monitoring harmonization progress. In addition to legislative gap analyses, annual questionnaires on the status of EU law harmonization and implementation provided a basis on which the Commission formulated its yearly position on the candidates' accession progress.

Other examples of EU capacity-building programs include the appointment of long-term legal advisors to CEE environmental ministries, the publication of the

3. On flexibility in compliance with the EU environmental *acquis*, see Holzinger and Knoepfel (2000).

Working Document on the Preparation of the Associated CEECs for the Approxima-tion of the EU Environmental Legislation and the *Guide to the Approximation of European Union Environmental Legislation*, the establishment of a telephone hotline on approximation issues managed by DG Environment, and the preparation of implementation indicators to assess the level of harmonization in different environmental areas. After 2001, when accession negotiations on the environment chapter of most of the countries were complete, the Commission shifted its assistance toward supporting environmental infrastructure investment through the Instrument for Structural Policies for Pre-Accession (ISPA) and monitoring implementation (Ecotech 2001b).

This brief overview of EU environmental pre-accession assistance demonstrates that mechanisms of social learning as well as of strategic bargaining and monitoring have been used to assure compliance with EU legislation by candidate countries. These mechanisms reinforced each other rather than acting as alternative instruments of EU influence. However, the above examples of pre-accession capacity-building also indicate that the process of social learning within EU accession was clearly subordinated to strategic objectives of bargaining and reaching agreements on the course of EU law approximation, the extent of transition periods, and the monitoring of its implementation.

The prevalence of external incentives in the EU environmental approximation process is also evident in the policy results it produced. Following the legislative screening projects, many of the CEECs' framework environmental laws adopted in the early 1990s, which followed EU principles only in a broad way, were amended to better reflect specific provisions of EU legislation. Similar amendments were also undertaken for issue-specific laws, driven by specific EU requirements. In this policy adjustment of the late 1990s, EU conditionality, multilevel bargaining between international and domestic interests dominated the reform process, overshadowing transnational learning and norm diffusion (Andonova 2003). To illuminate the shift in the dominant mechanisms of EU influence over domestic environmental politics and policies, the next two sections analyze air pollution regulations adopted in the Czech Republic and Poland in the course of the 1990s.[4]

Czech Air Pollution Policy

The reform of Czech air pollution policies was undertaken by the first postcommunist government of Czechoslovakia in 1990.[5] As in other postcommunist coun-

4. The analysis of the Czech and Polish cases is based on detailed case material presented in Andonova (2003).

5. Czechoslovakia split in 1992, and in 1993 the Czech Republic and Slovakia were established as independent countries. I refer to the federal government of Czechoslovakia when describing policy up to 1992. When describing the implementation of air pollution legislation, which proceeded largely after 1992, I refer to the experience of the Czech Republic.

tries, awareness of the environmental effects of communist-era industrialization was high in the aftermath of the democratic revolution. Czechoslovakia was one of the most industrialized socialist economies, relying heavily on highly polluting lignite coal for energy. The health effects of heavy air pollution, particularly in "hot spot" areas, were well publicized by the dissident movement and by international accounts that became widely available after 1989. Parts of Northern Bohemia in the Czech Republic, Lower Silesia in Poland, and Saxony in East Germany formed the infamous "Black Triangle" region, characterized by some of the heaviest concentration of air pollutants in Europe.

Public concern about the severity of the air pollution problem and its health effects motivated air pollution reforms early in the transition period. The first post-communist government included prominent activists including the Federal Minister of the Environment Josef Vavrousek and the Minister of the Environment of the Czech Republic Bedřich Moldan. The ruling Civic Forum–Public Against Violence coalition had proclaimed "the return to Europe" as its campaign slogan and leading foreign policy objective. Improved environmental performance was thus in line with the government's objectives of democratization and promotion of the country's image as a responsible citizen of Europe.

Czechoslovakia was party to the Long Range Transboundary Air Pollution (LRTAP) convention and its 1985 First Sulfur Protocol, which required a 30 percent reduction of 1980 sulfur emission levels by all European countries. However, as with the other former communist countries, Czechoslovakia had signed on to the accord to support the Soviet Union's strategic objective of *détente* with the West but had done little to reduce emissions of sulfur and other acidifying pollutants. The high international and domestic visibility of air pollution gave the proactive environmental administration of Czechoslovakia additional leverage to promote rapid reforms.

The strong domestic perception of a policy failure in managing air pollution, an entrepreneurial environmental administration, and the high salience of air pollution internationally created both a window of opportunity for policy reform and a strong motivation to seek policy lessons within the European community of states. The Rainbow Program of 1991, which outlined the national environmental strategy, emphasized health concerns, international reputation, and normative convergence with European environmental standards as leading considerations in setting priorities for reform (Ministry of the Environment of the Czech Republic 1991). Policymakers involved in the drafting and promulgation of air protection legislation in the early 1990s emphasized similar motivations.[6]

The Czechoslovak Act on Clean Air was one of the first pieces of environmental legislation introduced by the government. Federal Minister of the Environment of Czechoslovakia Josef Vavrousek was personally engaged in its drafting and assured political support for the legislation, capitalizing both on public concern

6. Author interviews with Bedřich Moldan and with representatives of Green Circle, November 1997.

Table 7.2 The 1988 Large Combustion Plant Directive: Emission limits for new sources

	Thermal capacity (MW)	SO2 (Mg/Nm³)	Desulfurization rate (%)	NOx (Mg/Nm³)	Dust (Mg/Nm³)
1. Solid fuels	50–100	2,000		650	100
	100–500	2,000–400	40 (100–167 MW) 40–90 (167–500 MW)	650	100
	>500	400	90	650	50
2. Liquid fuels	50–300	1,700		450	50
	300–500	1,700–400 linear decrease		450	50
	>500	400		450	50
3. Gaseous fuels				350	5
3.1. Gaseous fuels in general		35			
3.2. Liquefied gas		5			
3.3. Low calorific		800			

Source: European Council 1988, Directive 88/609/EEC, Annex III–VIII.

and the proclaimed desire of the government to move quickly to the policy styles and practices of Western Europe. According to close associates of the minister and participants in the policy drafting process, the Clean Air Act of 1991 was based on the German law on air pollution, considered one of the strictest in Europe.[7]

Germany had already successfully tackled an acid rain problem of similar magnitude to that in Czechoslovakia, and its legislation had strongly influenced EU regulations on emissions from large combustion sources. Moreover, the command and control, technology-based standards of German legislation were perceived as appropriated for the Czechoslovak context and corresponded to the priorities of the environmental administration, which sought rapid and visible reductions in polluting emissions from large power-generating utilities. As a consequence of these considerations, the air emission standards adopted by the Czechoslovak Clean Air Act of 1991 were almost identical to the ones set by the 1988 Large Combustion Plant Directive of the EU. If anything, Czechoslovak legislation was somewhat stricter in regulating emissions of smaller combustion units (see tables 7.2 and 7.3).

The Czech Republic adopted the 1991 Czechoslovak Clean Air Act after the split with Slovakia in 1992. The implementation of its provisions proceeded surprisingly quickly given the high technology and emission reduction standards it mandated at great cost to the electricity generation sector. In dealing with this powerful economic sector, the Ministry of the Environment capitalized on the early

7. Author interviews with Bedřich Moldan, at the Green Circle, and at the Air Protection Department of the Czech Ministry of the Environment, November 1997.

Table 7.3   Air emission standards for large combustion sources in the Czech Republic

	Thermal capacity MW	Solid pollutants mg/m³	SO₂ Mg/m³	NOx Mg/m³
Solid fuel	5–50	150	2,500	650
	50–300	100	1,700	650
	>300		500	650
Smelting boilers				1,100
Liquid fuels	5–50	100	1,700	450
	50–300	50	1,700	450
	>300	50	500	450
Gaseous fuels	5–50	10	35	200
	50–300	10	35	200
	>300	10	35	200

Source: Act on Clean Air of the Czech and Slovak Federal Republic (309/1991), Appendix 3.

political support in the Czech Republic for air protection regulation in line with West European standards. The government also ensured the cooperation of the electricity sector by granting policy concessions that made the implementation of pollution reductions more feasible. Such concessions included maintaining the monopolistic and vertically integrated structure of the electricity sector, increasing the share of nuclear-based electricity production through the completion of the Temelín nuclear power plant, and supporting investments in desulfurization equipment through international assistance and the resources of the national environmental fund. The strong governmental commitment to reintegration in Europe and the adoption of European norms also motivated industry to take a long-term perspective on regulatory reform and to cooperate with the government early in striking a deal on its own terms that would make implementation feasible (Andonova 2003).

Czechoslovakia and, later, the Czech Republic thus adopted legislation compatible with that of the EU early in the transition period, prior to any specific EU commitment to enlargement. The adoption of strict air pollution legislation also preceded the negotiation of the Europe-wide Second Sulfur Protocol (1994) under the LRTAP convention. As a consequence of the ability of a proactive environmental administration to lock in strong air pollution legislation in the early transition period and to negotiate incentives for its power industry to comply, by 1998, the year it started negotiations for EU accession, the Czech Republic achieved dramatic reduction in the emissions of acidifying pollutants. It overcomplied both with its own norms and with EU regulations on emissions from large combustion sources. In the period 1990–98, the Czech Republic reduced its SO2 emissions by 76 percent, its dust emissions by 86 percent, and its NOx emissions by 45 percent (Ministry of the Environment of the Czech Republic 1999, 2000, 2001). In the power sector alone, for the period 1993–98, the SO2 emissions dropped by 79 percent, dust emissions by 89 percent and NOx emissions by 56 percent (ČEZ

2002), while most utilities achieved compliance with technology standards compatible with those of the EU. That regulations compatible with EU legislation were implemented prior to the onset of accession negotiations, and that compliance exceeded EU and LRTAP standards—these indicate the weak impact of external incentives and bargaining in the Europeanization of Czech air pollutions standards.

The principal objective of EU membership had a clear impact on the Czechoslovak air pollution legislation of the early 1990s, but this influence materialized chiefly through policy diffusion and learning rather than through strict conditionality. There were domestic scope conditions that facilitated such lesson-drawing: policy dissatisfaction with air pollution, an active environmental administration engaged in a trans-European epistemic network, a search for policy models, a perceived transferability of rules of EU members and Germany in particular, and an ability of the government to both preempt opposition and compensate industrial interests that incurred a high cost of regulations. While lesson-drawing was probably the leading mechanism of incorporating EU air pollution rules in Czechoslovak legislation in 1991, the role of the EU was not entirely passive. Transboundary air pollution was an important concern of EU member states, which actively promoted air pollution mitigation policies and technology through technical assistance and political pressure, facilitating the process of social learning and policy diffusion.

Air Pollution Reforms in Poland

In the early 1990s, Poland, similar to the Czech Republic, inherited severe air pollution problems associated with communist industrialization and strong reliance on coal. Public support for the environment and for addressing air pollution was high. Poland had one of the best-organized dissident environmental movements, which took part in the Round Table negotiations that ended the communist regime and influenced the agenda of the first postcommunist Solidarity government. Thus, as in the Czech Republic, conditions for lesson-drawing and social learning existed in the early 1990s in Poland, including a perception of policy failures in managing the environment, an active search for new policy options by bureaucrats and epistemic communities, and a linkage of environmental reforms to democratic principles embodied by western democracies. However, these conditions did not suffice to induce the early adoption of EU air emission standards, as in the Czech Republic. Two domestic factors worked against the adoption of air emission regulations compatible with those of the EU. First, high adoption costs and inability of the government to circumvent the opposition of the politically influential power sector limited the transferability of rules. Secondly, concerns about cost effectiveness made models of regulation based on economic instruments more appropriate than the technology-based approach prevalent in EU environmental law.

The first postcommunist government initiated environmental reforms shortly after it came to power in 1990. It adopted the National Environmental Program in

1990 that outlined a broad strategy for reforms and institutional changes to strengthen the environmental protection system. Although the Polish environmental administration was actively engaged in policy learning and transnational policy diffusion, it chose to apply western regulatory models that were deemed to fit better domestic political and institutional conditions rather than seek early adherence to EU regulations. Poland adopted a regulatory style that was more flexible and emphasized the use of economic instruments, stronger institutional capacity, decentralization of regulatory authority, creation of a system of environmental funds, and increased enforcement capacity. The emphasis on decentralization and economic efficiency in the Polish environmental reforms was facilitated by the presence of western-trained environmental economists in the environmental administration in Poland (Andersson 1999). These policy circles were backed by IFIs, which also emphasized economic incentives as "win-win" solutions for many environmental problems. The World Bank in particular supported the early institutionalization of the Polish environmental reform with an environmental management loan of $18 million in 1990 (World Bank 1991).

The flexible regulatory approach emphasizing institutional capacity and cost-minimizing economic instruments also corresponded to the objective of the Polish environmental administration to design "implementable" regulations in consensual decision-making with industry. The electricity and coal production sectors were influential veto actors in Polish environmental reform, whose opposition to costly standards could not be ignored. In Czechoslovakia, the environmental administration was able to circumvent the veto of the power sector by capitalizing on high public concern and co-opting it with an energy policy deal. In Poland, the strong environmental concern of the early 1990s was not sufficient to overcome the opposition of the electricity sector to costly air emission standards.

The energy sector in Poland was highly unionized, with strong trade union ties to both left- and right-wing parties. Moreover, unlike in the Czech Republic, where the government and industry agreed on an energy policy that would decrease reliance on coal in the medium term and increase the share of nuclear power, such a deal was not an option in Poland. Because of the abundance of coal resources and their social importance, the fuel base of electricity generation in Poland was unlikely to change in the near future. Nuclear development was not publicly accepted. Immediately after the democratic changes, environmental groups succeeded in halting the only nuclear power project in the country started by the communist regime.

The anticipation of continued high reliance on coal made Poland unwilling to adopt wholesale the command and control standards of the EU, nor to ratify the Second Sulfur Protocol adopted in 1994. Instead, the country followed a more gradual and flexible approach to curbing air emissions from the power sector and other sources, emphasizing as in its broader environmental policy economic incentives and the capacity to support environmental investments.

In 1990, the Ministry of the Environment adopted an Ordinance on the Protection of Air (based on the provisions of the 1980 Act on Environmental Protection), which set specific air emission standards for combustion sources. These standards tended to be stricter for smaller combustion sources than the ones of the EU but were more lenient than European emission limits for dust and SO2 from the largest combustion sources with capacity of over 500 megawatts. This was an important concession to the power sector, as most of the electricity in Poland was produced by facilities with capacity greater than 500 megawatts. The 1990 ordinance also differed from European Community legislation in that it did not impose technology-based requirements for specific rates of desulfurization in combustion units, thus allowing greater flexibility in the mechanisms power plants could choose to comply with air protection regulations. The government and the World Bank sponsored a number of pilot projects that considered the implementation of a U.S.-style tradable permit scheme for acidifying emissions—a regulatory model not applied in EU regulations, but one that could substantially reduce the overall cost of emission reductions and the burden on some of the most polluting enterprises.

The Polish government also adopted a range of economic incentives to motivate the reduction of air emissions in the power sector. In the period 1990–92, the price of coal increased by more than 200 percent in dollar terms, electricity prices for industry tripled, and residential heating and electricity tariffs increased substantially. The fees for SO2 emissions also increased, reaching €85 per ton in 2000, one of the highest rates in Europe. The penalty for noncompliance with SO2 regulations was ten times higher, or about €850 per ton. The real increase in the fees and penalties for air emissions motivated a more proactive approach to emission abatement on the part of industry, and it had an important revenue-generating function that combined with other resources to create a strong system of environmental funds. The funds and other financing options enabled the government to subsidize investment in air pollution abatement equipment in the power sector and to maintain a dialogue with the sector for continued emission reductions.

As a consequence of both regulatory incentives and government support, the Polish electricity sector achieved consistent emission reductions throughout the 1990s, although not as dramatic as in the case of the Czech Republic. In 1996, the government concluded an agreement with the power sector for further reduction in SO2 emissions from power plants as a prerequisite for the country to meet its international obligations, including those associated with EU accession and compliance with LRTAP protocols. In the period 1990–98, Poland had reduced its total SO2 emissions by 41 percent, its NOx emissions by 23 percent, and its dust emissions by 55 percent (GUS 1997, 1998, 1999). For the same period, the power industry reduced SO2 emissions by 34 percent, NOx emission by 42 percent, and dust emissions by 85 percent.[8]

In the process of EU accession preparations, which intensified in the second half of the 1990s, Poland was required to continue its reform of the air protection

8. Calculated on the basis of emissions data provided by the Polish Power Grid Company in 2002.

system to approximate more closely the EU regulations, including the technology-based standards of the 1988 Large Combustion Plant Directive (Karaczun 1996; World Bank 1997, 1998). The European Commission also pushed informally for compliance with the Second Sulfur Protocol, as Poland was an important contributor to transboundary acidification. Faced with the task of adopting the EU air pollution *acquis* as an accession condition, Poland used technical support from the EU and the World Bank for cost assessments of alternative strategies for compliance with EU air pollution norms. These were intended as a tool for learning and consensus-building among domestic actors, the government, and the EU. Some of the studies took the notion of cost minimization seriously and concluded that allowing Poland some flexibility in the application of EU standards, such as the use of emissions trading or a temporary exemption of some of the strictest technology standards for power utilities, would reduce the cost of compliance (Energysys 1998; Krakow Academy of Economics 1996). Based on such assessments, Poland argued for a more flexible approach to compliance with EU standards that would allow it to delay the application of strict source-based standards to some of its installations built before the 1990s. Official estimates of the cost of compliance with EU air emission standards in Poland ranged from $1.5 billion to $10 billion, with the higher end of these estimates assuming a stricter interpretation of the EU *acquis* and the Second Sulfur Protocol (Council of Ministers of the Republic of Poland 2000).

Ultimately, however, Poland was hard-pressed by the EU to adopt standards that corresponded closely to the 1988 EU Large Combustion Plant Directive, with little opportunity to apply flexible mechanisms such as emissions trading. In effect, Poland had to "unlearn" some of the early lessons of cost minimization and economic flexibility, which did not fit the policy requirements of the EU. The EU saw close compliance with the 1988 Large Combustion Plant Directive as a necessary step for accession with a view to Poland's future ability to comply as a member country with an even stricter directive on emissions from large combustion sources that was in preparation in the late 1990s and adopted in 2001.

In 1998, the Polish Ministry of the Environment adopted two new air pollution regulations, which replaced the 1990 Ordinance on Air Protection. The 1998 Ordinance on the Emissions of Pollutants from Technological Processes and Technical Operations followed the requirements of the 1988 EU Large Combustion Plant Directive, but, unlike the EU directive, it did not introduce requirements for the application of Best Available Technology or specific desulfurization rates for large combustion units. In addition, while the EU directive applies to all sources that obtained a construction permit after 1987, the cut-off date in the Polish regulation was 28 March 1990. This was a concession to the power industry, which bargained for an even later cut-off date of 1996. The emission standards for "new sources," e.g. combustion units built after the cut-off date, were significantly stricter than the standards for existing sources and were expected to pose difficulties for plants built between 1987 and 1996. In 2001, the 1998 ordinance on air emissions was amended to achieve even closer alignment with EU provisions. While the 2001 ordinance still defines new and old combustion sources differently from the EU Large Combustion Plant Directive, it mandates that all sources (old and new) that have obtained a construction permit after 1987 must comply with standards compatible with those of the 1988 Large Combustion Plant Directive starting in January 2003.

The analysis of air pollution reforms in Poland illustrates unambiguously the prevalence of the logic of conditionality as a mechanism of EU environmental influence. During the early 1990s, Poland had greater leeway to pick and choose from a wider menu of policy lessons and instruments promoted by international institutions. But as accession negotiations gained speed, Poland became considerably more constrained by the EU model of regulations, even in instances where other policy instruments were deemed better suited for the national context. As accession negotiations progressed, both the determinacy and credibility of environmental conditions for accession increased, as did the power of the EU to offer and withdraw rewards. The size of domestic costs of the adoption of EU air emission standards also appeared lower in the late 1990s as a result of earlier regulations and government subsidies to achieve a consistent reduction of air pollution emissions in the electricity generation sector. Ultimately, the adoption of EU air pollution rules was dominated by hard strategic negotiations among multiple interests at the international and domestic levels.

There is little dispute that the aspiration of the CEECs to join the EU has exerted a considerable influence on the policy agendas of candidate states. I set out to examine the mechanisms of EU influence in the area of environmental policy. More specifically, I sought to determine the relevance of the external incentives model against two alternative models emphasizing lesson-drawing and social learning as mechanisms of international influence. I argue that the lesson-drawing and social learning logic prevailed in the early 1990s, when CEECs faced fewer constraints in seeking policy tools to mend their ailing environments and multiple international institutions were eager to offer advice and assistance to promote western regulations. However, the logic of external incentives became dominant later in the decade as accession preparations and negotiations with the EU accelerated. The analysis used the suggested temporal variation in the force of normative and rationalist factors to explore empirically their significance in two broad institutional frameworks of European environmental cooperation (the Environment for Europe process and the EU pre-accession cooperation) and in two cases of national policy reform (the adoption of EU air emission regulations in the Czech Republic and Poland).

The empirical material demonstrates that constitutive and interest-based mechanisms of international influence are not truly "alternative," as they often coexist in a given institutional setting. Thus, the staunch theoretical juxtaposition of the two perspectives may actually be misleading rather than illuminate international relations, a point recognized recently by other scholars of institutions as well

(Checkel 1997; Schimmelfennig 2001). In the Environment for Europe process described in this chapter, while most outcomes can be explained primarily in terms of normative diffusion, the process was not at all devoid of strategic consideration and bargaining, although the latter produced few measurable results. While conditionality and bargaining were dominant in the EU accession cooperation, programs of transnational norm diffusion, learning, and consensus building have supported the bargaining process and facilitated a greater overall level of adoption of the EU environmental *acquis*. Institutional influence is thus enhanced when norm diffusion and external incentives mechanisms reinforce each other to shape the behavior of states, an interactive effect that deserves further exploration and research (see also Cowles, Caporaso, and Risse 2001; Eising 2002; Héritier et al. 2001; Tallberg 2002).

The simultaneous presence of constitutive and rationalist mechanisms of institutional influence, however, often poses the problem of disentangling empirically their relative significance. Constructivists in particular have been challenged by rationalist approaches for failure to tackle empirically the null hypothesis of their argument, e.g., that despite the presence of mechanisms of constitutive influence their measurable impact is small if any and subordinated to rationalist interests and calculations. This study demonstrates that by specifying the conditions for prevalence and influence of mechanisms of institutional influence we can design studies to test their independent effects.

The cases of EU accession assistance and conditionality for policy reforms presented in this chapter unveiled the dominance of external incentives and constraints by demonstrating that norm diffusion mechanisms were often designed to serve strategic objectives and were trumped by powerful opposing interests. The Environment for Europe process and Czech air pollution reforms, by contrast, illuminated some of the conditions for strong normative influence of international institutions. Notable in these two cases is that transnational normative diffusion through lesson-drawing and social learning produced measurable policy results despite incongruence with strong material interests and in the absence of well-defined strategic and material incentives. What facilitated transnational normative influence in these cases were some of the conditions identified in other instances of international norm diffusion: perceived policy failures that opened windows of opportunity for learning, active transnational entrepreneurship on the part of policymakers and epistemic communities, pressure to incorporate the norms of groups and institutions to which states belong or aspire to join, close correspondence between domestic priorities and the imported policy lesson, and relatively weak or diffuse conditionality or linkage with material interests. The condition of weak or diffuse conditionality that emerged from the cases of strong normative diffusion presented in this chapter has been rarely recognized in the constructivist literature and deserves further empirical exploration using either quantitative methods to disentangle diffusion and conditionality effects in a large number of controlled cases, or temporal analyses to examine the force of each mechanism in different stages of international regime evolution.

CHAPTER EIGHT

The Transfer of EU Social Policy to Poland and Hungary

Beate Sissenich

E conomic disparities between old and new members of the European Union (EU) have never been as vast as when eight Central and Eastern European countries (CEECs) joined in 2004. In 1998, the average GDP per capita of these new entrants was 44 percent of the EU level.[1] Economic projections indicate that it will take these countries anywhere from one year (Slovenia) to thirty-three years (Poland) to reach three quarters of the per capita GDP of current EU member states (Commission DG for Economic and Financial Affairs 2001b). Given this income gap, member states and organized labor have called for speedy implementation of the social *acquis* in the CEECs. This chapter examines the adoption of EU social policy by Poland and Hungary. Both have consistently ranked among the most advanced candidates and therefore constitute most likely cases of compliance with EU rules. By focusing on an existing EU policy and its transfer to candidate countries, my investigation begins from a supply-side perspective and concentrates on those mechanisms of "Europeanization" that entail the EU's active promotion of rules—external incentives and social learning.

I start by spelling out expectations of both models and identifying factors that favor either external incentives or social learning. This discussion is summarized

I gratefully acknowledge the support provided by the following institutions: the Peace Studies Program and Institute for European Studies at Cornell University, European Trade Union Institute (Brussels), Central European University (Budapest and Warsaw), the Max Planck Institute for the Study of Societies (Cologne), the Institute for Social and Economic Research and Policy at Columbia University, and the International Dissertation Field Research Fellowship Program of the Social Science Research Council. I thank the numerous interviewees who graciously shared their time and insights with me. Uli Sedelmeier, Frank Schimmelfennig, and Dorota Dakowska provided useful comments on this chapter.

1. By contrast, Spain, Portugal, and Greece had an average per capita GDP of 66 percent of EC members in 1980 (Commission DG for Economic and Financial Affairs 2001a).

in table 8.1. Because social policy comprises three distinct areas, my analysis is cross-sectional in terms of policies *and* countries. I show that, consistent with the external incentives model, adoption of the social *acquis* in both countries has focused on approximating secondary legislation, with behavioral adoption lagging far behind. But contrary to the external incentives model, local stakeholders have not in any way responded to the opportunities and constraints inherent in EU social policy. Limited organizational resources and EU ambiguity about stakeholder involvement explain why the social *acquis* has failed to alter state-society relations despite its inherent potential. Evidence comes from official documents and interviews with EU and government officials as well as trade union and employer representatives conducted between 1999 and 2001.

Transferring EU Social Policy Eastward: External Incentives versus Social Learning

Which mechanism operates in rule adoption depends in part on the form and substance of these rules—in other words, on *rule density* and *rule clarity/consistency*. All else being equal, external incentives are more likely to operate in the case of hard legislation that spells out the responsibility of national governments than in the case of practices that lack specific directions for national institutions. In the latter case, social learning might be a more effective transfer mechanism. But there are other factors to consider, as Schimmelfennig and Sedelmeier point out (chapter 1). The *credibility* of external incentives depends on the salience of the policy area, the cost of enforcement for the EU, consistency, willingness to reward compliance, and available information on rule infractions. *Adoption costs* faced by accession candidates are affected by payoffs that alternative courses of action might generate, as well as by domestic opposition. *Perceptions of EU policy as legitimate* facilitate social learning.

Determinacy of Rules (External Incentives and Social Learning)

The legal basis of EU social policy consists of the Treaty on European Union (TEU) and the Treaty Establishing the European Community (TEC).[2] Treaty-based social and employment provisions relate to the free movement of workers, employment policy, social policy, the promotion of economic and social cohesion,

---

2. Article 2 of TEU calls for the Union to promote "economic and social progress which is balanced and sustainable" and for the "strengthening of economic and social cohesion." Article 2 of TEC lists among Community goals a "high level of employment and social protection, equality between men and women, . . . raising the standard of living and the quality of life, and economic and social cohesion and solidarity among the Member States." As specified in Article 3 of TEC, the activities of the Community include measures ensuring the free movement of persons, a strategy to coordinate member state employment policies, a European Social Fund, increasing economic and social cohesion, health protection, and contributions to education and training. Article 13 enables the Council to take action against discrimination based on sex, race, ethnic origin, religion, belief, disability, age, or sexual orientation.

and the protection of health. Note that EU social policy is strictly regulatory; it does not involve any redistributive or distributive dimensions. In other words, the EU does not constitute a welfare state; its social policy does not generate welfare expenditures.

There are three main components of EU social policy: secondary legislation, policies requiring member state coordination, and European social dialogue. First, treaty law serves as the basis for secondary EU legislation, in particular directives that require transposition into national law and implementation by member states. Chapter 13 in the accession negotiations, which concerns employment and social affairs, contains legislation on labor relations, equal treatment, workplace health and safety, the coordination of social security systems for migrant workers, public health, and the European Monitoring Center on Racism and Xenophobia.[3] Second, EU employment guidelines require the coordination of member state policies around annual guidelines set jointly by the member states.

Finally, European social dialogue is a procedure for peak-level consultations between European-level employer and labor organizations with the option of concluding agreements that will lead to EU legislation. Such legislation may then be implemented in the member states by labor and employers themselves or through legal transposition. Though the social dialogue is an EU-level procedure, it does implicitly require functioning structures of socioeconomic interest representation at the national level. Yet member states do not share a single model of industrial relations and socioeconomic consultation but retain nationally specific structures and practices. Hence, the Commission's case for adjusting any national social dialogue to EU-level practices is functional rather than legal, which limits the scope for EU sanctions against noncompliant candidates.

All else being equal, according to the external incentives model, rule determinacy makes the adoption of secondary social legislation highly probable: Expectations for rule adoption are outlined in EU law and further specified in court rulings. Compliance can be measured. Noncompliance may result in prolonged negotiations and, in the extreme case, deferred accession. After accession, noncompliance is likely to generate infringement proceedings and court action. Employment coordination is different. Though this area of social policy requires a certain level of institutional capacity, there are no binding results. Without clearly specified expectations, noncompliance is difficult to detect. Nor does EU employment policy prescribe any sanctioning mechanisms for national noncompliance. Therefore, the external incentives model would predict a lower level of adoption in employment policy than in secondary legislation. As for social dialogue, the absence of legally defined member state responsibilities suggests low rule adoption, as candidates are

---

3. Equal treatment legislation focuses on sex equality in the workplace as relevant to pay, occupational social security, self-employment, pregnancy and motherhood, parental leave, and the burden of proof in cases of sex discrimination. Recent secondary legislation expands the concept of equal treatment from gender relations to racial and ethnic origin, religion and belief, disability, age, and sexual orientation.

kept guessing as to what constitutes an appropriate arrangement for social dialogue. The Commission may express disapproval of existing institutions without being able to offer candidates any positive guidelines to work with.

Slightly different predictions follow from rule determinacy under the model of *social learning*. Here, questions of legitimacy may significantly interfere with rule determinacy and thus adoption. While the clarity of secondary legislation does facilitate its adoption under social learning, the fact that all of it was made by and for (mostly advanced) capitalist democracies may well detract from its legitimacy as perceived by candidate countries. The looseness of rules in employment policy and especially social dialogue would enable candidates to explore what arrangements best suit their own needs, whereas secondary legislation might be overly constraining. Thus, in the social learning model, rule determinacy suggests that rule adoption is more likely in social dialogue and employment policy than in secondary legislation.

In sum, rule density is considerable across all three components of EU social policy, though higher in secondary legislation than in employment policy and social dialogue. But rule clarity varies. Where there is secondary legislation, rules are well-specified (though not always eagerly followed by member states, as we will see). In employment policy, by contrast, rules have emerged only recently. Though they do specify government responsibilities, they lack depth. Social dialogue is the most interesting aspect of social policy, because rule density at the European level is high, but rules for government conduct are vague and grounded in functional expectations rather than in explicit law. Consequently, the external incentives model predicts the highest level of rule adoption in secondary social legislation, followed by employment policy and social dialogue. Social learning predicts a higher level of rule adoption where rules are loose, i.e. in employment policy and social dialogue, than in secondary legislation, where rules may be overly rigid.

Credibility of Conditionality (External Incentives)

How likely is the EU to wield the ultimate threat of denied entry if a candidate does not comply with its social policy? The answer to that depends on the political salience of social policy in the EU, on competing rules that may be in effect elsewhere, on the EU's willingness to reward compliance, and on its ability to monitor infractions. The evidence on social policy salience is mixed (Sissenich 2002b, 2003). On the one hand, EU citizens are highly concerned about the social and economic implications of European integration and, in contrast to their government leaders, tend to consider enlargement a low priority. On the other hand, there is no evidence that EU citizens view the existing social *acquis* as crucial to alleviating their concerns. One European-level stakeholder group, the European Trade Union Confederation (ETUC), endorsed enlargement early on and has called for the full implementation of the social *acquis* in the candidate countries and the swift closing of income gaps between Eastern and Western Europe (ETUC 1999, 2000).

Despite the mixed salience of EU social policy in the current member states, the Commission has not hesitated to criticize repeatedly the lagging adoption of the social *acquis* in all candidate countries. In the case of Hungary, the Orbán government's revamping of existing tripartite institutions led to protracted negotiations with the EU on the issue of social dialogue. Yet notwithstanding outspoken EU criticism of candidates' shortfalls in social dialogue, Commission officials readily admit that noncompliance in social policy is unlikely to trigger a response as drastic as delayed admission into the EU. They argue that some slippage in implementation is less disruptive than negotiations for transition periods that might result if the Commission were to insist on full adoption of the social *acquis* at once.[4]

Credibility also suffers if there are competing rules from other sources with which countries must also comply. This is because competing and contradictory commitments make enforcement less likely. In the case of social policy, EU legislation exceeds the requirements of other relevant international organizations. The EU's closest competitor in this field, the International Labor Organization (ILO), establishes minimum social standards that constitute the lowest common denominator between advanced and less developed countries. Because the current and future EU is less economically diverse than the ILO's members, in most instances EU policy tends to be more restrictive than ILO standards. Exceptions deal with gender-specific rules, where ILO conventions protect women against a limited set of working conditions while EU rules call for sex equality in the workplace. However, since the benefits of ILO membership do not override the more far-reaching payoffs of EU membership, candidates have found it in their interest to reconcile any gaps between ILO and EU requirements in favor of EU law.

Finally, the EU's ability to actually monitor infractions depends on candidate country cooperation and capacity, specifically in health and safety inspection. Hence, the EU has invested in building up candidates' administrative capacity in all areas of the *acquis*. The Commission also relies on labor and employer organizations for gathering information on compliance and expects these actors to be actively involved in the implementation of social policy. Monitoring capacity is likely to vary across sectors and enterprises and will be least effective with respect to small and medium-sized enterprises. One might add that the Union's enforcement record for social legislation in the member states is rather poor.[5]

Overall, accession conditionality is not very credible in social policy. Though citizens worry about social costs of European integration, there is no evidence that this translates into direct public pressure for candidates' compliance with the social *acquis*. Similarly, though the question of free labor mobility is highly politicized in some member states, this is not the case for social policy as such. The low political salience of social policy combined with patchy monitoring capacity suggests

---

4. Author interviews with Commission officials, 20 March 2001 and 11 April 2001 (Brussels).

5. In 2000, social policy accounted for 3.7 percent of all directives, but for 5 percent of all infringement proceedings against member states (Sissenich 2003, 110).

that conditionality is hardly credible in social policy, especially with respect to employment coordination and social dialogue. While there are few competing commitments to other international organizations in this field, the likelihood that the EU would disrupt the enlargement process because of poor compliance in social policy is slim indeed.

Adoption Costs and Benefits (External Incentives)

How costly is adoption of the social *acquis* for the candidate countries? What benefits might candidates obtain by implementing the social *acquis*—and what benefits by *not* doing so? What might be the domestic political fallout of rapid compliance? How many and what kinds of actors need to consent to rule adoption in social policy? As per the rules of EU social policy and the Commission's stated preferences, employer and labor organizations should be involved in the implementation of the social *acquis*, including hard legislation. Thus, by granting domestic actors an explicit role in rule adoption, the social *acquis* might very well have the effect of empowering domestic actors. This is most obvious with respect to social dialogue, but it should apply to substantive policies as well, notably employment coordination and secondary legislation.

Empowerment of domestic actors does not mean, of course, that nonstate actors (NSAs) embrace all substantive elements of EU social policy. Hard legislation may impose costs on employers that have implications for workers as well. Health and safety legislation, in particular, may require investment in expensive new equipment, which may be particularly challenging for small and medium-sized enterprises. Government agencies may oppose elements of social legislation because they are difficult to implement. While workers have an interest in occupational health and safety, they are unlikely to accept job losses if these were to result from overly costly EU legislation. On the other hand, some elements of secondary social legislation might resonate with labor interests. We would therefore expect employer organizations to oppose costly health and safety legislation, while trade unions should back laws implementing sex equality in the workplace, labor consultation, and restrictions on working time. Both employers and labor can be expected to endorse the soft elements of the *acquis*—employment policy and social dialogue. Specifically, regular and meaningful consultation with the government would upgrade the potential input of both sides in policymaking. Overall, examining costs and benefits of the social *acquis* to domestic actors suggests that both employers and labor are likely to promote the adoption of EU rules in employment policy and social dialogue. In secondary social legislation, by contrast, we would expect employers to resist costly rules, while trade unions should favor rule adoption. Note that for governments, EU social policy does not constitute a heavy budget item, though some investment is necessary in improving inspection capacities.[6]

---

6. Compared with other sectors such as environment, the investment needed in implementing EU social policy is minor.

Perceived Legitimacy and Domestic Resonance of EU Social Policy
(Social Learning)

Though candidate countries have had no say in shaping existing EU rules, they are more likely to adopt these rules if they perceive them as legitimate, internally coherent, and consistent with values of the European Union (see Schimmelfennig and Sedelmeier, chapter 1). CEEC officials are perfectly well aware that they may be held to more stringent standards than member states. Still, following the logic of appropriateness, evidence of flagrant disregard for EU social policy in the member states would weaken their willingness to take on EU rules. Indeed, a poor record of member state compliance affects perceptions of legitimacy as much as it affects credibility in the external incentives model. Practices that are inconsistent with stated values are likely to communicate to candidate countries that member states view social policy as a low priority. On the other hand, candidate countries tend to argue that their own legislation is already in line with the hard social *acquis* and therefore poses no fundamental problems for them. As for social dialogue, given that national practices vary among member states, candidate governments view Commission interference with domestic tripartism as problematic. Orbán's government in Hungary (1998–2002) deliberately sought to replace existing tripartite institutions with a more pluralistic and voluntaristic form of interest representation. For his center-right coalition, EU demands for tripartite and bipartite social dialogue carried little weight.

For socioeconomic stakeholders (including employers) and some elites in the candidate countries, social dialogue holds symbolic appeal. Seeking to identify with perceived "European" values, CEE political leaders and trade unionists sometimes evoke the "European social model"—but generally in reference to advanced capitalist welfare states rather than EU social policy. Overall, candidate governments tend to find the social *acquis* unproblematic but also rather insignificant compared with other EU policies. With the exception of the Orbán government, candidate countries tend to endorse some abstract form of social dialogue but fail to practice it in day-to-day policy formation. Societal stakeholders tend to express support for social dialogue and frustration with their governments' limited commitment to tripartite consultation. However, they strongly resent attempts by European-level confederations to consolidate their fragmented organizational landscapes. When European umbrella organizations push for greater cooperation among national groups, domestic stakeholders in the candidate countries regard as illegitimate intrusions by West Europeans who do not understand the ideological, organizational, and historical complexities of politics in new democracies.

Table 8.1 sums up this discussion of factors promoting rule adoption in the external incentives and/or social learning models. *Rule determinacy* varies within social policy, but it is particularly weak in the case of social dialogue. For the external incentives model, this implies that we would expect the greatest degree of adoption in secondary legislation and the lowest degree of adoption in social dialogue. In the social learning model, by contrast, the absence of clearly specified legal

Table 8.1 Factors promoting rule adoption based on external incentives or social learning and expected outcomes

	Secondary legislation (SL)	Employment policy (EP)	Social dialogue (SD)	Expected degree of rule adoption (*external incentives*)	Expected degree of rule adoption (*social learning*)
Determinacy of rules	High	Medium	Low	SL: high EP: medium SD: low	SL: medium EP: medium. SD: high
Credibility of conditionality	Low-medium (criticism in Regular Reports, institution-building measures)	Low	Low (criticism in Regular Reports, protracted negotiations, but entry not conditional on compliance)	SL/EP/SD: low	N/A
Adoption costs/benefits	Potentially considerable costs for small and medium enterprises, as well as for government agencies; medium potential benefits for labor	Low costs; medium to high benefits for labor and employers	Low costs and high benefits for labor and employers. Medium costs and benefits for government.	SL: low EP: medium-high SD: high	N/A
Perceived legitimacy of EU rules and domestic resonance	Medium	High	Medium-high	N/A	SL: medium-low EP: medium-high SD: medium-high

obligations in social dialogue allows candidate countries to modify this procedure to suit their own needs and practices, whereas secondary legislation may be too constraining and therefore elicit less adoption, with employment policy somewhere in between. Compared to some other policy areas, the *credibility of accession conditionality* in social policy is rather low, partly because it is less politically salient and barely relevant to addressing the Union's real socioeconomic problems. The *costs of adopting EU social policy* are generally considered low, though in the case of secondary legislation they are not really known and might in fact be considerable. Trade unions might *benefit* from employment policy, social dialogue, and even secondary legislation. Employers can expect to benefit from employment policy and social dialogue, but less from social legislation. For governments, by contrast, social dialogue would require time-consuming negotiations with stakeholders, which might constitute a problem for the rapid transformation necessary before accession. Finally, candidate countries tend to *consider EU social policy legitimate* and consistent with their own practices but resent outside interference in areas in which EU rules are insufficiently specific or frequently violated by member states. Secondary legislation, which reflects the needs of advanced capitalist countries, may resonate less with candidate countries than do employment policy and social dialogue. To the extent that candidates acknowledge gaps between their own arrangements and EU policy, they can easily point to similar gaps in member states in this area. Overall, these factors add up to a scenario in which the external incentives model would predict formal compliance with all three components but possible lags in behavioral adoption, especially due to contestation over costly legislation and government rejection of social dialogue. Social learning, by contrast, would predict discursive, formal, and behavioral adoption of social dialogue and possibly employment policy but little adoption (in any form) of secondary legislation.

Outcomes: Degree and Form of Rule Adoption

I will show in this section that the empirical record favors the external incentives model, albeit with some unexpected variations. Given that strict EU rule enforcement is less likely in areas that lack political salience in member states, we should not be surprised that candidates have focused on *formal* adoption. Consistent with the external incentives model, candidates have privileged secondary legislation, the social policy component with the highest level of rule determinacy, and been slow to improve social dialogue, the area in which national responsibilities are least clear.

But contrary to external incentives predictions, there are no strong stakeholder preferences for or against EU social policy. Despite the potential costs of secondary social legislation, employers in both Poland and Hungary remain largely indifferent. For its part, labor has not seized upon any element of substantive social legislation, presumably because EU directives do not address the socioeconomic concerns of workers in transition economies. Both labor and employers are in favor of EU accession in general and the social *acquis* in particular but tend to be poorly informed about its content. Both sides also endorse employment policy but have not identified an active role for themselves. Overall, the actual response to social policy transfer, by societal stakeholders as much as by government, has been lukewarm.

The following sections discuss rule adoption in each of the three components of social policy. Social dialogue has the greatest potential for altering state-society relations but has produced the least amount of change in the CEECs. I argue that social dialogue suffers from more than just the unwillingness of governments to include stakeholders in the policy process. Labor and employer organizations are ill-equipped for participating in policymaking and implementation. At the same time, the EU sends contradictory signals by rewarding the candidates' executive-driven approach to policy reform and accession preparations while insisting on social dialogue.

Adopting EU Secondary Social Law

Hungary has moved more swiftly and consistently than Poland in formally adopting EU social legislation. The Commission's 2001 Regular Report on Hungary noted "considerable progress" in adopting EU social and employment policy, particularly in transposing directives on labor relations, equal pay and the burden of proof in cases of sex discrimination, and various areas of health and safety (Commission 2001b, 60). According to Hungary's 2001 National Program for the Adoption of the *Acquis* (NPAA), roughly half of EU secondary law on social and employment policy was in effect in Hungary by mid-2001 (Hungarian Ministry of Foreign Affairs 2001). Three directives impose particularly high costs on employers and were scheduled for transposition only in the last year before accession.[7]

About Poland, the Commission's 2001 report noted "some progress" in the area of social and employment policy. Legal harmonization had progressed on working time, equal treatment, and certain aspects of health and safety. Nevertheless, the bulk of Polish law remained unaligned with EU social directives (Commission 2001c). Poland's NPAA indicated that even where harmonization had taken place, the new laws would not take effect until 2003, making implementation and enforcement rather difficult in the run-up to accession. Though Poland's pace of legal harmonization might seem slow, the government made considerable efforts after a negative Commission report in 2000 (Commission 2000b).

Implementation, i.e. behavioral adoption, of EU law is the responsibility of member states. In general, the EU provides little guidance on how states may achieve the required results. This leaves much room for slippage (Duina 1999; Haas 1998; Knill and Lenschow 1999; Mény et al. 1996, 1–24; Tallberg 2002; Vervaele 1999). Without binding institutional prerequisites, the Commission evaluates

---

7. The three directives are on display screens, the manual handling of loads, and the organization of working time with respect to transport (90/269/EEC, 90/270/EEC, and 93/104/EC). Author interviews, 23 February and 13 March 2000 (Budapest). See also Lantos (1997).

candidates based on qualitative criteria that consider the practical implications of the *acquis.*[8] An informal Commission document details the agencies and procedures required by each chapter under negotiation and explicitly calls for NSAs to be involved in implementing Community social law (Commission 2001a, 45–47).

In both countries, implementation capacity lags behind legal harmonization. Hungary's NPAA offers more information than Poland's on present and future activities to implement EU law. Poland's program focuses entirely on future measures and lacks specificity—a telltale sign of discursive but not behavioral adoption. Largely missing at this point is the active involvement of stakeholders (employers and trade unions) in implementing health and safety legislation, a gap that will likely compromise the laws' effectiveness in both countries. Tables 8.2, 8.3, and 8.4 detail planned or ongoing implementation measures for labor law, equal opportunity legislation, and workplace health and safety in both countries. Poland's discursive commitment to raise awareness among stakeholders contrasts with Hungary's hands-on approach to enhancing institutional capacity by training staff and improving technical infrastructure (Hungarian Ministry of Foreign Affairs 2001; Republic of Poland 2001, ch. 13).

Companies and employer organizations thus far know very little about EU legislation and hence lack preferences about specific directives (Eurochambres 2001). For both government and stakeholders, it is often difficult to assess the impact of individual health and safety directives, not only because of the novelty of the task, but also because costs that may be trivial and hard to trace at the micro-level may nevertheless add up to significant amounts in the aggregate. Small and medium-sized enterprises are likely to suffer most from costly EU laws.[9] Poland has recruited French technical assistance for developing methods of impact analysis to justify departures from the *acquis.* While this may look like a subversive use of PHARE funds, pre-accession advisors from member states argue that the benefits of developing impact assessment methods far outweigh the costs of a candidate's temporary noncompliance.[10]

In sum, both Poland and Hungary have concentrated on formal rule adoption. Implementation remains questionable and suffers from inadequate institutional capacity and the absence of stakeholder input. Hungary has advanced faster than Poland in both formal and behavioral adoption.

Adopting EU Employment Policy

Employment policy is the least controversial aspect of the social *acquis* in the enlargement process, even though active employment policy requires considerable

8. Author interviews, 7 and 27 March 2001 (Brussels).

9. Small and medium-sized enterprises tend to account for most new jobs in the region. In Poland, 99 percent of enterprises are small and medium-sized and contribute 45 percent of GDP; enterprises of up to 250 employees account for over 60 percent of employment (Republic of Poland and European Commission 2001, 3; OECD 2001, 75).

10. Author interviews, 8 and 10 November 2000 (Warsaw).

Table 8.2   Adoption of EU labor law

	Poland	Hungary
Formal adoption	• four directives transposed (in force in 2003) • legislation in preparation for four directives	• five directives in effect • legislation in preparation for six directives
Behavioral adoption	• no institutional changes planned • information campaign on new legislation • budget: €51,000 (2001–2002)	• training for labor inspectors and judges • staff increases in National Labor Inspectorate and labor courts • upgrading information technology • budget: €1.4 million (2000–2002)

Sources: Hungarian Ministry of Foreign Affairs 2001; Republic of Poland 2001.
Notes: There are eleven directives in labor law. Exchange rates: €1 = PLN 4.62; €1 = HUF 272.

Table 8.3   Adoption of directives on equal opportunities for men and women

	Poland	Hungary
Formal adoption	• one directive transposed (in force in 2003); • legislation in preparation for three directives	• two directives in effect; • legislation in preparation for four directives
Behavioral adoption	• raising awareness among social partners and others implementing the new legislation • no budget allocation specified	• upgrading human resources in Ministry for Social and Family Affairs • improving technical infrastructure in Ministry for Social and Family Affairs • audit programs to monitor companies • pilot projects (with PHARE funding) to reintegrate women into the workforce • participation in Community Action Program • NGO support • promotion of atypical forms of employment in social and childcare services • budget: €2.9 million (2000–2004)

Sources: Hungarian Ministry of Foreign Affairs 2001; Republic of Poland 2001.
Note: There are ten directives on equal treatment.

administrative efforts and labor market institutions capable of cooperation with multiple government agencies (Commission 2001a). Institutionally, EU employment policy involves coordination rather than harmonization. Candidate countries have gathered extensive experience in employment policy during the transformation period and drawn up national action plans similar to those now used in the EU. The EU concluded Joint Employment Policy Assessments with Hungary and Poland in 2001, a voluntary exercise that the candidate countries welcomed because it allowed them to demonstrate their competence in this area. Governing elites in

Table 8.4   Adoption of directives on health and safety in the workplace

	Poland	Hungary
Formal adoption	• eight directives transposed (in force 2001–2003) • legislation in preparation for seven directives	• twenty directives in effect • legislation in preparation for six directives
Behavioral adoption	• improved funding for ministerial agencies responsible for legal harmonization and implementation • information and training for social partners and health and safety personnel • development of methods for assessing risk and ascertaining conformity with EU law • budget: €3.5 million (2001–2002)	• establishment of a shared database for three government agencies in charge of workplace health and safety • information for social partners and small and medium enterprises • training of inspectors and workplace hygiene experts • impact studies for individual directives • staff increases • budget: €2.8 million (2001–2002)

Sources: Hungarian Ministry of Foreign Affairs 2001; Republic of Poland 2001.
Note: There are thirty-one directives on health and safety in the workplace.

the EU, meanwhile, are eager to see unemployment in the CEECs reduced so that electorates have less reason to fear low-wage competition from the East.[11]

The Joint Assessments analyze developments in the labor market. Based on this evaluation, the candidate countries commit to certain priorities in employment policy. These commitments do not have the status of legal obligations but will be subject to Commission monitoring. Discursive commitments, formal adoption, and implementing measures are summarized in table 8.5.

Policy compatibility and the relative lack of burdensome demands by the EU have made employment policy coordination an uncomplicated exercise, despite considerable administrative implications. Candidates retain much room to set their own priorities, as table 8.5 demonstrates. Hungary's approach has been more specific and practical than Poland's and therefore has greater potential for actually yielding benefits.[12]

Adopting and Improving Social Dialogue

Concerning social dialogue, the reality has diverged from the expectations of both theoretical models. Stakeholders have had little substantive input in the accession process. There are several reasons for this: First, speed and complexity of accession preparations make democratic deliberations challenging even for well-intentioned governments. Second, employers in particular tend to be fragmented and poorly organized and have often had few incentives to coordinate their efforts.

11. Author interview, 20 March 2001 (Brussels).
12. Whereas Hungary has allocated specific amounts of money for employment policy approximation, Poland has not.

Table 8.5 Employment policy priorities and implementation

	Poland	Hungary
Discursive and formal adoption: policy priorities	• complete reform of education system • establish coherent adult/continuing education system • expand legislation and enforcement against discrimination based on gender • improve coordination of tax and social benefit public sector structures to create jobs and reintegrate long-term unemployed • improve regional and local housing markets and infrastructure	• reform tax and social benefit structures to bring informal economy into mainstream • improve loan facilities for small and medium enterprises • reduce wage gap between private and public sector to attract better staff in public sector • intensified social partner involvement in Labor Market Fund and National Labor Council, especially in flexible and responsible wage formation
Behavioral adoption	• decentralization of Public Employment Service • intensified social partner involvement in Public Employment Service, Pact for Employment, and Tripartite Commission • Commission criticism regarding human resource technological shortages in labor offices	• since 1996 use of annual employment guidelines, since 2000 oriented toward European employment guidelines • advanced system of statistical monitoring of labor market • modernize Public Employment Service, i.e. improve information flow on labor supply and demand • employment programs targeting marginalized groups (youth, Roma) • budget: €6.1 million

Sources: Republic of Poland and European Commission 2001; Republic of Hungary and European Commission 2001; Hungarian Ministry of Foreign Affairs 2001.

For their part, unions, while better organized, are also mired in rivalry. Third, the impact of EU legislation is difficult to estimate and hinges on a basic level of information among social partners. Each individual health and safety directive may impose minimal costs, but combined effects may be very expensive. Whereas multinational subsidiaries tend to comply with EU law, small and medium-sized enterprises struggle with the constantly changing legal environment and the resulting lack of coherence.[13] Consequently, employers in the CEECs have little knowledge of EU law, as a recent survey shows (Eurochambres 2001). Lack of knowledge about legal requirements combines with uncertainty of outcomes to make employer resistance to the social *acquis* unlikely. To both employers and labor, employment policy and social dialogue tend to be more important than secondary social legislation. Both employers and trade unions tend to be dissatisfied with social dialogue in their countries, in particular with the lack of consultation on EU accession. Given the Commission's repeated criticisms of social dialogue in both Poland and Hungary, it is surprising that neither labor nor employers has taken advantage of Commission pressure to strengthen their own position vis-à-vis the government.

Social dialogue has attracted the most explicit criticism from the Commission, compared to other social policy components. The Commission has consistently used its Regular Reports to exert pressure on CEEC governments. Social dialogue thus illustrates the limits of rule transfer. Insufficient rule determinacy is part of the reason. In the absence of EU law that specifies the obligations of national governments, the EU has been unable to shape state-society relations in the CEECs. But what is striking is that NSAs who would benefit from better social dialogue have not made this their rallying cause. This is even more surprising given that the Commission supports stakeholder involvement in rule adoption and seeks out the insights of labor and employer organizations in the candidate countries.

The 2000 Regular Report warned Hungary's government not to use consultative institutions as simple top-down information devices and placed the responsibility for improving the situation squarely on the government (Commission 2000a, ch. 13). Its urgent tone paralleled EU pressure in the accession negotiations. Hungary had to agree to semiannual Commission inspections of social dialogue.[14] The Commission reacted negatively to Hungary's shift from tripartite to decentralized and pluralistic consultation procedures imposed by the center-right coalition in 1999. In 2001, the Commission reaffirmed its dissatisfaction and called for measures to strengthen the administrative capacity of social partners and the government, specifically by "helping the social partners to build their own research and negotiation capacity" as a way to enrich consultative procedures, thereby moving from general criticisms to more concrete suggestions (Commission 2001b, ch. 13). Some improvement was noted in 2002, when the newly elected leftist government reestablished Hungary's tripartite institutions (Commission 2002b, 85).

13. Author interview, 24 March 2000 (Budapest).
14. Author interviews, 11 April 2001 (Brussels) and 23 April 2001 (Budapest).

With respect to Poland, the Commission has been particularly concerned about the weakness of employer organizations and the exclusive reliance on tripartite consultations. The latter were "hampered" by the withdrawal of the All-Poland Trade Union Confederation (OPZZ), Solidarity's postcommunist rival, in 1999 (Commission 1999b, 46–47; 2000b, ch. 13). The 2001 Regular Report emphasized the need for active use of tripartite and bipartite institutions, closer coordination between different levels of consultation, and full representation of all relevant organizations.

Such explicit EU criticism has remained largely without consequences. Given these ineffective transfer pressures, we may wonder to what extent the EU can interfere with fundamentally political conflicts in the candidate countries when it does not wield the power of clear legal prescriptions. Participants agree that the Commission's margin of action in this case is rather constrained. From the perspective of social learning, candidates rightly question the legitimacy of EU rule transfer in an area in which member state practices diverge considerably.

The weakness of social dialogue in the CEECs manifests itself in four ways: inadequate organizations representing labor and employers; ineffective tripartite procedures; little bipartite social dialogue and collective bargaining, especially at the intermediate level; and absence of social partners from accession preparations. First, interest organizations in both countries have been feeble due to fragmentation, ideological bifurcation, close relations with political parties, low representativeness, and insufficient enforcement capacity (Casale 2001; Draus 2000; European Industrial Relations Review 1999; Héthy 1999, 2001). In Poland, employer organizations have been slow to evolve and labor is bifurcated between Solidarity and the postcommunist OPZZ, with additional fragmentation among smaller trade unions. In Hungary, both labor and employer organizations are highly fragmented. More generally, employer organizations have developed only haltingly in CEE, in part because of the uncertainties arising from property restructuring, in part because trade unions have not presented formidable challenges to employers. Fragmentation has been extensive and weakens the ability of both management and labor to conclude agreements. At a minimum, fragmentation raises transaction costs in bipartite and tripartite negotiations. More problematically, fragmented organizations tend to compete against one another and undercut their peers' agreements. Bifurcation, on the other hand, reflects a polarized environment in which even less mutual coordination is possible than under conditions of fragmentation. In most candidate countries, trade unions are divided between independent organizations and postcommunist successor organizations. Both blocs often maintain close links with political parties, though they vary in the extent to which their officials simultaneously hold political office. Frequently both sides compete for members within the same enterprises, duplicating functions and requiring resources that could be better spent addressing the challenges of economic transformation. An additional problem is poor labor representation at small and medium-sized enterprises, which make up 90 percent of enterprises in the region (Vaughan-Whitehead 2000).

Second, though tripartite institutions exist in all CEEC candidates, they remain poorly utilized. Tripartite structures were generally established at the beginning of the transformation period, often under the pressure of international organizations such as the ILO, the IMF, and others (Iankova 1998, 258; 2002). Regular consultation with employers and trade unions has enabled CEE governments to carry out far-reaching macroeconomic reforms while maintaining social peace (Greskovits 1998, 170; Martin 1999, 110). Incidentally, tripartite institutions have helped trade unions gain new political standing in democratization (Pollert 1999, 14). However, the tripartite label is misleading in light of prevailing gaps between formal institutions and actual consultation practices in CEE (Kubicek 1999b; Ost 2000). State actors tend to utilize the institutions as channels for disseminating government information. At the same time, socioeconomic interest organizations have not availed themselves of all the opportunities for participation that the formal structures offer (Crowley and Ost 2002, 227). Rapid economic transformation, combined with EU accession preparations, has not encouraged meaningful social dialogue. Macroeconomic constraints have left little room for competing policy proposals. The vast majority of voters, including workers, have supported market reforms and EU accession. Social democratic and conservative governing coalitions in CEE have been equally committed to market reform. This broad policy consensus has made it difficult for organized labor to justify demands for concrete policy input from trade unions (Ost and Weinstein 1999). Governments and external actors such as the EU have privileged speed in the transformation process and accession preparations at the expense of participatory decision-making.

In Hungary, the tripartite National Council for Interest Reconciliation was created in 1988 and reinforced after the regime change in 1989–90. Its responsibilities included consultation on economic, social, and labor bills and general policy orientation, as well as the conclusion of agreements on wage policy (Héthy 1999, 2001; Ladó and Tóth 1996; Tóth 2002). Significant modifications occurred under Orbán's conservative coalition government. In 1999, the tripartite Interest Reconciliation Council was replaced by several policy-specific forums that lacked horizontal coordinating structures. Membership was opened up to other types of organizations, notably chambers of commerce, representatives of banks and foreign investors, and social service providers (Neumann 2000). By fragmenting consultative bodies and shifting to a more pluralist composition, the Orbán government weakened Hungary's structures of socioeconomic consultation. Because the membership of the new forums did not overlap, NSAs were less able to advocate coherent policy agendas and hence have any impact. This system functioned primarily as a vehicle for the dissemination of government information but, in the absence of horizontal links, participants deplored the de facto loss of information depth. The leftist government in power after 2002 has reestablished the National Interest Reconciliation Council and sought to negotiate substantively with the social partners in this and more specialized forums.

Poland's Tripartite Commission for Social and Economic Affairs was established in 1994, much later than in other CEECs. Because the regime change was achieved by Solidarity as a labor-based political movement and because workers widely supported market transformation, the perceived need to generate legitimacy through tripartite consultation was less urgent than elsewhere in the region (Ost 2000). In 1997, the principle of social dialogue was anchored in the constitution.[15] Nevertheless, the Tripartite Commission lacked a formal legal base until 2001, when the Act on the Tripartite Commission for Social and Economic Affairs was passed (European Industrial Relations Review 1999). In practice, dominance of state actors and politicization of trade unions by parties have undermined the work of the Tripartite Commission (Crowley 2002; Pollert 1999, 139, 144).[16] In late 1998, one of the two main labor confederations withdrew from tripartite consultations. The postcommunist confederation OPZZ accused the Solidarity-affiliated government of excluding labor from legislative and policy consultation (OPZZ 1998; Ost 2002). OPZZ filed a complaint with the ILO, which responded by reprimanding the Polish government (Kohl et al. 2000). Overall, therefore, the record of tripartite institutions in both countries has been unimpressive. While Hungarian tripartism deteriorated because of the Orbán government's deliberate restructuring of consultative institutions, in Poland the main obstacle to constructive consultation has been the politicization of trade unions by parties.

A third way in which the sluggish adoption of social dialogue rules can be seen is bipartite consultations between labor and employers. Collective bargaining is even less developed in the region than tripartism. Both sides tend to rely on the state as mediator. Consequently, both territorial and sectoral intermediate structures of industrial relations are inadequate. National-level wage policy sets minimum and maximum levels of wage increases, usually via tripartite consultation. Beyond that, collective bargaining takes place mostly at the enterprise level. Company-level agreements predominate in most types of enterprises (Kohl et al. 2000; Martin 1999; Neumann 1997, 2000; Frege 2000; Vaughan-Whitehead 2000). High unemployment and capital mobility weaken labor's bargaining position at the sectoral level, as do the widely differing wage levels in foreign-owned versus domestic enterprises. In addition, organizational structures remain weak at the sectoral level, especially among employers.

Finally, several observers have noted the puzzlingly low profile of the social partners in the accession process despite the opportunities that EU social dialogue rules and explicit Commission support would seem to create (Borbély 2000; Kohl et al. 2000, 409; Vaughan-Whitehead 2000). Multiple forums allow social partners to engage with the issues of EU accession. The Commission utilizes national and transnational participatory forums to strengthen the international presence of CEE

15. Constitution of the Republic of Poland, adopted 2 April 1997, Preamble and Art. 20 ("A social market economy, based on the freedom of economic activity, private ownership, and solidarity, dialogue and cooperation between social partners, shall be the basis of the economic system of the Republic of Poland").

16. Avdagić calls such cooptation "party paternalism" (2003, 149). More optimistically, Iankova interprets the overlap of party and syndicalist functions in Poland as "'parliamentarian' tripartism" based on the direct presence of union representatives in parliament (2002, 176).

NSAs and prepare them for EU membership. Interaction with European umbrella organizations helps CEE organizations gain access to financial resources, information, and expertise.[17] Social partner organizations from the candidate countries also often pursue international affiliation as a means for increasing their domestic legitimacy. Regular participation in meetings in Brussels can socialize CEE social partners into the EU policymaking process. Both Poland and Hungary have national consultative forums on European integration that either include the social partners officially or provide access to opportunities if social partners take the initiative. In the logic of rational cost-benefit calculations, through such networking opportunities the EU may empower domestic actors as potential rule entrepreneurs or veto players. In the logic of appropriateness, such regular encounters encourage elite socialization and persuasion. Though the EU does not directly manage all of these forums, it supports them politically and often provides technical and financial assistance.

Given all these opportunities for European multilateral networking and domestic state-society consultation, what explains the lack of substantive stakeholder involvement? I argue that two proximate factors have made it difficult for social partners to use consultative forums in the accession process effectively: resource constraints and ambiguous EU signals about prevailing opportunity structures.

Resource constraints, combined with the complexity of the accession tasks, have placed societal actors at a real disadvantage relative to the government. Much of EU legislation remains to be translated into CEE languages. Yet outside the international affairs departments of trade unions and smaller employer organizations, foreign language skills are in short supply. CEE NSAs have not enjoyed the intensive coaching in EU law that the EU offered to CEE governments. The social partners argue that their substantive input would be most useful at the sectoral level, yet resource constraints make international cooperation even more difficult for sectoral organizations than for national ones.[18] Neither financial nor technical assistance from the EU has been sufficient to resolve the difficulties faced by trade unions and employer organizations wishing to insert themselves into the accession preparations.

Beyond material constraints, the political opportunity structure of accession preparations has remained ambiguous for stakeholder organizations. The EU itself sends mixed signals about political participation in the enlargement process. Its rhetoric of social dialogue contrasts sharply with the intergovernmental style of accession negotiations. Consequently, the EU turns to NSAs for informal background information but places the formal responsibility of consulting with social partners on candidate country governments. Negotiation procedures aside, the accession criteria also implicitly favor a strong executive (Ágh 2002). Since speed

17. ETUC began affiliating CEE unions in the mid-1990s, whereas the two employer confederations UNICE and CEEP did not do so until the late 1990s.
18. Author interviews with representatives of employer and labor organizations in Poland and Hungary, 2000–01.

has generally been rewarded more highly than quality in adopting EU law, partic-ipatory decision-making has not been a priority. Consequently, opportunities for civil society input have been limited. Even national legislatures have been reduced to the rather passive approval of accession preparations and legal harmonization (Grabbe 2001a; Williams 2001). As one Polish government official put it: "We have enough to do as it is. If the social partners themselves don't initiate an exchange of opinions, then we don't necessarily seek it out either, since it would just be another pain in the neck."[19]

Divergent institutional mandates within the Commission go some way toward explaining mixed signals toward interest organizations. Among officials of the Directorate-General (DG) for Employment and Social Affairs, the prevalent view tends to be that the "European social model" provides a valuable counterweight to variants of globalization that feature even less democratic control and social pro-tection. From this perspective, European social dialogue holds significant oppor-tunities that have yet to be fully explored. This view justifies activism by EU officials with an interest in cultivating constituencies and thereby expanding their own scope of influence. For officials from DG Employment and Social Affairs, social purpose *and* bureaucratic self-interest call for promoting social dialogue in the candidate countries.

A different incentive structure prevails in DG Enlargement, whose function is to manage the overall accession process by balancing speed and quality of prepa-rations. From the perspective of DG Enlargement, social dialogue and stakeholder involvement in policy implementation are desirable to the extent that they help advance the goal of *acquis* compliance, but certainly no country should be denied membership because of the poor quality of its social dialogue.[20] Organizational self-interest thus compels each agency to cultivate its constituency. In the process, a complex organization such as the Commission sends contradictory signals about political opportunities that EU accession may create for NSAs.

In light of weak labor and employer organizations, poorly developed collective bargaining, and meaningless tripartite mechanisms, it is clear that the transfer of social dialogue rules to candidate countries has thus far failed (see summary in table 8.6). NSAs have participated only marginally in accession preparations and have not used their direct ties to EU institutions and other international actors to enhance their domestic influence, as conditionality would predict. Multilateral contacts may allow for elite socialization and persuasion, but among CEE governments we can see little more than discursive and formal commitment to social dialogue. The development of meaningful interest mediation has been limited by resource con-straints among NSAs and an ambiguous structure of political opportunities. Thus, the EU rewards intergovernmentalism while urging organized interests to get involved. Rather than offer alternative points of leverage for NSAs, EU accession has reinforced domestic weaknesses in state-society relations.

19. Author interview, 19 October 2000 (Warsaw).
20. Author interview, 20 March 2001 (Brussels).

Table 8.6 Social dialogue in Poland and Hungary—Formal and behavioral rule adoption

	Poland	Hungary
Organizational configuration	• labor: organizational bifurcation at national level (highly politicized), fragmentation at subnational level • employers: fragmentation, but tendency toward bifurcation at national level	• labor: fragmentation among six national confederations • employers: fragmentation among nine national confederations
Tripartite consultation (formal and behavioral adoption)	• Tripartite Commission since 1994, grounded in law since 2001 • since 2001, two labor confederations and three employer organizations represented • 1999–2001: consultations boycotted by OPZZ (labor) • Polish law requires that organized interests be consulted on all legislative drafts	• relatively strong tripartism through Interest Reconciliation Council 1989–98 • weakening of tripartism 1999 to 2002: fragmentation of consultative forums, pluralization of membership to include other economic and social actors
Collective bargaining (behavioral adoption)	• extremely weak national-level bipartism; tendency to rely on state mediation • weak intermediate (regional and sectoral) structures of industrial relations • overwhelming predominance of company-level agreements	• extremely weak national-level bipartism; tendency to rely on state mediation • weak intermediate (regional and sectoral) structures of industrial relations • predominance of company-level agreements
Social partner involvement in EU accession preparations (formal and behavioral adoption)	• one of two labor confederations associated with ETUC; two employer confederations associated with UNICE • participation in Joint Consultative Committee of EU Economic and Social Committee • national-level consultation on EU: National Council for Integration and Chief Negotiator's Consultation Committee includes interest groups; formal rather than substantive consultation	• six labor confederations associated with ETUC, eight employer confederations formed umbrella organization associated with UNICE • participation in Joint Consultative Committee of EU Economic and Social Committee • national-level consultation on EU: European Integration Council (includes social partners)—primarily serves to disseminate government information

The transfer of social policy to Poland and Hungary largely confirms the expectations of the external incentives model: formal adoption of secondary legislation and employment policy has proceeded at reasonable speed in both countries. Implementation is lagging behind, partly due to insufficient institutional capacity, partly because of the absence of societal stakeholders whose active involvement would help "pull in" the new rules (Jacoby 2000). Also consistent with external incentives has been governments' sluggish adoption of social dialogue: Without secondary law prescribing domestic institutions and practices, candidate countries have resisted EU pressure to create meaningful structures of social consultation. Their resistance has been made easier by the EU's own ambivalence: Despite normative pressure to include interest organizations in the accession preparations, the accession negotiations follow a thoroughly intergovernmental format and reward rapid transformation rather than in-depth societal involvement. This ambivalence is reflected in the different working styles of DG Enlargement and DG Employment and Social Affairs within the Commission. Whereas DG Employment allows NSAs ample access, DG Enlargement favors intergovernmentalism.

However, the case of social policy is instructive primarily for what has *not* happened: Despite predictions of both external incentives and social learning, the arguably most significant element of EU social policy, namely social dialogue, has had the least impact on the two countries. Neither model predicted the passivity of NSAs concerning social dialogue. At a rhetorical level at least, social dialogue enjoys great legitimacy in the EU as well as in most candidate countries. This should have aided rule transfer through social learning. Despite the weakness of explicit EU rules on domestic social dialogue, conditionality could have operated by changing the opportunity structures faced by trade unions and employer organizations. The EU has provided material and political support for greater involvement of societal stakeholders in policymaking and accession preparations. It has helped establish transnational links that enable NSAs to access government and EU institutions to voice their preferences. Yet neither trade unions nor employer organizations have mobilized these resources to gain greater domestic leverage, whether as rule entrepreneurs or as veto players. The case of EU social dialogue thus shows the limits of external influence on state-society relations even when conditions appear to render such influence very likely. Ambiguity among external actors about organized interests is likely to limit the latter's ability to participate in rule adoption.

Diverging Effects of Social Learning and External Incentives in Polish Central Banking and Agriculture

Rachel Epstein

W hy, despite domestic opposition, did Poland ultimately institutionalize central bank independence (CBI) in ways consistent with European
Union (EU) and Bretton Woods expectations in the first decade of transition? Why,
on the other hand, has the restructuring of Polish agriculture in compliance with
European demands remained a contentious domestic political issue? A central aim
of this chapter is to explain the variation in the level and form of Europeanization
in Poland's postcommunist economic policy. Europeanization in this context refers
to the degree of formal compliance with rules and norms of European economic
policy as well as the societal acceptance of those rules and norms. The process
through which international institutions impart knowledge to Polish policymakers—or fail to do so—has had political consequences for reform (Jacoby 2001).
Judging from a comparison of central banking and agricultural policy in Poland,
processes of social learning and lesson-drawing tend to foster rule and norm adoption at multiple levels, whereas conditionality tends to elicit formal acceptance
accompanied by multilevel resistance.

The principal dependent variable under consideration in this volume is the
degree of adoption of western rules among postcommunist states. The introductory chapter stresses the exclusivity in explanatory power of three distinct models.
In a slightly different vein, I argue that two of those models, social learning and
external incentives, may be equally powerful in explaining the transposition of
formal rules from West to East. Indeed, in both central banking and agriculture,
western states saw not only their rules implemented in Poland but also their own
patterns of political conflict reproduced. What differed, however, was the degree
of discursive adoption. Discursive compliance was greater in the central banking
case than in the agricultural case, which is explained by variation in the role of
social learning in the respective cases.

178

The line of inquiry in this chapter is two-fold. First, I seek to explain how two models, both the preferred explanation of the introductory chapter, "external incentives" as well as one of the alternative explanations, "social learning," can account for the formal transfer of western rules and norms to postcommunist economic policy. Second, I explore the potential political consequences that accompany each of the explanatory models. Whereas with social learning we can expect acceptance of western rules and norms without the radicalization of domestic political party platforms against western institutions, under conditionality it is more likely we will find formal rule implementation accompanied by discursive resistance.

Consistent with these claims, Poland institutionalized CBI through the constitution. The sequence of events that led to this outcome was roughly as follows: social learning leading to institutionalization of CBI followed by contestation and ultimately additional institutionalization of CBI. The contrast between central banking and agricultural reform supports the argument that different processes of rule and norm transfer may result in similar modes of formal compliance but have divergent political ramifications.

In December 2002, Poland, with nine other candidates, agreed to the conditions of EU accession in 2004, including lower initial levels of agricultural subsidies from the Common Agricultural Policy (CAP) than their western counterparts. The sequence of events this time was roughly as follows: conditionality followed by growing skepticism in Polish public opinion of EU membership and mobilization of political parties on the basis of the threat that EU membership posed to Polish agriculture. When Polish fears of unequal treatment under accession rules were confirmed by the January 2002 EU proposal on graduated subsidies for Central and East European (CEE) farmers, sections of Poland's polity were further radicalized against EU membership.

Poland adopted CBI on multiple levels, while the country accepted rules for agricultural reform on the elite negotiating level only—and after considerable acrimony at that. I argue that a crucial difference between these two cases is in the processes of rule transfer. Whereas social learning embeds new rules in the target society, conditionality may not, and if it does, only after a prolonged period of institutionalization and habitualization. In the cases of central banking and agriculture, the result was limited politicization of CBI against domestic proponents of CBI versus intensified politicization of Polish agricultural political parties against the EU.

Of course, monetary policy and agricultural reform are structurally distinct issue areas. Because between 20 and 30 percent of the Polish population is dependent on agricultural production or processing for employment, we might expect any kind of agricultural reform, whether in response to domestic imperatives or international demands, to be fraught with conflict. Monetary policy, the conventional wisdom suggests, is by contrast relatively technical in nature and therefore above the political fray. These facts, rather than the process of rule transfer, may more plausibly explain the level and form of rule adoption than the process of rule transfer.

Although I acknowledge the structural differences that figure into the alternative explanation outlined above, the respective structures of central banking and agriculture do not explain the principal difference in which I am interested. That is, the degree to which the level and form of rule adoption affects the orientation and severity of politicization. In the agricultural case, limited rule adoption manifested itself in radicalization of agriculturally based political parties *against* the EU. This outcome, I argue, stemmed directly from EU conditionality coupled with the EU's conduct.

Moreover, if agriculture appears to be naturally politically contentious whereas monetary policy does not, it is only because the peculiarities of European integration have made it seem that way. Historically, monetary policy has been the source of political conflict because of its hypothesized relationship to unemployment, inflation, economic stimulus, and national sovereignty. In fact, despite the institutionalization of CBI in the Polish constitution, monetary policy continued to be the subject of some controversy. By November 2002, unemployment in Poland was nearing 20 percent and growth had plummeted. This suggests that under different international conditions, opponents of CBI might indeed have prevailed. That CBI is not as visible a source of political conflict now as it has been traditionally is a consequence of Western Europe's commitment to depoliticizing monetary policy through supranational arrangements (McNamara 2001, 164). Monetary policy continued to be highly politicized in selected European states, most notably in Britain (Gamble and Kelly 2002). Arguably, the tensions surrounding agriculture in connection with EU enlargement were as much a result of Western Europe's refusal to subject agriculture to market liberalization as they were to the size of the farming sector in Poland and other CEE states.

Both central banking and agriculture were politically contentious in the first decade of postcommunist transition, and, I argue, would have developed differently had international institutions not interfered in these policy areas. The Polish central bank is more independent than it otherwise would have been without Bretton Woods and EU intervention. The agricultural lobby, on the other hand, is more radicalized than it otherwise would have been, and against the EU. The radicalization of the agricultural sector was manifested most recently in the 2001 election with the victory of two Euro-skeptic parties in Poland, one of which is agriculturally based. These parties gained still further discursive power against the EU after the EU submitted its graduated subsidy proposal in January 2002. Because of this variation in outcomes, central banking and agriculture provide good empirical settings in which to evaluate the explanatory power of the scope conditions.

The agricultural case in particular highlights the variable political effects of embarking on EU accession for postcommunist states. On the one hand, the EU has certainly improved the "informational environment" in Romania, Bulgaria, Slovakia and elsewhere by bolstering both the material and ideological resources of pro-EU reformers (Vachudova 2001). The EU has also encouraged the adoption of politically progressive laws on minority protection, antidiscrimination, and independent civil administrations (see Schwellnus, chapter 3, and Dimitrova, chapter 4). In contrast to these welcome developments, it is important to note how the EU can also play into the hands of its critics. Rather than improve the quality of the informational environment in the Polish agricultural case, the EU's offer on agriculture actually provided additional fuel for Euro-skeptics in Poland who mobilized support on the basis of the country's purported exploitation by Western Europe.

What follows is a discussion of four scope conditions, drawn from the introduction to this volume, which indicate when policy implementation consistent with the agenda of international institutions is most likely. I then consider the central banking and agricultural cases in the first decade of Poland's postcommunist transition. In these sections, I address the scope conditions, the immediate and long-term effects of international institutions on domestic political debates in these issue areas, and alternative explanations for these outcomes.

Scope Conditions

The conceptualization of "transition" depends on moving from one set of norms to another. Both material inequality between East and West and the West's ideological ascendancy marked the power asymmetry between Western and Eastern Europe in the post–Cold War era. This underlying condition would suggest that the logic of consequences has informed the compliance of East European states' with western norms because of the advantages of winning membership in western institutions.[1]

Despite the power asymmetry and the East's drive to "re-join" the West, the logic of appropriateness has nevertheless been central to transition. Three pieces of evidence support this claim. First, not all of the international institutions' policy prescriptions were explicitly tied to either material gains or membership in organizations. The Polish central banking case is one such example. Second, because East European states wanted to adopt western systems of governance and economic organization, much of the rule transfer appears to have been voluntary, albeit with western institutions subtly exercising their power. Third, despite the relatively weak position of East European states, they have resisted complying with some western demands, even when those demands were tied to material incentives.

In an effort to understand the conditions under which actors adopt rules and ultimately take them for granted, recent constructivist work has focused on the

---

1. The "logic of consequences" refers to choice based on a self-interested cost-benefit calculation. The "logic of appropriateness" underlies behavior that is "taken for granted" and is consistent with an actor's identity (March and Olsen 1998).

role of socialization in rule or norm transfer (Checkel 2001, Gheciu 2003). Constructivists in international relations have turned to social psychology in order to specify the conditions under which persuasion takes place (Checkel 2001; Johnston 2001). Work on persuasion seeks to specify the process through which actors move from one set of rules and norms to another. What emerges is a more refined picture of how transition states learn what their western interlocutors take for granted, i.e., how they learn to act in ways consistent with westerners' views of themselves (Wolff 1994; Poznanski 2001a, 2001b; Janos 2001).

I test four scope conditions in reference to the central banking and agricultural cases in Poland. These scope conditions correspond to lesson-drawing and social learning in the introduction to this volume. Persuasion of policymakers in a transition state will take place if:

(1) the target actors are in the wake of policy failure and have few prior convictions about how to conduct reform (*policy dissatisfaction/resonance—social learning and lesson-drawing*);
(2) the persuader is a member of an organization from which the persuadee seeks membership or affirmation (*identity—social learning*); and
(3) the persuader acts out the principles he or she hopes to transfer to the target state (*legitimacy—social learning*).

Assuming these three conditions are present, then rule adoption that is normatively consistent with prior efforts at persuasion is most likely to take place if:

(4) international institutions have cultivated strategic transnational coalitions with politically positioned domestic actors who can implement policy (*domestic empowerment—social learning*).

These scope conditions define the circumstances under which arguments are likely to matter in transferring new rules to a target society.[2] Arguments, however, are never divorced from the social and political context in which they are made. Prestigious actors confer legitimacy on ideas, and this fact certainly figures into the deliberative process in which actors debate the validity of competing ideas. Where international institutions with the power to confer legitimacy argue with normative consistency and where pre-existing domestic interests are not well defined, international institutions will be able to embed new ideas in a domestic policy setting. This "embeddedness" is marked by high-level domestic support for the new ideas, which politically positioned domestic actors in turn lobby for. Without these conditions, even in the face of an overwhelming power asymmetry between two parties, it is possible that the targets of persuasion will lead a backlash against international institutions and their policy prescriptions.

---

2. This is in contrast to studies that suggest conditionality tends to produce compliance more often than other forms of influence (Schimmelfennig, Engert, and Knobel 2003a). For a theoretical approach to understanding how arguments affect actors, see Risse (2000).

Methodology and Case Selection

I begin by investigating the reasons for variation on the dependent variable. With respect to central banking and agriculture, "politicization" refers to the degree to which rules are openly contested and become or remain the points of political departure among parties. In my case, having found variation in the degree of politicization in two policy areas, I explore the origins in that variation. Unconvinced that the structure of the issue areas in question can account for the severity and direction of politicization, I have researched the mechanisms by which rule transfer in central banking and agriculture occurred. Although Polish policymakers have accepted EU demands in both cases, the political ramifications of rule adoption differed as the processes through which rule transfer varied. Because the cases are not perfectly homogeneous, however, the applicability of the hypotheses, particularly concerning normative consistency, may be limited.

There are advantages and disadvantages to having selected two cases from within one country. On the one hand, comparing cases from within Poland controls for an array of political and economic variables that tend to vary from country to country and that may bear on the degree of rule adoption and on the political ramifications stemming from rule adoption. On the other hand, cases from a single country may also introduce an omitted variable bias since it may be something peculiar to Poland that accounts for the outcomes in question rather than the explanatory variables that I have suggested. Poland's exceptionally large agricultural sector and its close encounter with hyperinflation in 1989 and 1990 are two such peculiarities that could also account for outcomes in the agricultural and central banking cases. It would therefore be useful to test this series of hypotheses in other cases and in other countries in order to better understand the broader applicability as well as the limitations of the theoretical framework outlined here.

Central Banking in the First Decade: Lesson-Drawing and Social Learning

The debate about CBI in Poland concerned the appropriate role of the government in setting monetary policy. By the mid-1990s, there were two competing views. The Bretton Woods institutions, USAID, and the EU empowered Polish political figures who favored preserving CBI. Poland's center-left political parties, on the other hand, made the case for a more politicized bank. They wanted greater government control over monetary policy and the diffusion of the central bank's decision-making power. By 1999, however, according to international standards, Poland had institutionalized CBI. Without the intellectual, technical, and social power of the international institutions, proponents of CBI in Poland during this period might not have prevailed.

International Institutions and Central Bank Policy in Poland: 1986–93

The first steps toward the creation of Poland's central bank began in 1986 when Poland rejoined the International Monetary Fund (IMF) and the World Bank.[3] During the period from 1986–90, World Bank activity was limited to "getting to know Poland" (World Bank 1997a, 26). Later, in the run-up to Poland's macro-economic stabilization program ("shock therapy"), the World Bank and IMF were active in analyzing the Polish economy and in encouraging successive governments to pursue economic reform (World Bank 1997a, 9). This included the provision of the intellectual and technical support necessary for the conceptualization of the reform of Poland's banking sector.[4]

USAID was also building reform capacity and a network of contacts within Poland in the late 1980s. In 1989, before revolutionary political changes had accelerated, Poland began restructuring its financial sector. Early that year, Poland passed the Banking Act and the Act on the National Bank of Poland. These laws converted the communist-era monobank into a two-tiered banking system modeled explicitly on western capitalist principles. It was USAID affiliates who advised Poland on how to design the structures and write the bylaws for the National Bank of Poland (NBP) and the nine state-owned commercial banks (SOCBs) that emerged from that legislation (Stirewalt and Horner 2000, 20).[5]

Once macroeconomic stabilization was under way, the primary concern of both the international financial institutions (IFIs) and the first wave of Polish reformers from Solidarity was to formulate monetary policy consistent with anti-inflationary goals. Related to this was the perceived need to build competence within Poland's banking supervision department, the General Inspectorate of the National Bank (GINB, Generalny Inspektorat Nadzoru Bankowego). This regulatory capacity became increasingly important in 1992, when the extent of the banking sector's fragility became apparent (Borish 1998, 5).[6]

Polish volunteerism and compliance with foreign advice characterized this early phase of financial sector reform. The low level of conflict between Polish reformers and their foreign interlocutors did not signify a lack of foreign influence, however. On the contrary, international institutions were able to wield a great deal of power in this initial period because they were dealing with a sector that was

3. Poland had been a founding member of the Bretton Woods institutions, but then left in 1950 to join the Council for Mutual Economic Assistance (CMEA).

4. Although he did not arrive in Poland until 1990 to serve as the World Bank's resident head in Warsaw, one official acknowledged that the World Bank helped lay plans for reform even when it was not lending. Author interview with resident head in Warsaw for the World Bank, Warsaw, 5 June 2000.

5. With regard to legislation, the report states that "USAID advisors have provided detailed written and oral advice during the drafting of the Banking Act and the Act on the National Bank of Poland." A USAID advisor to the National Bank of Poland confirmed that USAID "provided direct advice to the bylaws and the structure as they were proposing to create these separate bodies." Author interview with USAID advisor A to the NBP, participant in USAID's project on "Strengthening Bank Supervision in Poland," Warsaw, 15 June 2000.

6. Since that time, the report states, "banking supervision at NBP has evolved to contain systemic risk in the banking sector and to support NPB's larger objective of price stability."

largely discontinuous between state-socialism and free market enterprise (*policy dissatisfaction*), because they represented organizations from which Polish reformers sought approbation (*identity*), and because they were normatively consistent in what they were prescribing (*legitimacy*).

It is easier to observe the effects of international institutions where there was conflict rather than where there was none. In fact there were some points of disagreement and misunderstanding between Polish officials at the National Bank of Poland (NBP) and the international institutions. For example, one high-ranking NBP official recalled that her colleagues initially believed that bank supervision was a matter for military authorities and had to be persuaded of the legal nature of enforcement.[7] Similarly, a U.S. Treasury advisor to NBP noted the "problem of convincing bankers in Poland that supervision would be good for them . . . that it would strengthen and protect the banking sector and would therefore benefit them rather than just be a nuisance."[8] A third conflict emerged between Polish central bank authorities and Bretton Woods over the concept of government deposit insurance. Although World Bank officials eventually prevailed in the debate by arguing that this was a fundamental feature of a sound banking system and thus of a market economy, to Poles the initiative resonated with the "soft budget constraint," a phenomenon most often associated with the misallocation of resources under state socialism (Kornai 1990).[9]

The early efforts of international institutions at persuasion and coalition-building around the idea of central banking in keeping with western models would prove essential to preserving CBI in subsequent challenges. These same individuals would use the technical knowledge they had gained from international institutions to defend the original principles on which reform was based. Building a technically competent central banking bureaucracy significantly broadened the coalition in favor of CBI beyond the few sophisticated Polish economists who had already developed an enthusiasm for free market institutions before transition began. It is important to note, however, that it was the IMF, the World Bank, and USAID that provided the mobilizing force behind the coalition, not Polish politicians.

The fact that international institutions were normatively consistent in their policy prescriptions also explains the broadly volunteeristic attitude of Polish reformers (*legitimacy*). The promise of CBI's effects, although notoriously untestable empirically (Eijffinger and De Haan 1996; Grabel 2002; Posen 1993, 1995), has resulted in a worldwide rush to institutionalize independent central banks (Maxfield 1997; Loungani and Sheets 1997). By helping to design Polish structures according to their own expertise, international institutions emphasized the technical correctness of their plans, thereby eliding the distributional consequences (Johnston 2001). Representatives of international institutions do not

7. Author interview with Polish General Inspectorate for Banking Supervision (GIBS) official, Warsaw, 9 June 2000.
8. Author interview with U.S. Treasury advisor to NBP, Houston, 16 May 2001.
9. Author interview with World Bank resident head in Warsaw.

acknowledge such political consequences because they themselves take the apolitical nature of their ideology for granted. As one World Bank representative explained, the process is "all market driven, and is primarily about creating transparency, increasing efficiencies, and so on. We are trying to help countries with strategies to get them where they want to go."[10]

NBP Phase II: 1994–1998

As the senior partner in the governing coalition, the SLD led the drive for institutional reform at NBP. SLD's approach was at odds with what Polish reformers and the IFIs had pursued, both before and at the outset of transition. The conflict began when Minister of Finance Grzegorz Kołodko criticized NBP's monetary policy as overly restrictive. Specifically, Kołodko claimed that NBP's execution of bank supervision was "inefficient," arguing that it should be removed from the central bank and institutionalized separately. With regard to monetary policy, he argued that, in connection with NBP's reduction in the złoty devaluation rate and the consequent drop in the relative price of foreign currency, the central bank should also lower the price of domestic credit.[11] Further, he argued that interest rates should be set according to expected inflation rather than past inflation, a change in NBP policy that would have also resulted in lower interest rates. He concluded that the level at which interest rates were set encouraged speculative capital inflows, thus disturbing the capital account balance and bringing inflationary effects. It also contributed to the government's cost of servicing the public debt, thus limiting the state's resources for other uses.[12] Finally, Kołodko and his colleagues in parliament questioned the wisdom of concentrating the central bank's power in just one official—the NPB president.

Consistent with these objections to central bank policies, SLD and PSL deputies in the Sejm, the lower house of the Polish parliament, submitted legislation both to create a separate body for banking supervision and to create a National Bank of Poland Council.[13] According to the August 1995 proposal, the NBP Council would have nine members serving six-year terms. The government and the Sejm would appoint three members each, while the Polish Union of Banks would appoint two. The President of NBP would also serve on the Council, but that appointment would be subject to greater political participation. According to the legislation, the

10. Author interview with the World Bank Resident head in Warsaw.

11. Until 1995, when the Polish złoty was freed, Poland had a crawling peg exchange rate regime. The basket to which it was pegged included the U.S. dollar, the German mark, and several other European currencies. The reduction in the rate of devaluation of the złoty in question here was from 1.6 to 1.5 percent.

12. *Polish News Agency*, 6 September 1994; *Financial Times*, 3 March 1995, 4; Kołodko 2000, 35–36. It is important to note, however, that even as Kołodko was critical of central bank policy, he claimed to support central bank independence.

13. Although the source of the legislation was never revealed, it was widely believed that Kołodko was crucial to the legislation's content. Author interview with Research Department official National Bank of Poland, Warsaw, 14 June 2000.

bank head would be appointed by the parliament at the nomination of the prime minister instead of the president. The NBP Council's primary responsibility would be to manage monetary policy. In addition, this bill would enable the central bank to lend the government an amount of up to 5 percent of the state budget, although the coalition eventually removed that provision.[14]

There was immediate domestic opposition to the bill. The president of NBP, Hanna Gronkiewicz-Waltz, against whom the policy critiques were directed, repeatedly stressed in interviews with the media that these proposals would threaten Poland's standing abroad.[15] She emphasized that it was not only inconsistent with how most western states had designed their central banks, but that it was in violation of the EU standards for Economic and Monetary Union set out in the 1992 Maastricht criteria. Leszek Balcerowicz supported her position and argued that central bank independence should be written into the constitution. Because the NBP was forbidden by law to submit its own legislation, the Freedom Union (UW), of which Balcerowicz was a member, submitted the NPB-drafted legislation on the central bank's behalf that was intended to serve as an alternative to the SLD bill.[16]

When USAID first learned of the proposed changes to the NBP structures, it called on officials from the World Bank and the IMF to assist their Polish allies in using their strategic coalition to defeat the SLD legislation.[17] Neither Bretton Woods nor USAID had any conditionality agreements pending with Poland on banking (World Bank 1997b). And while Polish officials debated the merits of the competing proposals on CBI with reference to the EU's Maastricht criteria, Polish accession to the EU was not contingent on them. In fact, EU officials had repeatedly stressed that candidate countries should focus their energies on fulfilling the Copenhagen criteria first and foremost (Mayhew 2001, 6). Thus international institutions and their fellow champions of CBI in Poland had to rely on argumentation and legitimacy rather than incentives to make their case.

The strategic coalition functioned in three ways to undermine and discredit the SLD's legislation. In a pivotal instance of social learning, Gronkiewicz-Waltz, for example, changed her views on CBI considerably during the course of her tenure as NBP president. Prior to her appointment, she had argued that banking supervision should be institutionalized outside the central bank, a claim that Finance Minister Grzegorz Kołodko later used against her to justify the SLD's legislation to reduce the NBP's independence. Moreover, as an advisor to President Wałęsa

---

14. *Polish News Bulletin*, 5 October 1995. Although the SLD proposed this legislation, the head of banking supervision from 1992 until 2000 recalled that opposition to CBI was not limited to the SLD. She reported that representatives from all the political parties had tried at various points to gain political influence by making direct appeals to NBP officials. Author interview with Polish GIBS official.

15. *Polish Press Agency*, 21 September 1995. Gronkiewicz-Waltz also said that the proposed reforms to NBP signaled a return to the communist era.

16. *Polish News Agency*, 7 May 1996. This legislation was authored in large part by World Bank and USAID representatives. Many of these advisors were contracted from the U.S. Treasury. Author interview with USAID advisor B to NBP, 2 June 2001.

17. Author interview with USAID advisor A.

in 1991, she had recommended that he veto amendments to banking laws that would have increased the NBP president's independence.[18]

One could argue that Gronkiewicz-Waltz was naturally adapting her political views to the office she occupied in order to maximize the power of the institution in which she resided. However, there have been plenty of central bankers the world over who consolidated their own power precisely by cooperating with politicians on monetary policy. The CBI phenomenon is relatively new (Maxfield 1997). The most compelling factor making the preservation of CBI appear "natural" as opposed to "unorthodox" in the post–Cold War period is IFI support for it and western insistence that CBI reflect the norm among industrialized democracies (Grabel 2002).

The second way in which the strategic coalition functioned to defeat the SLD proposal was to foster communication between international institutions and Polish officials. One consultant in particular whom the World Bank contracted in the early 1990s to advise Poland and whom Polish officials cite as crucial to the process of CBI institutionalization was Robert L. Clarke.[19] A trusted advisor of Ewa Sleszynska-Charewicz (NBP's head of supervision), Clarke provided the commentary, language, and arguments for the NBP to defend itself against political pressure.[20] He told NBP officials what, in his view, they were risking by potentially allowing supervisory functions to be removed from the central bank.[21] NBP officials in turn used these arguments to try to persuade their domestic critics. This kind of assistance included USAID meetings with NBP officials (including the president) to prepare them before appearances in the Sejm to ensure that they would convey competence and professionalism as they explained that CBI and low inflation should be maintained at the expense of competing policy goals.[22]

The third and final way in which this strategic coalition discredited the SLD legislation was to use the EU's prestige to narrow the definition of what constituted appropriate policy, even without using explicit conditionality. The president of the European Monetary Institute visited Poland to cast doubt on the SLD's claims that their legislation was in sync with the EU. At a 1996 press conference from the National Bank of Poland, Baron Alexandre Lamfalussy announced that Poland was "a credible partner for membership of the European Union and the Monetary Union." But he also emphasized, with NBP President Gronkiewicz-Waltz standing at his side, that striving for lower inflation and preserving CBI

18. Gronkiewicz-Waltz was trained as a lawyer; her doctoral dissertation, entitled "The Central Bank: From a Centrally Administered Economy to a Market Economy: Legal Issues," contained her earlier views on CBI.

19. In 2000, Clarke was a partner at the Bracewell and Patterson law firm in Houston, Texas. From 1985 to 1992, he was comptroller of the currency of the United States. His areas of legal practice include bank holding company regulation, corporate banking law, federal regulatory law, regulatory investigations, and bank securities.

20. Author interview with Polish GIBS official.

21. Author interview with USAID official A.

22. Author interview with USAID official B.

would remain important in Poland's quest to join Europe (*Polish Press Agency*, 17 September 1996).[23]

This was not a reordering of the EU's earlier prioritization, which placed greater importance on the Copenhagen criteria than the Maastricht criteria for candidate countries. Poland's membership in the EU was still not explicitly tied to the structure of its central bank institutions. However, this event clearly delegitimized SLD claims that its own legislation was more consistent with EU norms than that supported by Balcerowicz. Lamfalussy was conveying which side he favored in this debate, and, in so doing, he conferred credibility on NBP's president. This strengthened her position against her detractors in the Ministry of Finance and in the Sejm by limiting the range of arguments they could deploy. No longer could they credibly claim that the EU would be just as willing to support their plans as not.

This political conflict over CBI was ultimately resolved with the SLD legislation being "quietly shelved."[24] The SLD/PSL-dominated Sejm ultimately passed the UW legislation on institutional reform at NBP. Moreover, the 1997 ratification of Poland's new constitution further strengthened the institutional weight of CBI in Poland. Finally, after waging an eighteen-month campaign against NBP to win lower interest rates, Marek Belka replaced Kołodko at the Ministry of Finance.

Had there not been an international consensus in favor of CBI (*legitimacy*), and had that international consensus not been backed by the active engagement of international institutions in Polish policy, it is unlikely that the debate over CBI would have been resolved as quickly as it was. The strongest evidence for this thesis is the first phase of financial sector reform, when Polish officials were particularly open to foreign advice. When there was little experience with managing a market economy (*policy dissatisfaction*) and Poland was eager to join the western community of states (*identity*), international institutions cultivated a strategic coalition that later defended the CBI agenda (*domestic empowerment*). It is less clear in the second phase how crucial international advice was. Although foreign advisors no doubt contributed to the coherence of NPB's arguments—according to NBP officials—it is also true that Polish CBI proponents might have prevailed in the domestic debate in any case.

Polish Agriculture and EU Conditionality: Reluctant Rule Adoption

In the September 2001 elections, Polish voters, already skeptical of the potential economic consequences of competing on the European market, elected two agriculturally based political parties to the Sejm. The returning Polish Peasant Party (PSL) won 9 percent of the vote and later entered the governing coalition with the

---

23. *Polish Press Agency*, 17 September 1996.
24. *Financial Times*, 26 March 1997.

Democratic Left Alliance (SLD). For the first time, the Union of Self Defense (Samoobrona), an explicitly Euro-skeptic party, entered the Sejm with just over 10 percent of the popular vote. In addition, the League of Polish families, an explicitly anti-EU populist party, won just shy of 8 percent of seats in the Sejm. Although it was clear from the beginning of transition that the Polish agricultural lobby would pose particular challenges to European integration because of its size (20–30 percent of Poland's population is dependent on agriculture for income) and inefficiency (Polish agriculture accounts for less than 5 percent of GDP), it was not clear how its political influence would be channeled.

The January 2002 release of the EU's proposal for incorporating candidate countries into the Common Agricultural Policy (CAP) and the Polish response to it shed some light on how the agricultural lobby would exercise its political power in the future (Commission 2002c). The proposal confirmed what was already feared in Poland: that the EU, despite its formal ideology of equal rights for all members, planned to create a two-tiered system within the CAP. The initial reactions from Poland and other CEE states were resoundingly negative. Polish Foreign Minister Włodzimierz Cimoszewicz since softened his position, however, suggesting that Poland would do whatever it takes to enter the European Union in 2004, as scheduled.[25] But Deputy Prime Minister Jarosław Kalinowski, who is also the PSL's party leader and agriculture minister, argued that if the EU failed to improve its offer, Poland would maintain trade barriers against EU farm products.

In contrast to the central banking case in which a transnational coalition succeeded in institutionalizing CBI and containing the debate over monetary policy, Polish agriculture remained an intensely politicized subject, more than a decade after the start of transition. As EU policy on the subject became clearer, the politicization became directed more against the EU and threatened to undermine Polish political elites' efforts to encourage the Polish public to support the 2003 referendum on Poland's membership in the EU. The central question I will address here is why this intensification of politicization occurred in the agriculture case. I argue, in reference to the central banking case, that the four hypotheses outlined earlier account for some of the variation, but not all of it. In other words, because it was a not a social learning process through which Poland ultimately adopted EU rules on agricultural reform but rather a conditionality process, the levels at which EU rule adoption took place were more limited than in the central banking case.

The EU Proposal and the Polish Response

The EU proposed a transitional approach to integrating new members into the CAP. Starting in 2004, CEE farmers would receive direct payments at a rate of 25 percent of what their West European counterparts receive. That percentage would increase to 30 percent in 2005, to 35 percent in 2006, and would reach West European levels in 2013. These direct subsidies are calculated according to

25. *Agence France Presse*, 22 February 2002.

production levels. The greater the productivity, the larger the subsidy. The EU proposed using CEE production levels from the 1995–99 period as a baseline for allocations. National governments are allowed to supplement EU subsidies, but not beyond existing EU levels.

Recognizing the dual and underdeveloped structure of CEE agriculture (that there is both commercial and subsistence farming), the EU has justified this transitional approach in part by arguing that higher levels of direct payment would inhibit needed restructuring in the East. In addition, the EU has pointed to purchasing power disparities between East and West as well as the EU's own budgetary limitations, which were laid out in Agenda 2000 to support its case for a phasing in of direct payments to farmers (Commission 2002c).[26] In connection with incorporating CEE states into the CAP, the EU has also proposed production quotas. At the same time, much of the EU subsidy is directed at making the potentially profitable subsistence farms more market-oriented. Finally, in order to qualify for EU subsidies, Poland must unconditionally open its market to European food products.

Polish politicians initially objected to the proposal on a number of grounds. First, they argued, it violated the principle that all member states in the EU have equal rights and privileges. This arrangement threatened to create two classes of EU members. The lower level of reimbursement exacerbated the EU's decision to use the 1995–99 period as the baseline for calculating subsidies, since those years represent the nadir of CEE agricultural production due to the economic difficulties associated with transition.[27] German or French farmers might produce two to three times as much of a particular product on the same amount of land as their Polish counterparts, and they would receive proportionately larger subsidies according to those ratios. This disparity fueled the fear among Polish farmers that their own products would not be competitive with more highly subsidized products from Western Europe, thus pushing many Polish farmers out of production altogether. In addition, although the EU has stated its intention to subsidize CEE farmers at commensurate levels beginning in 2013, the EU will renegotiate its budget in 2006, so there was no guarantee that the current system would endure in its proposed form.

The disparity in subsidies was not the only point of dispute. Whereas Polish farmers in 2002–03 produced as much as they could, within the EU they face production quotas. Much like uneven competition created by disparate levels of subsidy, this could cut into Polish farmers' livelihoods. Joining the EU would also mean an end to preferential credit for machinery and production costs.[28] Given these restraints, Polish officials pointed out that it was hypocritical of the EU to

26. The EU plans to spend €40.2 billion between 2004 and 2006, at the end of which the EU budget is to be renegotiated. This is actually slightly less than was negotiated at the EU summit in Berlin in 1999, when enlargement was expected to include only six countries instead of ten.

27. *European Report*, 2 February 2002.

28. *Polish News Bulletin*, 14 February 2002.

claim vis-à-vis the World Trade Organization (WTO) that it must maintain sub-sidies to stay competitive while telling CEE farmers that they must limit subsidies and other forms of assistance to their farmers in order to become competitive.[29] The perceived inequality built into the proposal justified claims to the Polish public made by Polish Euro-skeptic and nationalist politicians that the European project is exploitive and threatens to undermine centuries of Polish tradition. Observing how little the EU had done to defend its proposal, one news editor wondered whether EU officials "don't half want the Poles to vote against membership, and get them off the hook."[30] So instead of improving the informational environment in this instance (Vachudova 2001), the EU, up until the September 2001 elections in Poland and beyond, perversely played into the hands of its most powerful critics.

Many of the provisions of the EU agricultural proposal were known before its formal release in January 2002. Thus the reconfiguration of Polish political inter-ests began in the run-up to the September 2001 elections. The most alarming inter-pretation of those election results from the EU's perspective was that fully 27 percent of the vote went to Euro-skeptic parties.

Although the most moderate of the Euro-skeptic parties (the PSL) ended up pledging its support for Polish accession to the EU before the referendum in June 2003, it is also notable that the radicalization of Polish public opinion against the EU manifested itself in the growth of Samoobrona, whose support came in large measure from former PSL voters.[31] Precisely because many voters viewed the PSL as too passive with regard to Polish interests vis-à-vis the EU, after the 2001 national elections Samoobrona's support also grew from its level of 10 percent. Had new elections been held in July 2003, for example, Samoobrona would have attracted 14 percent support.[32] In the European Parliament elections of June, 2004, support for Euro-skeptic parties remained substantial, with the anti-EU Catholic national party, the League of Polish Families, winning 15.9 percent of the vote, and Samoobrona receiving 10.8 percent.[33]

A Modified Constructivist Approach to Explaining Reluctant Rule Adoption

The formal rule adoption outcomes for central banking and agriculture were vir-tually the same even though a social learning process was operative in one case and conditionality was operative in another. Despite domestic opposition, the Polish government accepted the terms of EU accession in December 2002 with the addi-tion of a token increase in the funds for Polish agriculture. However, in terms of

29. *European Report*, 13 February 2002.
30. *Economist*, 18 February 2002.
31. *Gazeta Wyborcza*, 26 September 2001.
32. *Rzeczpospolita*, 26 June 2003.
33. Note that European Parliament results are not a commensurate indicator of political party support to national elections because voter turnout is usually much lower. In June 2004, Poland was no exception, with only 21% participation.

the political conflicts that emerged, the outcome for Polish agriculture is largely the reverse of the outcome for central banking insofar as an international institution (the EU) in the agricultural case had aligned itself against a unified domestic political coalition. In contrast, by 1997, a strategic coalition of international institutional actors and domestic reformers institutionalized CBI in Poland and depoliticized the issue by removing it from public debate from 1997 until 2001.

Consistent with other sectors of Polish society, Polish peasants overwhelmingly supported the demise of the communist regime in 1989 and the introduction of free market enterprise. Shortly after macroeconomic stabilization began in 1990, however, a process that included price liberalization, "their enthusiasm about the free market suddenly abated" (Kowalski 1993, 349). After that, Polish agricultural reform became increasingly politicized with the growth of agricultural interests in government and the mounting conflict with the EU over how best to integrate Polish farmers into the Union's existing institutional arrangements.

In order to demonstrate that the four scope conditions are relevant to the political ramifications of the agricultural case, I would have to show that the reverse conditions would have resulted in less Euro-skepticism and less political conflict around agricultural reform than was the case in early 2002. Moreover, in order to make the constructivist case, I must show that the reverse conditions could bring about multilevel rule adoption and thus less politicization of agriculture through the manipulation of the normative framework and the cultivation of strategic coalitions rather than through material incentives. The scope conditions do reveal in part why the EU faced a backlash in Poland from the agricultural lobby, but they do not provide a complete explanation.

Policy Dissatisfaction

Persuasion of target policymakers will take place if the target sector in question is in the wake of policy failure and target actors have few prior convictions of their own about how to structure reform.

The agricultural case confirms this hypothesis. Agriculture was largely continuous with the communist past, so the pre-existing interests were not very susceptible to change through argumentation or deliberation. That Poland had largely escaped Soviet-mandated agricultural collectivization meant that private property remained an organizing principle of the Polish peasantry throughout the Cold War (Krok-Paszkowska 2002, 15–16).[34] This explains why the Polish agricultural lobby was still so large in 1989. It also explains why marketization required limited and not all-encompassing reform. Unlike in the central banking case, in which domestic actors were dependent on foreign technical expertise to remake the sector, the Polish agricultural sector already partly embodied a market logic with private property, even if the social structures were centuries old.

---

34. There were some state-owned farms under the communist regime, but 76 percent of Poland's two million farms were still family-owned in 1989.

Identity

Persuasion will take place if the persuader is a member of an organization from which the persuadee seeks membership or affirmation.

The agricultural case in Poland does not confirm this hypothesis. Despite the broad consensus in Poland that the country's rightful place is in the "heart of Europe," this has done little to persuade Polish policymakers that the EU's approach to integrating CEE agriculture is appropriate. With regard to other issue areas, Poland has been eager to demonstrate its solidarity with western states through the enactment of democratic and capitalist norms.[35] However, Poland has been very unresponsive to EU criticisms of its failure to reform agriculture.

There are two possible explanations for why the EU has no persuasive power in this case, despite holding the key to Poland's acceptance as a member of the European community of states. The first is that Poland is divided between those who are susceptible to the EU's persuasion because they believe the EU is a legitimate institution and those who have a nationalist, Catholic worldview that does not value membership in a secular superstate. Although this divide does exist in Poland, the Polish rejection of the recent proposal on agriculture transcended this divide. Those who would normally be most susceptible to the EU's persuasion in this case initially were not, and they were never persuaded by the logic of unequal levels of subsidy. The second possible explanation leads to the third hypothesis.

Legitimacy

Persuasion will take place if the persuader acts out the principles it hopes to transfer to the target state.

This hypothesis goes the furthest in explaining the EU's failure to mobilize Polish political support for its enlargement strategy. The EU was attempting to apply different standards to CEE states than those it enforces among member states. In fact, Poland stands to reap massive financial benefits from EU accession, even in the area of agriculture. For example, it is slated to receive about half of the more than €40 billion budgeted for enlargement between 2004 and 2006. One of the EU's greatest concerns about Polish accession in early 2002 was whether Poland would have the administrative capacity to absorb the heavy influx of funding. The central sticking point that Polish politicians repeatedly highlighted was that the EU proposal to create of two classes of EU members—and therefore unfair competition—appeared to be hypocritical. This gave Polish agricultural lobbyists argumentative weapons with which to critique the EU proposal. The EU's double standard also made Euro-skeptical views more plausible while weakening Euro-enthusiasts' claims for joining. Essentially, because agricultural policy is so heavily politicized in Western Europe, it was impossible for EU negotiators to act with normative consistency in Poland without bankrupting the EU.

---

35. Other cases include defense planning, civil-military relations, central bank policy, and the restructuring of Poland's state-owned commercial banks.

Domestic Empowerment

Assuming the three previous conditions are present, then policy implementation that is normatively consistent with prior efforts at persuasion is most likely to take place if international institutions have cultivated strategic transnational coalitions with politically positioned domestic actors who can implement policy.

This hypothesis receives partial confirmation from the agricultural case. The continuity of the agricultural sector coupled with the failure of the EU to conduct normatively consistent policy interfered with the EU's capacity to cultivate a strategic coalition that includes domestic actors who support the EU's position. It is too difficult to promote domestically, not because the benefits of EU accession are not great for Poland (they are) but because they overtly contradict the basic democratic principles that putatively underlie the European project. This is only important from a rhetorical point of view. In fact, international organizations use undemocratic methods to achieve particular outcomes all the time. The issue is only whether that contradiction is publicly known. If so, it becomes much more difficult for domestic politicians to support it (Gheciu 2001).

Policy implementation in Poland that is consistent with EU demands on agriculture may yet take place in Poland. If it does, however, it will not be because the EU cultivated a strategic coalition with persuasive tactics. It is likely that the EU will have to resort in coercion in this case.[36] If the theoretical framework presented here is correct, this will lead to intensified politicization of agricultural reform and a larger backlash against the EU.

Competing Hypotheses

There are a number of competing hypotheses from the introductory chapter that might also explain rule compliance in central banking and agriculture. Most of these competing hypotheses are from the external incentives model. Following a review of the competing hypotheses, I conclude that in most cases the process-tracing approach reveals the centrality of the social learning hypotheses that I have selected. Moreover, to the extent that international institutions did provide material incentives, these incentives did not correspond with the outcomes under consideration here—that is, central bank independence in one case and rule compliance with anti-EU politicization in the other.

From the social learning and the lesson-drawing model, I have argued that persuasion of target actors is most likely to occur in the wake of policy failure when

36. Shortly after Polish officials objected to the EU's 30 January proposal, EU Commissioner for Enlargement Günter Verheugen said in a press interview that if Poland does not accept the deal as is, the country may face delays in winning membership (*Süddeutsche Zeitung*, 7 February 2002, 8). Verheugen also complained that Polish politicians had been "downright criminal" in suggesting that Polish farmers would receive benefits equal to those of existing EU member states before the EU had launched its own proposal (*Bloomberg News*, 30 January 2002).

domestic reformers are unsure of how to proceed with reform (*policy dissatisfaction*). This corresponds to the hypothesis of the external incentives model that states that rule adoption decreases with the number of veto players. Although neither monobank employees nor farmers qualify as institutional veto players (as bureaucratic or business interest groups would), their political power is nevertheless substantial. One might assume an absence of bureaucratic interests in the central banking case because under state socialism there was no "central bank" as such undergirding a free market system of finance. Rather, in the wake of communism's collapse, Poland was essentially building a new institution with a new set of rules. In fact, however, all of Poland's monobank employees were held over from the communist period into the transition period. There was no purging of potential "veto players." It was not the elimination of veto players in this case that facilitated rule adoption, but rather inculcation of Poland's monobank employees by international institutions that accounts for compliance.

In the agricultural case, there actually was rule compliance, albeit in a very reluctant form, despite the strength of agricultural opposition. On the other hand, when one is considering the degree of politicization against the EU in response to its graduated approach to expanding the CAP, the political strength of skeptics could be instructive in understanding the mobilization of political parties around the issue of protecting farming interests against the EU. Thus, both the structural continuity of Poland's agricultural sector and the array of "veto players" this created provide redundant explanations for why selected Polish political parties rejected the EU's CAP extension strategy and even EU accession.

From the social learning model, I have also argued that target actors who seek social affirmation from international institutions are susceptible to persuasion (*identity*). Sometimes that social affirmation comes in the form of membership in an international institution. Two possible alternative hypotheses from the external incentives model are that rule adoption will take place in issue areas where there are well-defined rules and where an international institution threatens to withhold a reward. While it is true that the Bretton Woods institutions and the EU have a highly developed set of expectations about the benefits of CBI, it is also true that neither the World Bank nor the IMF ever tied Poland's compliance to material rewards or membership. Moreover, the EU made it clear that, for membership, fulfilling the Copenhagen criteria was far more important than fulfilling Maastricht.

With respect to agriculture, Polish negotiators did ultimately agree to the EU's terms of accession, including to a graduated schedule of subsidies to CEE farmers. Neither the highly developed set of rules governing the CAP nor the material incentives promised with EU membership, however, prevented the radicalization of selected Polish political parties against the EU. Thus, while incentives and power asymmetries largely explain Poland's willingness to compromise on the issue of agricultural subsidies, the external incentives model does not address the full range of political ramifications—namely the popularity of political parties in Poland that opposed EU accession on the grounds that the terms of Poland's entry were unjust.

The third hypothesis of my preferred explanation, also from the social learning model, claims that normative consistency contributes to the persuasive power of international institutions (*legitimacy*). There is no hypothesis within the conditionality framework that addresses this issue. There is, however, a second lesson-drawing hypothesis that may explain the lack of contestation in the central banking case and the heightened contestation in the agricultural case. The *epistemic communities* hypothesis from lesson-drawing states that rule adoption increases with the institutionalization of expert advice in a given policy area. This hypothesis suggests that we should find more contestation around agriculture than around CBI because while there has been a worldwide rush to establish central bank independence, the structure of the CAP is peculiar to the EU and goes against the institutionalized ideologies of international institutions, not least the WTO.

The *legitimacy* hypothesis and the *epistemic communities* hypothesis similarly convey the importance of the process through which target actors begin to take new norms for granted. The *legitimacy* argument, however, is more powerful in explaining the variation between central banking and agriculture for two reasons. First, it was not the agricultural subsidies themselves that Poland rejected. Rather, it was the principle of unequal treatment between existing and new members of the EU. Second, while there has been a growing international expert consensus behind CBI, Poland's discourse on CBI nevertheless departed dramatically from this consensus in the mid-1990s. Thus lesson-drawing was part of the process of rule adoption when Poland faced the threat of hyperinflation. But clearly not everyone drew the same lesson. What proved crucial to the abandonment of efforts to politicize NBP was the portrayal by international institutions of the SLD-PSL policy proposals as illegitimate.

Finally, I have argued that rule adoption depends on who the targets of persuasion are. Only if target actors are politically positioned both within the ministry and within the sector undergoing reform can we expect persuasion to have enduring political consequences (*domestic empowerment*). This is similar to explanations derived from the external incentives model that claim that rule adoption increases with the number and strength of domestic rule entrepreneurs and the degree of information asymmetry they enjoy. The first distinction I make between my hypothesis concerning the political positioning of persuadees and the external incentives hypothesis is that coalitions that implement reform are not pre-existing. Rather, they are largely the creation of international institutions, which, through persuasion, cultivate a domestic consensus around a particular set of ideas. Any information asymmetry they enjoy is also the consequence of their ties to international institutions. Second, both "number" and "strength" are underspecified in the conditionality model, making it difficult, except with hindsight, to assess whether a coalition with a particular structure would lead to policy implementation.

Bretton Woods, in cooperation with USAID and later the EU, cultivated a Polish coalition in favor of CBI at a moment when policy failure, the desire for social affirmation, and the association between CBI and legitimacy facilitated rule transfer.

Through technical transfer, economists and bureaucrats at the National Bank of Poland developed information asymmetries vis-à-vis their domestic opponents. The failure of the EU to cultivate a similarly reform-minded coalition in the agricultural case partly explains the EU's lack of influence in shifting the terms of the Polish domestic debate to curb the development of anti-EU sentiment.

Central bank policy and agricultural politics might at first seem unfit for comparison. According to conventional wisdom, they are structurally distinct issue areas in that central bank independence is a technical institutional arrangement whereas agricultural politics is all about defending entrenched interests. Given that CBI is increasingly a worldwide phenomenon, we would expect Poland to adopt that norm. Equally, agriculture would seem to be universally politicized because farmers across Europe—and not only there—are unusually good at political mobilization. Given these facts, why should events in Poland fail to reflect these general trends?

One purpose of this chapter was to show that Polish politics not only reflects these global trends, but is in fact inextricably linked to them. The relationship between domestic politics and international factors, however, is not a mechanistic response to market pressures and material incentives, as strictly rationalist accounts of politics imply. Where there are competing views on the political value of CBI, for example, international institutions can use their legitimacy to impose their own agenda by manipulating the normative framework. This is why, despite the lack of empirical evidence that CBI causes economic prosperity, there is a global rush to depoliticize monetary policy.

Equally, international institutions might inadvertently construct a normative framework that complicates the imposition of their agenda. The politicization of European agriculture through the CAP has ensured that Polish farmers would use the same argumentative logic against the EU to improve their own position. A constructivist ontology is not instructive for understanding all political outcomes. However, in a transition state where interests are fluid, sociological insights highlight how particular rationalities are remade or reproduced, primarily as a consequence of arguments rather than of incentives.

CHAPTER TEN

Europeanization Research East and West:
A Comparative Assessment

Adrienne Héritier

How does Europeanization research in this volume with its focus on accession states differ from Europeanization research that has been conducted in the context of the existing member states? To what extent are the two strands of research distinctive? Where do they show commonalities? What are the underlying reasons for their distinctiveness and commonality? These are the questions discussed in this chapter. I will start out by presenting the concept of Europeanization as developed in the research on the old member states ("Europeanization West") and elaborate its central features. I will then proceed to point out differences between Europeanization West and "Europeanization East," i.e. the research on Europeanization in the Central and Eastern European countries (CEECs). I will conclude by pointing out commonalities between research on Europeanization West and Europeanization East.

Europeanization: Definition, Concepts, and Theoretical Explanations

Definition

There are three different definitions of Europeanization that are applied in the literature documenting research on the European Union (EU). Under the first definition, Europeanization is used as an equivalent of European integration. As such it denotes the pooling of national competences in different policy areas at the supranational level in order to engage in joint policymaking. This research describes and systematically explains why more and more member state policies are being drawn into the political and judicial processes at the European level. The most important theories that are employed in order to describe and explain this process are neofunctionalism (Haas 1964; Sandholtz and Stone Sweet 2001), which emphasizes the ever-deepening institutionalization that results from increasing transnational economic exchanges and communication, and liberal intergovernmentalism (Moravcsik 1998), which emphasizes the intentional delegation of national powers of policymaking to EU institutions.

Under the second notion, Europeanization is defined in a more restrictive sense, conceived of as the impact of clearly defined, individual EU policy measures on the existing policies, political and administrative processes, and structures of member states. This process of influence is not understood as a unilateral adjustment on the part of member states resulting mechanistically from a good or bad fit with respect to EU policy demands. Rather, it is seen as a specific EU policy input into a national policymaking process, which is then used by key actors to strengthen their political positions in the domestic conflict, thereby increasing their chances to obtain their policy goals.

This notion of Europeanization also explicitly includes the endeavors of individual member states to take strategic influence on the formation of the particular EU policy measures that they must subsequently comply with. If successful, such endeavors of "uploading" national policy practices to the European level save adjustment costs which would otherwise occur at the national political and administrative levels. In a further step, this bottom-up perspective relinquishes the assumption of member states as unified actors and draws attention to the fact that subnational public and private actors may seize the opportunity of the existence of another arena at the supranational level in order to circumvent a political deadlock situation in the domestic arena. By addressing supranational actors, they shift their policy concerns to the European arena, hoping to find new coalition partners at this level (vertical dimension) (Héritier et al. 1996; Héritier et al. 2001).

This notion of Europeanization, understood as a policy influence exercised by one polity vis-à-vis another, also focuses on the voluntary transfer of policymaking practices or mutual learning about specific policy instruments among member states. It may involve a simple process of emulation, in the course of which one country copies the policy practice of another country because the policy proved to be successful; or, alternatively, it may consist of a process of social learning where, in the context of transnational policymaking fora or transnational networks, an exchange of information and arguments takes place, which subsequently leads to a mutual adjustment of policy goals and policy instruments (horizontal dimension).

The third notion of Europeanization, finally, defines Europeanization in terms of the influence of EU policies and values on the "rest of the world," i.e. non-member states. It encompasses a broad variety of processes featuring direct and indirect influence of EU policies and economic, social, and cultural activities on political, economic, social, and cultural processes well beyond Western Europe. In the context of this volume, it is the *second* notion of Europeanization, i.e. the impact of well-specified individual EU policy measures on member states' policies and administrative and political processes and structures, which is at the center of the analytic attention and hence serves as a point of reference for the following remarks.

Theoretical Background

What are the explanatory factors, causal mechanisms, and explananda that constitute the explanatory program of Europeanization research West as defined above? Looking at the vertical dimension first, the following analytical factors have been at the center of the explanation of the outcome of Europeanization. Assuming identical EU policy demands for all countries under investigation and starting from the assumption of rational strategic actors, different groups of factors (independent variables) have been investigated in terms of the most important factors on the outcomes of Europeanization: existing policy practices in the issue area under study viewed in terms of their fitting well or not well with European policy requirements; policy types in terms of their specificity or framework nature and in terms of the underlying problem types, including redistributive or distributive Prisoner's Dilemma problems; and issues of coordination. A further important factor is the institutional political and administrative structure of member states at the national and sectoral level in terms of the number of formal and factual veto players involved. And, finally, the prevailing national belief systems characterizing existing policy practices in their distinctiveness from and similarity to EU policy demands.

On the side of the outcomes of Europeanization (dependent variable), research attention has focused on policies at the level of outputs (legislative decisions or transposition), outcomes in terms of short-term practical implementation measures as well as policy impact in terms of mid- and long-term behavioral adjustments of target groups. With respect to the nature of change brought about, policy transformations have been measured in terms of typical patterns, such as absorption, patching up, substitution, and innovation (Héritier 2001b). Research attention has also focused on how EU policy demands, by creating new needs for administrative processes and organizational measures or by favoring some national political actors over others, have brought about changes in existing administrative and political structures and processes (Sverdrup 2000). Thus, they may have a centralizing or decentralizing effect on national political and administrative structures (Knill 2001; Börzel 2002; Eliassen 1993; Egeberg 2001). Patterns of change, again, have been measured in terms of absorption, patching-up, substitution, or innovation. Still other research has investigated the impact of European policy demands on state-association relationships (Lehmkuhl 1999; Haverland 2000; Schmidt 2001) and on institutions of democratic legitimation in member states (Olsen 1995; Jachtenfuchs and Kohler-Koch 1996), but also on overall state structures (Olsen 2002; Eberlein and Grande 2000).

Different causal mechanisms have been invoked in order to explain the link between the different independent and dependent variables (Héritier et al. 2001; Knill and Lehmkuhl 2002; Ladrech 2000; Knill and Lenschow 2000; Börzel and Risse 2003; Radaelli 2000; Falkner 1998; Treib 2003), whose analytical fruitfulness has been shown under particular, well-defined scope conditions. The first theoretical strand is based on a rational actor approach and argues that actors seek to achieve their policy objectives in a given institutional context that has a restrictive, but also facilitating, function. Assuming a lack of policy fit, it is submitted that domestic actors favoring similar policies will use EU policy requirements as a resource in order to strengthen their position in the national political conflicts. The EU policy demands may help overcome the resistance of formal and factual domestic veto players that would otherwise have blocked the policy reform because of the adjustment costs they accrue. As a result, a change in national policies may ensue.

However, in analyzing the impact of a delimited EU policy input into a national political arena in such terms, the respective temporal sequences of national and EU reform cycles have to be taken into account. Depending on whether a country is in a pre-reform, reform, or post-reform stage, EU reform requirements may buttress the domestic power of completely different actors. If, for instance, in the area of deregulation, country X is in a pre-reform stage, an EU deregulation claim will strengthen the position of the pro-liberalizers. If, by contrast, country Y is already in a post-reform stage of re-regulation, deregulation requirements will trigger a counterreaction and reinforce the re-regulation party (Héritier et al. 2001).

A second theoretical strand that has been very important in the Europeanization West literature is historical institutionalism, with its argument of the inertia of existing policies and institutions (Thelen 1999; Mahoney 2000; Pierson 2001). This argument states that existing national policies are susceptible to EU influences, but only within limits. These limits are set by the "stickiness" of existing policies and institutions that—once having embarked upon a path of development—due to increasing returns, learning effects, and coordination effects tend to be stable over time and can be changed only incrementally. According to the logic of this argument, the changes expected to result from EU adjustment pressure are marginal at best. Member states would be expected to "absorb" EU policy demands into existing policy repertoires or to "patch them up" by adding new elements while at the same time maintaining the old policy instruments, in a process that has been called "layering" (Thelen 1999). Only under exceptional circumstances would member states completely substitute policy instruments or engage in innovation.

A third theoretical strand in Europeanization research West—taking both the vertical and horizontal view—is the socialization and learning approach (Radaelli 1999; Börzel and Risse 2003; Checkel 2001; Schmidt 2001). This argument accounts for the impact of Europeanization in terms of a process of socialization, i.e. the internalization of EU norms. Since norms, defined as regularities of behavior, are claimed to influence compliance behavior, i.e. again regularities of behavior, there is a danger of tautology.[1] An additional variable that is clearly independent from compliant behavior has to be introduced to account for when, i.e. under which well-specified conditions, social learning takes place. Such conditions could be uncertainty about the problem at hand, the existence of an authoritative reference model or an insulated institutional context (Checkel 2001), all of which favor the willingness to learn, that is, change held beliefs or preferences on the basis of new information and arguments (Risse 2000). An example would be the aforementioned horizontal cooperation in transnational regulatory networks, such as biotechnological regulation. Under such conditions, it is claimed, learning occurs without any pressure or obligation on the part of supranational institutions. By contrast, it is doubtful whether such voluntary learning in Europeanization would take place if clear redistributive issues had to be decided.

Hence, taking the particular policy type or problem type into account when analyzing Europeanization processes and their outcomes has been an important argument in Europeanization research. The problem types that are most frequently used are the analytical problem types used in game theory. Since they reflect diverse interest configurations, they allow for the derivation of likely political cleavages (Scharpf 1997). Thus, it has been argued that redistributive problems and Prisoner's Dilemma problems represent the problematic cases, rendering Europeanization cumbersome, whereas coordination or distributive or discrete problems (with no transboundary effects) allow for smooth implementation.

If viewed against the background of the basic features of Europeanization West described above, what are the differences that emerge when we consider Europeanization East, as presented by the research in this volume?

Differences between Europeanization East and Europeanization West

Europeanization East and Europeanization West differ considerably; however, they reveal commonalities as well. It appears that the differences which, from the perspective of Europeanization research West, are most striking, to a large extent derive from the particular starting situation from which Europeanization research East takes its inception. These starting conditions are the coexistence of Europeanization East with the transition of CEECs to democratic political systems and their transformation into market economies, on the one hand; and the link of Europeanization East with accession negotiations, on the other hand. I claim that these two structural conditions are reflected in the particular features of the

---

1. The empirical identification of norms as a factor of influence is difficult because norms often are incomplete, internally inconsistent, or only weakly given. Moreover, they may still be valid even if they are not observed (Lichbach 2003).

Europeanization processes in accession states. These specific features relate to the *scope* and the *types* of the policies at stake; they are also reflected in particular *process* features, i.e. the *direction* of influence-taking and types of *controls* applied in the implementation process.

The Different Starting Situation

Europeanization research East coincides with research on democratic transition and on the transformation of state-led economies into market economies. Transition research (among many others, Elster, Offe, Preuss 1998; Ágh 1998) constitutes in itself an important branch of research and should be kept in principle analytically separate from Europeanization research as defined above (Dimitrova, chapter 4). However, the conjunction of the two strands of development is so obvious that their interdependence has to be taken into account. In the process of transition, the EU plays an important role by reinforcing and accelerating transition to democracy and market economies. It acts as "a conduit," giving transition a certain shape (Schmidt 2001).[2]

In the process of Europeanization West, by contrast, in the large majority of countries, the EU did not play a role in reinforcing national democratic institutions because such institutions were already in place.[3] On the contrary, it could be argued that the accession of the Scandinavian member states significantly spurred the debate about democratic transparency and access to information in EU decision-making processes and led to the establishment of such procedures, such as in the Council. This constituted an important "bottom-up" influence from member states, uploading their institutional policy traditions onto the European arena. Furthermore, some old member states are preoccupied because the influence of EU decision-making may jeopardize the existing national democratic institutions. Thus, supranational decision-making may undercut the role of national parliaments. Since the national governments have to commit themselves to supranational decision-making in the Council or comitology, it becomes difficult for national parliaments to question these decisions later in the domestic decision-making process.

The second crucial starting condition that makes Europeanization East different from Europeanization West is the accession negotiations.

The Shadow of Accession Negotiations

Europeanization East is intrinsically linked with accession negotiations and the overpowering external incentives associated with EU membership conditionality (Schimmelfennig and Sedelmeier, chapter 1). There is enormous pressure on

2. Schmidt analyzes the role of Europe in the context of the overall influence of economic internationalization for the existing member states (2001).

3. Except in Greece, Portugal, and Spain, where the European Community did have a positive impact on the consolidation of democracy.

applicant states to take on EU policy outputs, i.e. the entire *acquis*, without any "ifs and buts."[4] Thus, in the case of environmental policy, over 250 policy regulations had to be adopted, "a bitter pill that candidates have to swallow" (Andonova, chapter 7). Or, as Heather Grabbe (chapter 6) quotes a Hungarian official, "accession on any terms is better than no accession." Considering, moreover, that accession negotiations are very limited in scope and have been dominated by executive politics (see Sissenich, chapter 8), questions arise as to what extent they enjoy broad popular support.

Given the shadow of accession talks and the strong incentives linked with potential membership, could nontransposition be plausibly expected as a response? Under these conditions, adjustment costs would have to be very high, threatened sanctions very much lacking credibility, or the promised gains (i.e. membership) unconvincing in order to motivate non-transposition (see Schimmelfennig, Engert and Knobel, chapter 2). Considering, furthermore, the circumstance of recent democratic and economic transition, it seems rather likely that, in a first period, Europeanization will remain very much at the level of mere transposition and is not very likely to proceed to the level of policy outcomes, not to mention policy impacts (or behavioral adjustment, in the terms of Schimmelfennig and Sedelmeier, chapter 1).

Compared to the threat of being excluded from membership altogether, such as has been the case in Europeanization East, noncompliance in Europeanization West is linked with relatively mild sanctions.[5] Positive incentives consist in the sectorally limited monetary or nonmonetary benefits bestowed by EU policy measures; negative incentives can be applied by the Commission and the European Court of Justice in many policy areas, such as in structural policy and agricultural policy, for reasons like an illegal spending of funds or an infringement of EU competition law. But these sanctions—positive or negative—are very sectorally limited.

The Wide Scope of Europeanization Research East

Again, due to the link with accession negotiations, Europeanization research East is more encompassing in its approach, looking at the entire *acquis*, or an entire sector, e.g. agricultural policy, structural policy, environmental policy, or social policy (see, respectively, Andonova, chapter 7; Epstein, chapter 9; Jacoby, chapter 5; Sissenich, chapter 8). Even when focusing on one policy area, under the shadow of accession talks, compliance performance in this area would always be viewed in the context of the overall *acquis* (substantive and institutional), because the

4. The exception are transition periods that can be obtained in accession negotiations. Such transition periods allow for important delays in the application of the *acquis*, but they can cover only a very limited part of the entire *acquis*. A large part of the *acquis*, according to the same sources of information, was accepted "wholesale." Personal communication, Wim van Aken, 21 November 2003.

5. Systematic comparison of compliance across all policy areas shows that even formal compliance (transposition) in some areas leaves much to be desired in large member states such as Germany, France, and Italy (Börzel 2002).

Commission would assess the viability of accession in the light of this overall assessment.

By contrast, Europeanization research West has tended to focus on narrow policy areas or individual issues. Research would typically study one or two EU measures in a particular closely circumscribed policy area and raise the question of how the latter affect member states' policies and administrative and political structures across a limited number of countries (Börzel 1999; Héritier et al. 1994, 1996; Knill 2001; Kerwer 2001; Lehmkuhl 1999). Only more recently have large-N studies of compliance across many measures and many countries been conducted, using correlation and regression analysis (Börzel 2003; Falkner et al. 2002).

Types of Policy Demands

More Institutional Requirements in Europeanization East. On account of the link to accession negotiations and the basic starting conditions of democratic and economic transition, EU policy demands directed at the CEECs to an important degree include requirements to change national political, administrative, and judicidial structures—in other words, to accept the institutional *acquis* (Schimmelfennig and Sedelmeier, chapter 1), such as the institutionalization of human rights (Schimmelfennig, Engert, and Knobel, chapter 2) or the introduction of administrative reforms (Dimitrova, chapter 4). Interestingly, even substantive policies are seen by accession states as a vehicle to introduce democratic institutions, as pointed out for environmental policy (Andonova, chapter 7).

In Europeanization West, such explicit demands for institutional reform are only made under exceptional circumstances. Such rare instances of EU institutional requirements are the obligation to introduce procedures allowing for the public to have access to information to administrative documents regarding the environment; or the demand to establish independent regulatory authorities after the liberalization of the network industries; or, in the case of structural policies, the requirement to establish social partnership schemes for the implementation of structural funds.

Problem Type and Europeanization Research West. Europeanization research West has asked how the particularities of a problem dealt with in a Community policy are linked to the smoothness or difficulty of its implementation. In the case of redistributive policy, it is expected that resistance to implementation will be considerable because the losers will try to alter the redistributional objectives in order to reduce the costs imposed upon themselves. From this it was derived that if implementing actors are granted a lot of discretion, the realization of a redistributive policy objective is unlikely unless the supposed winners of the redistributive measure organize and insist on implementation (Pressman and Wildavsky 1984; Windhoff-Héritier 1980; also, Sissenich points to the "pull factor" important for implementation in social policy, chapter 8).

Another policy or problem type whose target is at risk of getting lost during implementation are policies that take the form of Prisoner's Dilemma problems.

During implementation, all involved actors have an incentive to cheat on the agreed outcomes and defect unless the Commission has provided substantial monitoring mechanisms. Thus, an EU policy of deregulation introducing an integrated market for electricity seeks to establish a collective good: the integrated market should allow for free access for new market entrants from all member states. However, national governments may be tempted to maintain or reintroduce measures of process regulation that de facto prevent new market accessants from entering the market (Coen and Héritier 2004).

By contrast, if distributive policies that treat all actors similarly are at issue and there are no losers and winners, adjustment to EU policy demands is expected to be much smoother. The same holds for coordination problems where all actors prefer coordination over noncoordination.

While it is implausible that there is an inherent difference between Europeanization research East and West regarding the question of how a particular problem type affects compliance with European policy requirements, it is nevertheless striking that the problem aspect plays only a marginal role in Europeanization research East as presented in this volume, as where the saliency of a policy is mentioned as an important factor in the implementation of the free movement of people (see Grabbe, chapter 6). This may be linked to the wide policy scope that is at the center of Europeanization research East. A broad scope does not reveal the analytical problem-type features. Put differently, one has to define a policy measure in quite a narrowly limited sense in order to identify clearly redistributive, distributive, Prisoner's Dilemma, or coordination features of an issue (Snidal 1995).

Process

One-Way Street vs. Two-Way Street. A further difference between Europeanization West and Europeanization East is that Europeanization West is a two-way street when it comes to shaping EU policy measures, whereas Europeanization East, at this stage, seems to be more of a one-way street. Europeanization research West, when analyzing the impact of a particular EU policy measure on member states' policies and political and administrative structures also reverses the research perspective and investigates how individual member states have sought to influence or even propose the very policy measure they subsequently are expected to comply with. The Commission by no means starts all policy initiatives. Member states frequently try to influence the policy agenda of the Commission. National governments do so in order to avoid policy and institutional adjustment costs. They engage in what we call a "political regulatory competition" in order to attain a more privileged position on the Commission's policy agenda and to "upload" a particular policy practice onto the European level. Thus we could show in the field of environmental policy that different environmental legislative acts were very much influenced by national administrators who had been "seconded" to Brussels in order to "write the legislative draft." However, it is not always the same member states that most influence the shaping of Commission drafts, instead the "leaders" change over time and across policies. The Commission takes care not to let the influence of one member state become predominant (Héritier et al. 1994, 1996). In brief, Europeanization West is a two-way street with changing member states functioning as policy initiators.

Quite the opposite seems to be the case in Europeanization East, if one considers the research presented in this volume. There seem to have been few policy initiatives on the part of accession states to actively shape the individual EU policies that then have to be adopted. According to information by the Commission, accession negotiations are about "bits and pieces here and there," and transition periods negotiated in the accession treaties cover only a small part of the *acquis.*[6] Given the initial situation of democratic and economic transition and the looming shadow of accession negotiations, that Europeanization East is a one-way street does not come as a surprise.

Process: Scrutiny by the Commission. Another feature differentiating Europeanization East from Europeanization West is that implementation seems much more extensively to be subject to routine Commission monitoring and control in a variety of policy areas. Even if the formal policy requirements are relatively vague and lack determinacy, "a continuous stream of evaluations, Commission communications" served to specify the adjustment requirements (Schimmelfennig, Engert, Knobel, chapter 2).

In Europeanization West, by contrast, implementation competences as a matter of principle lie with member states. Only in exceptional cases are they subject to direct control and monitoring by the Commission, such as in competition policy and, to a limited extent, in structural funds and agricultural policy. Again, this difference can be traced to the basic difference in the initial starting conditions of Europeanization East, i.e. political and economic transition, which may have motivated the Commission to engage in a much closer and continuous scrutiny of performance across all policy areas.

In conclusion, the differences between Europeanization East and West largely originate in the fundamentally different conditions from which Europeanization East began, that is democratic and economic transition, and the link with accession negotiations. Thus, the focus on a wide scope of policies (East) as opposed to a more narrow focus (West), the importance of institutional expectations (East) as opposed to the rarity of institutional requirements (West), the one-way street of influence vis-à-vis EU policies (East) as opposed to a two-way street of influencing as well as being influenced (West), and the relative frequency of routine implementation controls (East) as opposed to their relative infrequency (West)—these are all causally linked to the nature of the starting situation in the East.

But there are also similarities between the two Europeanization processes. The causal mechanisms explaining adjustment or non-adjustment applied in research

6. Personal communication, Wim van Aken, Florence, 22 November 2003.

on Europeanization West and East are basically the same. Once the overpowering shadow of accession conditionality and transition circumstances recedes in Europeanization East, these mechanisms will emerge more clearly, and the scope conditions will emerge in a way very similar to that documented by Europeanization research West. Already at this point, several cases presented in this volume clearly indicate the particular conditions under which predominantly goal-oriented strategic action on the one side or social learning on the other come to bear (see, for instance, Epstein, chapter 9).[7]

It is with respect to historical institutionalist explanations that one would expect the largest differences in the causal mechanisms explaining Europeanization. Since the political and economic conditions in CEECs have been fundamentally transformed, a "stickiness" of policy practices and institutional traditions seems much more unlikely.

---

7. It seems, however, that in the analysis of the differential impact of central bank policy as opposed to agricultural policy in Poland, where different causal mechanisms of Europeanization are at play, a control variable might be causally important for the outcome. The central bank policy is clearly a political elite issue, whereas the agricultural policy issue is of interest to a large portion of the Polish population.

CHAPTER ELEVEN

Conclusions: The Impact of the EU on the Accession Countries

Frank Schimmelfennig and Ulrich Sedelmeier

W hat have we learned? What drives the Europeanization of Central and Eastern Europe and under what conditions do nonmember states adopt the rules of the EU? Having tested three models of EU impact—external incentives, social learning, and lesson-drawing—in a great variety of policy fields and countries, our contributions suggest, first of all, that the influence of the EU depends crucially on the context in which the EU uses its incentives.

In the context of *democratic conditionality*, the influence of the EU depends on the initial conditions in the candidate countries. The EU's influence remains largely limited to a particular set of countries, namely the more fragile and unstable democracies. In the democratic front-runners, the EU's incentives were unnecessary; in undemocratic countries, they were ineffective. These differences can be explained mainly with the costs that incumbent governments incur if they adopt EU rules. Governments that fear that implementing EU rules will erode their domestic power base are unresponsive to the EU's incentives.

In the context of *acquis* conditionality, the key distinction is whether or not the EU sets the adoption of its rules as conditions for the accession of countries with a credible membership perspective. Before the EU used its conditionality, rule adoption was limited and selective, but it increased dramatically after conditionality set in. Thus, while none of the three models specified in the introductory chapter explains the Europeanization of Central and Eastern Europe entirely, the external incentives provided by the EU can largely account for the impact of the EU on candidate countries. Furthermore, depending on the context, a more

We thank the anonymous reviewers, Guido Schwellnus and the participants of the workshop "External Governance in the European Union" at the Mannheim Center for European Social Research (MZES) and of the MZES research seminar for their comments.

limited set of factors explains variations in rule adoption. Credible conditionality and adoption costs are the key variables in the context of democratic conditionality. In the context of *acquis* conditionality, the scope conditions are a credible membership perspective and the setting of EU rules as requirements for membership, while adoption costs and veto player structure only explain variation in the timing of rule adoption.

Social learning and lesson-drawing are primarily relevant in the context of *acquis* conditionality. The two models explain instances of rule adoption in the absence of EU conditionality. In the presence of EU conditionality, however, they only explain particular aspects of the adoption process. The social learning model may explain the political ramifications of compliance, namely why rule adoption is accompanied by a low level of domestic contestation. The lesson-drawing model helps us to understand which rules nonmember states choose when conditionality does not fully determine their choice. But even in these cases, rule adoption as such is primarily driven by the conditional external incentives of the EU.

In this concluding chapter, we analyze the findings of the individual empirical chapters for the influence of the EU on the CEE candidate countries in the two contexts of EU conditionality. We then assess the contribution of these findings to the literatures on EU enlargement, transition, EU governance and Europeanization, and international institutions. Finally, we offer some thoughts on the future perspectives of Europeanization in Central and Eastern Europe as well as on future research in this field.

Contexts of Conditionality and Models of Europeanization

We suggest distinguishing two main contexts of Europeanization in Central and Eastern Europe: democratic conditionality and *acquis* conditionality. The former concerns the general EU rules of liberal democracy. In this area, the EU has applied its conditionality from the very start of the transformations in the CEECs. The latter concerns the specific rules of the EU's *acquis communautaire*. In this context, the EU started to apply its conditionality only at a later stage, roughly from 1995, when it began to spell out in increasingly explicit terms the content of legislation that the CEECs had to adopt as preconditions for membership. The main rationale for distinguishing these contexts is theoretical. We suggest that, in each of them, different processes and factors of Europeanization are operative. While the external incentives model generally explains Europeanization in both contexts, the explanatory power of alternative models and specific factors varies among them.

The contexts of conditionality refer to different (stylized) historical stages in the Europeanization process. In the period starting with the beginning of post-communist transition in the CEECs, EU conditionality was mainly *democratic conditionality*: EU external incentives were linked to the fundamental political principles of the EU, the norms of human rights and liberal democracy, and the institutions of the market economy. These rules are not only fundamental for the EU, but for the entire western community of states. EU conditionality thus goes hand in hand with efforts of other organizations of this community (NATO, the OSCE, the OECD, or the Council of Europe) to support the democratization and democratic consolidation of the transformation countries. Democratic conditionality prepares the political ground for the accession process and the transfer of more specific EU rules. The main external incentive of democratic conditionality is, first, the establishment of institutional links with the EU, such as association agreements. In addition, the EU has linked technical and financial assistance to the fulfillment of basic political conditions. At a second stage, the incentive is the opening of accession negotiations. The decision to open these negotiations signifies that the EU considers the major conditions of democratic conditionality to be fulfilled. Even though the European Commission continues to monitor the democratic and human rights situation—with the threat that negotiations may be broken off still looming in the background—democratic conditionality recedes into the background.

Acquis conditionality sets in once candidate countries start to prepare for full membership, which becomes the major external incentive for rule adoption. In the case of the CEECs, the EU formulated rather strict *pre*-accession conditionality. It not only demanded full compliance prior to accession but insisted on significant progress with adopting the *acquis* as a precondition for starting accession negotiations.

In principle, each CEEC has found itself, at different times and for different issues, in these contexts of Europeanization. For some countries, however—in particular the democratic front-runners of Central Europe—democratic conditionality was not applied or did not need to be used heavily. Others have not been subject to *acquis* conditionality—yet—because they failed to adopt the basic liberal-democratic rules. Finally, the temporal distinction between the two contexts is not always perfectly clear-cut. In many cases, *acquis* conditionality already began to apply before all the problems of democratic conditionality had been sorted out. In eastern enlargement, regulatory alignment (such as the process triggered by the 1995 White Paper on the adoption of internal market rules) had started for the associated countries, although the EU still criticized the authoritarian politics of the Slovak government and the lack of respect for minority rights in the Baltic countries.

Democratic Conditionality

Explanatory Power of External Incentives

With regard to the general political rules of liberal democracy, EU conditionality has been present from the very beginning of the postcommunist transition process. What do our cases tell us about the relevant conditions and mechanisms of rule adoption in this context?

Generally, given high credibility of threats (exclusion) and promises (membership), the size of governmental adoption costs mattered most. The size of the ultimate reward—membership—was constantly high in all of the cases analyzed here. The cases of Turkey and, to some extent, the western Balkans indicate, however, that the promise of membership also needs to be credible. When the EU officially accorded Turkey the status of a candidate for membership and indicated that it would treat Turkey according to the same criteria as the other CEE candidates, it strongly enhanced the credibility of the membership promise it had already made in principle in the Ankara Agreement of 1963. This enhanced credibility did a lot to trigger the wave of liberal-democratic reforms in the country. In other cases, credibility concerned primarily the threat of exclusion. In the laggard states, the EU's decision in 1997 to begin accession negotiations with only five CEECs (plus Cyprus) dispelled any illusions about cheap EU membership that the state elites might have had or might have created to placate their societies.

However, even high benefits and credibility did not guarantee rule adoption. Studies of reluctant democratizers (Vachudova 2003; Schimmelfennig, Engert, and Knobel[1]) show that the benefits of EU membership often did not balance the domestic political costs of complying with democratic conditionality. For these governments, compliance would have meant giving up the very instruments on which the preservation of their political power rested. This is not only true for authoritarian governments, however. In the Baltic countries, for instance, the fear that citizenship and political rights for the Russian-speaking minority would dramatically change the composition of the electorate and undermine the dominant position of the Latvian or Estonian national parties was strong enough to produce noncompliance. In these cases, the likelihood of rule adoption only increased when the costs of rule adoption decreased (as a result of slow naturalization and the failure of a "Russian vote" to materialize). By contrast, other factors of the external incentives model—variations in determinacy and the speed of benefits—did not affect the likelihood of governmental rule adoption in any significant or systematic way. Whether democratic conditionality focused on the more determinate rules of democracy and general human rights or on the less determinate minority rights did not make a difference. And governments with high adoption costs also failed to comply when high benefits were close, as in the case of the Mečiar government in Slovakia.

But what if domestic adoption costs did not decrease? Under these circumstances, rewards-based intergovernmental bargaining alone has not been effective. Rather, rule adoption required prior political change, that is, the coming to power of democratic, reform-oriented political forces. It is a contested issue whether the EU has been able to contribute significantly to such political change via the domestic empowerment of democratic parties and NGOs and the mobilization of the electorate (Schimmelfennig, Engert, and Knobel 2003a; Vachudova 2004). In the wave of "second democratizations" in Romania, Bulgaria, Slovakia, Croatia, and

---

1. References to other chapters in this volume are noted by author name alone.

Serbia, it is hard to tell whether the electorate consciously voted for parties supporting democratization and European integration, following the advice and pressure of the EU and other western organizations, or whether they would have ousted the incumbent governments regardless of EU conditionality. At any rate, in the following round of elections in these countries, the electorate generally failed to vote according to EU preferences (except for Slovakia in 2002), suggesting that voters are more concerned with government performance on domestic problems than with European integration. Thanks to a highly credible EU conditionality and a high resonance of democratic norms, Slovakia may indeed be the only case in which EU democratic conditionality spurred the democratic parties to cooperate for the goal of EU membership and mobilized the electorate in their favor.

How effective, then, was democratic conditionality as a strategy of reinforcement by rewards? Whereas the cases of reform laggards and late democratizers analyzed in this volume suggest that democratic conditionality is likely to work eventually, either as a result of credible intergovernmental bargaining or domestic empowerment, the broader picture shows that it was neither necessary nor sufficient to bring about democratic change. The democratic front-runners of the region, such as Hungary, Poland, the Czech Republic, and Slovenia, began to democratize and consolidate their democracies without specific EU prodding. Even though it is always risky to put forward counterfactual arguments, it is plausible to assume that these countries would have continued on the path of democratic reform in the absence of democratic conditionality. In other countries of the region, EU democratic conditionality was not sufficient to bring about democratization and democratic consolidation. Such failure is likely to be the case, first, if societies are not sufficiently interested in EU membership to oust their authoritarian governments or if autocracy is sufficiently consolidated to suppress the democratic opposition and manipulate elections. One typical case is Belarus. Second, the reward of membership may be too distant, or the promise of membership may not be perceived as credible. This appears to be an additional factor in the European successor states of the Soviet Union such as Ukraine or Moldova. Third, EU democratic conditionality is likely to be ineffective in the case of failed states, primarily those affected by severe ethno-political conflict, such as many successor states of Yugoslavia. In the latter cases, the EU would need to go beyond reinforcement by reward and use both coercive and supportive strategies to have a positive impact.

Alternative Explanations

What do the models of social learning and lesson-drawing contribute to the explanation of rule adoption in the context of democratic conditionality? The chapters by Schwellnus and by Schimmelfennig, Engert, and Knobel concur in the finding that the legitimacy of EU conditions was causally irrelevant. Legitimate EU rules (democratic rules shared and implemented by the member states) did not produce more compliance than the minority protection rules, which have remained outside the *acquis* and are not generally accepted by the member states. Neither identity nor resonance account for variation in rule adoption. Thus the social learning model fails to explain the substantive impact of EU democratic conditionality. However, rule resonance may explain which pathway of democratic conditionality is most suitable. In cases of high societal resonance, domestic empowerment is an option, whereas in cases of low resonance, the EU must rely on intergovernmental bargaining.

The chapters on democratic conditionality did not explicitly test the lesson-drawing model against the external incentives model. Quite obviously, however, for the authoritarian governments of the region, democratization and the introduction of minority rights was an issue of lesson-avoidance rather than lesson-drawing (Schimmelfennig, Engert, and Knobel). Since it is derived from a study of the EU impact on reform laggards only, this conclusion has to be qualified, however. In the democratic front-runner countries, democratic reform and, to some extent, minority rights have been introduced without specific EU external incentives but are more readily explained as an effect of lesson-drawing (Schwellnus).

Acquis Conditionality

Explanatory Power of External Incentives

Acquis conditionality is the context in which the EU's influence has been particularly pervasive. Our contributions show that the most important distinction for the likelihood of rule adoption in this context is whether or not the EU had made rules subject of its conditionality. We do observe some rule adoption even before the EU's conditionality was spelled out, but it was patchy and selective. However, once a given issue area became subject of the EU's conditionality, rule adoption increased dramatically and became a consistent feature across countries and issue areas.

How can we explain the impact of the EU in this context? The key conditions were a credible membership perspective for a country and the setting of EU rules as conditions for membership. The external incentives model thus explains these cases well, but not all of the factors that it postulates as relevant are equally important. The most important factor influencing the cost-benefit calculations of CEEC governments is the *credibility* that the EU will reward rule adoption with membership. This credibility increased significantly once accession negotiations started.

The importance of adoption costs contrasts sharply with the context of democratic conditionality. As *acquis* conditionality does not concern the political system and the bases of political power as such, governments generally do not have to fear that the costs of rule adoption in individual policy areas will lead to a loss of office. Costs are thus unlikely to be prohibitive. Moreover, once a credible membership perspective has been established, adoption costs in individual policy areas are discounted against the (aggregate) benefits of membership, rather than just the benefits in this particular policy area. Thus, *adoption costs* and domestic *veto players* do not play as decisive a role as in the case of democratic conditionality. In some cases, they explain variation in the speed of rule adoption across issue areas and countries. Adoption costs and veto players therefore often influence the *timing* of rule adoption, but they do not lead to systematic variation in the likelihood of rule adoption as such.

In the cases analyzed by Beate Sissenich and Heather Grabbe, high adoption costs did not have a negative effect on rule adoption. Quite to the contrary, in the area of social policy, the more costly rules relating to secondary legislation (such as health and safety at the workplace) were adopted more fully than the less costly rules relating to the Social Dialogue. Concerning the free movement of persons, behavioral rule adoption was more pronounced for the more costly Schengen rules than for the internal market rules. Both Wade Jacoby and Liliana Andonova suggest that veto players account for variation in the *speed* of rule adoption. In the Czech Republic, regionalization increased after the Klaus government had lost office (see also Brusis 2003a). In the area of environmental policy, opposition from the energy sector in Poland prevented the adoption of control and command instruments that the EU prescribed to combat air pollution. In contrast to the Czech Republic, EU rules were thus only adopted in the late 1990s, once the EU applied its conditionality.

Further factors specified by the external incentives model appear even less significant and do not systematically account for variation in the cases examined in this volume. First, once *acquis* conditionality sets in, the *determinacy* of conditions is generally high: the EU regularly communicates in progress reports its expectations about which rules have to be adopted and specifies what further efforts are necessary. The clarity of EU rules that are part of its conditionality thus increased continuously in this context. Second, as the EU's *acquis* conditionality concerns conditions for membership, rather than, say, association, the *size* of the EU's rewards is high and does not vary in this context. Third, since our contributions predominantly focus on countries involved in accession negotiations that were designed to lead to the collective admission of most candidates at the same time, there is also no great variation with regard to the expected *speed* of the rewards. Still, we can ask whether the stage of accession negotiations makes a difference, i.e. how far advanced in the negotiations a country is and whether it can consider itself a front-runner for accession or a laggard.

Yet the stage of the accession process does not seem to have a systematic impact on compliance in our cases. On the one hand, we observe that toward the final stages of accession negotiations, rule adoption increases particularly in the more costly areas, in which the CEECs had delayed rule adoption. This is the case, for example, with regard to Schengen rules in Hungary and Poland, as Heather Grabbe demonstrates. On the other hand, we also observe a negative impact on rule adoption in countries that considered themselves front-runners and thus did not fear exclusion in the late stages of enlargement negotiations. Antoaneta Dimitrova provides the example of civil service reform in the Czech Republic, where rule adoption was much less in line with the EU's requirements than in most countries further down the line of accession. At the same time, we witness particularly vigorous efforts at rule adoption by countries further down the accession line, if these are coupled with "intermediary" rewards. For example, in the run-up to the Helsinki European Council in 1999, the EU identified specific issue areas in which rule adoption was presented as a precondition for the inclusion of Romania and Bulgaria into accession negotiations. Likewise, Heather Grabbe shows that these two countries made particularly strenuous efforts to implement the Schengen rules in order to achieve a lifting of the EU's visa requirements.

The broader picture that emerges is that it is not necessarily the stage of accession negotiations as such, but rather the *salience* the EU attaches to a particular area, that is a key factor that renders the EU's conditionality credible, and hence leads to an increase in rule adoption. CEEC governments know that the Commission and member states monitor adoption of these rules particularly closely and give them a higher weight in their enlargement decision. EU actors clearly communicated to the CEECs that the Schengen rules were a key condition for membership (Grabbe), while parts of the Commission and some member states indicated that in other policy areas rather superficial rule adoption would not present an obstacle to concluding negotiations. This was the case in social policy (Sissenich) and, maybe paradoxically in view of the repeated emphasis on the need for institutional capacity, in the area of civil service reform (Dimitrova).

The external incentives model thus fares rather well in explaining the broader picture of the impact of the EU in the context of *acquis* conditionality. Furthermore, its explanatory power can rely on a narrow range of factors: the main scope conditions for rule adoption are a credible membership perspective and the setting the adoption of its rules as conditions for membership. Variation in the timing of rule adoption can be explained primarily with domestic veto players and the salience of an issue area for accession.

Alternative Explanations

How well do the alternative explanatory models fare in the context of *acquis* conditionality? There are three main issues on which the models suggest competing hypotheses: i) the significance of the *legitimacy of rules* that the social learning model postulates as key for rule adoption but the external incentives model considers irrelevant; ii) time periods or issue areas in which EU *conditionality is absent* and for which the external incentives model would not expect rule adoption; and iii) the *form of rule adoption*, for which the external incentives model would primarily suggest that candidates choose the less costly form of merely formal rule adoption (as long as this is not detected by EU monitoring), while the social learning and lesson-drawing model envisage a much higher likelihood of behavioral adoption.

Our contributions suggest fairly conclusively that the legitimacy of rules did not matter for the likelihood of rule adoption. Rule adoption did not suffer when the

EU demanded compliance with the rule in question only from candidate countries, without any EU competence vis-à-vis the member states. This concerns, for example, administrative capacity and civil service reform (Dimitrova), but such a special "enlargement *acquis*" is most notable in the context of democratic conditionality (Schimmelfennig, Engert, and Knobel; Schwellnus). This finding also holds for issue areas in which the EU did not play by its own rules by delaying the benefits of rules adoption for the new members. This concerned, for example, the phasing in of the receipts from the Common Agricultural Policy (CAP) (Epstein), the transitional period that delays the free movement of workers from the new members, or membership in the Schengen area, the latter of which will require a separate decision by the member states (Grabbe). Finally, in areas in which the implementation and compliance record in the member states itself is patchy, such as social policy (Sissenich), the damaged legitimacy was not detrimental to rule adoption.

Yet whereas rule legitimacy did not have an impact on rule adoption by the accession countries, it does seem to have constrained the member states and their overwhelming bargaining power in the accession negotiations. When the member states deviated from the *acquis* rules for economic or financial reasons, they could only do so for a defined transition period (as in the phasing in of CAP payments) and felt compelled to grant similar derogations to the candidate countries (as in the equally long transitional periods for labor mobility granted to the member states and for land sales granted to the accession countries).[2]

The key challenge to the external incentives model is rule adoption during time periods or in issue areas in which EU conditionality is absent. Rule adoption without EU incentives for doing so should be an important validation of alternative explanations for the influence of the EU in the candidate countries. While the broader picture is of only limited rule adoption before the EU spelled out its (pre-)accession requirements in the context of *acquis* conditionality, we can indeed observe some rule adoption, albeit in a patchy, selective, and adaptive form. Thus, although EU incentives become a sufficient condition for rule adoption and trump all alternative mechanisms once the EU provides a credible membership perspective and spells out its requirements, *EU incentives are not a necessary condition for rule adoption.*

Examples of such rule adoption that predates the EU's conditionality include the adoption of command and control rules against air pollution in the Czech Republic (Andonova); moves toward regionalization in Hungary, which started even prior to 1989, and elements of health policies in Hungary and the Czech Republic (both Jacoby); and central bank independence in Poland (Epstein). Furthermore, some contributions show the importance of the lesson-drawing model in cases in which external incentives would predict rule adoption but are indeterminate as to what specific rules will be adopted, as the EU's requirements leave some room for choice within a larger universe of acceptable rules.

---

2. We thank one of the reviewers for alerting us to this point.

These contributions provide important evidence for the mechanisms of social learning and lesson-drawing. After the collapse of communism in the CEECs, the widespread perception of policy failure and of the need to replace "old" socialist rules or to adopt new rules in areas where none existed before, created conditions conducive for both mechanisms. Nonetheless, adoption of EU rules was far less pervasive than in the period after EU conditionality set in. Even in some cases in which learning from abroad led to the adoption of new rules, these rules were not imported from the EU. Poland, for example, chose U.S.-style instruments for air pollution control that relied on economic incentives rather than the technology-based command and control regulations used in the EU. In yet other cases, the rules in question were not specific to the EU. For example, Polish central banking rules were promoted more broadly by the IFIs (Epstein).

Which factors were most important in determining whether candidate countries imported rules from the EU? Our contributions demonstrate that while it is possible to show that certain rules drew on practices in the EU or particular member states, it is much more difficult to identify clearly which factors consistently predict whether or not (and which) EU rules will be chosen. Most contributions emphasize the presence or absence of epistemic communities promoting EU rules as a key factor. The presence of EU-centered networks of experts and officials was an important condition for the transfer of EU rules, while the dominance of more U.S.-centered IFI experts led, for example, to the adoption of different clean air policies in Poland (Andonova). Dense interactions between CEEC officials and experts with their EU counterparts also facilitated social learning, as in the case of Polish central banking (Epstein) or of officials in CEEC interior ministries who—in contrast to their colleagues from foreign ministries or prime ministers' offices—appear to have largely internalized the ideas underpinning the EU's Schengen rules (Grabbe). At the same time, the presence of such epistemic communities alone is not a reliable indicator. For example, in contrast to earlier periods, consultations with EU health policy experts had little impact on Hungarian policies after 1998 (Jacoby).

Our contributions point to a second area in which alternative explanatory models appear relevant. Many contributors find that while external incentives played an important role in the process of rule adoption, they went hand in hand with other mechanisms. Whether external incentives account exclusively for rule adoption or not makes an important difference for the *form* of rule adoption. Rules that are adopted through social learning or lesson-drawing are much less contested domestically. Implementation is more likely to result in behavioral rule adoption and sustained compliance.

Rachel Epstein demonstrates that central bank independence in Poland, which was adopted as the result of a social learning process, enjoyed wide acceptance and was successfully defended against governmental attacks by a broad coalition of societal actors. By contrast, the coercive process that led to the adoption of agricultural policy resulted in widespread domestic resistance and contestation. Heather Grabbe shows that social learning and lesson-drawing by officials in

CEEC interior ministries led to a behavioral adoption of Schengen rules, despite the concerns of foreign ministries and prime ministers' offices.

As we will elaborate below, the importance of the adoption mechanism for the form of rule adoption and implementation should become particularly important after the CEECs have become full members. Rules that are adopted through social learning processes or lesson-drawing should facilitate sustained compliance by creating domestic stakeholders. Rule adoption motivated by external incentives and bargaining are more likely to cause domestic resistance and poor implementation in the absence of continued monitoring and threats of sanctions.

In sum, the external incentives model captures well the influence of the EU in the context of *acquis* conditionality. External incentives explain why rule adoption increased dramatically after EU conditionality set in, and why it was generally only limited and patchy before. However, it cannot explain those instances of rule adoption in the earlier period. In these cases, social learning and/or lesson-drawing explain rule adoption. But why was rule adoption not more widespread, given strong policy dissatisfaction, high identification with Western Europe and a generally high legitimacy of western rules and models? There are two possible explanations. First, one may argue that social learning and lesson-drawing need a long time and that the period between transition and the start of *acquis* conditionality was too short for both processes to fully unfold. This explanation, however, is not entirely convincing. In some cases reported in this volume, there was obviously enough time for social learning and lesson-drawing to have a positive effect, or the same duration of exposure to EU rules led to divergent outcomes in rule adoption. By contrast, the second explanation is able to explain the variation in rule adoption. The transferability of EU rules was generally problematic, as adoption costs were often high, veto players resisted outside rules, and resonance was low. These considerations underline the conclusion that, in the absence of *acquis* conditionality, the Europeanization of Central and Eastern Europe would have remained limited and patchy.

A final and more general challenge to the external incentives model might be based on the argument that the entire Europeanization process has been embedded in a larger social learning process. According to this argument, the CEECs' decision to seek accession to the EU resulted from their strong identification with the European international community and the high legitimacy of the European integration project. The smooth transfer of EU rules during the accession process could then be attributed to "a mimetic logic based on the search of legitimacy" (Maniokas 2002, 6).[3] However, whereas we agree that, for most of the candidate countries, their desire to join the EU was a corollary of their "return to Europe," this fact still leaves central features of the Europeanization process unexplained. First, as we have shown, the CEECs' early interest in EU membership was not accompanied with an early adoption of EU rules. Rather, *acquis* conditionality provided the necessary link between the two. Second, even though all candidates in

---

3. We thank one of the reviewers for bringing up this point.

the end adopted the EU rules during the accession negotiations, there was variation in timing and accuracy, a fact best explained by the variation in domestic costs,
veto players, and salience emphasized in the external incentives model.

Contributions to Related Bodies of Literature

In the introductory chapter, we suggested that the study of Europeanization in
Central and Eastern Europe might be able to address lacunae in several related
bodies of literature. In light of our findings, what are the major contributions?

Enlargement

Our research has confirmed the extremely important and strong links between
enlargement and Europeanization in Central and Eastern Europe. The extension
of EU membership to the CEECs is, at its core, a process of Europeanization, a
massive export of EU rules. Compliance with the fundamental liberal-democratic
rules of the EU is the central precondition for entering into accession negotiations
with the EU, and the negotiations are mainly a process of rule transfer.

Moreover, our research has shown that enlargement is the main driving force
and the main condition of effective EU rule export in this region. For the CEECs,
the massive benefits of EU membership and the perception that EU accession was
a top priority and an absolutely essential policy have been the core incentive for
adopting EU rules. In the absence of enlargement and accession conditionality, the
export of EU rules would have remained limited, patchy, and slow—as demonstrated by the pattern of rule adoption in the absence of conditionality. The
massive transfer of EU rules cannot be explained simply by lesson-drawing or
social learning. Policy dissatisfaction in the CEECs was widespread and led their
governments to look abroad for alternative rules and solutions. The search for new
rules alone, however, did not ensure that they would look to the *EU* (rather than
other international organizations or nation states) or adopt EU rules in cases where
they would be costly and inconvenient. It required the credible prospect of EU
membership and the credible linkage of membership with rule adoption to focus
the CEECs on *EU* rules and to overcome domestic inertia and resistance.

One might ask, of course, whether the sheer importance of access to the EU's
internal market would not have led the small economies of Central and Eastern
Europe to adopt EU rules unilaterally even in the absence of accession. This is
certainly true with regard to the product regulations that otherwise present non-
tariff barriers (NTBs) for CEEC goods and services. The adoption of EU rules
by nonmember countries like Norway or Switzerland provides ample evidence for
this process.[4] However, rule adoption in the context of enlargement goes much
further than the elimination of NTBs. The issues of Europeanization analyzed in

4. We thank Andreas Dür for alerting us to this point.

this volume would not have been affected by market integration alone—above all, political and minority rights, regionalization, and civil service reform—or in a much more limited way, as in the cases of central banking, agriculture, social, and environmental policy.

Transition

It follows from the finding of massive rule transfer driven by enlargement and accession conditionality that the transformation of the former communist systems of the CEECs cannot be adequately understood without analyzing the impact of the EU. True as it is, this general statement requires some modification. As for democratic transition and consolidation, we detected a significant causal impact of the EU only with regard to a specific group of countries: the unstable democracies that had not yet been consolidated. Both for the democratic front-runners of the region and the consolidated authoritarian and autocratic countries, domestic factors are indeed sufficient to explain the divergent transition pathways. In these groups of countries, EU democratic conditionality has largely been either redundant or ineffective. By contrast, the EU has made a real difference in the countries in between those two extremes.

First, if domestic adoption costs for governments were moderate, a credible promise of membership and a credible threat of exclusion from membership provided governments with a sufficiently strong incentive to change their cost-benefit assessments or strengthened reform-oriented forces within these governments. Second, the EU "locked in" democratic reforms in unstable democracies with governments alternating between reform-friendly liberal democratic forces and reform-adverse authoritarian or populist forces: EU integration advanced when these countries had reform-friendly governments and thereby made it more and more costly for their reform-adverse opponents to reverse course.

The impact of the EU, however, goes beyond democratic transition and consolidation. Europeanization implies a more far-reaching transformation of the state in Central and Eastern Europe. Studies of postcommunist transformation generally point to the fact that transition in the region was not just a political transition from communist dictatorship to democracy but also an economic transition from a socialist central planning to a capitalist market economy, a foreign policy transition from Soviet domination to state autonomy, and, in many cases, a territorial transition from multinational states to new or resurrected nation states.

Europeanization affected, complemented, and, to some extent, superseded all of these dimensions of postcommunist transition in ambivalent ways. First, whereas it furthered democratic consolidation in the unstable democracies of the region, it also undermined the democratic and parliamentary processes in the accession countries by imposing large parts of the legislative agenda (Innes 2002a).

Second, by integrating the CEECs into the internal market, the EU helped to promote the capitalist market economy. At the same time, however, the EU not only transferred its market-distorting rules (e.g. in agriculture) to the CEECs but also complemented markets with the institutions of the "regulatory state" (Majone 1996; McGowan and Wallace 1996), both at the national and the European levels. As a result, the CEEC markets became more regulated and their administrations more charged with regulatory policies (such as environmental and consumer protection, regional policy and competition policy) and the accompanying regulatory agencies than they had been after the roll-back of the command economy and under the influence of the IFIs (Grzymała-Busse and Innes 2003; Maniokas 2002).

Third, EU integration (together with NATO integration) removed the specter of Russian domination for good. At the same time, however, accession to the EU was again a highly asymmetrical process and involved a substantial loss of autonomy for the polities of Central and Eastern Europe. Likewise, the new or reborn nation states that emerged from the ruins of the multinational communist countries are on the way to being integrated in another multinational and multilevel polity.

In sum, any study of transition that is limited to domestic processes and outcomes and overlooks the parallel process of Europeanization will fail to grasp the complex and sometimes contradictory transformation of the state in Central and Eastern Europe. Our finding that the EU as an actor matters but that its influence is context-dependent, furthermore, raises questions for both actor-centered and structuralist approaches in the debate on post-socialist transformation.[5] At a minimum, we suggest that each side in this debate has to make greater efforts to include the EU in their explanatory frameworks. Actor-centered models of strategic decision-making that dominated the debate in the early period of democratic transition (see, e.g., Przeworski 1992) would need to include the credibility and size of EU rewards in order to fully understand the politics of democratic consolidation and market-making. Structuralist approaches tend to consider the structural conditions as largely emanating in the past, regardless whether they refer to the socialist legacies (e.g., Jowitt 1992), extrication modes (e.g., Karl and Schmitter 1991; Munck and Leff 1997) or initial macroeconomic conditions (e.g., Haggard and Kaufman 1997). These explanations would do well not only to consider the EU as part of the structural context but to conceptualize the dynamic nature of the EU's conditionality for both the material and normative structure in which governments and other domestic actors operate. By including the EU as an actor that has the power to modify existing institutional structures and to build new ones, our findings suggest one possible way for transformation researchers to integrate agency- and structure-based approaches in their analyses.

EU Governance

EU governance in the enlargement process hardly bears any resemblance to the "new" or "network" governance that is claimed, by some of the literature, to characterize a broad range of governance within the Community (Eising and

---

5. We thank Sabina Avdagić for pushing us to clarify this point.

Kohler-Koch 1999, 275) and even the external relations of the EU (Filtenborg, Gänzle, and Johansson 2002). Rather, EU governance in the accession countries exhibits many basic features of "old governance," including vertical control, command, and steering. Although it is not based on any formal hierarchical relationship and is located outside the EU's legal system of rule creation and rule enforcement, the highly asymmetrical relationship between insiders and outsiders gives the EU a degree of power that it does not enjoy either vis-à-vis its own member states nor vis-à-vis other external actors.

Accession negotiations are negotiations only by name. They start from predetermined and nonnegotiable formal rules decided by the member states alone. The scope for change is restricted to bargaining over transition periods. Rather, "negotiations" serve the EU to explain its organizational rules to the representatives of the external states and to tell them what they have to do in order to adopt them.

Moreover, EU governance in the enlargement process has been dominated by bureaucratic actors, intergovernmental or inter-bureaucratic relations, and a top-down process of rule transfer. Within the EU, governmental and supranational bureaucracies possess a high degree of autonomy in enlargement. First, the role of the public has been very limited. Given the widespread skepticism of EU public opinion toward enlargement, EU governments are under virtually no public pressure to accommodate nonmember interests. On the other hand, this skepticism has not constrained governments in pursuing enlargement (see, e.g., Harris 2002). Second, EU norms and policies are generally transferred in a top-down mode to the external states. In their relations with the candidate countries, the EU mainly relies on intergovernmental bargaining. It privileges central governments and bureaucracies charging them with implementing EU rules (Grabbe 2001a). Even in social policy, where transnational networks were in place and societal actors should have played an important role (above all, for the requirement of Social Dialogue), their input was irrelevant (Sissenich, chapter 8; Sissenich 2002b).

Europeanization

In the introductory chapter, we asked whether the Europeanization of Central and Eastern Europe differed from Europeanization in the member states and whether the study of "Europeanization East" could shed new light on the theoretical debate on the mechanisms and conditions of EU-induced domestic change. First of all, we must start with a caveat. The CEECs are still at an early stage of the process of Europeanization. Therefore we most often observe the formal, legislative, and institutional adoption of EU rules, rather than their implementation. That being said, however, we find that accession conditionality, as an instrument that the EU obviously does not possess in its relations with the member states, does make a big difference for the process and the conditions of Europeanization (Héritier).

First, the dominant logic of external incentives corroborates the "actor-based rational-choice approach" to the study of Europeanization, which highlights the change of opportunities and constraints and the redistribution of resources as the main mechanisms of domestic change (Héritier 2001a, 3). By contrast, our comparative case studies provide little support for the "institution-based" sociological institutionalist or constructivist approach with its emphasis on the logic of appropriateness, identification, and resonance (Börzel and Risse 2003, 66; Héritier 2001a, 3–5). The fact that the adoption of EU rules in the context of accession conditionality—with its concomitant high adaptational pressure—was quick and general also confirms rationalist expectations where sociological or historical institutionalism would have predicted more inertia (Börzel and Risse 2003, 70).

Second, however, the main mediating factor emphasized in the rationalist analysis of Europeanization—domestic structures defined as veto points or players—only played a minor role in the accession process. In the context of democratic conditionality, the adoption costs of governments were paramount; in the context of *acquis* conditionality, the veto player structure mattered for the speed but not the likelihood of rule adoption. Apparently, the high benefits and the time pressures of accession significantly reduce the causal impact of veto players and other intervening domestic structures. Similarly, institutional legacies or specific national traditions and situations only played out to the extent that EU rules were flexible enough to leave room for them. Moreover, except for the difference between democratic and *acquis* conditionality, we did not detect any systematic variation between policy types and the mechanisms and outcomes of Europeanization (Knill and Lehmkuhl 2002). Thus, for the peculiar context of accession conditionality, our findings go against the thrust of the Europeanization literature, which highlights the relevance of domestic mediating factors and institutional inertia.

Can we attribute the weak causal relevance of domestic structures to the overpowering impact of accession conditionality alone or is it (also) an effect of the simultaneity of systemic transformation in the CEECs that reduced institutional inertia (Héritier)? An answer to this question would require a careful comparative analysis of the Europeanization of Central and Eastern Europe with, say, the EFTA candidates with their stable political institutions. Our analysis of democratic conditionality, at least, suggests that inertia was of minor relevance compared with the credibility and adaptation costs of accession conditionality. On the one hand, Turkey's entrenched political institutions began to change rather quickly once the membership perspective became credible; on the other hand, the Slovak government under Mečiar stuck to its authoritarian practices (for reasons of domestic power preservation) although these practices had been introduced only very recently.

Finally, it appears as if Europeanization in Central and Eastern Europe not only proceeded at a much quicker pace than in the member states, it also produced more homogeneous and convergent outcomes. To substantiate this assumption, however, we would not only need comparative East-West research but also a longer time-frame for the analysis.

International Institutions

At the theoretical level, the conclusions for "Europeanization" also hold for the study of international institutional effects more generally: whereas they broadly support a rationalist-institutionalist explanation of international institutional effects on domestic change, they reduce the causal role of domestic intervening variables.

More specifically, they add new evidence to the debate on the effectiveness of international conditionality. In contrast to the literature, which generally sees the effectiveness of IFI conditionality as mixed, our study draws a more unambiguously positive picture. There is no theoretical quarrel here, however. That EU accession conditionality was so successful can be attributed to exactly those conditions that are lacking or found wanting in the case of IFI conditionality. First, the size of benefits was significantly higher: EU membership and IFI loans are hardly comparable in this respect. Second, cross-conditionality was absent in the EU case. For one thing, there was no alternative to EU membership for the CEECs. Moreover, in the context of democratic conditionality, other attractive international organizations such as NATO set the same conditions. Third, the fact that eastern enlargement was costly to the EU and—in contrast with IFI lending—did not constitute a core activity defining the very purpose of the organization, enhanced the credibility of conditionality significantly.

Future Perspectives on the Europeanization of Central and Eastern Europe

It is the main finding of this volume that, in the context of accession conditionality, the EU has had a tremendous impact on the Europeanization of Central and Eastern Europe and that this impact has been a product of the size of the net benefits of EU accession to the candidate countries and of the credibility of EU conditionality. This finding immediately triggers a question for the future: what will happen after accession when these instruments of Europeanization are no longer available? Once the candidates have joined the EU, they will already reap the benefits of membership and cannot be induced to comply with EU rules by conditional incentives. Will this new context slow down, stall, or even reverse the Europeanization process in the CEECs? This question is not only of practical importance, it is also a challenge to future research on Europeanization in this region.

There are, indeed, many good reasons for concern in light of our findings. First, many EU rules have been only formally transposed into national legislation but are not fully or reliably implemented. Since rule adoption has been driven mainly by external incentives, the absence of these incentives should significantly slow down or even halt the implementation process.

Second, in the absence of high conditional external benefits, domestic structures such as adoption costs, veto players, and resonance that were superseded in the conditionality context will again have a causal impact. This will be particularly relevant because rule adoption via external incentives is generally more likely to be contested than if it resulted from social learning or lesson-drawing.

Third, many of the policymakers or "core executives" who are responsible for the quick transposition of EU rules and are knowledgeable in EU affairs—and are also those most likely to have been influenced by social learning—will move to Brussels to assume the posts in the EU organizations allotted to the new member states.

Fourth, the new member states might not be willing to accept further rules of the "enlargement *acquis*," which were specifically designed for accession candidates but are not binding on the old members. Moreover, as we know from British and Spanish experiences, accession deals that are considered unfair impositions lead to disgruntled newcomers that spend much of their early accession years trying to renegotiate perceived wrongs. Under all these circumstances, the short-term effectiveness of rule transposition in the context of conditionality might well be compromised by medium-term ineffectiveness of implementation.

Yet the absence of conditionality need not necessarily result in the stagnation or breakdown of Europeanization—if other mechanisms efficiently replace external incentives. First, in areas of the regular *acquis*, the new member states will be subject to the same noncompliance procedures as current members, such as the infringement procedure, which allows the Commission to bring member states before the Court (which might impose fines), or private litigation in national courts (see, e.g., Börzel 2001; Tallberg 2002). In the area of former democratic conditionality, the new Article 7 of the Treaty on European Union gives the EU the power to sanction and eventually exclude countries that violate its fundamental democratic rules. Moreover, the Commission has already attempted to introduce instruments developed initially to monitor compliance in the candidate countries inside the EU, such as the publication of annual "scoreboards" on implementation records with internal market legislation. New policy instruments, such as benchmarking or the open method of coordination, are also in part inspired by enlargement practices.

However, these old and new EU instruments rely more on shaming and social influence than on effective material sanctioning mechanisms (Héritier). Large-scale breaches and infringement procedures in themselves would be detrimental to mutual trust in the ability and willingness of all members to play by the rules on which the internal market is based. In addition, the EU does not possess instruments to sanction breaches of the rules of the "enlargement *acquis*" that were adopted during the accession process.

Second, the mechanisms of lesson-drawing and social learning that were crowded out by the massive impact of external incentives in the context of conditionality might again come to the fore and gain in relevance after accession. Among other factors, the active participation in EU policymaking may be conducive to such processes.

Third, as suggested by historical institutionalist analyses, the formal rules and institutions transposed to the new member states may prove "sticky" even in the

228 Frank Schimmelfennig and Ulrich Sedelmeier

absence of external enforcement. They may nurture domestic interest in preservation, e.g. the interest of bureaucratic actors whose turf and income are based on them, or they may simply be difficult to abolish for institutional reasons.

Finally, the enlargement *acquis* might feed back into rule creation in the EU. In part, actors in the EU might promote the transfer of competences to EU institutions in areas of democracy conditionality, in order to have continued leverage over newer members that might slip back into authoritarian rule. The Article 7 provisions mentioned above are one example. At the same time, norm entrepreneurs may seize on the EU's apparent double standards as well as on the discursive validation of democratic and human right norms as constitutive principles of the EU in the enlargement discourse in order to promote a legalization of these norms at the EU level.

Thus, the contributions to this volume analyze stages in the Europeanization process of Central and Eastern Europe that come to an end with EU accession. However, they should also provide a useful baseline for the next steps in research—the post-accession Europeanization of the new member states.

REFERENCES

Abbott, Kenneth, Robert Keohane, Andrew Moravcsik, Anne-Marie Slaughter, and Duncan Snidal. 2000. The Concept of Legalization. *International Organization* 54:401–19.

Adler, Emanuel, and Peter Haas. 1992. Conclusion: Epistemic Communities, World Order, and the Creation of a Reflective Research Program. *International Organization* 46:367–90.

Ágh, Attila. 1998. *Emerging Democracies in East Central Europe and the Balkans.* Cheltenham, UK: Edward Elgar.

———. 2002. The Reform of State Administration in Hungary: The Capacity of Core Ministries to Manage the Europeanization. *Budapest Papers on Europeanization* 7. Budapest: Hungarian Centre for Democracy Studies Foundation.

Allen, David. 2000. Cohesion and the Structural Funds. In *Policy-Making in the European Union,* 4th ed., ed. Helen Wallace and William Wallace, 243–66. Oxford: Oxford University Press.

Anderson, Richard Jr., Steven Fish, Stephen Hanson, and Philip Roeder. 2001. *Postcommunism and the Theory of Democracy.* Princeton: Princeton University Press.

Andersson, Magnus. 1999. *Change and Continuity in Poland's Environmental Policy.* Boston: Kluwer Academic Publishers.

Andonova, Liliana. 2003. *Transnational Politics of the Environment. The EU and Environmental Policy in Central and Eastern Europe.* Cambridge, MA: MIT Press.

Andreescu, Gabriel. 2001. Universal Thought, Eastern Facts: Scrutinizing National Minority Rights in Romania. In *Can Liberal Pluralism be Exported? Western Political Theory and Ethnic Relations in Eastern Europe,* ed. Will Kymlicka and Magda Opalski, 270–82. Oxford and New York: Oxford University Press.

Avdagić, Sabina. 2003. Shaping the Paths to Labor Weakness: The Interplay of Political Strategies and Institutional Structures in Post-Communist Central Eastern Europe. Ph.D. dissertation. Central European University, Budapest.

Avery, Graham. 1995. The Commission's Perspective on the EFTA Accession Negotiations. Sussex European Institute Working Paper No. 12. Brighton, UK: Sussex European Institute.

229

Avery, Graham, and Fraser Cameron. 1998. *The Enlargement of the European Union.* Sheffield, UK: Sheffield Academic Press.

Bachtler, John, Ruth Downes, and Grzegorz Gorzelak. 2000. Transition, Cohesion, and Regional Policy in Central and Eastern Europe: Conclusions. In *Transition, Cohesion, and Regional Policy in Central and Eastern Europe*, ed. Bachtler, Downes, and Gorzelak, 355–78. Burlington, VT: Ashgate.

Bachtler, John, Ruth Downes, Irene McMaster, Philip Raines, and Sandra Taylor. 2002. The Transfer of EU Regional Policy to the Countries of Central and Eastern Europe: Can One Size Fit All? Working Paper No. 10. European Policies Research Centre, Future Governance Series.

Bajda, Piotr, Magdalena Syposz, and Dariusz Wojakowski. 2001. Equality in Law, Protection in Fact: Minority Law and Practice in Poland. In *Diversity in Action: Local Public Management of Multi-Ethnic Communities in Central and Eastern Europe*, ed. Anna-Mária Bíró and Petra Kovács, 205–39. Budapest: IGI Books.

Baldwin, Richard. 1994. *Towards an Integrated Europe.* London: Centre for Economic Policy Research.

Baldwin, Richard, Joseph Francois, and Richard Portes. 1997. The Costs and Benefits of Eastern Enlargement: The Impact on the EU and Central Europe. *Economic Policy* 24:125–76.

Bartsch, Sebastian. 1995. *Minderheitenschutz in der internationalen Politik: Völkerbund und KSZE/OSZE in neuer Perspektive.* Opladen, Germany: Westdeutscher Verlag.

Baun, Michael J. 2000. *A Wider Europe: The Process and Politics of European Union Enlargement.* Lanham, MD: Rowman and Littlefield.

Betten, Lammy, and Nicholas Grief. 1998. *EU Law and Human Rights.* London and New York: Longman.

Beyme, Klaus von. 1994. *Systemwechsel in Osteuropa.* Frankfurt: Suhrkamp.

Bigo, Didier. 1998. Frontiers and Security in the European Union: The Illusion of Migration Control. In *The Frontiers of Europe*, ed. Malcolm Anderson and Eberhard Bort, 148–64. London: Pinter.

Birch, Sarah. 2000. Elections and Representation in Post-Communist Eastern Europe. In *Elections in Central and Eastern Europe: The First Wave*, ed. H.-D. Klingemann, E. Mochmann, and K. Newton, 13–35. Berlin: Edition Sigma.

Birckenbach, Hanne-Margret. 1997. The Citizenship Issue in Estonia and Latvia: A Success Story of Preventive Diplomacy? In *Preventive Diplomacy through Fact-Finding: How International Organisations Review the Conflict over Citizenship in Estonia and Latvia*, ed. H.-M. Birckenbach, 17–91. Hamburg: Schleswig-Holstein Institute for Peace Research (SHIP).

Blažek, Jiří. 1996. Regional Patterns of Economic Adaptability to the Transformation and Global Processes in the Czech Republic. *Geographica* 37:61–70.

———. 1997. The Czech Republic on Its Way Towards West European Structures. *European Spatial Research and Policy* 4: 57–58.

Blažek, Jiří, and Sjaak Boekhout. 2000. Regional Policy in the Czech Republic and the EU Accession. In *Transition, Cohesion, and Regional Policy in Central and Eastern Europe*, ed. John Bachtler, Ruth Downes, and Grzegorz Gorzelak, 301–17. Burlington, VT: Ashgate.

Blumenwitz, Dieter, and Markus Pallek. 2000. *Draft of a Minority Protection Clause in the Charter on Fundamental Rights of the European Union: Contribution by the International Institute for Right of Nationality and Regionality.* CHARTE 4301/00 CONTRIB 173.

den Boer, Monika, and William Wallace. 2000. Justice and Home Affairs. In *Policy-Making in the European Union*, 4th ed., ed. Helen Wallace and William Wallace, 493–522. Oxford: Oxford University Press.

Bohle, Dorothee. 2002. The Ties that Bind the New Europe: Neoliberal Restructuring and Transnational Actors in the Deepening and Widening of the European Union. Paper presented at the ECPR joint sessions workshop Enlargement and European Governance. Turin, Italy, 22–27 March.

Borbély, Szilvia. 2000. Hungary: EU Enlargement and Trade Unions. *South East Europe Review* 3:97–108.

Borish, Michael. 1998. An Assessment and Rating of the Polish Banking System. Washington, DC: USAID.

Börzel, Tanja. 1999. Towards Convergence in Europe? Institutional Adaptation to Europeanisation in Germany and Spain. *Journal of Common Market Studies* 37:573–96.

———. 2001. Non-Compliance in the European Union: Pathology or Statistical Artefact? *Journal of European Public Policy* 8:803–24.

———. 2002. Pace-Setting, Foot-Dragging, and Fence-Sitting: Member State Responses to Europeanization. *Journal of Common Market Studies* 40:193–214.

———. 2003. Shaping and Taking EU Policies: Member State Responses to Europeanisation. Institute of European Studies. Queen's University of Belfast. Queen's papers on Europeanisation No. 2003–5.

Börzel, Tanja, and Thomas Risse. 2002. Die Wirkung internationaler Institutionen: Von der Normanerkennung zur Normeinhaltung. In *Regieren in internationalen Institutionen: Festschrift für Beate Kohler-Koch*, ed. Markus Jachtenfuchs and Michelle Knodt, 141–82. Opladen, Germany: Leske and Budrich.

———. 2003. Conceptualizing the Domestic Impact of Europe. In *The Politics of Europeanization*, ed. Keith Featherstone und Claudio Radaelli, 55–78. Oxford: Oxford University Press.

Bossaert, Danielle, and Christoph Demke. 2003. *Civil Services in the Accession States: New Trends and the Impact of the Integration Process.* Maastricht, Netherlands: EIPA.

Botcheva, Liliana. 2001. Expertise and International Governance: Eastern Europe and the Adoption of European Union Environmental Legislation. *Global Governance* 7:197–224.

Brunner, Georg. 1999. Minderheitenrechtliche Regelungskonzepte in Osteuropa. In *Das Recht der nationalen Minderheiten in Osteuropa*, ed. Georg Brunner and Boris Meissner, 39–73. Berlin: Spitz.

Brusis, Martin. 2003a. Instrumentalized Conditionality: Regionalization in the Czech Republic and Slovakia. Paper presented at the workshop The Europeanization of Central and Eastern Europe. European University Institute. Florence, Italy, 4–5 July.

———. 2003b. The European Union and Interethnic Power-Sharing Arrangements in Accession Countries. *Journal of Ethnopolitics and Minority Issues in Europe* 1.

Bruszt, Laszlo. 2002. Making Markets and Eastern Enlargement: Diverging Convergence? In *The Enlarged European Union: Diversity and Adaptation*, ed. Peter Mair and Jan Zielonka, 121–40. London: Frank Cass.

Bunce, Valerie. 1999. *Subversive Institutions: The Design and Destruction of Socialism and the State.* Cambridge: Cambridge University Press.

Bungs, Dzintra. 2000. Lettland und Litauen: Sichere Zukunft durch EU-Beitritt. In *Osterweiterung der Europäischen Union—Die doppelte Reifeprüfung*, ed. B. Lippert, 223–49. Bonn: Europa Union Verlag.

Bútora, Martin, and Zora Bútorová. 1999. Slovakia's Democratic Awakening. *Journal of Democracy* 10:80–95.

Bútorová, Zora. 1998. Transformation Challenges in Public Perception. In *Democracy and Discontent in Slovakia: A Public Opinion Profile of a Country in Transition*, ed. Z. Bútorová, 21–36. Bratislava: Institute for Public Affairs.

Bútorová, Zora, and Ol'ga Gyárfasová. 1998. Social Climate Three Years After the 1994 Elections. In *Democracy and Discontent in Slovakia: A Public Opinion Profile of a Country in Transition*, ed. Z. Bútorová, 51–37. Bratislava: Institute for Public Affairs.

Carlsnaes, Walter, Thomas Risse, and Beth Simmons, eds. 2002. *Handbook of International Relations*. London: Sage.

Casale, Giuseppe. 2001. Social Dialogue and Tripartism in Poland: Evolution and Trends. In Focus Program on Strengthening Social Dialogue Working Paper No. 2 (November). Geneva: International Labor Office.

Červený, Miloš, and Alois Andrle. 2000. Czech Republic. In *Transition, Cohesion, and Regional Policy in Central and Eastern Europe*, ed. John Bachtler, Ruth Downes, and Grzegorz Gorzelak, 85–98. Burlington, VT: Ashgate.

ČEZ (Czech Electricity Company) 2002. ČEZ and the Environment. Accessed in November 2002 at http://www.cez.cz.

Chayes, Abram, and Antonia Chayes. 1995. *The New Sovereignty. Compliance With International Regulatory Agreements*. Cambridge, MA: Harvard University Press.

Checkel, Jeffrey. 1997. International Norms and Domestic Politics: Bridging the Rationalist-Constructivist Divide. *European Journal of International Relations* 3:473–95.

———. 1999a. Social Construction and Integration. *Journal of European Public Policy* 6:545–60.

———. 1999b. Norms, Institutions, and National Identity in Contemporary Europe. *International Studies Quarterly* 43:83–114.

———. 2000. Compliance and Conditionality. ARENA Working Paper 00/18. Oslo: ARENA.

———. 2001. Why Comply? Social Learning and European Identity Change. *International Organization* 55:553–88.

Christiansen, Thomas, Knud Erik Joergensen, and Antje Wiener, eds. 2001. *The Social Construction of Europe*. London: Sage.

Chruściak, Rzyszard, ed. 1997. *Projekty Konstytucji, 1993–1997*. 2 volumes. Warsaw: Wydawnictwo Sejmowe.

Coen, David, and Adrienne Héritier. 2004. Refining Regulatory Regimes. Manuscript. Florence, London.

Commission. 1997a. *Agenda 2000—Summary and conclusions of the Opinions of Commission concerning the Applications for Membership to the European Union presented by the Candidate Countries*. DOC/97/8, 15 July.

———. 1997b. *Agenda 2000: For a Stronger and Wider Union*. COM(97) 2000. Vol. 1, 15 July.

———. 1997c. *Opinion on the Czech Republic*. Luxembourg: Office of Official Publications of the European Communities (OOPEC).

———. 1999a. *Regular Report from the Commission on Hungary's Progress Towards Accession*. COM(1999) 505 final, 13 October.

———. 1999b. *Regular Report from the Commission on Poland's Progress Towards Accession*. COM(1999) 509 final, 13 October.

———. 1999c. *The Structural Funds and Their Coordination with the Cohesion Fund, Guidelines for Programmes in the Period 2000–2006*. Luxembourg: OOPEC.

———. 2000a. *2000 Regular Report on Hungary's Progress towards Accession*. Brussels.

———. 2000b. *2000 Regular Report on Poland's Progress towards Accession*. COM(2000) 709F, 8 November. Brussels.

———. 2000c. *Regular Report on the Czech Republic's Progress Towards Accession*. Luxembourg: OOPEC.

———. 2000d. *Proposal for a Decision of the European Parliament and of the Council Adopting a Programme of Community Action in the Field of Public Health (2001–2006)*. Luxembourg: OOPEC.

———. 2000e. *2000 Regular Report of the Commission on Romania's Progress towards Accession.* COM(2000) 710F, 8 November.

———. 2001a. Main Administrative Structures Required for Implementing the *Acquis.* Informal working document. Brussels, Belgium, 13 February.

———. 2001b. *Regular Report from the Commission on Hungary's Progress Towards Accession.* SEC(2001) 1748. 13 November, Brussels.

———. 2001c. *Regular Report from the Commission on Poland's Progress Towards Accession.* SEC(2001) 1752, 13 November. Brussels.

———. 2001d. *Regular Report on the Czech Republic's Progress Towards Accession.* Luxembourg: OOPEC.

———. 2001e. *Staff Working Paper: Health and Enlargement.* Luxembourg: OOPEC.

———. 2001f. *Regular Report on Romania's Progress towards Accession.* SEC(2001) 1753, 13 November.

———. 2002a. *2002 Regular Report On Turkey's Progress Towards Accession.* COM 700 final, SEC(2002) 1412, 9 October.

———. 2002b. *Regular Report on Hungary's Progress Towards Accession.* COM 700 final, SEC(2002) 1404, 9 October. Brussels.

———. 2002c. *Enlargement and Agriculture: Successfully Integrating the New Member States into the CAP.* Issues paper, 30 January.

Commission DG for Economic and Financial Affairs. 2001a. The Economic Impact of Enlargement. *Enlargement Papers* No. 4. II/419/01-EN. Brussels.

———. 2001b. Real Convergence in Candidate Countries: Past Performance and Scenarios in the Pre-Accession Economic Programmes. ECFIN/708/01-EN. Brussels.

Connolly, Barbara, Tamar Gutner, and Hildegard Bedarf. 1996. Organizational Inertia and Environmental Assistance to Eastern Europe. In *Institutions for Environmental Aid: Pitfalls and Promise,* ed. R. Keohane and M. Levy, 281–324. Cambridge, MA: MIT Press.

Coombes, David. 2001. Politics and Bureaucracy in the Modern Administrative State: Comparing Western and Eastern Europe. In *Politico-Administrative Relations: Who Rules?* ed. T. Verheijen, 26–45. Bratislava: NISPAcee.

Cortell, Andrew, and James Davis. 1996. How Do International Institutions Matter? The Domestic Impact of International Rules and Norms. *International Studies Quarterly* 40:451–78.

———. 2000. Understanding the Domestic Impact of International Norms: A Research Agenda. *International Studies Review* 2:65–87.

Council of Ministers of the Republic of Poland. 2000. Poland's Position Paper in the Area of Environment for the Accession Negotiation with the European Union. Warsaw.

Cowles, Maria Green, James Caporaso, and Thomas Risse, eds. 2001. *Transforming Europe: Europeanization and Domestic Change.* Ithaca, NY: Cornell University Press.

Cowles, Maria Green, and Thomas Risse. 2001. Transforming Europe: Conclusion. In *Transforming Europe: Europeanization and Domestic Change,* ed. Cowles, J. A. Caporaso, and Risse, 271–37. Ithaca: Cornell University Press.

Cox, Robert. 1993. Creating Welfare States in Czechoslovakia and Hungary: Why Policymakers Borrow Ideas from the West. *Government and Policy* 11:349–64.

Crowley, Stephen. 2002. Explaining Labor Quiescence in Post-Communist Europe. Paper presented at the 13th Biennial Conference of Europeanists. Chicago, Illinois, 14–16 March 2002.

Crowley, Stephen, and David Ost, eds. 2002. *Workers after Workers' States: Labor and Politics in Eastern Europe.* Lanham, MD: Rowman and Littlefield.

Czech Republic, Ministry of Environment. 1991. *The Rainbow Program: Environmental Recovery Program for the Czech Republic.* Prague: Academia.

——. 1999. *Statistical Environmental Yearbook of the Czech Republic 1999.* Prague.

——. 2000. *Statistical Environmental Yearbook of the Czech Republic 2000.* Prague.

——. 2001. *Statistical Environmental Yearbook of the Czech Republic 2001.* Prague.

Czech Republic, Ministry of Industry and Trade: Budget and Support to Business Division. 1999. *Conception of the Consumer Policy for the Years 1999–2000.* Prague.

Czech Republic, Ministry of Regional Development. 2000. *Regional Development Strategy of the Czech Republic.* Government Document 682/2000. Prague.

Czech Social Democratic Party (ČSSD). 1997. *An Alternative for Our Country.* ČSSD Party Program, 15 March 1997, chapter I.2. Accessed on 13 March 2001 at http://www.socdem.cz.

Dembinski, Matthias. 2001. *Bedingt handlungsfähig: Eine Studie zur Türkeipolitik der Europäischen Union.* HSFK-Report 5. Frankfurt: Hessische Stiftung für Friedens- und Konfliktforschung.

Deutsch, Karl. 1963. *The Nerves of Government.* London: Free Press.

De Witte, Bruno. 2000. *Politics Versus Law in the EU's Approach to Ethnic Minorities.* EUI Working Papers RSC 2000/4. San Domenico, Italy: European University Institute.

Dimitrova, Antoaneta. 2002. Enlargement, Institution-Building, and the EU's Administrative Capacity Requirement. *West European Politics* 25:171–90.

Dolowitz, David, and David Marsh. 2000. Learning from Abroad: The Role of Policy Transfer in Contemporary Policy-Making. *Governance* 13:5–24.

Downes, Ruth. 2000. Regional Policy Evolution in Hungary. In *Transition, Cohesion, and Regional Policy in Central and Eastern Europe*, ed. John Bachtler, Ruth Downes, and Grzegorz Gorzelak, 209–26. Burlington, VT: Ashgate.

Draus, Franciszek. 2000. Les organizations patronales dans les pays de l'Europe centrale et orientale (Pologne, République tchèque, Hongrie). *ETUI Report* No. 64. Brussels: European Trade Union Institute.

Duina, Francesco. 1999. *Harmonizing Europe: Nation-States within the Common Market.* Albany: State University of New York Press.

Eberlein, Burkhard and Edgar Grande. 2000. Regulation and Infrastructure Management: German Regulatory Regimes and the EU Framework. *Politikfeldanalyse* 1:39–66.

Ecotech. 2001a. The Benefits of Compliance with the Environmental Acquis for the Candidate Countries: Report for DG Environment. Accessed in April 2003 at http://europa.eu.int/comm/environment/enlarg/publications_en.htm.

——. 2001b. Administrative Capacity for Implementation and Enforcement of EU Environmental Policy in the 13 Candidate Countries: Report for DG Environment. Accessed in April 2003 at http://europa.eu.int/comm/environment/enlarg/publications_en.htm.

Egeberg, Morten. 2001. An Organisational Approach to European Integration: Outline of a Complementary Perspective. ARENA Working Paper 18–2001. Oslo: ARENA.

Eijffinger, Sylvester C. W., and Jakob De Haan. 1996. *The Political Economy of Central Bank Independence.* Special Papers in International Economics, No. 19. Princeton, NJ: Princeton University Press.

Eising, Rainer. 2002. Policy Learning in Embedded Negotiations: Explaining EU Electricity Liberalization. *International Organization* 56:85–120.

Eising, Rainer, and Beate Kohler-Koch. 1999. Governance in the European Union: A Comparative Assessment. In *The Transformation of Governance in the European Union*, ed. B. Kohler-Koch and R. Eising, 267–85. London: Routledge.

Eliassen, Kjell A. 1993. European Challenges for Administration in the Nordic Countries. *Nordisk Administrativt Tidsskrift* 74:420–31.

Elster, Jon, Claus Offe, and Ulrich Preuss. 1998. *Institutional Design in Post-Communist Societies: Rebuilding the Ship at Sea.* Cambridge: Cambridge University Press.

Energysys. 1998. Poland—Compliance with the European Union Air Emission Standards: Cost of Alternative Strategies for Reducing Sulfur Emissions. Final Report for the World Bank.

Eurochambres. 2001. *Corporate Readiness for Enlargement in Central Europe: A Company Survey on the State of Preparations for the Single Market.* Summary Report. Brussels: Eurochambres.

European Council. 1993. Conclusions of the Presidency. Copenhagen, Denmark, 21–22 June 1993.

European Industrial Relations Review. 1999. Industrial Relations Background: Poland. *European Industrial Relations Review* 307:22–27.

European Observatory on Health Care Systems. 1999. *Health Care Systems in Transition: Hungary.* Copenhagen: World Health Organization.

———. 2000. *Health Care Systems in Transition: Czech Republic.* Copenhagen: World Health Organization.

European Trade Union Confederation. 1999. *ETUC Activity Report 1995–1998.* Brussels: ETUC.

———. 2000. Post-Nice Enlargement of the European Union: Executive Committee Resolution of 13th–14th December 2000. Brussels. Accessed on 12 February 2002 at http://www.etuc.org/EN/Decisions/execCom/Resolutions/English/0012_Enlargement.cfm.

Faini, Riccardo, and Richard Portes, eds. 1995. *European Union Trade with Eastern Europe: Adjustment and Opportunities.* London: Centre for Economic Policy Research.

Falkner, Gerda. 1998. *EU Social Policy in the 1990s: Towards a Corporatist Policy Community.* London: Routledge.

Falkner, Gerda, Miriam Hartlapp, Simone Leiber, and Oliver Treib. 2002. Opposition through the Backdoor? The Case of National Non-Compliance with EU Directives. Working Paper Political Science 83. Vienna: Institut für Höhere Studien.

Ferguson, Alan. 1991. Eastern Block Seeks Environmental Aid. *The Toronto Star*, 24 June 1991, A3. Accessed via LexisNexis, March 2003.

Figueras, Josep, Martin McKee, and Suszy Lessof. 2002. Ten Years of Health Sector Reform in CEE and NIS: An Overview. Paper presented at USAID Conference. Washington DC, 29–31 July.

Filtenborg, Mette, Stefan Gänzle, and Elisabeth Johansson. 2002. An Alternative Theoretical Approach to EU Foreign Policy: "Network Governance" and the Case of the Northern Dimension Initiative. *Cooperation and Conflict* 37:387–407.

Finnemore, Martha, and Kathryn Sikkink. 1998. International Norm Dynamics and Political Change. *International Organization* 52:887–917.

Fournier, Jacques. 1998. Administrative reform in the Commission opinions concerning the accession of central and eastern European countries to the European Union. In *Preparing Public Administration for the European Administrative Space.* Paris: OECD, SIGMA Paper No. 23, CCNM/SIGMA/PUMA (98) 39:111–18.

Francis, Patrick, Jürg Klarer, and Nelly Petkova, eds. 1999. *Sourcebook on Environmental Funds in Economies of Transition.* Paris: OECD.

Franck, Thomas. 1990. *The Power of Legitimacy among Nations.* New York: Oxford University Press.

Frege, Carola. 2000. The Illusion of Union-Management Cooperation in Postcommunist Central Eastern Europe. *East European Politics and Societies* 14:636–60.

Friis, Lykke. 1998. Approaching the "third half" of EU grand bargaining: The post-negotiation phase of the "Europe Agreement game." *Journal of European Public Policy* 5:322–38.

Friis, Lykke, and Anna Murphy. 1999. The European Union and Central and Eastern Europe: Governance and Boundaries. *Journal of Common Market Studies* 37:211–32.

Gamble, Andrew, and Gavin Kelly. 2002. Britain and EMU. In *European States and the Euro: Europeanization, Variation, and Convergence*, ed. Kenneth Dyson, 97–119. Oxford: Oxford University Press.

Garrett, Geoffrey, and Barry R. Weingast. 1993. Ideas, Interests, and Institutions: Constructing the European Community's Internal Market. In *Ideas and Foreign Policy: Beliefs, Institutions, and Political Change*, ed. Judith Goldstein and Robert O. Keohane, 173–206. Ithaca, NY: Cornell University Press.

Gawrich, Andrea. 2001. Ethnische Minderheiten im Transformations- und Konsolidierungsprozess Polens: Verbände und politische Institutionen. Ph.D. dissertation, University of Bochum.

Gheciu, Alexandra. 2001. Security as Community? NATO and the Politics of State Crafting in Post—Cold War Central and Eastern Europe. Ph.D. dissertation. Cornell University.

———. 2003. Security Institutions as Agents of Socialization? NATO and Post—Cold War Central and Eastern Europe. Manuscript, European University Institute.

Goetz, Klaus, ed. 2001a. *Executive Governance in Central and Eastern Europe*. Special issue of the Journal of European Public Policy 8(6).

———. 2001b. Making Sense of Post Communist Central Administration: Modernization, Europeanization, or Latinization? *Journal of European Public Policy* 8:1032–51.

Goetz, Klaus, and Hellmut Wollmann, 2001. Governmentalizing Central Executives in Post-Communist Europe: A Four-Country Comparison. *Journal of European Public Policy* 8:864–87.

Goldman, Minton F. 1999. *Slovakia since Interdependence: A Struggle for Democracy*. Westport, CO: Praeger.

Government of Hungary. 1990. *Programme for the Nation's Renewal*. Budapest: Government Printing Office.

Grabbe, Heather. 1999. *A Partnership for Accession? The Implications of EU Conditionality for the Central and East European Applicants*. EUI Working Papers RSC 99/12. San Domenico, Italy: European University Institute.

———. 2001a. How Does Europeanization Affect CEE Governance? Conditionality, Diffusion, and Diversity. *Journal of European Public Policy* 8:1013–31.

———. 2001b. *Profiting from EU Enlargement*. London: Centre for European Reform.

Grabel, Ilene. 2002. Ideology and Power in Monetary Reform: Explaining the Rise of Independent Central Banks and Currency Boards in Emerging Economies. In *Monetary Orders: Ambiguous Economics, Ubiquitous Politics*, ed. Jonathan Kirshner, 25–52. Ithaca, NY: Cornell University Press.

Green, Peter. 1991. Environment Ministers Call for Cleanup in Europe. U.P.I., 23 June 1991. Accessed via LexisNexis, March 2003.

Greskovits, Béla. 1998. *The Political Economy of Protest and Patience*. Budapest: Central European University Press.

Grzymała-Busse, Anna, and Abby Innes. 2003. Great Expectations: The EU and Domestic Political Competition in East Central Europe. *East European Politics and Societies* 17:64–73.

Gunter, Michael. 2000. The Continuing Kurdish Problem in Turkey. *Third World Quarterly* 21:849–69.

GUS (Głowny Urzad Statystyczny). 1997. *Ochrona Środowiska 1997*. Warsaw: ZWS.

———. 1998. *Ochrona Środowiska 1998*. Warsaw: ZWS.

———. 1999. *Ochrona Środowiska 1999*. Warsaw: ZWS.

Gutner, Tamar. 2002. *Banking on the Environment: Multilateral Development Banks and Their Environmental Performance in Central and Eastern Europe*. Cambridge, MA: MIT Press.

Haab, Mare. 1998. Potentials and Vulnerabilities of the Baltic States. In *The Baltic States in World Politics*, ed. B. Hansen and B. Heurlin, 1–23. Richmond, VA: Curzon Press.

Haas, Ernst. 1964. *Beyond the Nation-State: Functionalism and International Organization.* Stanford: Stanford University Press.

———. 1990. *When Knowledge is Power.* Berkeley: University of California Press.

Haas, Peter. 1992. Introduction: Epistemic Communities and International Policy Coordination. *International Organization* 46:1–35.

———. 1998. Compliance with EU Directives: Insights from International Relations and Comparative Politics. *Journal of European Public Policy* 5:17–37.

Haggard, Stephan, and Robert Kaufman. 1997. The Political Economy of Democratic Transitions. *Comparative Politics* 29:263–83.

Haggard, Stephan, Marc Levy, Andrew Moravcsik, and Kalypso Nicolaïdis. 1993. Integrating the Two Halves of Europe: Theories of Interests, Bargaining, and Institutions. In *After the Cold War: International Institutions and State Strategies in Europe, 1989–1991*, ed. R. Keohane, J. Nye, and S. Hoffmann, 173–95. Cambridge, MA: Harvard University Press.

Haggard, Stephan, and Steven Webb. 1994. Introduction. In *Voting for Reform: Democracy, Political Liberalization, and Economic Adjustment*, ed. Haggard and Webb, 1–36. Oxford: Oxford University Press.

Hall, Peter. 1989. Conclusion: The Politics of Keynesian Ideas. In *The Political Power of Economic Ideas: Keynesianism Across Nations*, ed. Hall, 361–92. Princeton, NJ: Princeton University Press.

———. 1993. Policy Paradigms, Social Learning, and the State: The Case of Economic Policymaking in Britain. *Comparative Politics* 25:275–96.

Hanne, Gottfried. 1996. Ethnische Konfliktkonstellationen in Lettland seit Perestroika: Eine Bestandsaufnahme der Auseinandersetzungen bei der Wiederherstellung des lettischen Nationalstaats. BIAB Report No.3. Berlin: Freie Universität, Inter-University Working Group on the Baltic States (BIAB).

Hanson, Stephen E. 2001. Defining Democratic Consolidation. In Richard D. Anderson Jr., M. Steven Fish, Stephen E. Hanson, and Philip G. Roeder, *Post Communism and the Theory of Democracy*, 126–52. Princeton, NJ: Princeton University Press.

Hargreaves Heap, Shaun, and Yanis Varoufakis. 1995. *Game Theory: A Critical Introduction.* London: Routledge.

Harris, Geoffrey. 2002. The Democratic Dimension of EU Enlargement: The Role of Parliament and Public Opinion. In *Norms and Nannies: The Impact of International Organizations on the Central and East European States*, ed. R. H. Linden, 33–57. Lanham, MD: Rowman and Littlefield.

Haverland, Marcus. 2000. National Adaptation to European Integration: The Importance of Institutional Veto Points. *Journal of Public Policy* 20:83–103.

Héritier, Adrienne. 1996. The Accommodation of Diversity in European Policy-making and its Outcomes: Regulatory Policy as a Patchwork. *Journal of European Public Policy* 3:149–67.

———. 2001a. Differential Europe: The European Union Impact on National Policymaking. In *Differential Europe: The European Union Impact on National Policymaking*, ed. Héritier et al., 1–21. Lanham, MD: Rowman and Littlefield.

———. 2001b. Differential Europe: National Administrative Responses to Community Policy. In *Transforming Europe: Europeanization and Domestic Change*, ed. M. G. Cowles, T. Risse, and J. Caporaso, 44–59. Ithaca, NY: Cornell University Press.

Héritier, Adrienne, Martina Becka, Christoph Knill, and Susanne Mingers. 1994. *Die Veränderung von Staatlichkeit in Europa: Ein regulativer Wettbewerb: Deutschland, Großbritannien und Frankreich in der Europäischen Union.* Opladen, Germany: Leske and Budrich.

Héritier, Adrienne, Dieter Kerwer, Christoph Knill, Dirk Lehmkuhl, Michael Teutsch, and Anne-Cécile Douillet. 2001. *Differential Europe: The European Union Impact on National Policymaking*. Lanham, MD: Rowman and Littlefield.

Héritier, Adrienne, Christoph Knill, and Susanne Mingers. 1996. *Ringing the Changes in Europe: Regulatory Competition and the Transformation of the State: Britain, France, Germany*. Berlin: Walter de Gruyter.

Héthy, Lajos. 1999. Tripartism and Industrial Relations in Hungary. In *Social Dialogue in Central and Eastern Europe*, ed. G. Casale, 180–99. Budapest: International Labor Office, Central and Eastern Europe Team.

———. 2001. Social Dialogue and the Expanding World: The Decade of Tripartism in Hungary and in Central and Eastern Europe, 1989–1999. *ETUI Report* No. 70. Brussels: European Trade Union Institute.

Hix, Simon, and Klaus Goetz. 2000. Introduction: European Integration and National Political Systems. *West European Politics* 23:1–26.

Hofmann, Rainer. 1992. Minderheitenschutz in Europa: Überblick über die völker- und staatsrechtliche Lage. *Zeitschrift für ausländisches öffentiches Recht und Völkerrecht* 52:1–69.

Holoboff, Elaine. 1995. National Security in the Baltic States: Rolling Back the Bridgehead. In *Statebuilding and Military Power in Russia and the New States of Eurasia*, ed. Bruce Parrott, 111–33. Armonk, NY: M. E. Sharpe.

Holzinger, Katherina and Peter Knoepfel, eds. 2000. *Environmental Policy in a European Union of Variable Geometry? The Challenge of the Next Enlargement*. Basel, Switzerland: Helbing and Lichtenhahn.

Hooghe, Liesbet, ed. 1996. *Cohesion Policy and European Integration: Building Multi-Level Governance*. New York: Oxford University Press.

Horváth, Gyula. 1998. *Regional and Cohesion Policy in Hungary*. Pécs, Hungary: Centre for Regional Studies.

Horváth, István, and Alexandra Scacco. 2001. From the Unitary to the Pluralistic: Fine-Tuning Minority Policy in Romania. In *Diversity in Action. Local Public Management of Multi-Ethnic Communities in Central and Eastern Europe*, ed. Anna-Mária Bíró and Petra Kovács, 241–71. Budapest: IGI Books.

Huba, Mikulas, and Pavel Novacek, eds. 2000. *The World Perceived by the Heart of Europe*. Published by Society for Sustainable Living and Palacký University Olomouc in cooperation with the Slovak and Czech Associations of the Club of Rome and The European EcoForum Issue Group "Values for a Sustainable Future." Bratislava: Olomouc.

Hughes, James. 2001. The Impact of EU Conditionality on Regionalization in CEE States: A Case of Europeanization? European Forum Discussion Paper, European University Institute. San Domenico, Italy, 13 December 2001.

Hughes, James, and Gwendolyn Sasse. 2003. Monitoring the Monitors: EU Enlargement Conditionality and Minority Protection in the CEECs. *Journal of Ethnopolitics and Minority Issues in Europe* 1/2003.

Hungarian Ministry of Agriculture and Regional Development. 1998. *Regional Development in Hungary*. Budapest.

Hungarian Ministry of Foreign Affairs. 2001. *National Program for the Adoption of the Acquis*. Revised version, vol. 2. 15535–3/2001. Budapest: State Secretariat for Integration.

Huntington, Samuel. 1991. *The Third Wave: Democratization in the Late Twentieth Century*. Norman: University of Oklahoma Press.

Hyde-Price, Adrian. 1994. Democratization in Eastern Europe: The External Dimension. In *Democratization in Eastern Europe: Domestic and International Perspectives*, ed. Geoffrey Pridham and Tatu Vanhanen, 220–52. London: Routledge.

Iankova, Elena. 1998. The Transformative Corporatism of Eastern Europe. *East European Politics and Societies* 12:222–64.

———. 2002. *Eastern European Capitalism in the Making.* Cambridge: Cambridge University Press.

Immergut, Ellen. 1992. *Health Politics: Interests and Institutions in Western Europe.* Cambridge: Cambridge University Press.

Innes, Abby. 2002a. Party Competition in Postcommunist Europe: The Great Electoral Lottery. *Comparative Politics* 35:85–104.

———. 2002b. The Changing Power of the State in Eastern Europe. Paper presented at the ECPR joint sessions workshop Enlargement and European Governance. Turin, Italy, 22–27 March.

Jachtenfuchs, Markus. 2001. The Governance Approach to European Integration. *Journal of Common Market Studies* 39:245–64.

Jachtenfuchs, Markus and Beate Kohler-Koch. 1996. Einleitung: Regieren im dynamischen Mehrebenensystem. In *Europäische Integration*, ed. M. Jachtenfuchs and B. Kohler-Koch, 15–44. Opladen, Germany: Leske and Budrich.

———. 2004. Governance and Institutional Development. In *European Integration Theory*, ed. Antje Wiener and Thomas Diez, 97–115. Oxford: Oxford University Press.

Jacoby, Wade. 1999. Priest and Penitent: The European Union as a Force in the Domestic Politics of Eastern Europe. *East European Constitutional Review* 8:62–67.

———. 2000. *Imitation and Politics: Redesigning Modern Germany.* Ithaca, NY: Cornell University Press.

———. 2001. Tutors and pupils: International organizations, Central European elites, and Western models. *Governance* 14:169–200.

———. 2002. Talking the Talk and Walking the Walk: The Cultural and Institutional Effects of Western Models. In *Postcommunist Transformation and the Social Sciences: Cross-Disciplinary Approaches*, ed. Frank Bönker, Klaus Müller, and Andreas Pickel, 129–52. Boulder, CO: Rowman and Littlefield.

———. 2004. *The Expansion of the European Union and NATO: Ordering from the Menu in Central Europe.* Cambridge: Cambridge University Press.

Jacoby, Wade, and Pavel Černoch. 2002. The EU's Pivotal Role in the Creation of Czech Regional Policy. In *Norms and Nannies: The Impact of International Organizations on the Central and East European States*, ed. Ronald Linden, 317–40. Lanham, MD: Rowman and Littlefield.

James, Oliver and Martin Lodge. 2003. The Limitations of "Policy Transfer" and "Lesson Drawing" for Public Policy Research. *Political Studies Review* 1:179–93.

Janos, Andrew C. 2001. From Eastern Empire to Western Hegemony: East Central Europe under Two International Regimes. *East European Politics and Societies* 15:221–49.

Jansone, Dace, and Iveta Reinholde. 2001. Politico-administrative relations: The case of Latvia. In *Politico-Administrative Relations: Who Rules?* ed. Tony Verheijen, 203–26. Bratislava: NISPAcee.

Jendroska, Jerzy. 1998. UN ECE Convention on Access to Information, Public Participation in Decision Making, and Access to Justice in Environmental Matters: Towards More Effective Public Involvement in Monitoring Compliance and Enforcement in Europe. *National Environmental Enforcement Journal* 13:34–41.

Johnston, Alastair Iain. 2001. Treating International Institutions as Social Environments. *International Studies Quarterly* 45:487–515.

Jordan, Andrew. 2000. *The Europeanisation of UK Environmental Policy, 1970–2000: A Departmental Perspective.* "One Europe or Several?" Working Paper 11/00. Brighton, UK: Sussex European Institute.

Jowitt, Kenneth. 1992. *New World Disorder: The Leninist Legacy.* Berkeley: University of California Press.

Jubulis, Mark. 1996. The External Dimension of Democratization in Latvia: The Impact of European Institutions. *International Relations* 13:59–73.

Jupille, Joseph, James Caporaso, and Jeffrey Checkel. 2003. Integrating Institutions: Rationalism, Constructivism, and the Study of the European Union. *Comparative Political Studies* 36:7–40.

Kahan, James, and László Gulácsi. 2000. Envisioning Health Care Quality in Hungary. *Eurohealth* 6:2–4.

Kahler, Miles. 1992. External Influence, Conditionality, and the Politics of Adjustment. In *The Politics of Economic Adjustment*, ed. Stephan Haggard and Robert Kaufman, 89–133. Princeton, NJ: Princeton University Press.

Kaldor, Mary, and Ivan Vejvoda. 1999. Democratization in Central and Eastern European Countries: An Overview. In *Democratization in Central and Eastern Europe*, ed. M. Kaldor and I. Vejvoda, 1–24. London: Pinter.

Kallas, Marian. 1995. Parlamentarische Arbeiten am Status der nationalen und ethnischen Minderheiten in Polen. *Osteuropa Recht* 41:173–92.

Karaczun, Zbigniew. 1996. *Policy of Air Protection in Poland. Part IV—January 1994–December 1996.* Warsaw: Institute for Sustainable Development.

Karl, Terry Lynn, and Philippe Schmitter. 1991. Modes of Transition in Latin America, Southern, and Eastern Europe. *International Social Science Journal* 128:269–84.

Katzenstein, Peter, ed. 1997. *Mitteleuropa: Between Europe and Germany.* Providence, RI: Berghahn Books.

Katzenstein, Peter, Robert Keohane, and Stephen Krasner, eds. 1999. *Exploration and Contestation in the Study of World Politics.* Cambridge, MA: MIT Press.

Kelley, Judith. 2001. Norms and Membership Conditionality: The Role of European Institutions in Ethnic Politics in Latvia, Estonia, Slovakia, and Romania. Ph.D. dissertation, Harvard University.

———. 2004. *Ethnic Politics in Europe: The Power of Norms and Incentives.* Princeton, NJ: Princeton University Press.

Keohane, Robert, Joseph Nye, and Stanley Hoffmann, eds. 1993. *After the Cold War: International Institutions and State Strategies in Europe, 1989–1991.* Cambridge, MA: Harvard University Press.

Kerwer, Dieter. 2001. *Regulatory Reforms in Italy: A Case Study in Europeanisation.* Aldershot, UK: Ashgate.

Killick, Tony. 1996. Principals, Agents, and the Limits of BWI Conditionality. *The World Economy* 19:211–29.

Kirschbaum, Stanislav. 1999. Slovakia: The End to a Confused Sense of Direction? *International Journal* 54:582–602.

Knill, Christoph. 2001. *The Europeanisation of National Administrations: Patterns of Institutional Change and Persistence.* Cambridge: Cambridge University Press.

Knill, Christoph and Dirk Lehmkuhl. 2002. The National Impact of European Union Regulatory Policy: Three Europeanization Mechanisms. *European Journal of Political Research* 41:255–80.

Knill, Christoph, and Andrea Lenschow. 1999. New Concepts—Old Problems? The Institutional Constraints for the Effective Implementation of EU Environmental Policy. *Politische Vierteljahresschrift* 40:591–620.

———. 2000. *Implementing EU Environmental Policy: New Directions and Old Problems.* Manchester, UK: Manchester University Press.

Koh, Harold Hongju. 1997. Why Do Nations Obey International Law? *Yale Law Journal* 106:2599–2659.

Kohl, Heribert, Wolfgang Lecher, and Hans-Wolfgang Platzer. 2000. Transformation, EU Membership, and Labour Relations in Central Eastern Europe. *Transfer* 6:399–415.

Kohler-Koch, Beate. 1999. The Evolution and Transformation of European Governance. In *The Transformation of Governance in the European Union*, ed. Kohler-Koch and Rainer Eising, 14–35. London: Routledge.

Kolodko, Grzegorz. 2000. *Post-Communist Transition: The Thorny Road*. Rochester, NY: University of Rochester Press.

Kopstein, Jeffrey and David Reilly. 2000. Geographic Diffusion and the Transformation of the Postcommunist World. *World Politics* 53:1–37.

Kornai, János. 1990. *The Road to a Free Economy: Shifting from a Socialist System: The Example of Hungary*. New York: W. W. Norton.

Kornai, János, and Karen Eggleston. 2001. *Welfare, Choice, and Solidarity in Transition: Reforming the Health Sector in Eastern Europe*. Cambridge: Cambridge University Press.

Kowalski, Zbigniew. 1993. Back to Market: Polish Family Farming in the 1990s. *Canadian Journal of Agricultural Economics* 41:349–56.

Krakow Academy of Economics. 1996. Developing of Cost Methodologies and Evaluation of Cost-Effective Strategies for Achieving Harmonization with EC Environmental Standards. Final Report for the Ministry of the Environmental Protection, Natural Resources, and Forestry of the Republic of Poland.

Kramer, Heinz. 2000. *A Changing Turkey. The Challenge to Europe and the United States*. Washington, DC: Brookings.

Krizsán, Andrea. 2000. The Hungarian Minority Protection System: A Flexible Approach to the Adjudication of Ethnic Claims. *Journal of Ethnic and Migration Studies* 26:247–62.

Krok-Paszkowska, Ania. 2002. Samoobrona: The Polish Self Defense Movement. In *Uncivil Society? Contentious Politics in Eastern Europe*, ed. Petr Kopecky. London: Routledge.

Kubicek, Paul. 1999a. Turkish-European Relations: At a New Crossroads? *Middle East Policy* 6:157–73.

———. 1999b. Organized Labor in Postcommunist States: Will the Western Sun Set on It, Too? *Comparative Politics* 32:83–102.

Kuniholm, Bruce. 1996. Sovereignty, Democracy, and Identity: Turkey's Kurdish Problem and the West's Turkish Problem. *Mediterranean Politics* 1:353–70.

Kurtz, Marcus, and Andrew Barnes. 2002. The Political Foundations of Post-Communist Regimes: Marketization, Agrarian Legacies, or International Influences. *Comparative Political Studies* 35:524–53.

Kux, Stephan, and Ulf Sverdrup. 2000. Fuzzy Borders and Adaptive Outsiders: Norway, Switzerland, and the EU. *Journal of European Integration* 22:237–70.

Kymlicka, Will. 2001. Reply and Conclusion. In *Can Liberal Pluralism be Exported? Western Political Theory and Ethnic Relations in Eastern Europe*, ed. Kymlicka and Magda Opalski, 347–413. Oxford: Oxford University Press.

Lackó, László. 1994. Settlement Development Processes and Policies in Hungary. In *European Challenges and Hungarian Response in Regional Policy*, ed. Zoltán Hajdú and Gyula Horváth, 151–56. Pécs, Hungary: Centre for Regional Studies, Hungarian Academy of Sciences.

Laczko, Frank, Irene Stacher, and Jessica Graf, eds. 1999. *Migration in Central and Eastern Europe: 1999 Review*. Geneva: International Organization for Migration.

Ladó, Mária, and Ferenc Tóth. 1996. The Interest Reconciliation Council in 1995: The Year of Warfare. In *Magyarország politikai évkönyve 1995-röl* [Hungarian Political Yearbook of 1995], ed. S. Kurtán, P. Sándor, and L. Vass, 303 (abstract). Budapest: Demokrácia Kutatások Magyar Közponja Alapítvány.

Ladrech, Robert. 2000. *Social Democracy and the Challenge of the European Union*. Boulder, CO: Lynne Rienner.

Lantos, Géza. 1997. Arbeitsschutz und Unfallversicherung in Ungarn. In *Die soziale Unfall-versicherung in Europa*, ed. Hauptverband der Gewerblichen Berufsgenossenschaften, 105–11. Bielefeld, Germany: Erich Schmidt Verlag.

Leff, Carol Skalnik. 1997. *The Czech and Slovak Republics: Nation versus State*. Boulder, CO: Westview.

Legro, Jeffrey. 1997. Which Norms Matter? Revisiting the "Failure" of Internationalism. *International Organization* 51:31–64.

Lehmkuhl, Dirk. 1999. *The Importance of Small Differences: The Impact of European Integration on the Associations in the German and Dutch Road Haulage Industries*. Amsterdam: Thela Thesis.

Leibfried, Stephan, and Paul Pierson. 2000. Social Policy: Left to Courts and Markets? In *Policy-Making in the European Union*, 4th ed., ed. Helen Wallace and William Wallace, 267–92. Oxford: Oxford University Press.

Levy, Jack. 1994. Learning and Foreign Policy: Sweeping a Conceptual Minefield. *International Organization* 48:279–312.

Lichbach, Marc. 2003. *Is Rational Choice Theory All of Social Science?* Ann Arbor: University of Michigan Press.

Linden, Ronald, ed. 2002. *Norms and Nannies: The Impact of International Organizations on the Central and Eastern European States*. Lanham, MD: Rowman and Littlefield.

Linz, Juan, and Alfred Stepan. 1996. *Problems of Democratic Transition and Consolidation: Southern Europe, South America, and Post Communist Europe*. Baltimore: Johns Hopkins University Press.

Łodziński, Sławomir. 1999. *Minority Rights in Poland: Report by the Helsinki Committee in Poland*. Warsaw: Helsinki Foundation of Human Rights.

Loungani, Prakash, and Nathan Sheets. 1997. Central Bank Independence, Inflation, and Growth in Transition Economies. *Journal of Money, Credit, and Banking* 29:381–99.

Lynch, Diahanna. 2000. Closing the Deception Gap: Accession to the European Union and Environmental Standards in East Central Europe. *Journal of Environment and Development* 9:426–37.

Mahoney, James. 2000. Path Dependence in Historical Sociology. *Theory and Society* 29:507–48.

Mair, Peter, and Jan Zielonka, eds. 2002. *The Enlarged European Union: Diversity and Adaptation*. London: Frank Cass.

Malova, Darina, and Tim Haughton. 2002. Making Institutions in Central and Eastern Europe and the Impact of Europe. *West European Politics* 25:101–20.

March, James, and Johan Olsen. 1989. *Rediscovering Institutions: The Organizational Basis of Politics*. New York: Free Press.

———. 1998. The Institutional Dynamics of International Political Orders. *International Organization* 52:943–69.

Marek, Dan, and Michael Baun. 2002. The EU as a Regional Actor: The Case of the Czech Republic. *Journal of Common Market Studies* 40:895–919.

Majone, Giandomenico, ed. 1996. *Regulating Europe*. London: Routledge.

Marrée, Jörgen, and Peter Groenewegen. 1997. *Back to Bismarck: Eastern European Health Care Systems in Transition*. Aldershot, UK: Ashgate.

Martin, Lisa, and Beth Simmons. 1998. Theories and Empirical Studies of International Institutions. *International Organization* 52:729–59.

Martin, Roderick. 1999. *Transforming Management in Central and Eastern Europe*. Oxford: Oxford University Press.

Maxfield, Sylvia. 1997. *Gatekeepers of Growth: The International Political Economy of Central Banking in Developing Countries*. Princeton, NJ: Princeton University Press.

Mayhew, Alan. 2000. Enlargement of the European Union: An analysis of the negotiations with the Central and Eastern European candidate countries. *SEI Working Paper* No. 39, Sussex.

——. 2002. The Negotiating Position of the European Union on Agriculture, the Structural Funds, and the EU Budget, *SEI Working Paper* No. 52, Sussex.

McDermott, Gerald. 2002. *Embedded Politics: Industrial Networks and Institutional Change in Postcommunism.* Ann Arbor: University of Michigan Press.

McFaul, Michael. 2002. The Fourth Wave of Democracy and Dictatorship. Noncooperative Transitions in the Postcommunist World. *World Politics* 54:212–44.

McGowan, Francis, and Helen Wallace. 1996. Towards a European Regulatory State? *Journal of European Public Policy* 3:560–76.

McKee, Martin, Elias Mossialos, and Rita Baeten, eds. 2002. *The Impact of EU Law on Health Care Systems.* Brussels: Peter Lang.

McNamara, Kathleen. 2001. Where do Rules Come From? The Creation of the European Central Bank. In *The Institutionalization of Europe*, ed. Alec Stone Sweet, Wayne Sandholtz, and Neil Fligstein. Oxford: Oxford University Press.

Melvin, Neil. 2000. Post-Imperial Ethnocracy and the Russophone Minorities of Estonia and Latvia. In *The Politics of National Minority Participation in Post-communist Europe*, ed. J. P. Stein, 129–66. Armonk, NY: M. E. Sharpe.

Mény, Yves, Pierre Muller, and Jean-Louis Quermonne, eds. 1996. *Adjusting to Europe: The Impact of the European Union on National Institutions and Policies.* London: Routledge.

Merkel, Wolfgang. 1999. *Systemtransformation: Eine Einführung in die Theorie und Empirie der Transformationsforschung.* Opladen, Germany: Leske and Budrich.

Meyer-Sahling, Jan-Hinrik. 2001. Getting on Track: Civil Service Reform in Post Communist Hungary. *Journal of European Public Policy* 8:960–79.

Mineshima, Dale. 2002. The Rule of Law and EU Expansion. *Liverpool Law Review* 24:73–87.

Mohlek, Peter. 1994. Der Minderheitenschutz in der Republik Polen. In *Der Minderheitenschutz in der Republik Polen, in der Tschechischen und in der Slowakischen Republik*, ed. Mohlek and Mahulena Hošková, 9–82. Bonn: Kulturstiftung der deutschen Vertriebenen.

Moldan, Bedřich. 2000. Environment After 10 Years. Press release of the Regional Environment Center. Hungary, 18 June 2000. Accessed in March 2003 at http://www.rec.org/.

Monar, Jörg. 1999. *Flexibility and Closer Cooperation in an Emerging European Migration Policy: Opportunities and Risks*, Laboratorio CeSPI, No. 1, Rome: CeSPI.

——. 2000. *Enlargement-related Diversity in EU Justice and Home Affairs: Challenges, Dimensions, and Management Instruments*, Working Document W112. The Hague: WRR Scientific Council for Government Policy.

Moravcsik, Andrew. 1998. *The Choice for Europe: Social Purpose and State Power from Messina to Maastricht.* Ithaca, NY: Cornell University Press.

Moravcsik, Andrew, and Milada Vachudova. 2003. National Interests, State Power, and EU Enlargement. *East European Politics and Societies* 17:42–57.

Morlino, Leonardo. 2002. What we know and what we should know on Europeanization and the reshaping of representation in SE democracies. Paper delivered at the conference on "EU and Democracy in Southern Europe." University of California, Berkeley, 31 October–2 November 2002.

Munck, Gerardo, and Carol Skalnik Leff. 1997. Modes of Transition and Democratization: South America and Eastern Europe in Comparative Perspective. *Comparative Politics* 29:343–62.

Nelson, Joan. 2001. The Politics of Pension and Health-Care Reforms in Hungary and Poland. In *Reforming the State: Fiscal and Welfare Reforms in Post-Socialist Countries*, ed. János Kornai, Stephan Hagggard and Robert Kaufman, 235–66. Cambridge: Cambridge University Press.

Neumann, László. 1997. Circumventing Trade Unions in Hungary: Old and New Channels of Wage Bargaining. *European Journal of Industrial Relations* 3:183–202.

——. 2000. Decentralised Collective Bargaining in Hungary. *International Journal of Labour Law and Industrial Relations* 16:113–28.

Niewerth, Johannes. 1996. *Der kollektive und der positive Schutz von Minderheiten und ihre Durchsetzung im Völkerrecht*. Berlin: Duncker and Humblodt.

O'Donnell, Guillermo, Philippe Schmitter, and Laurence Whitehead, eds. 1986. *Transitions from Authoritarian Rule*. Baltimore: Johns Hopkins University Press.

OECD. 2001. *OECD Economic Surveys 2000–2001—Poland*. Paris: OECD.

Offe, Claus. 1998. Designing Institutions in East European Transitions. In *The Theory of Institutional Design*, ed. R. E. Goodin, 199–226. Cambridge: Cambridge University Press.

Olsen, Johan. 1995. European Challenges to the Nation-State. ARENA Working Paper 14–1995. Oslo: ARENA.

——. 2002a. The Many Faces of Europeanization. *Journal of Common Market Studies* 40:921–52.

——. 2002b. Towards a European Administrative Space? Arena Working paper 02/26. Oslo: Arena.

Open Society Institute. 2001. *Minority Protection in the EU Accession Process: Monitoring the EU Accession Process: Minority Rights*. Budapest: Open Society Institute.

OPZZ [All-Poland Alliance of Trade Unions]. 1998. The Black Paper on the Social Dialogue in Poland. *Trybuna*, 2 October. Accessed on 26 April 2002 at http://opzz.org.pl/end/english/cont3.html.

Orenstein, Mitchell, and Martine Haas. 2002. Globalization and the Development of Welfare States in Postcommunist Europe. BCSIA Discussion Paper 2002–02, Kennedy School of Government, Harvard University.

Orosz, Éva, and Andrew Burns. 2000. *The Health Care System in Hungary*. Working Paper No. 241. OECD, Economics Department.

Orosz, Éva, Guy Ellena, and Melitta Jakab. 1998. Reforming the Health Care System: The Unfinished Agenda. In *Public Finance Reform During the Transition: The Experience of Hungary*, ed. Lajos Bokros and Jean-Jacques Dethier, 221–53. Washington, DC: World Bank.

Orosz, Éva, and Imre Holló. 2001. Hospitals in Hungary: The Story of Stalled Reforms. *Eurohealth* 7:22–25.

Ost, David. 2000. Illusory Corporatism in Eastern Europe: Neoliberal Tripartism and Postcommunist Class Identities. *Politics and Society* 28:503–30.

——. 2002. The Weakness of Symbolic Strength: Labor and Union Identity in Poland, 1989–2000. In *Workers after Workers' States*, ed. Stephen Crowley and Ost, 79–96. Lanham, MD: Rowman and Littlefield.

Ost, David, and Marc Weinstein. 1999. Unionists Against Unions? Towards Hierarchical Management in Post-Communist Poland. *East European Politics and Societies* 13:1–33.

Pabriks, Artis. 1999. From Nationalism to Ethnic Policy: The Latvian Nation in the Present and in the Past. BIAB Report No. 17. Berlin: Freie Universität, Inter-University Working Group on the Baltic States (BIAB).

Pentassuglia, Gaetano. 2001. The EU and the Protection of Minorities: The Case of Eastern Europe. *European Journal of International Law* 12:3–38.

Peterson, John, and Elizabeth Bomberg. 1999. *Decision-Making in the European Union*. London: Macmillan.

Petite, Michel. 1998. The Treaty of Amsterdam, Jean Monnet Paper 98–2–03, Harvard Law School.

Pierson, Paul, ed. 2001. *The New Politics of the Welfare State.* Oxford: Oxford University Press.

Plakans, Andreijs. 1997. Democratization and Political Participation in Postcommunist Societies: The Case of Latvia. In *The Consolidation of Democracy in East-Central Europe,* Democratization and Authoritarianism in Postcommunist Societies, vol. 1, ed. K. Dawisha and B. Parrott, 245–89. Cambridge: Cambridge University Press.

Pollert, Anna. 1999. *Transformation at Work in the New Market Economies of Central Eastern Europe.* London: Sage.

Posen, Adam. 1993. Why Central Bank Independence Does Not Cause Low Inflation: There is No Institutional Fix of Politics. In *Finance and the International Economy,* vol. 7, ed. R. O'Brian, 40–65. Oxford: Oxford University Press.

———. 1995. Declarations Are Not Enough: Financial Sector Sources of Central Bank Independence. *NBER Macroeconomic Annual 1995,* vol. 10, 253–74. Cambridge: MIT Press.

Poznanski, Kazimierz. 2001a. Transition and its Discontents: An Introduction. *East European Politics and Societies* 15:207–20.

———. 2001b. Building Capitalism with Communist Tools: Eastern Europe's Defective Transition. *East European Politics and Societies* 15:320–55.

Pravda, Alex. 2001. Introduction. In *Democratic Consolidation in Eastern Europe, Vol. 2: International and Transnational Factors,* ed. J. Zielonka and A. Pravda, 1–27. Oxford: Oxford University Press.

Preece, Jennifer Jackson. 1998. National Minorities and the International System. *Politics* 18:17–23.

Pressman, Jeffrey, and Aaron Wildavsky. 1984. *Implementation.* Berkeley: University of California Press.

Preston, Christopher. 1997. *Enlargement and Integration in the European Union.* London: Routledge.

Pridham, Geoffrey, George Sanford, and Eric Herring, eds. 1994. *Building Democracy: The International Dimension of Democratisation in Eastern Europe.* Leicester, UK: Leicester University Press.

Prymula, Roman, Juri Pavlicek, and Alena Petrakova. 1997. University Partnership Project in Health Services Management Education: The Driving Force Behind the Czech Republic Educational Network. *Journal of Health Administration Education* 15:190–99.

Przeworski, Adam. 1992. The Games of Transition. In *Issues in Democratic Consolidation: The New South American Democracies in Comparative Perspective,* ed. S. Mainwaring, G. O'Donnell, and J. S. Valenzuela, 105–52. Notre Dame: Notre Dame University Press.

Radaelli, Claudio. 1999. The Public Policy of the European Union: Whither Politics of Expertise? *Journal of European Public Policy* 6:757–74.

———. 2000. Whither Europeanization? Concept Stretching and Substantive Change. *European Integration Online Papers* 4(8). http://eiop.or.at/eiop/texte/2000–008a.htm.

Ram, Melanie. 2001. Minority Relations in Multiethnic Societies: Assessing the European Union Factor in Romania. *Romanian Journal of Society and Politics* 1:63–90.

Ratner, Stephen. 2000. Does International Law Matter in Preventing Ethnic Conflict? *Journal of International Law and Politics* 32:591–698.

Reinholde, Iveta. 2004. Challenges for the Latvian public administration in the European integration process. In *Driven to Change: European Union enlargement viewed from the East,* ed. A. L. Dimitrova, 163–93. Manchester, England: Manchester University Press.

Republic of Poland. 2001. *National Program for the Preparation of Membership in the European Union,* 12 June. Warsaw: Council of Ministers of the Republic of Poland.

Republic of Poland and European Commission. 2001. *Joint Assessment of Employment Priorities in Poland*, 30 January 2001. Accessed on 20 May 2002 at http://europa.eu.int/comm./employment_social/intcoop/news/prioritiespol_en.htm.

Risse, Thomas. 2000. "Let's Argue!": Communicative Action in World Politics. *International Organization* 54:1–39.

Risse, Thomas, Maria Green Cowles, and James Caporaso. 2001. Europeanization and Domestic Change: Introduction. In *Transforming Europe. Europeanization and Domestic Change*, ed. Green Cowles, Caporaso and Risse, 1–20. Ithaca, NY: Cornell University Press.

Risse, Thomas, and Kathryn Sikkink. 1999. The Socialization of International Human Rights Norms into Domestic Practices: Introduction. In *The Power of Human Rights: International Norms and Domestic Political Change*, ed. Risse, Stephen C. Ropp, and Sikkink, 1–38. Cambridge: Cambridge University Press.

Risse-Kappen, Thomas. 1994. Ideas Do Not Float Freely: Transnational Coalitions, Domestic Structures, and the End of the Cold War. *International Organization* 48:185–214.

———. 1995. Bringing Transnational Relations Back In: Introduction. In *Bringing Transnational Relations Back In: Non-State Actors, Domestic Structures, and International Institutions*, ed. Risse-Kappen, 3–33. Cambridge: Cambridge University Press.

Rollo, Jim, Judy Batt, Brigitte Granville, and Neil Malcolm. 1990. *The New Eastern Europe: Western Responses*. London: Pinter.

Rose, Richard. 1991. What is Lesson-Drawing? *Journal of Public Policy* 11:3–30.

———. 1993. *Lesson-drawing in Public Policy: A Guide to Learning across Time and Space*. Chatham, NJ: Chatham House Publishers.

———. 1997. *Baltic Trends: Studies in Co-operation, Conflict, Rights and Obligations*. Studies in Public Policy No. 288. Glasgow: University of Strathclyde.

Rouleau, Eric. 2000. Turkey's Dream of Democracy. *Foreign Affairs* 79:100–114.

Ruggie, John. 1998a. *Constructing the World Polity: Essays on International Institutionalization*. New York: Routledge.

———. 1998b. What Makes the World Hang Together? Neo-Utilitarianism and the Social Constructivist Challenge. *International Organization* 52:855–86.

Samson, Ivo. 2001. Slovakia: Misreading the Western Message. In *Democratic Consolidation in Eastern Europe, Vol. 2: International and Transnational Factors*, ed. J. Zielonka and A. Pravda, 363–82. Oxford: Oxford University Press.

Sandholtz, Wayne, and Alec Stone Sweet, eds. 2001. *European Integration and Supranational Governance*. Oxford: Oxford University Press.

Sasse, Gwendolyn, and James Hughes. 2002. The Ambivalence of Conditionality: Europeanization and Regionalization in Central and Eastern Europe. Paper presented at the ECPR joint sessions workshop Enlargement and European Governance. Turin, Italy, 22–27 March.

Scharpf, Fritz. 1997. *Games Real Actors Play: Actor-Centered Institutionalism in Policy Research*. Boulder, CO: Westview.

Scheffler, Richard, and Franci Duitch. 2000. Health Care Privatisation in the Czech Republic: Ten Years of Reform. *Eurohealth* 6:5–7.

Schimmelfennig, Frank. 1997. Rhetorisches Handeln in der internationalen Politik. *Zeitschrift für Internationale Beziehungen* 4:219–54.

———. 2000. International Socialization in the New Europe: Rational Action in an Institutional Environment. *European Journal of International Relations* 6:109–39.

———. 2001. The Community Trap: Liberal Norms, Rhetorical Action, and the Eastern Enlargement of the European Union. *International Organization* 55:47–80.

———. 2002. Introduction: The Impact of International Organizations on the Central and Eastern European States—Conceptual and Theoretical Issues. In *Norms and Nannies: The Impact of International Organizations on the Central and Eastern European States*, ed. Ronald Linden, 1–29. Lanham, MD: Rowman and Littlefield.

———. 2003a. *The EU, NATO, and the Integration of Europe: Rules and Rhetoric.* Cambridge: Cambridge University Press.

———. 2003b. Internationale Sozialisation: Von einem "erschöpften" zu einem produktiven Forschungsprogramm? In *Die neuen Internationalen Beziehungen: Forschungsstand und Perspektiven in Deutschland*, ed. Gunther Hellmann, Klaus Dieter Wolf, and Michael Zürn, 401–27. Baden-Baden, Germany: Nomos.

Schimmelfennig, Frank, Stefan Engert, and Heiko Knobel. 2003a. Costs, Commitment, and Compliance: The Impact of EU Democratic Conditionality on Latvia, Slovakia, and Turkey. *Journal of Common Market Studies* 41:495–517.

———. 2003b. Europäisierung in Osteuropa: Reaktionen auf die demokratische Konditionalität. *Österreichische Zeitschrift für Politikwissenschaft* 32:321–37.

Schimmelfennig, Frank, and Ulrich Sedelmeier. 2002. Theorizing EU Enlargement: Research Focus, Hypotheses, and the State of Research. *Journal of European Public Policy* 9:500–28.

Schmidt, Vivien. 2001. Europeanization and the Mechanics of Economic Policy Adjustment. *European Integration Online Papers* 5(6). http://eiop.or.at/eiop/texte/2001-006a.htm.

Schneider, Eleonora. 1997. *Quo vadis, Slowakei? Von der eingeleiteten Demokratie zum Autoritarismus?* Bericht des BIOSt 36. Cologne: Bundesinstitut für internationale und ostwissenschaftliche Studien.

Schönbohm, Wulf. 2002. *Die Türkei am Wendepunkt.* KAS-Länderberichte, 30 July 2002. http://www.kas.de/publikationen/2002/561-dokument.html.

Sedelmeier, Ulrich. 1998. The European Union's Association Policy towards the Countries of Central and Eastern Europe: Collective EU Identity and Policy Paradigms in a Composite Policy. Ph.D. dissertation. University of Sussex, UK.

———. 2001. Enlargement of the European Union: Impacts on the EU, the Candidates, and the "Next Neighbors." *ECSA Review* 14:2–7.

———. 2002. Sectoral Dynamics of EU Eastern Enlargement: Advocacy, Access, and Alliances in a Composite Policy. *Journal of European Public Policy* 9:627–49.

Sedelmeier, Ulrich, and Helen Wallace. 2000. Eastern Enlargement: Strategy or Second Thoughts? In *Policy Making in the European Union*, 4th ed., ed. Helen Wallace and William Wallace, 427–60. Oxford: Oxford University Press.

Sissenich, Beate. 2002a. State Building by a Nonstate: How the EU Strengthens Institutional Capacity in Candidate Countries, Ms.

———. 2002b. The Diffusion of EU Social and Employment Legislation in Poland and Hungary. In *Norms and Nannies: The Impact of International Organizations on the Central and East European States*, ed. Ronald Linden, 287–315. Lanham, MD: Rowman and Littlefield.

———. 2003. State Building by a Nonstate: European Union Enlargement and Social Policy Transfer to Poland and Hungary. Ph.D. dissertation. Cornell University, Ithaca, New York.

Shafir, Michael. 2000. The Political Party as National Holding Company: The Hungarian Democratic Federation of Romania. In *The Politics of National Minority Participation in Post-Communist Europe: State-Building, Democracy, and Ethnic Mobilization*, ed. Jonathan P. Stein, 101–28. Armonk, NY: M. E. Sharpe.

Sitter, Nick. 2001. Beyond Class vs. Nation? Cleavage Structures and Party Competition in Central Europe. *Central European Political Science Review* 2:67–91.

Smith, Alasdair, Peter Holmes, Ulrich Sedelmeier, Edward Smith, Helen Wallace, and Alasdair Young. 1996. *The European Union and Central and Eastern Europe: Pre-Accession Strategies.* Sussex European Institute Working Paper No. 15. Brighton, England: Sussex European Institute.

Smith, Graham, Vivian Law, Andrew Wilson, Annette Bohr, and Edward Allworth. 1998. *Nation-Building in the Post-Soviet Borderlands: The Politics of National Identities.* Cambridge: Cambridge University Press.

Smith, Karen. 2001. Western Actors and the Promotion of Democracy. In *Democratic Consolidation in Eastern Europe, Vol. 2: International and Transnational Factors,* ed. Jan Zielonka and Alex Pravda, 31–57. Oxford: Oxford University Press.

Snidal, Duncan. 1995. The Politics of Scope: Endogenous Actors, Heterogeneity, and Institutions. In *Local Commons and Global Interdependence,* ed. Robert Keohane and Elinor Ostrom, 47–70. London: Sage.

Sootla, Georg. 2001. Evolution of Roles of Politicians and Civil Servants during the Post-Communist Transition in Estonia. In *Politico-Administrative Relations: Who Rules?* ed. Tony Verheijen, 109–47, Bratislava: NISPAcee.

Stankovsky, Jan, Fritz Plasser, and Peter Ulram. 1998. *On the Eve of EU Enlargement: Economic Developments and Democratic Attitudes in East Central Europe.* Schriftenreihe des ZAP 16. Vienna: Zentrum für Angewandte Politikforschung.

Stark, David, and Laszlo Bruzst. 1998. *Postsocialist Pathways: Transforming Politics and Property in East Central Europe.* Cambridge: Cambridge University Press.

Steunenberg, Bernard. 2002. Enlargement and Reform in the European Union. In *Widening the European Union: The Politics of Institutional Change and Reform,* ed. Bernard Steunenberg, 3–21. London: Routledge.

Stirewalt, Bryan, and James Horner. 2000. *Poland-National Bank of Poland: Final Report,* 1 March. KPMG Peat Marwick and Barents Group, for USAID.

Sverdrup, Ulf. 2000. Ambiguity and Adaptation: Europeanization of Administrative Institutions as Loosely Coupled Processes. ARENA Report 8–2000. Oslo: ARENA.

Szilágyi, Tibor. 2001. The Unwanted Child of Transition and Health Reform: Health Development in Hungary. *Health Promotion Journal of Australia* 11:78–83.

Tallberg, Jonas. 2002. Paths to Compliance: Enforcement, Management, and the European Union. *International Organization* 56:609–43.

Tank, Pinar. 2001. Turkey as a "Special Case" for the EU: Will the Generals Retreat from Politics? *Security Dialogue* 32:217–30.

Thelen, Kathleen. 1999. Historical Institutionalism in Comparative Politics. *Annual Review of Political Science* 2:369–404.

Thornberry, Patrick. 1991. *International Law and the Rights of Minorities.* Oxford: Clarendon.

Tkaczynski, Jan Wiktor, and Ulrich Vogel. 1997. Sieben Jahre nach der Wende: Die polnische Verfassung zwischen Oktroi und Obstruktion. *Osteuropa Recht* 43:169–81.

Toggenburg, Gabriel. 2000. A Rough Orientation Through a Delicate Relationship: The European Union's Endeavours for (its) Minorities. *European Integration Online Papers* 4, 16.

Tontsch, Günther. 1999. Die Rechtsstellung der Minderheiten in Rumänien. In *Das Recht der nationalen Minderheiten in Osteuropa,* ed. Georg Brunner and Boris Meissner, 231–54. Berlin: Spitz.

Toonen, Theo. 2001. The Comparative Dimension of Administrative Reform: Creating Open Villages and Redesigning the Politics of Administration. In *Politicians, Bureaucrats, and Administrative Reform,* ed. B. Guy Peters and Jon Pierre, 183–201. London: Routledge.

Tóth, András. 2002. The Failure of Social-Democratic Unionism in Hungary. In *Workers after Workers' States*, ed. Stephen Crowley and David Ost, 37–58. Lanham, MD: Rowman and Littlefield.

Treib, Oliver. 2003. Die Umsetzung von EU-Richtlinien im Zeichen der Parteipolitik: Eine akteurzentrierte Antwort auf die Misfit-These. MPIfG Discussion Paper 03/3. Cologne: Max-Planck-Institut für Gesellschaftsforschung.

Tsebelis, George. 1995. Decision Making in Political Systems: Veto players in Presidentialism, Parliamentarism, Multicameralism, and Multipartism. *British Journal of Political Science* 25:289–325.

———. 2002. *Veto Players: How Political Institutions Work*. Princeton, NJ: Princeton University Press.

Turan, Ilter. 2002. The Turkish Political System: Instability and Hurdles. In *Turkey: the Road Ahead?* ed. B. Dunér, 5–22. Stockholm: Swedish Institute of International Affairs.

Vachudova, Milada. 2001. The Leverage of International Institutions on Democratizing States: Eastern Europe and the European Union. EUI Working Papers RSC 33. San Domenico, Italy: European University Institute.

———. 2003. EU Leverage and the Empowerment of Domestic Actors. Paper presented at the workshop The Europeanization of Central and Eastern Europe, European University Institute. Florence, Italy, 4–5 July.

———. 2004. *Europe Undivided: Democracy, Leverage, and Integration Since 1989*. Oxford: Oxford University Press.

Van Waarden, Frans, and Michaela Drahos. 2002. Courts and (epistemic) communities in the convergence of competition policies. *Journal of European Public Policy* 9:913–34.

Vass, Laszlo. 1999. Hungarian Public Administration Reform and EU accession. Paper presented at the conference "EU enlargement to the East: Public Administration in Eastern Europe and European Standards." Warsaw, Poland, 22–24 November.

———. 2001. Civil service development and politico-administrative relations in Hungary. In *Politico-Administrative Relations: Who Rules?* ed. Tony Verheijen, 147–74. Bratislava, Slovakia: NISPAcee.

Vaughan-Whitehead, Daniel. 2000. Social Dialogue in EU Enlargement: *Acquis* and Responsibilities. *Transfer* 6:387–98.

Verheijen, Tony. 2001. Introduction. *Politico-Administrative Relations: Who Rules?* ed. Verheijen, 6–10. Bratislava, Slovakia: NISPAcee.

———. 2003. Administrative reform: public administration in post communist states. In *Handbook of Public Administration*, ed. B. Guy Peters and Jon Pierre, 489–97. London: Sage.

Vermeersch, Peter. 2003. EU Enlargement and Minority Rights Policies in Central Europe: Explaining Policy Shifts in the Czech Republic, Hungary, and Poland. *Journal of Ethnopolitics and Minority Issues in Europe* 1.

Vervaele, John, ed. 1999. *Compliance and Enforcement of European Community Law*. The Hague: Kluwer Law International.

Vidláková, Olga. 2001. Politico-administrative Relations in the Czech Republic. In *Politico-Administrative Relations: Who Rules?* ed. Tony Verheijen, 86–109. Bratislava, Slovakia: NISPAcee.

Wallace, Helen. 2000. The Domestication of Europe and the Limits to Globalization. Paper presented at the International Political Science Association Meetings. Quebec, Canada, 1–5 August.

Wälzholz, Gunnar. 1998. Lettische Nationenbildung im Transformationsprozeß: Gemeinschafts- und gesellschaftsbildende Aspekte unter besonderer Berücksichtigung der Sprach- und Staatsangehörigkeitsproblematik. BIAB Report No. 15. Berlin: Freie Universität, Inter-University Working Group on the Baltic States (BIAB).

Whitehead, Laurence, ed. 1996. *The International Dimensions of Democratization: Europe and the Americas.* Oxford: Oxford University Press.

Wiener, Antje. 2001. Zur Verfassungspolitik jenseits des Staates: Die Vermittlung von Bedeutung am Beispiel der Unionsbürgerschaft. *Zeitschrift für Internationale Beziehungen* 8:73–104.

———. 2003. Constructivism: The Limits of Bridging Gaps. *Journal of International Relations and Development* 6:253–76.

Williams, Margit Bessenyey. 2001. Exporting the Democratic Deficit: Hungary's Experience with EU Integration. *Problems of Post-Communism* 48:27–38.

———. 2002. European Integration and Minority Rights: The Case of Hungary and Its Neighbors. In *Norms and Nannies: The Impact of International Organizations on the Central and East European States*, ed. Ron Linden, 227–58. Lanham, MD: Rowman and Littlefield.

Windhoff-Héritier, Adrienne. 1980. *Politikimplementation: Ziel und Wirklichkeit politischer Entscheidungen.* Königstein, Germany: Hain.

Wolff, Larry. 1994. *Inventing Eastern Europe: The Map of Civilization on the Mind of the Enlightenment.* Stanford: Stanford University Press.

World Bank. 1991. Poland. Environmental Management. Project Report.

———. 1994. Environmental Action Program for Central and Eastern Europe. Report No. 10603-ECA. Washington, DC: World Bank.

———. 1997a. *Poland Country Assistance Review, Volume I.* Report No. 16495. Washington, DC, 14 April.

———. 1997b. *Implementation Completion Report, Poland: Enterprise and Financial Sector Adjustment Loan.* Report No. 16743, 16 June. Washington, DC: World Bank.

———. 1997c. Poland—Country Economic Memorandum: Reform and Growth on the Road to the EU. Document of the World Bank No. 16858-Pol.

———. 1998. Poland. Complying with EU Environmental Legislation: Final Report. World Bank Discussion Paper.

———. 1999. Czech Republic towards EU Accession. Washington, DC: World Bank.

———. 2001. Bulgaria—Country Economic Memorandum: The Dual Challenge of Transition and Accession. Document of the World Bank.

Yavuz, Hakan. 2000. Turkey's Fault Lines and the Crisis of Kemalism. *Current History*, January, 33–38.

Young, Oran R., ed. 1999. *The Effectiveness of International Environmental Regimes: Causal Connections and Behavioral Mechanisms.* Cambridge, MA: MIT Press.

Zielonka, Jan, and Alex Pravda, eds. *Democratic Consolidation in Eastern Europe, Vol. 2: International and Transnational Factors.* Oxford: Oxford University Press.

INDEX

251

Cornell Studies in Political Economy
A SERIES EDITED BY
PETER J. KATZENSTEIN